CONTENTS

THE HEBREW BIBLE TODAY

An Introduction to Critical Issues

Steven L. McKenzie
M. Patrick Graham
editors

WESTMINSTER JOHN KNOX PRESS
LOUISVILLE, KENTUCKY

Scripture quotations, unless otherwise noted, are from the New Revised Standard Version of the Bible, copyright © 1989 by the Division of Christian Education of the National Council of the Churches of Christ in the U.S.A., and are used by permission. However, in some cases the divine name is rendered Yahweh where the NRSV has "the LORD."

Book design by D & G Limited, LLC
Cover design by Brooke Griffiths

First edition
Published by Westminster John Knox Press
Louisville, Kentucky

This book is printed on acid-free paper that meets the American National Standards Institute Z39.48 standard. ∞

PRINTED IN THE UNITED STATES OF AMERICA

98 99 00 01 02 03 04 05 06 07 — 10 9 8 7 6 5 4 3 2 1

Library of Congress Cataloging-in-Publication Data

The Hebrew Bible today : an introduction to critical issues / edited
   by Steven L. McKenzie and M. Patrick Graham.
        p.   cm.
   Includes bibliographical references and index.
   ISBN 0-664-25652-X
   1. Bible. O.T.—Criticism, Interpretation, etc.   I. McKenzie,
Steven L., 1953–   .   II. Graham, Matt Patrick.
BS1188.H47 1998
221.6—dc21   98-10294

PREFACE

The basic idea behind this book is simply to make the very latest scholarship on the Hebrew Bible or Old Testament available to the widest possible audience. A word of explanation is in order concerning the three elements in this statement, that is, scholarship, the Hebrew Bible, and audience.

First, with regard to the *Hebrew Bible*, the use of this term in the title, as well as the organization of the book according to the three parts of the Hebrew or Jewish canon of scripture (Law, Prophets, and Writings), reflects the traditional effort of scholars to interpret or at least to begin to interpret the Bible within its original historical and literary context. This is not meant, however, in any way to exclude less traditional or other-faith approaches. Indeed, to the contrary, the most recent research on parts of the Bible often incorporates a diversity of methodological and theological/ideological perspectives, and this situation is represented in the essays included in this volume. The terms "Hebrew Bible" and "Old Testament," for instance, are used interchangeably throughout depending on the preference of the individual contributors. The main thrust of the book and the essays that comprise it is to present the best and most recent *academic* work on the Hebrew Bible/Old Testament, which, to a greater or lesser extent, transcends differences in religious affiliation, theological outlook, and ideological stance.

What the contributors to this volume, therefore, share in common is that they represent *biblical scholarship* of the very highest order. Each author is someone who has devoted his or her life to the study of the Hebrew Bible, focusing on a particular portion of it. They come from a variety of religious backgrounds, work at a variety of institutions, and represent a variety of nationalities. But they are all in every way "on top of" their field. They are well equipped to describe the direction of current biblical scholarship, to sketch its origins, and to speculate on its future, because their own work has helped to determine it. Their credentials, which are outlined below, speak for themselves so that I need not belabor the point here. I would be remiss, however, not to mention that it has been a pleasure and an honor to work with them in this project, and I express to each of them my sincere gratitude.

The real challenge for the panel of authorities assembled in this volume was to make their scholarship accessible to a broad audience. This they have accomplished admirably. "Updates" of this kind have been attempted before, although it is clearly time for another one.[1] What separates this book from previous ones of the same kind is its effort to speak to readers on an introductory level. Contributors were asked not to assume any real familiarity with the Hebrew Bible on the part of their readers. Hence, while we hope that other scholars will find the book useful, it is designed primarily for the average reader, who is not initially aware of the issues and complexities involved in understanding the origin and nature of the Hebrew Bible/Old Testament. In addition to students in colleges and seminaries, who we hope will profit from the surveys, clergy and professors in other academic areas should be able to gain here a rudimentary acquaintance with the academic study of the Hebrew Bible or bring themselves up to date with the topics involved in its critical study.

For purposes of this volume the books of the Hebrew Bible are divided into eight sections. For the most part these sections follow the traditional divisions and groupings of the Hebrew Bible itself. Thus the Torah, the Former Prophets, the three "major" Latter Prophets (Isaiah, Jeremiah, Ezekiel), the book of the Twelve ("minor") prophets, and the so-called "Chronicler's History" (Ezra, Nehemiah, Chronicles) are all recognized as traditional "units" of one form or another that make up the Hebrew Bible. They are also generally treated as such within scholarship, although the exact relationship of the Torah and the Former Prophets is a matter of considerable debate, as will become clear from the articles that deal with them, and Isaiah, Jeremiah, and Ezekiel are independent books, each with its own set of issues. The grouping together of Job, Proverbs, and Ecclesiastes (Qoheleth) as the "Wisdom books" was also a natural choice because of their widely recognized similarity to each other in distinction from the rest of the books, which is reflected in the long-standing tradition of scholarship on wisdom literature. The rest of the Writings were more difficult to group together, and the divisions represented here are somewhat arbitrary. Psalms and Lamentations have in common that they are both poetry, and the lament, of which Lamentations is an example, is a genre encountered in Psalms. However, Ruth, Song of Songs, Esther, and Daniel have little in common and are treated in one chapter in this volume more for convenience than for similarities in content or in traditional or critical discussion.

The authors were asked to follow a specific format for each biblical unit (or in some cases each book) that they treated. They were asked first to characterize the contents of the section they were discussing and its place in the Hebrew Bible, that is, how it relates to other sections of the Bible. This included describing what the books in the section share and why they were treated together. As suggested above, this was not possible for every section or group of books represented in each chapter. Sometimes authors were compelled, therefore, to characterize individual books and their place in the Bible.

Next, authors were asked to sketch the history of critical scholarship for their section. Here they attempted to address a series of questions such as: How have early observations shaped the course of scholarship? What methods have scholars employed in treating this material, and what critical approaches have arisen in this section? What points of consensus have been reached or have deteriorated?

Finally, authors were asked to isolate and discuss the most crucial issues that have arisen in the critical interpretation of each section and its component books. They were to focus particularly on changes in orientation or approach in recent decades that have led to current trends. For several authors, this meant focusing on their own work and showing how it has moved in a new direction. Throughout these discussions the authors have made a concerted effort to define important terms that may be unfamiliar to readers and to provide specific illustrations from the texts in their sections for the points in their discussion, particularly by isolating a single passage and using it repeatedly for illustration. I am once again extremely grateful to the eight authors represented here for the care with which they have followed this format, while at the same time exercising their creativity and expert judgment in adapting it to the circumstances presented by each section and book.

STEVEN L. McKENZIE

Rhodes College

CONTRIBUTORS

John Van Seters is James A. Gray Professor of Biblical Literature at the University of North Carolina, Chapel Hill. It is fair to say that no single individual has exercised more influence on the direction of biblical studies worldwide over the past two decades than Prof. Van Seters. His many publications on the Pentateuch and on historiography in the ancient world and in the Bible have effected a revolution in these areas that has led to the rethinking if not the revision of theories that were formerly nearly universally held. He has been invited to lecture at universities throughout North America, Europe, and Israel. He also began the Pentateuch Section of the Society of Biblical Literature and has been an active participant in it for many years.

A. Graeme Auld is professor of Hebrew Bible and head of the Department of Hebrew and Old Testament Studies in the Divinity Faculty of the University of Edinburgh, Scotland. He is also former Dean of the Divinity Faculty. He served for three years (1969–72) as the Assistant Director of the British School of Archaeology in Jerusalem and has studied and lectured throughout Europe and North America. He is the author of numerous books and articles on the Hebrew Bible, concentrating above all on the books of the Former Prophets (Joshua, Judges, 1–2 Samuel, 1–2 Kings). His most recent volume (*Kings without Privilege* [T. & T. Clark, 1994]) proposes a new perspective on the origin of the books of Samuel and Kings and their relationship to Chronicles. He is currently writing commentaries on Joshua and 1–2 Samuel for two major series.

Marvin A. Sweeney is professor of Hebrew Bible at Claremont School of Theology in Claremont, California and a trustee of the Ancient Biblical Manuscript Center affiliated with Claremont University. He is on the editorial board of the *Journal of Biblical Literature* and is editor for Hebrew Bible and Ancient Near Eastern Religions of *Religious Studies Review*, as well as editor of the Forms of the Old Testament Literature commentary series (Eerdmans). He is also former editor of the Resources for Biblical Study Monograph Series published by Scholars Press. He has been instrumental in founding program units on Isaiah and Ezekiel in the Society of Biblical Literature. Among his many publications are a monograph on Isaiah 1–4 and a commentary on Isaiah 1–39 in the FOTL series.

David L. Petersen is professor of Old Testament at Iliff School of Theology and the University of Denver. A leading figure in the Society of Biblical Literature, he is on the SBL Executive Committee and is chair of its Research and Publications Committee. He has also served as editor of the SBL Dissertation Series and has chaired the Section on Israelite Prophetic Literature in the SBL. He was the book review editor for all publications on Israelite prophecy for *Religious Studies Review* (1978–86) and is currently the Senior Old Testament Editor for *The New*

Interpreter's Bible, as well as a member of the Editorial Advisory Board for the Old Testament Library, a major commentary series. He is author of two volumes in the OTL (*Haggai and Zechariah 1–8* and *Zechariah 9–14 and Malachi*) as well as several other books on prophecy in Israel.

Kathleen A. Farmer is professor of Old Testament at United Theological Seminary in Dayton, Ohio. Her publications reflect her interest in all parts of the Hebrew Bible/Old Testament but especially in wisdom and in feminist interpretation. She wrote the commentary on Proverbs and Ecclesiastes entitled *Who Knows What Is Good?* in the International Theological Commentary Series (Eerdmans) and is also the author of a number of study guides on the Bible, especially wisdom literature, for laypeople. She was a contributor to *The Women's Bible Commentary* (Westminster John Knox) and has written articles for a variety of other important publications dealing with the interpretation of the Bible by and for modern women.

John H. Hayes is professor of Old Testament at Candler School of Theology, Emory University, Atlanta. He is past editor of several books, periodicals, and series dealing with biblical interpretation, including *The Journal of Biblical Literature*, the main publishing instrument of the Society of Biblical Literature. He has written books on a variety of topics dealing with both the Old and New Testaments. He is probably best known for his works with Max Miller, also of Emory, on Israelite history. In addition to his numerous publications, he has directed many doctoral dissertations at Candler and thus continues to have an impact on the field of biblical studies not only through his writings but also through his students.

Kirsten Nielsen is professor of Old Testament at the Institute of Biblical Studies, Aarhus University, Denmark. She also served from 1984–89 as Dean of the Faculty of Theology of the university. She has studied a large number of ancient languages and writes in a variety of modern ones (Danish, English, German, and French). She has put her language skills to use in the translation of the Bible into Danish. One of the most recent of her many publications is her commentary on Ruth in the Old Testament Library series (1997). She also contributed several entries to the prestigious *Theologisches Wörterbuch zum Alten Testament* (*Theological Dictionary of the Old Testament*) and to the recent *Dictionary of Deities and Demons in the Bible* (Brill, 1995).

M. Patrick Graham is both a contributor to this volume and its coeditor. He is used to dual roles, because he is both a biblical scholar and a librarian. He is Director of Pitts Theology Library at Candler School of Theology, Emory University, Atlanta, and the Margaret A. Pitts Associate Professor of Theological Bibliography at Candler as well as an adjunct faculty member in Old Testament of Emory's Graduate Division of Religion. He served for six years (1991–97) as the Chair of the Chronicles-Ezra-Nehemiah Section in the Society of Biblical Literature and is still on the steering committee of that program unit as well as the one for the Literature and History of the Achaemenid [Persian] Period Group. At the same time, he is the current President of the Board of Directors of the American Theological Library Association. Amazingly, he maintains an active publishing career in both fields.

ABBREVIATIONS

AASF	Annales academiae scientiarum fennicae
AB	The Anchor Bible
ABD	*The Anchor Bible Dictionary*
ABRL	The Anchor Bible Reference Library
AThANT	Abhandlungen zur Theologie des Alten und Neuen Testaments
BEATAJ	Beiträge zur Erforschung des Alten Testaments und des antiken Judentums
BEvT	Beiträge zur evangelischen Theologie
BETL	Bibliotheca ephemeridum theologicarum lovaniensium
BI	*Biblical Interpretation*
Bib	*Biblica*
BKAT	Biblischer Kommentar: Altes Testament
BLS	Bible and Literature Series
BTS	Biblisch-Theologische Studien
BWANT	Beiträge zur Wissenschaft vom Alten und Neuen Testament
BZAW	Beihefte zur *ZAW*
ConBOT	Coniectanea biblica, Old Testament
CRBS	*Currents in Research: Biblical Studies*
EI	*Eretz Israel*
EVV	English versions
FAT	Forschungen zum Alten Testament
FOTL	Forms of Old Testament Literature
FRLANT	Forschungen zur Religion und Literatur des Alten und Neuen Testaments
GBS	Guides to Biblical Scholarship
GHAT	Göttinger Handkommentar zum Alten Testament
HBT	*Horizons in Biblical Theology*
HKAT	Handkommentar zum Alten Testament
HTR	*Harvard Theological Review*
ICC	The International Critical Commentary
IDB	*The Interpreter's Dictionary of the Bible*
IDBSup	*The Interpreter's Dictionary of the Bible, Supplemental Volume*
ISBL	Indiana Studies in Biblical Literature
ITC	International Theological Commentary
JBL	*Journal of Biblical Literature*
JSOT	*Journal for the Study of the Old Testament*

JSOTSup	*JSOT* Supplement Series
JTS	*Journal of Theological Studies*
NCB	New Century Bible
NIC	The New International Commentary
OBO	Orbis biblicus et orientalis
OBT	Overtures to Biblical Theology
OTG	Old Testament Guides
OTL	The Old Testament Library
OTS	*Oudtestamentische Studiën*
SBAB	Stuttgarter biblische Aufsatzbände
SBLDS	Society of Biblical Literature Dissertation Series
SBLMS	Society of Biblical Literature Monograph Series
SBT	Studies in Biblical Theology
SJT	*Scottish Journal of Theology*
SSN	Studia semitica neerlandica
TB	Theologische Bücherei
TL	*Theologische Literaturzeitung*
VT	*Vetus Testamentum*
VTSup	Supplements to *VT*
WBC	Word Biblical Commentary
WMANT	Wissenschaftliche Monographien zum Alten und Neuen Testament
YOS	Yale Oriental Series
ZAW	*Zeitschrift für die alttestamentliche Wissenschaft*
ZB	Zürcher Bibelkommentare

Part I

Law (*Torah*)

1

THE PENTATEUCH

Genesis, Exodus, Leviticus, Numbers, Deuteronomy

JOHN VAN SETERS

I. CONTENTS

The term "Pentateuch" (meaning the "five-part" book) refers to the first five books of the Old Testament: Genesis, Exodus, Leviticus, Numbers, and Deuteronomy. In the Christian Bible they are not set apart in any way from the rest of the books, but in the Hebrew Bible these five books constitute the first of three divisions: *Torah* ("the Law"), *Nevi'im* ("the Prophets"), and *Ketuvim* ("the Writings"). The Law (*Torah* or Pentateuch) was regarded by all branches and groups within early Judaism (including Christianity) as the most complete revelation and authoritative religious document handed down from ancient Israel.

The term "Law" as a description of the content of the Pentateuch is somewhat misleading, since it consists of about half law and half narrative. Most of the laws are concentrated in large blocks within Exodus 19– Numbers 10 and Deuteronomy 5 and 12—26 and are closely associated with the figure of Moses and his reception of the laws at Mount Sinai (hence the designation of the Pentateuch as the "Law of Moses"). However, some laws are imbedded in narrative outside of these blocks, such the account of the exodus from Egypt (Exodus 12—13) or the wilderness journey (Numbers 15—19; 26—31; 34—36), and some are found in Genesis in connection with Noah (Genesis 9) and Abraham (Genesis 17). The narrative provides an extensive historical framework for the laws from the creation of the world to the death of Moses as sketched in the following outline:

Genesis 1—11: The Primeval History

1—3	Creation and the origin of evil
4:1–16	The story of Cain and Abel and the first murder
4:17–5:32	The genealogies of Cain and Seth
6:1–9:19	The story of the Flood and Noah's ark
9:20–27	Noah's discovery of wine and the curse of Ham
10	The table of nations and the origin of the world's peoples
11:1–9	The tower of Babel (Babylon)
11:12–32	The genealogy of Shem (son of Noah) down to Abraham

Genesis 12—50: The Patriarchs of Israel

12:1–25:11; 26	The lives of Abram (Abraham) and Isaac
25:19–33; 27–35	The adventures of Jacob
36	The genealogy of Esau
37—50	The story of Joseph and his brothers

Exodus 1—15: The Sojourn in Egypt and the Liberation from Slavery

1	The oppression of the Hebrews
2–4 (6)	The birth, youth, and calling of Moses
5	The first audience with Pharaoh
7—11	The plagues
12—13	The death of the firstborn and the departure from Egypt, the institution of the Passover and Feast of Unleavened Bread
14—15	The crossing and rescue at the Red Sea

Exodus 15—Numbers 10: The Revelation of the Law at Sinai

15—18	The journey through the wilderness to Sinai
19	The theophany (appearance of God) at Sinai
20—24	The giving of the Ten Commandments and a code of laws followed by a covenant-making ceremony
32—34	The violation of the covenant through the making of the golden calf (in Moses' absence), his intervention, and covenant renewal
25—31; 35—40	The construction of the Tabernacle
Lev. 1—7	Laws for sacrifice
8—16	Regulations on the investiture of priests and rituals for purity and atonement
17—26	The Holiness Code
Lev. 27—Num. 10	Various laws and regulations

Numbers 10—36: The Journey through the Wilderness

10:11–36	Departure from Sinai
11	Two episodes of "murmurings" and the appointment of elders
12	Aaron and Miriam contest Moses' authority
13—14	The failed southern campaign to capture Canaan
15; 18—19; 26—31	Various priestly laws and regulations
16—17	The rebellion of Korah, Dathan, and Abiram
20—21	The journey around Edom, the death of Aaron, war for the possession of the territory east of the Jordan (Transjordan)
22—24	The story of Balaam
25	The sin of Baal of Peor
32—36	Distribution of the Transjordan and preparations for conquest of the West

Deuteronomy: The "Second Law"

1—3	Recapitulation of the wilderness journey by Moses
4—5	Another version of the Ten Commandments
6—11	Prologue of exhortations on keeping the laws
12—26	The Deuteronomic law code
27—28	Blessings and curses
29—33	Final instructions in the land of Moab
34	The death of Moses

II. AN OVERVIEW OF PENTATEUCHAL CRITICISM

A. Traditional Authorship

Early Jewish and Christian tradition holds the view that Moses wrote the Pentateuch—not just the laws, but the entire narrative from creation to the end of his own life on the threshold of the promised land. This tradition is reflected in the New Testament and in contemporary Jewish writings, but it does not go back to the Hebrew Bible itself, at least in this form. Some laws, a poem, and an itinerary are attributed to Moses directly within the Pentateuch. The rubric, "book of the law [of Moses]," is also used elsewhere with a meaning that is more limited than the entire Pentateuch. In fact, the Pentateuch itself looks back on the time of Moses as being in the distant past: "There has not arisen a prophet since in Israel like Moses whom Yahweh knew face to face" (Deut. 34:10). The Pentateuch, like much of the rest of the Hebrew Bible, is anonymously written.

The rabbis of early Judaism and the early church fathers defended Moses' authorship of the Pentateuch as essential to the prestige and authority of their scriptures, and this viewpoint predominated until the Protestant Reformation. Nevertheless, those biblical scholars who were concerned with understanding the literal and historical meaning of the text were often confronted by statements in it or its manner of presentation that proved problematic for Mosaic authorship. Thus the statement in Deut. 1:5, "Beyond the Jordan, in the land of Moab, Moses undertook to expound this law," cannot be by Moses himself, because he died in the land of Moab and could not have referred to this region as "beyond the Jordan." The statement could only be made by a later writer who lived in the land west of the Jordan. Furthermore, in this text and in much of the Pentateuch from Exodus to Numbers, Moses is referred to in the third person—not what one would expect if he were writing his own memoirs.

Following the beginning of the modern period and the Enlightenment, philosophers and humanists such as Benedict Spinoza and Thomas Hobbes questioned whether Moses was the author of the Pentateuch in order to dispute the authority of the church and the Bible over scientific truth. In the seventeenth century scholars within the church, such as Richard Simon, began to apply a critical method to the study of the Pentateuch that did not assume the single authorship of the whole by Moses but saw it as the work of a number of different hands over a long period of time. Thus from the seventeenth century to the present, biblical scholars have debated possible explanations for the Pentateuch's compositional history.

B. More than One Author

Several features in the Pentateuch suggest that it was the work of more than one author. Scholars often speak of "sources" or "documents," meaning a plurality of authors. Before we consider such modern literary theories, however, we need to review some of the features that have evoked explanations different from the traditional view.

1. Literary Style and Vocabulary

There is a diversity of style, terminology, and ideological and theological perspective distributed throughout the Pentateuch—sometimes in large blocks, at other times in shorter units—that often disrupts the narrative flow of the text. For instance, one style reflects a special interest in chronology and genealogy construed as a framework into which stories of a very different character have been set. This combination can sometimes create a conflict between the framework and the stories themselves. Thus, in the story of the expulsion of the slave Hagar and her child Ishmael from the household of Abraham (Gen. 21:7–20), Ishmael is viewed as quite young. However, according to the chronology of the framework (Gen. 12:4; 16:3; 17:1; 21:5) Ishmael is about sixteen years old. Hence the ridiculous picture of Abraham putting a teenaged youth on his mother's shoulder as she set out into the desert (Gen. 21:14) and the subsequent scene of the crying child being rescued by God.

Sometimes the stylistic difference is reflected in various choices for the designation of deity. One narrative prefers the divine name "Yahweh" (= "the LORD" in English versions), while another simply uses "Elohim" ("God"), the generic term for deity. Sometimes divine titles such as El Shaddai ("God Almighty") or El Elyon ("God Most High") are also used. What makes this significant is the remark in Exod. 6:2–3: "God (Elohim) said to Moses, 'I am Yahweh (the LORD). I appeared to Abraham, Isaac, and Jacob as God Almighty (El Shaddai), but by my name, the LORD, I did not make myself known to them.'" In at least one place in Genesis God says to Abraham, "I am Yahweh" (15:7), which contradicts Exod. 6:3. But on another occasion God tells him, "I am El Shaddai" (Gen. 17:1), and this agrees with Exod. 6:3. The Jacob narratives contain the same kind of parallel divine appearances, one using Yahweh (Gen. 28:13), the other El Shaddai (Gen. 35:9–11). So scholars have argued that at least for the book of Genesis (i.e., before the time of Moses) one narrator used the name Yahweh for the deity, while another used only Elohim or El Shaddai. This principle of distinguishing authors or sources on the basis of the terms used for God became very important, and we will return to it below.

2. Parallel Stories

There are a number of cases in the Pentateuch of parallel narratives: two creation accounts in Genesis 1—3, parallel episodes in the lives of the patriarchs, in the desert journey of the Israelites, and in the accounts of the conquest of the eastern territories, to name just a few examples. There are parallel accounts of the giving of the law at Sinai/Horeb and parallel versions of the laws themselves (such as the two versions of the Ten Commandments in Exodus 20 and Deuteronomy 5). These parallels are not simply a repetition of the same thing in different places; they are different enough in style, perspective, and details to suggest that they come from different authors. The parallels, in fact, coincide with the distinctions noted earlier in literary style and terminology, such as the use of the divine name. For instance, both Genesis 15 and 17 describe God's covenant with Abraham; in chapter 15 it is Yahweh who addresses Abraham, while in Genesis 17 God identifies himself as El Shaddai (compare also God's appearances to Jacob at Bethel in Gen. 28:10–22 and 35:9–15).

3. Additions to Older Narratives

Some stories appear to contain later additions that give them a new context or theme. We will see below that in a number of the patriarchal stories the theme of a divine promise of land and great progeny has been added by one author, and the stories have been given a precise chronology that fits them into a larger historical context by another author. These additions also fit the stylistic differences mentioned above.

These features have been observed in scholarly biblical study for a long time and have led to the conclusion that more than one author is at work in the Pentateuch. This is especially apparent when the different accounts of stories contain contradictions in a close proximity that no single author could tolerate. Yet a number of questions remain matters of long-standing and continuing debate: Exactly how did the works of these authors come together into one work? Which is the oldest version and which later, and how are they related to each other?

C. The Problem of Genre: Myth, Legend, History, Law?

During the past century another mode of inquiry into the nature of the Pentateuch has arisen, and this has to do with the question of the genre or type of literature that is present in it. Among the vast quantity of archaeological finds from the ancient Near Eastern world over the last century are numerous myths about creation and the great flood that resemble those of the Genesis 1—11, as well as classical stories about wandering heroes and ancestors who set off for distant lands to found new nations. A number of Near Eastern law codes have also come to light, the most famous being Hammurabi's code, which predate the laws of Moses yet contain many similar laws. All of this suggests that the Pentateuch is a compendium of traditional materials corresponding to the broad range of literary types that existed in the ancient world. One important task in the study of the Pentateuch, therefore, is to sort out, by means of a comparative study with other ancient literatures, just what genres the Bible shares with other peoples. This kind of study yields important clues about the kinds of traditional materials at the disposal of the biblical authors as well as the kinds of literature they were trying to produce.

D. The Scope of the Work

Once there is reason to believe that the Pentateuch is not the work of one author, Moses, and that it is not a single genre of law but an organized body of traditional materials, of which law is only one large component, then we must further explore whether tradition has correctly identified the scope of those literary works contained within it. If Moses is not the author of the Pentateuch, then we may not be justified in limiting our study to the point in the narrative at which he dies (Deuteronomy 34). From Num. 21:10 on, the people proceed in the final stage of their wilderness journey to the region east of the Dead Sea and the Jordan River, defeating all the Amorite kingdoms of the land that will be the home of the eastern tribes. They are now poised to cross the river and conquer the rest. But first (in Deuteronomy) Moses appoints Joshua as his successor and gives his farewell address before he dies. Is the story to end at this point? Everything in our present text speaks against it. One cannot read Deuteronomy 31 and 34 without the sense that they prepare for the time of Joshua. Some scholars, therefore, speak of a Hexateuch (= "six-part" book). However, the book of Joshua itself may be part of a larger history of the Israelite people that extends to the end of the book of 2 Kings (see the next chapter in this volume).

While it is not my purpose here to deal with the whole literary history of the corpus from Genesis–Kings, one cannot avoid considering the question of the relationship of the Pentateuch to this larger work. In the last few years that question has become one of the most pressing issues in Pentateuchal studies. Yet, if the Pentateuch is somehow related to this history of the nation, then we must also return to the question of genre, not in terms of the traditional sources of the authors, but in terms of how these authors make use of traditional myths, legends, laws, and so on in a historical work. We must consider the genre of the whole, the kind of history-writing of antiquity that could produce such a work as we have reflected in the Pentateuch.

To recapitulate, we have suggested reasons for believing that the Pentateuch was not written by Moses but is the work of more than one author. How these authors may be distinguished and what their relationship is to each other still must be considered. We also suggested that comparison with other bodies of ancient literature indicates that these authors made use of a body of lore (myths, legends, laws, etc.) as sources for their compositions. Furthermore, it appears that their literary works became part of a larger national history found within Genesis–2 Kings. We must now consider more closely the various theories and models of composition that scholars have used in attempting to explain these features.

E. First Approaches to a Solution

A number of different approaches have been attempted in the past to find an adequate explanation for these various literary features found in the Pentateuch. The following are a few of the most important suggestions.

1. The Fragmentary Hypothesis holds that the Pentateuch consists of many small, independent units that were brought together by an editor at a single stage. The existence of short, self-contained stories (e.g., the Tower of Babel in Gen. 11:1–9, or Abraham's trip to Egypt in Gen. 12:10–20) and law codes in the Pentateuch signals the collection of traditional materials. But this hypothesis does not take seriously enough the fact that the process of combining the smaller pieces often involved extensive literary activity by means of thematic and framing structures in a distinct style—in other words, the work of an author—and that this did not happen at one stage but involved two or three such authors/editors of distinct documents.

2. The Supplementary Hypothesis suggests that there was a basic core of stories, traditions, and so on, to which additions were made from time to time. Few scholars regard this as the whole answer, but some notion of repeated additions or expansions continues to play a part in Pentateuchal criticism.

3. The Documentary Hypothesis is the oldest and most persistent explanation of the literary features of the Pentateuch. It explains the parallels and the differences in style and use of the divine names as reflecting *independent* parallel sources or documents that were interwoven by a succession of editors to produce the final product. This theory has largely carried the day since Julius Wellhausen popularized it in 1883.[1] Advocates of this theory identified four sources: two that use "Elohim" alone and one that uses "Yahweh." These three were confined to Genesis–Numbers, with Deuteronomy considered as a separate work. Of the two sources with Elohim, one was priestly in character and one was nonpriestly. The results may be diagrammed as follows:

J = Yahwist
E = Elohist   } Genesis – Numbers (Tetrateuch)
P = Priestly Writer
+
D= Deuteronomy

There was much discussion about the dating and order of the sources. D was the fixed point since scholars, following de Wette,[2] dated it to the time of King Josiah's reform, ca. 625 B.C.E. P was associated with the priestly reforms of the second temple in the fifth century. J and E were dated earlier than D. J was considered to contain the most "primitive" traditions and therefore to be the earliest. E was thought to have been influenced by the early prophetic movement (eighth century B.C.E.). This resulted in the following order:

J (Yahwist)   = tenth-ninth century B.C.E.
E (Elohist)   = eighth century B.C.E.
D (Deuteronomy)   = seventh century B.C.E. (Josiah, 625)
P (Priestly Writer) = fifth century B.C.E. (postexilic, Ezra)

This scheme has since been modified in a variety of ways, as we will see.

F. Form Criticism

Once the documentary hypothesis had gained broad acceptance, scholars turned their attention to a consideration of genres and forms of literature within the source documents. Gunkel, Gressmann, and Alt[3] were interested in the nature of the smaller units—or "fragments"—within the sources of the Pentateuch. These units could be narratives or collections of laws. Gunkel studied the stories of Genesis, Gressmann the Moses stories, and Alt the various types of laws. These scholars believed that each individual unit, a story or group of laws, originally had a separate life of its own before it became part of a source in the Pentateuch, and that these stories and laws were handed down by *oral tradition* from the earliest period of Israelite history until they become fixed in writing. They also suggested that the form of the story or law was a clue to its "setting in life" (*Sitz im Leben*), the particular social setting where it was used and from which it was taken by the written source.

In Genesis, for example, there are many short stories that have little connection with one other. They usually center on an ancestor in a remote time. These are not history, that is, an account of political events within a fixed chronology, but rather have all the marks of legend (German: *Sage*). One common type of legend in Genesis that is found among many peoples is the *etiology,* which is an explanation, in story form, of the origin or cause of something. It may explain the sacredness of a particular place (e.g., Bethel in the story of Jacob's dream), a striking geological feature (e.g., the Dead Sea and salt pillars in the Sodom and Gomorrah story), the origin of certain peoples (e.g., Ishmael, the father of the Arabs), or the plurality of languages (e.g., the tower of Babel story). These stories of the Pentateuch have many parallels in the legends and folklore of other peoples. Thus Gunkel argued that in order to understand the biblical material one must grasp the nature of folklore, the role it plays in primitive, preliterate societies, and how it is transmitted by oral tradition.

G. Tradition History

Tradition history may refer either to *content*—the development of a tradition through various stages over time—or to the *process* of transmission from the past. Those like Gunkel who were concerned with tradition history believed that each small unit or individual story of Genesis was connected with a particular locality, such as a sanctuary, and was the special preserve of a tribe or clan. Each story or piece of tradition was handed down *orally* from one generation to another, as is common practice among many peoples at different periods of history. It is also suggested that as the tribes or clans of ancient Israel came together to form larger political entities—a twelve-tribe league in the time of the judges or the state of the United Monarchy—the individual traditions of the various tribes merged to become the possession of the entire nation. Following World War II, the tradition history of the Pentateuch was dominated by the views of two scholars, Gerhard von Rad and Martin Noth, who had both been students of Alt. It is hard to overestimate their influence.

1. Von Rad

Gerhard von Rad's concern in his 1938 study[4] was to try to explain the form of the Pentateuch—why the units of tradition were put together not in any random collection but in historical sequence as we now have it. This arrangement could hardly be accidental. Von Rad found his answer in a form of liturgy, the use of the historical summary as a *credo*. The best example is Deut. 26:5–9, "A wandering Aramean was my father. . . ." Von Rad found a number of other examples of this credo form in the Bible and concluded that early in Israel's history religious festivals were used to celebrate God's "saving acts" recited in the credos. In time the historical credo (salvation history) formed the nucleus of the expanded history (adding the account of creation and the life of the patriarchs). Von Rad further noted that the earliest form of the creeds made no mention of Sinai and the giving of the law but that the deliverance from Egypt was followed directly by conquest and settlement of the land. He concluded, therefore, that the tradition of the giving of the law was celebrated in a separate festival and was combined with the exodus-conquest theme only at a later stage. In the same way the patriarchal traditions were added as a new theme at the beginning of the saving events. For von Rad, this all took place before J wrote the first version of the Pentateuch during the time of Solomon.

2. Noth

Martin Noth developed the approach of von Rad a little differently.[5] He suggested that the Pentateuch consisted of five originally separate blocks of tradition: (1) exodus from Egypt, (2) entrance into the land of Canaan, (3) promise to the patriarchs, (4) guidance in the wilderness, and (5) Sinai. The combination of traditions took place before any written version in the time of the Judges and the twelve-tribe league. Writers of the Pentateuch such as J were collectors and recorders of the traditions handed down to them. Each of these traditions had its own complex development. For example, Noth suggested that the stories of Abraham, Isaac, and Jacob originally belonged to separate regions: the Jacob traditions in north and central Palestine (Shechem and Bethel), the Abraham ones in the Judean hill country of Hebron, and the Isaac stories in the south around Beersheba. When all these groups came together to form a tribal league the separate traditions were combined by means of a genealogical scheme. Abraham became the father of Isaac, who became the father of Jacob. Similar developments apply to the other major blocks of the Pentateuchal traditions and epitomize the idea of tradition history.

H. A Critique of Pentateuchal Method

1. Critique of Tradition History

Tracing the development of a theme or tradition is a fine idea in *principle* but becomes too speculative in *practice*. We simply do not have the oral stage of the biblical tradition, so one can only guess what it was like. Since there is no control, both the original shape of the tradition and its development over time are conjectural, and no two scholars ever propose the same tradition history for the stories of the Pentateuch. Von Rad and Noth furnish good examples of this. All of von Rad's examples of "little credos" occur in Deuteronomy or literary material influenced by it—late monarchic or exilic in date, not at the beginning of Israelite history. There is no evidence that they were ever part of a primitive liturgy. The model for von Rad's reconstruction is early Christian confessional creeds (e.g., the Apostles' Creed) rather than examples from ancient Israel or the Near East. Noth's theory of Pentateuchal growth depends on his ideas about a premonarchical twelve-tribe league having a certain religious structure in which the Pentateuchal traditions played an important role. But lately there has been much criticism of his notions of such a tribal league and of how he sees these blocks of tradition coming together. In particular there is no reason to believe that the five blocks of tradition developed in some way separate from each other.

In actuality little can be done with the oral level of the material, except to recognize that there are in the stories of the Pentateuch certain folkloristic features that may reflect the fact that popular stories about early times were in circulation in ancient Israel. The basic weakness with both von Rad and Noth is that they restricted the use of oral tradition to the earliest period of Israel's history. But Israel and Judah continued to be predominantly oral throughout their history to the end of the monarchy and beyond. We may therefore assume that the biblical writers could draw upon a body of oral tradition throughout this time period. Nevertheless, our primary concern must be an analysis of the *written* text.

2. Critique of Form Criticism

While Gunkel's treatment of the stories of Genesis was very influential in suggesting that behind the writers of the Pentateuch was a large body of folk tradition, the exact form and character of that folk tradition continues to be discussed. Does etiology provide an adequate criterion for identifying the nature of the material and its social setting in primitive Israelite society? A number of scholars have found fault with this idea and have offered other suggestions for dealing with the form of the stories,[6] but their proposals also seem flawed.

My own approach is quite different. Like von Rad, I am concerned first with the question of the form of the whole Pentateuch. I have suggested that the appropriate model for its form is historiography of the kind that was common in antiquity. For instance, Greek historians like Herodotus make abundant use of folk tradition —popular stories, myths, etiologies, genealogies—in order to fill out their presentation of the past. Some of this derives from oral tradition, but some was simply invented by the historian to fill in gaps in the material. The point is that these histories contain a great mixture of different forms and genres that are the result of collecting, arranging, and inventing. This is exactly what we have in the Pentateuch. The form of the whole is that of ancient history-writing. Everything can be accounted for by using this model.

3. Critique of the Documentary Hypothesis

After 100 years of relatively widespread agreement on the documentary hypothesis, the consensus has broken down. While there is still agreement that separate sources and multiple authors underlie the Pentateuch, a number of recent works, including my own, call for a new approach. The major problem areas are twofold. First, while scholars have continued to agree for the most part about the two distinct sources D and P, the material in J and E is another matter. Are there more than two sources here? Should J be further divided? Is E really a separate source or only variant traditions? Since it is only attested in a few places in Genesis, many scholars no longer regard E as a Pentateuchal source like the others.

Second, it is unclear whether the sources are *independent* of each other. Do we need redactors to account for the combination of sources with each other? Could these sources have existed in the same place or community and an earlier document *not* be known or used by a later writer? Along with a number of other scholars, I have advocated the view that the sources were very much *dependent* upon one another. Yet there is still considerable debate as to how this dependence is to be understood.

Out of the current debate there arc three dominant models of the historical-literary analysis of the Pentateuch.

a. The Documentary Hypothesis

There are still many who continue to defend this theory, although often in a strongly modified form.[7] While still advocating the idea that the sources were independent, they suggest a much larger role for the redactors. Instead of the redactors merely being responsible for combining sources (e.g., R_{je}), they are now seen as adding much material of their own. This combines the documentary idea of separate sources with the supplementary idea of source dependence.

b. The Tradition-Historical Hypothesis

This builds on Noth's notion of the separate development of tradition complexes discussed above and gives up the idea of sources altogether.[8] The approach is basically supplementary, with numcrous stages in the expansion of each block of tradition and in the redactional combination of the tradition complexes with each other. For example, in Genesis the primeval history (Genesis 1—11) is viewed as developing separately from the patriarchal tradition (Genesis 12—50). Within the latter group of stories the Abraham and Isaac traditions, the Jacob tradition, and the Joseph story are considered to have developed as independent blocks until they were gradually combined with each other. The traditions in Exodus–Numbers about the sojourn in Egypt, the exodus, the wilderness wanderings, and the giving of the law have their own complex development and only in the later stages of literary composition are combined with those of Genesis. While the source designations J and E are no longer used for these earlier stages, P is still viewed as the last phase of development in the process. This method applies primarily to the books of Genesis–Numbers, while Deuteronomy is considered separately.

c. The New Supplementary Hypothesis

This approach is critical of both the older documentary hypothesis and the tradition-historical approach. It emphasizes the work of a few authors who created documents out of traditional material. However, after the first document the later authors were also editors, adding their own work to the earlier one. There was no elaborate system of redaction as advocated in both of the previous options. Since this is the model that I have developed and advocate, we will consider it here in greater detail.

I. The New Supplementary Hypothesis—Van Seters

In my view there are only three main sources. D is an entirely separate entity, and P can be fairly easily separated from the rest of Genesis–Numbers; there is no serious debate about the extent and content of most of it. The entire JE corpus that remains has a clear overall design quite distinct from P and D. Within it is a body of diverse traditional material. Since the attempt to construct a separate E document has been a failure, I speak only of J. Behind J there are some earlier literary stages that can be traced in the written text, as we shall see. Hence, there are only three principal authors of the Pentateuch.

This leaves three further questions. First, how are the three sources related to each other? I suggest that they are directly dependent on one another. Each author —after the first—expanded the Pentateuchal tradition by supplementation. There were no redactors. Second, what is the relative order of the sources? The only way to establish this is by careful comparison of parallel texts of the same episode in more than one source or by analysis of the way in which one source supplements another in the same story. My conclusion based on such studies is that the relative order of the sources is D, J, P. Finally, what are the dates of these sources? This order obviously results in a radically different dating. The date of D remains firm, ca. 625 B.C.E., which means that J is likely exilic (ca. 540 B.C.E.) and P postexilic (ca. 400). This dating does not prejudge the age of all the material within the sources. But it indicates the historical perspective in which each author is to be understood. The radical shift for J—dating the work 400 years later than most scholars formerly did—results in a very different way of thinking about this source and the whole development of Israelite religion.

III. THE SOURCES OF THE PENTATEUCH

A. Deuteronomy

As the fifth book of the Pentateuch Deuteronomy takes the form of *retelling* some of the events having to do with the wilderness journey that were covered more fully in the earlier books. The setting of the book is the region east of the Jordan River opposite Jericho where Moses is addressing the people before they enter the promised land. Moses will not lead them in, but will die on Mount Nebo overlooking the northern end of the Dead Sea. It is Joshua who will be their new leader, and the story of the conquest will follow in the book of Joshua.

It may seem strange to begin the study of the Pentateuch at its end. But Deuteronomy is the key to understanding both the Pentateuch (Torah) and the historical books that follow in Joshua–2 Kings, as well as the relationship between them. This is true for at least three reasons. First, as we have already noted, Deuteronomy is a separate source in the Pentateuch and can be dated to a particular historical setting in Israel's history. The other "sources" must be dated and placed in relationship to Deuteronomy. Second, whenever the "book of the law of Moses" is mentioned in the history of Joshua–2 Kings, it is always Deuteronomy that is intended, not the law of the rest of the Pentateuch. Deuteronomy, therefore, has the closest relationship to this history. While we cannot explore this relationship in depth in this study of the Pentateuch, neither can we ignore it. Third, if one adopts my model for Pentateuchal study, whereby the Tetrateuch (Genesis–Numbers) is a later addition to the Deuteronomistic History (Deuteronomy–2 Kings), then the reason for starting here is all the more apparent. There is even a broad recognition in the current discussion of the Pentateuch that the way Deuteronomy is viewed as related to the Tetrateuch and to the "deuteronomic" elements within it determines the approach that one takes to the rest of the Pentateuch.

1. Form

Deuteronomy in its present form is one long farewell address by Moses, in the first person, to the Israelites east of the Jordan. Underneath this surface, of course, the work has a complex structure and history of development. But in its present form it is strikingly different from the other sources in the Pentateuch, and what makes it so different is its predominant sermonic, hortatory style. There is almost none of this in the rest of the Pentateuch. Yet the same style of language and form occurs in the later historical books in speeches by leaders and prophets, where it is given the designation "deuteronomistic." Even the form of a farewell address just before Moses' death is imitated in the later history by Joshua, Samuel, and David in the same sermonic style.

The occasion of Moses' final speech is also the point at which he gives to the people the laws which are to govern their behavior when they enter the promised land. Deuteronomy 5 suggests that at Horeb (= Sinai) God gave the Ten Commandments to the people by speaking to them directly. But the experience was so terrifying for them that they called on Moses to deal with God directly on their behalf and to receive the rest of the laws in private. It is this "whole law" that Moses passes on to the people in the land of Moab in the form of a book (i.e., Deuteronomy).

2. Structure

The core of Deuteronomy is the code of laws in chapters 12—26, which is framed by exhortation to obedience in chapters 5—11 and the "carrot and stick" of blessings and curses in chapters 27—28. This in turn is enclosed in a second framework of historical prologue in chapters 1—4 and concluding exhortation and covenant making in chapters 29—30, followed by Joshua's installation as Moses' successor in chapter 31 and Moses' death in chapter 34. Into this ending have been fitted two poems in chapters 32—33. This may be diagrammed as follows:

first prologue (chaps. 1—4)
   second prologue (5—11)
   laws (12—26)
   blessings and curses ([27] 28)
   the Moab covenant and concluding exhortation (29—30)
   Joshua's installation (31) and Moses' death (34)
(two poems: Moses' song and blessing [32—33])

We may comment on this structure by sections.

Deuteronomy 12—26: The laws make up only half the book's total. This is the oldest part of the book and the source around which the rest developed. These laws are of various kinds: laws governing Israel's worship (chaps. 12 —16A), laws dealing with appointment and regulation of community and religious leaders (16B—18), social laws (19—25), and confession of identity and loyalty (26). This code was subject to revision in the years that followed.

Deuteronomy 5—11: After a second introduction in 4:44—49, this prologue to the laws begins with the events at Horeb and the giving of the Ten Commandments by God in the hearing of all the people. It urges family instruction in the law (chap. 6). It also has frequent warnings about serving other gods (7, 9); it recalls some of the trials of the wilderness and conditions of blessing in the good land (8), and it ends with general exhortation to obedience (10—11).

Deuteronomy (27) 28: The blessings and curses in chapter 28 belong to the laws at an earlier stage of development. The cursing ceremony in chapter 27 to be held in Canaan at Shechem has no connection with the context and is a late addition.

Deuteronomy 1—4: There are two prologues to the book, and it is likely that the first one (chaps. 1—4) was added later than 5—11. It is in the form of a historical recapitulation of the route from Horeb to Kadesh to Moab (chaps. 1—3) and is parallel to the account in Numbers. Chapter 4 is a second version of the events at Horeb and parallels chapter 5. It was probably a later addition to this prologue.

Deuteronomy 29—30: This concluding discourse on the covenant in the land of Moab includes all the laws in chapters 12—26, after those given at Horeb. There is continued exhortation to obedience.

Deuteronomy 31, 34: The installation of Joshua (31:1–8; cf. 3:18–22), followed by the delivery of the law to the Levites (vv. 9–13), is the final act before the ascent of Pisgah/Nebo by Moses and his death (chap. 34; cf. 3:23–29). The connection between the prologue in chapters 1—3 and this epilogue is very close. The rest, however (i.e., 31:14–30 = a second version of the installation), is a later addition.

Deuteronomy 32—33: The two poems were probably independent before their inclusion into Deuteronomy. The first is built into its present context by means of 31:16–22, 24–30; 32:44–47. Deuteronomy 32:48-52 is a P addition.

This yields the following broad outline of development:

a Laws in 12—26* are the oldest (* = original content, before later additions).
b First framework of 5—11; 28* = the second stage.
c Second framework, 1—4 + 29-31; 34 = the third stage.
d Two poems, 32—33 = last addition?

Since scholars find evidence of late additions to the laws and to the first framework, the development of the whole is highly complex.

3. Origins

As mentioned above, scholars long ago noted a similarity between Deuteronomy and the reforms of King Josiah of Judah (2 Kings 22—23). During the process of renovations of the temple a "book of the law" was found that inspired the king to carry out a series of cultic reforms. It has been suggested that Deuteronomy was written in order to create this reform program. The authors of Deuteronomy have often been identified with the priests of Jerusalem who stood to gain a great deal of power and wealth from the centralization of worship in Jerusalem and all the offerings to be brought to this one place. But this proposal needs further examination.

It is clear that Deuteronomy contains a body of traditional material about Moses, the exodus, the wilderness journey, the conquest of the land, and a body of laws, all of which were not invented in the seventh century. Furthermore, it is doubtful that these traditions could have originated in Judah and Jerusalem. The prophecy of Isaiah of Jerusalem about a century before Josiah makes no mention of the exodus and covenant traditions. Also, in all of his criticism of temple worship and sacrifices and his catalogue of social sins Isaiah says nothing about disobedience to God's laws.

By contrast, the prophet Hosea, Isaiah's contemporary in the northern kingdom of Israel, makes frequent reference to the exodus and wilderness traditions. Hosea was also concerned about disobedience to God's laws, and he is the first to mention the idea of a covenant. Furthermore, he was especially concerned about the worship of "foreign" deities (such as Baal) and of singular loyalty to Yahweh. Indeed, much of the language and themes of Deuteronomy seem to grow out of the concerns expressed by this prophet. This has led scholars to the view that the traditions behind Deuteronomy have a northern origin.

The northern kingdom of Israel came to an end in 722/1 B.C.E. and was replaced by the Assyrian province of Samaria. A number of refugees from the north—the social and religious elite—moved to Judah. "Israel" came to have a religious, instead of political, meaning as the name of the exclusive "people of Yahweh" and as such the term was transferred to the people of Judah, where Yahweh was also worshiped. However, the reform movement inspired by prophets like Hosea did not immediately take hold in Judah. Under King Manasseh, Josiah's grandfather, who was pro-Assyrian, a diversity of cults and deities was permitted in the temple and elsewhere. Only with the decline of Assyrian power and the rise of a new king, Josiah, did this reform movement come into its own.

According to 2 Kings 22—23, the discovery and reading of the book of the law led King Josiah to institute a religious reform designed to get rid of all forms of "foreign" worship (including the cults of Baal, Asherah, and the astral deities), to destroy all the "high places" and depose their priests, to remove cult prostitutes from the temple, to prohibit child sacrifice, and to keep the Passover in Jerusalem. Since all of these measures have their counterparts in Deuteronomy but not in the rest of the Pentateuch, the book of the law is identified with Deuteronomy. From the time of Josiah on it was the divine law of the land, at least in some circles. The impact of this reform can be seen in the prophetic works that come after this time and in histories that were written at the end of the monarchy (Joshua to Kings).

Josiah's "book of the law" was not the whole book of Deuteronomy as we now have it. As we have seen, Deuteronomy in its present form consists of an older nucleus with later expansions. The book purportedly found in the temple included the greater part of the laws in chapters 12—26, the blessing and curses of chapter 28, and at least part of the prologue in chapters 5—11. Several additions were made to this book at the time that Deuteronomy became part of a larger national history that extended from the time of Moses to the end of the monarchy.

4. Themes

a. Centralization of Worship

The most distinctive theme of Deuteronomy and its reform is that of centralization of worship in one place ("the place that the LORD your God will choose out of all your tribes as his habitation to put his name there," Deut. 12:5) and the elimination of all other places of worship. The law as set forth in chapter 12 and elsewhere recognizes a longstanding practice of worship in many local sanctuaries as administered by Levitical priests. All of these are to be eliminated in this reform. Therefore, placing this law in the time of Moses before the people even entered the land is an obvious anachronism. Deuteronomy never says where the chosen place would be, but the book of Kings makes clear that it was understood to be Jerusalem and the temple there.

The centralization of worship had its basic motivation in a program of "purification" of worship by those who advocated the exclusive worship of Yahweh. During the monarchy there were many local sanctuaries of Yahweh scattered throughout Israel and Judah. The presence of other "foreign" cults was also in evidence. The intention of the reform was to eliminate all of these sanctuaries in the interest of one authorized place that could presumably be kept pure by the central authority. The kind of religious activity that was permitted locally was greatly restricted.

Centralization also leads to unity of authority, in this case religious authority. The idea of one deity with one sanctuary, one priesthood, and one religious law strongly points to a theocratic state. Deuteronomy's view of ultimate authority is that the law was supreme over political and civil authority (the king and his appointees), and the Levitical priests were to be the guardians and interpreters of the law. Deuteronomy, therefore, sets in motion a radical religious change, although it scarcely foresees the full implications of that process.

b. The "Promised Land"

This theme of the promised land of Canaan is basic to Deuteronomy and permeates all parts and levels of the book. In the laws (Deuteronomy 12—26) it is often expressed as the basis for the laws and institutions. "When Yahweh brings you into the land that he is giving you" is followed by instructions about the institutions to be set up: the law courts (16:18–20; 17:8–13), the appointment of a king (17:14–20), the cities of refuge (19:1–10), and above all, the single altar in the chosen place (12:1–28). The whole of the law code is viewed as a "constitution" given through Moses in anticipation to the people's inheriting the land.

In the prologue (Deuteronomy 1—11) it is repeatedly suggested that the land belonged previously to unworthy peoples, the "Amorites." It was because of their evil ways that God eliminated them and replaced them with the Israelites. However, if the Israelites behave in the same way as the former inhabitants, then they too will forfeit the land. So the gift of the land is conditional upon obedience to the law (the covenant).

The land is regularly spoken of as "promised by oath to the fathers." Originally this referred to the ancestors who came out of Egypt. All of that generation died in the wilderness because they failed the test of their obedience to God there. But their children became the heirs of the promise and were permitted to enter the land under Joshua. Only at a later stage in the development of the promised land theme did the reference to the "fathers" come to stand for the patriarchs—Abraham, Isaac, and Jacob.[9] Their names were added to some of the promise texts in Deuteronomy. We will return to this development below.

c. Election and Covenant

Closely linked with the theme of the promised land is that of the "chosen people" and their covenant with God. God's choice of Israel as his special people, the gift of the land to them, and their faithful commitment to exclusive worship of Yahweh is the way in which Deuteronomy sets out their sense of identity. This theme has several basic components. First, Israel is a people chosen by God through its deliverance in the exodus from Egypt. By means of this event the people were freed from slavery and created as a new people. Second, election by God is not a matter of pride or special distinction. It was not earned through obedience or goodness; they were a stubborn people and no better than other nations (7:6–11; 9:4). They were chosen because God loved them. But being the "elect" confers upon Israel a responsibility to obey the laws of God (26:16). Third, this relationship between Yahweh and Israel is expressed in a covenant. This is an oath, a sworn commitment. It has two sides to it. On God's part, God promises to give them the land of Canaan and to make it prosperous. On the people's part, they must be obedient to the law. The covenant includes the whole people and does not admit individual exceptions. Fourth, the "promised" land, taken from the wicked Amorites and given to Israel, is theirs on condition that everyone keep the covenant. If the covenant is broken, even by a few, then Israel can lose the land. So they must vigilantly safeguard against any such threat. Finally, the king and all the local officials—elders and judges (chaps. 16—17)—are under the authority of this Deuteronomic law. The Levitical priests are its guardians.

d. Prophetism: Moses as Model Prophet

Alongside these basic themes are three others that play an important support-ing role. The first of these, prophetism, answers the question: How could this re-form movement be given the authority to carry out such drastic changes in Is-raelite/Judean society? The answer is that Deuteronomy is viewed as the special and supreme revelation by God to the greatest of all the prophets, Moses: "Never since has there arisen a prophet in Israel like Moses" (Deut. 34:10). The laws in Deuteronomy 12—26 are the word of God given through Moses to the people (5:22–31) and therefore are prophecy. Moses is a preacher of obedience to the law. Most of chapters 5—11 is exhortation to be obedient to the law in chapters 12—26. In fact, Deuteronomy views the primary function of prophecy in general as urging obedience to the law. Thus prophecy becomes instruction in the law as given through Moses. Since the law is the complete and sufficient revelation of the divine will for the whole life of the people, nothing more is needed. Another prophetic role assumed by Moses is that of *intercessor,* representing the people be-fore God, especially when they have sinned and are threatened by the divine wrath (9:7–29). As a prophet Moses can also be expected to suffer on behalf of the peo-ple. Thus it is because of their disobedience that Moses may not enter the promised land (3:23–29).

e. Militarism: Holy War—Purity of the Land

Deuteronomy preaches uncompromising "holy war" against the aboriginal population of the land of Canaan, whom it labels the "Amorites," and against their cultural and religious practices, especially the worship of other gods. This mili-taristic rhetoric is carried over into the following historical books, especially Joshua. Its language of extermination or "ethnic cleansing" of the land (chap. 20) understandably makes modern readers uneasy. However, this is essentially a "re-ligious" polemic motivated by the concern for a distinct religious and ethnic iden-tity (chap. 7).

f. The Law Code—A Nation of "Brothers"

On a more positive note, the law code sets forth the view that one should treat all fellow Israelites, one's neighbors, as "brothers (and sisters)" (15:7–11; 22:1–4). This is often described as the humanitarian concern of the code, an ideal that is be-yond the limits of a set of rules and regulations. It is a moral code, an ethic that is preached and in fact reflects the passionate concern of the eighth-century prophets, as we shall see. It may relate to those who are one's equals. But it has special concern for the poor, the widow, and the "fatherless." In other words, Deuteronomy is a strong supporter of the welfare state. There is complete equality "under God," to whom all must answer for their actions to their fellows. Still, this brotherhood only includes those within the community of Israel. No such compassionate attitude holds for the foreigner who has another religion and way of life.

B. The Yahwist (J)

The next phase in the Pentateuch's growth is the work of a writer—whom we call the "Yahwist"—in the books of Genesis–Numbers. In contrast to Deuteronomy, which as we have seen is a retrospective farewell address by Moses at the end of Israel's wilderness journey, Genesis–Numbers takes the form of a historical narrative that stretches from the beginning of human history to the end of that same wilderness journey. We shall begin by considering what particular kind of history is represented in this part of the Pentateuch and especially in Genesis.

1. National "Antiquities" as a Literary Form

The genre of the book of Genesis is a matter that has long baffled scholars. The tendency has been to treat it as a unique collection of materials that are often folkloristic in nature. Many of the individual units in the book have close parallels from the surrounding world of the Near East. But Genesis as a whole is no more unique in form than it is in the content of its stories. The model for this type of literature lies in classical Greece and is known in Greek as "archaeology," or in Latin as "antiquities." Such antiquarian histories became very popular in the ancient world because they told of the earliest appearance on earth of human beings who were the ancestors of the various peoples and nations of later times. These ancestors were often *eponymic* figures like Jacob/Israel who gave their names to their descendants.

The early histories are set forth in elaborate genealogies of eponymic ancestors and heroes that are traced from earliest origins down to historic times. (Because of their form these books are often called "genealogies" in ancient book catalogs.) Within the framework of the genealogical structure were placed stories, anecdotes, and other pieces of tradition about the various heroes and ancestors. The genealogy served as a kind of chronology. The subject matter of the histories had to do with the invention of culture, the founding of cities, the origin of sacred places, and so forth. The relationships of ancestors to each other foreshadowed those of nations in later times. The wandering of heroes and ancestors was one way of explaining the origins of nations (e.g., Aeneas as the founder of Rome). This involved the migration of an ancestor or his group from one place of high culture to a new land, often at the impulse of a deity. Such journeys (called "itineraries") were an important means of providing additional structure (along with genealogies) to the literary work.

It is my thesis that Genesis represents just such an "antiquities" of the Israelite people. The form of this history was derived from the learned traditions of the Eastern Mediterranean peoples (Phoenician/Canaanite). These were combined with Mesopotamian traditions about primeval times, such as the flood story. This diversity of forms and sources is accounted for by the framework of genealogy and itinerary and the mixture of traditional stories within it. The book was produced in two editions, an earlier version by the Yahwist (J) and a later edition by the Priestly Writer (P). The second edition was not a separate literary work but a supplementation of J's edition, with new material added, as we shall see.

This proposed form of "antiquarian" history accounts for the nature of Genesis better than any previous suggestion, and it will guide our discussion of its literary character. Within the limitations of this literary genre we will try to hear what the authors, the Yahwist and P, have to say about Israel and its relationship to its deity.

2. Myth and History

Long before nations like Israel and Greece began to write history as a way of explaining the present by reference to causes in the past, they had their myths to account for origins. In myth, present reality is based on what happened to gods and heroes in the primeval time, and this establishes an eternal precedent or model. There is an explanation in myth and legend for every custom, institution, and other important aspect of life. Myths are usually separate stories or units of tradition handed on without any connection to each other. Consistency and chronology are not important to myths. They are basically *symbolic* stories.

Modern readers have no difficulty with myth or legend as symbolic story if it is told "once upon a time." But when it is placed in a historical sequence of events we find the mixture of genres inappropriate. However, that distinction is not yet part of the thinking of the earliest historians, including the biblical authors. When they began to put together accounts of the nation's past, they had very few historical traditions, and these were only about the recent past. They had to use myths and legends for earlier periods. In order to make sense out of the variety of different and often conflicting versions of stories, and to relate the stories to each other, they fitted them into a genealogical chronology.

3. The Primeval History in Genesis 2—11

a. Creation and Fall (Gen. 2:4b–3:24)

The Yahwist (J) opens the account with a story about the creation of the human race. "In the day that Yahweh-God made the earth and the heavens" (2:4b) is a typical storytelling introduction like "once upon a time." Similar introductions occur in Babylonian myths about the earliest period of human history. "Yahweh God" (LORD God) is a special designation for God used only in the creation story. The original state of the earth is *desert* (2:7), because no rain means no growth. The creation of *man* (the male) takes place before that of the plants and the animals. He is formed from clay by the divine potter. God then plants a *garden* in which he places the sole human. It is like the great parks that the kings of Baby-

Ionia and Assyria used to build for their temples and palaces, with every exotic plant in it. (The name Eden probably means "pleasant place.") The best guess for its location according to the story is lower Mesopotamia (Iraq), since two of the rivers mentioned in 2:10–14, the Tigris and the Euphrates, flow through that region. Two *special trees,* the tree of life and the tree of the knowledge of good and evil, are said to be in the midst of the garden (2:9). The man is commanded not to eat of the tree of knowledge of good and evil (2:15–17), in anticipation of the story of the fall in chapter 3, but nothing further is said about the tree of life at this point. However, creation is not yet finished. Yahweh God, in search of a "helper" for the man (vv. 18–23), creates the animals but finds none that is suitable as a mate. So woman is made from a part of man's body as an appropriate partner. This is understood as the basis for the attraction between the sexes and for marriage (an etiology).

The story of temptation and fall in Genesis 3 has given rise to centuries of interpretive tradition (e.g., Milton's *Paradise Lost*), so that it is sometimes hard to get back to the biblical story itself. The focus of this narrative is on the psychology of temptation. The tree of the knowledge of good and evil stands for the human ability to make decisions about one's own life without religious or social restriction. This was the teaching of Wisdom; it entailed carefully observing and weighing the evidence and possible consequences and then acting. (For more on Wisdom see chapter 5 of this book.) The woman is innocent and naive rather than evil. (Contrast the account of the origin of evil in Hesiod's story of Pandora's jar [*Works and Days* 62–105] where the treatment of woman is much more negative.) The snake is not Satan but one of God's creations. As was common in antiquity, the snake is viewed as having special wisdom. It draws the woman into a discussion about the fruit and questions the motive behind the command not to eat it (vv. 1–7). To take upon oneself the task of judging what is good and evil is to be like a god; religion calls for faith and obedience. The irony in the story is that the godlike gift of the knowledge of good and evil can come only at the expense of disobedience and a sense of guilt. Innocence is gone; the couple is naked.

When God confronts the human pair in the next scene (vv. 8–13), they "pass the buck" like children caught in the act. The man blames the woman and ultimately God ("the woman whom *you* gave"). The woman accuses the snake ("the serpent tricked me"). God then passes sentence (vv. 14-19). The man and woman do not die as threatened. The divine judge is not bound by his own prescribed penalties but may choose to be merciful. Still, there are consequences: the snake must crawl on the ground and eat dust; the woman must suffer the pain of childbirth and be submissive to her husband's authority; and the man must toil as farmer to sustain them instead of continuing to live in the garden of delight. These are all etiologies to explain why things are the way they are in the time of the writer. In the final scene of the story (vv. 20–24) the humans are expelled from the garden and denied access to the tree of life, instead to begin "normal" life as we know it.

A review of some of the characteristics of the J account in this unit will be useful for comparison with P's version of creation in Genesis 1.

—The divine name throughout the story is Yahweh God (LORD God).

—The creation serves as a background to the larger story of Adam and Eve.

—The order of the acts of creation is set down for the dramatic use of the story and differs substantially from that of chapter 1.

—Etiologies in the story explain conditions after the fall.

—Humankind becomes like God after the fall but also becomes mortal by expulsion from the garden.

—J's view of early times is pessimistic, as expressed by the curses.

—J's style is to "tell a good story."

b. The Story of Cain and Abel (Genesis 4)

The traditional material that J used for the story of Cain's murder of his brother Abel in 4:1–16 consisted of stories about cultural rivalry and an etiology explaining the origin of a nomadic people, the Kenites. It was J who put this material together and set the story in the second generation of humankind—but not without problems (e.g., who was Cain's wife?). J's main concern was theological, as expressed in the divine warning (vv. 6–7) that Cain should not be concerned about which sacrifice is better but about "doing good," which is the surest way to divine acceptance. Furthermore, sin (one's passions) is like a pet dog that must be controlled and disciplined or it will lead to trouble. Cain's murder leads to the curse of expulsion from the land, but within this divine judgment there is mercy, with the tribal tatoo (the "mark of Cain") as protection in his wanderings.

Two genealogies follow the story of Cain and Abel proper. The one for Cain (vv. 17–24) contains seven generations ending in a triad. This genealogy is interesting in that it consists of the first inventors of civilization (similar to Greek and Phoenician origin traditions). The genealogy of Seth then comes in vv. 25–26. The birth of a third son to Adam and Eve suggests a new beginning in place of Abel. The worship of Yahweh begins with "Enosh," son of Seth. Finally, the remark about Noah (5:29) originally belonged to J's genealogy of Seth.

c. The Flood Story (Genesis 6—9)

The story of the great flood is the third major episode in J's history. The theme also occurs in early Greek mythology and in ancient Mesopotamia. In fact, there are so many similarities between J's version and the one in the Epic of Gilgamesh, as the chart below shows, that J must have borrowed it from the Babylonians.

Gilgamesh tablet XI	Genesis 6—8 (J)
1. Divine warning and instruction to build a boat followed by detailed description: size of boat, seven levels, nine compartments in each level, with pitch used to secure the boat.	1. Divine warning given about destruction of humankind and command to build an ark having compartments and covered with pitch: size of ark given; ark is to have roof, door, and three levels.
2. Animals brought to the boat to preserve "the seed of all living	2. Animals and birds brought on board "to keep alive seed upon the face of the earth."

Gilgamesh tablet XI	Genesis 6—8 (J)
creatures." Family and animals enter the boat. Utnapishtim shuts the door. In some versions there is a seven-day respite before the flood.	Noah brings his family on board. God shuts the door. After seven days the flood comes.
3. Great storm of wind and rain for seven days. Flood destroys humankind.	3. Rain for forty days produces flood with destruction of all life.
4. Storm subsides. Utnapishtim opens the window. Boat lands on Mount Nisir. After seven days birds are sent out: dove, swallow, raven.	4. Flood subsides. Ark lands on Mount Ararat. Noah opens the window and releases birds: raven and dove in seven-day intervals.
5. Utnapishtim and all with him leave boat. He offers sacrifice to the gods, who smell the sweet savor and decide never to bring another flood.	5. Noah and family leave ark and offer sacrifice. God smells pleasing odor and promises never to bring another flood.
6. Utnapishtim is granted eternal life.	6. Noah becomes new founder of human race.

Yet J shapes the Israelite version according to his own perspective. In the Babylonian version the gods become upset with humans and try to do away with them because there is too much noise (= overpopulation), which disturbs their sleep. One god warns the hero, who builds his boat to save himself, his family, and the animals. After the flood the gods realize that they acted too hastily and decide not to do it again. In Genesis, one God brings the flood as a divine punishment on evil, but then the same God saves Noah and his family.

In the prologue to the flood story (Gen. 6:1–4) J tells of the sexual union of gods and human women. This union produces the heroic age of famous men. This detail is not in the Babylonian flood story but corresponds directly with the heroic age of the Greeks in which heroes were the semidivine offspring of gods and mortals and performed deeds of valor. In the Greek versions the heroic age is linked with a genealogical table of nations just as in Genesis 10. The flood story from Babylon has been fitted into this scheme as the divine judgment on the heroic age.

The flood story proper (Gen. 6:5–8:22) is widely recognized as a combination of two versions, J and P. The following chart highlights the repetitions and contradictions within the narrative that point to parallel accounts.

Comparison of J and P in the Flood Story

J	P
6:5–7: causes of the flood	6:9–10: new introduction
6:8: Noah's introduction	6:11–12: causes repeated
7:1–5: collecting the animals—seven pairs of clean, one pair of unclean	6:20–21; 7:8–9, 14, 16: one pair of all animals

J	P
7:4, 12, 17: flood caused by forty days of rain	7:11; 8:2–5: flood is a return to chaos ("windows of the heavens were opened")
8:6–12: flood lasts two months	8:11, 13: flood lasts a year
8:20–22: Noah leaves the ark, offers sacrifices; Yahweh vows never again to bring a universal flood	9:1–17: permission for animal slaughter, not murder; covenant with Noah and sign of the rainbow

It is clear that J provided the basic story (parallel to the Babylonian one). P supplements the story but does not provide any new element. The J story has the same basic features as the Adam and Eve story and the Cain and Abel story (e.g., the crime and punishment theme). Also of special note is J's love of paradox: God's judgment on humanity because they are habitually evil (6:5) is balanced by God's mercy towards humanity for the same reason (8:21).

The little episode at the end of the flood story in 9:18–27 belongs to the series of inventions of the arts of civilization as in Genesis 4. Here Noah, the first to cultivate the grape, also becomes the first drunk (cf. 5:29)! Once an independent story, this episode has been made to accommodate both the flood story and the Table of Nations. The story was originally about two sons—Canaan and Eber—in which Canaan is cursed, but later it was modified to fit the three brothers Ham, Shem, and Japhet. The political meaning is not clear (e.g., when did the Phoenicians serve the Israelites?).

d. The Table of Nations (Genesis 10)

The elaborate genealogy in this chapter is designed to explain all the known peoples of the world as deriving from Noah's three sons. The list is a combination of J and P sources. The form of the genealogy is the segmented (family tree) type, which is commonly used by many societies as a way of indicating the relationships between peoples as represented by their eponymous ancestors. The relationships are not ethnic but cultural and political. Included are nations, countries, peoples, tribes, and cities as well as kings and heroes. Nimrod, the "first of the heroes" (vv. 8–12), was actually an Assyrian king who conquered Babylon and the Kassites (= Cush), contrary to what is stated here. Not all the names found here can be identified, but a large number can, and it seems fairly clear that this is an attempt at global geography from sometime in the sixth–fifth century B.C.E.

The Greeks also had schemes of places and peoples represented as descendants from eponymous ancestors. The hero Deucalion, the first human, had three grandsons from whom the main branches of the Greek peoples came. They also included short narratives about heroes within their genealogies and many other features common to Genesis.

e. The Tower of Babel (Gen. 11:1–9)

This story was originally connected by J to the Table of Nations, but this connection became obscured by P additions to chapter 10 that speak of the diversity of peoples and languages. These contradict J's statement at the beginning of chapter 11 that "the whole earth had one language." The story is set in the plain of Shinar, which is Babylonia. The city and the tower are none other than Babylon with its great tower or "ziggurat," which was actually built between the eighth and sixth centuries B.C.E. Characteristic of this region, as the storyteller knows, is that there is no good building stone as in Palestine so that everything is made from clay. The intention of the people in the story is to create a great center of civilization "to make a name for ourselves." But this is regarded as pride (Greek: *hybris*) against God, who therefore confounds their speech so that they cannot understand each other. This is thus another etiology about the origin of the diversity of language. The name of the city, Babel (which actually means "Gate of God"), is taken to mean "incoherent speech" because it sounds something like a Hebrew verb, *balal*. This understanding of the name is then used as a polemic against the city of Babylon.

f. J's Primeval History as a Whole

The stories in J's primeval history form a pattern of unrelieved crime and punishment: Adam and Eve sin and are cursed and expelled; Cain's murder leads to curse and expulsion from the land; Cain's descendants and the heroes commit multiple crimes that lead to the flood; the humiliation of Noah by Ham leads to the curse on Canaan; the pride at the tower of Babel leads to confusion and scattering. Thus the themes of sin and disobedience that lead to death, expulsion, exile, and servitude predominate. They raise the question whether there is any hope for humankind; in this way the primeval history provides a backdrop for the coming of Abraham. In Gen. 12:1–3 God declares that through Abraham "all the families of the earth shall be blessed." This positive theme in J will be traced throughout the patriarchal stories. In my view, J is speaking here to the people of the exile in Babylon who have also experienced the curse of both expulsion from their homeland and servitude in a foreign land because of disobedience. In what follows, Abraham becomes a paradigm of hope for a new beginning for them.

4. The Stories about Abraham and Isaac (Genesis 12—26)

The patriarchs are the forefathers of Israel, presented in Genesis 12—50 as four successive generations of ancestors: Abraham, Isaac, Jacob/Israel, and the twelve sons of Israel, corresponding to the twelve tribes. A careful reading shows that the narrative about them is not unified but combines many stories and traditions. The patriarchal stories have developed to their present corpus through various stages of growth that are sketched here.[10]

a. Pre-J Traditions

The pre-J traditions in this section correspond to Gunkel's smaller units and developed in two phases. The first phase consisted of an early collection of folktales about Abraham represented by three stories.

i. Gen. 12:10–20. Abraham journeys to Egypt and lies about Sarah, saying that she is his sister rather than his wife. She is taken into Pharaoh's harem, for which

Abraham is paid a handsome bride-price. When divine plague strikes Pharaoh's household, he is forced to return Sarah to Abraham and send them out of the country. Abraham keeps his wealth. It is worth noting that in the verses before and after this story Lot, Abraham's nephew, is traveling with them, but he is not part of the story proper. Also, the later framework (P) makes Abraham seventy-five years old and Sarah sixty-five, but these details are not appropriate to this story. Such things indicate that the story was originally independent of its present context and that the latter two elements belong to later stages of development.

ii. Gen. 16:1–12. Sarah, who is childless, gives Abraham her Egyptian maid Hagar in order to bear children through her. When Hagar becomes pregnant, tensions between the women force Hagar to flee. Hagar's child Ishmael is promised a great destiny by a divine being. He will be the father of the Arabs.

iii. Gen. 18:1a, 10–14; 21:2, 6–7. God appears to Abraham and Sarah and promises them a child in their old age. In spite of Sarah's doubts, attested by her laughter, she gives birth to a son, calling him "Isaac" (= "laughter").

iv. Gen. 20:1–17; 21:25–31a. This story, which is directly parallel to the one in 12:10-20, represents a second phase in the development of the pre-J tradition. Abraham again goes into a foreign region where he passes his wife off as his sister; the king takes Sarah into his harem; the king is threatened by God; and the plot of Abraham is exposed. This story, however, is not just a variant tradition of Gen. 12:10–20. It depends upon the earlier story, because it assumes a knowledge of the general scheme to fool the inhabitants without giving an explanation, and it alludes to the earlier episode: "at every place to which we come" (20:13). The reason for the addition of the parallel version is that in it Abraham exonerates himself from the use of deceit. He tells the king, "She is indeed my sister" (20:12). This author further *moralizes* the story by explaining that Abimelech did not sleep with Sarah (20:4) and by having God give the innocent king a chance to clear himself. The story in chapter 12 was not removed or changed. Instead, the second story was added to modify the effect of the first story. This illustrates how biblical tradition develops by supplementation. Because the story in chapters 20 and 21 uses the divine name *Elohim* throughout, scholars have often cited it as an instance of the E source. But this is the only story belonging to this phase, and I do not regard it as a separate source.

b. J's Framework

Taking up the Abraham stories just surveyed, the Yahwist, as historian of the larger work, added new stories of his own and organized them by using his own framework and themes. J does this in three ways.

i. By means of a *genealogy*. Beginning in 11:28–31 J gives Abraham's family connections—son of Terah along with two brothers—and this family tree accounts for all the genealogical branches and descendants that became Israel and its neighbors: the main line of Abraham-Isaac-Jacob + the twelve sons; the line of Lot = Moabites and Ammonites; the Ishmaelites, from Abraham's other son; and the Edomites from Esau.

Genealogy of the Patriarchs

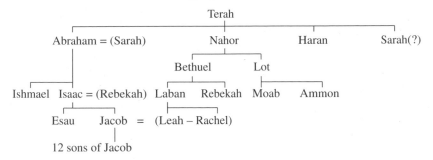

ii. By means of *itinerary*. The patriarchs travel from place to place, and all their stories are tied together by this device. Their wandering also connects them with important historical places: Shechem, Bethel, Hebron, Beersheba, and so on. This is a common feature of this kind of primitive historiography.

iii. By means of the *promises and blessings of God* (12:1–3, 7; 13:14–17; 15; 18:17–18; 22:15–18; 26:3–5, 24; 27:27–29; 28:13–15; 32:12; 46:1–4). These promises are repeated at important points in the patriarchal stories and provide a "red thread" that runs through the entire work.

c. The Promise Theme in J

i. The *call of Abraham (Gen. 12:1–3)*. The emphasis here is on the divine promise of blessing that will make Abraham and his offspring into a great nation and will make them prosperous and a blessing to other nations. The blessing contrasts with the curse in J's primeval history, and the "families of the earth" are set in the context of the Table of Nations. The call narrative in 12:1–3 serves as a bridge between the two units.

ii. The *land promise (Gen. 12:7; 13:14–17)* is given to Abraham when he arrives in the land of Canaan, and the extent of the land is specified after he separates from Lot, who chooses the Jordan plain. The promise of land is already implicit in the call to "go to the land that I will show you" (12:1). In fact, the two themes of call and promise cannot be separated.

iii. The *covenant of Abraham (Genesis 15)*. In this unit God repeats to Abraham his promise of numerous offspring and makes a covenant with him to give him the land from the Nile to the Euphrates. Some want to relate this land promise to the empire of David,[11] but there is little reason to believe that David ever controlled more than a small part of this region. Genesis 15 also highlights some important theological differences with Deuteronomy. While Deuteronomy emphasizes obedience to the law as the way of righteousness and future blessing, here righteousness is granted to those who have faith in God's promises of future blessing (15:6). Also, in D Yahweh is the God who brought Israel up out of the land of Egypt. But Gen 15:7 identifies Yahweh as the God of Abraham "who brought you from Ur of the Chaldeans to give you this land." This is an important shift in the defining event of who Israel is and who its deity is and reflects the concern of those in Babylonian exile (cf. Isa. 41:8–10; 51:1–3). The covenant God makes with Abraham and his offspring is an *unconditional* commitment in fulfillment of the promises of land and nationhood. The promises are repeated to each subsequent patriarch so that Yahweh becomes the God of Abraham, Isaac, and Jacob. In this way the Yahwist fashions a new identity for Israel, which is chosen not primarily through the exodus but through the call of Abraham and the covenant with the forefathers. This is an *ethnic*, not a national, identity. The nation was destroyed by the Babylonians and the people exiled. But they were still a people, and the Yahwist gave them a sense of identity that would overcome this crisis and be a hope for the future.

d. Major Episodes in J

To the earlier collection of stories and the framework J adds the following major episodes:

i. *Lot's separation from Abraham (Genesis 13)* is the result of Lot's choice to live near Sodom in the Jordan valley. This anticipates the story of the destruction of Sodom and Gomorrah.

ii. *Destruction of Sodom and Gomorrah (Genesis 18–19).* In order to incorporate this story into the earlier material J divided the account of Isaac's birth into two parts, placing the story between the promise of a child and its fulfillment. He also added some details to the first part (18:1b–9), using the familiar myth about how gods in disguise come to earth and are rudely received. The myth tells how a righteous couple shows the gods hospitality and is rewarded, while the rest of the region is destroyed. The dialogue between Abraham and Yahweh in 18:16–21 sets up the second visitation of the two "angels" to Lot in chapter 19. Lot shows hospitality to the two strangers whom the men of the city want to violate sexually ("sodomize"). The angels reveal to Lot that the city is to be destroyed and that he must flee with his family and not look back. Lot's wife looks back and becomes a pillar of salt, an etiology for the salt formations in the Dead Sea. The episode that follows about the incest between Lot and his daughters is a mocking ethnographic etiology for the origin of the Moabites and Ammonites. At this point chapter 20, the story of Abraham and Sarah in Gerar, was included, though it hardly fits since the context in chapters 18 and 21 indicates that Sarah is both very old and very pregnant; the king of Gerar would hardly be inclined to take her into his harem. She gives birth to Isaac in 21:1–7.

iii. *The story of Hagar's expulsion (Gen. 21:8–21)* was added as a sequel to the birth story of Isaac and becomes a parallel to chapter 16. In the earlier story Hagar was told to return and submit to her mistress. Now Sarah, fearful that Ishmael will get the inheritance in place of her son, Isaac, demands the expulsion of the slave mother and child. Reluctantly Abraham complies, and mother and child are sent off into the desert. They run out of water and are at the point of death when God reveals to Hagar a spring of water. Ishmael also receives a divine promise that he will become a great people (= Arabs) because he too is a son of Abraham!

iv. *The sacrifice of Isaac (Genesis 22)* is a remarkable story of the test of Abraham's faith. It is a touching narrative (v. 7—"The fire and the wood are here, but where is the lamb for a burnt offering?") with profound irony (v. 8—"God himself will provide a lamb for the burnt offering, my son"). Abraham is prepared to slaughter his son when a voice from heaven stops him, and Isaac is released. He thus passes the test of obedience and the promises are renewed. The obedience of Abraham is said to outweigh the disobedience of all his descendants.

v. *The story of the quest for a bride for Isaac (Genesis 24)* among Abraham's kinfolk in Mesopotamia illustrates the theme of divine guidance in answer to prayer. There is a clear emphasis in the story on not intermarrying with the Canaanite population, a concern of the late monarchic (D) and exilic period.

vi. *The story of Isaac in Gerar (Genesis 26)* contains the third version of the wife-sister motif. This account is a combination of elements from the two stories in chapters 12 and 20, but some problems remain. For example, the king of Gerar is Abimelech, as in the days of Abraham, making him a very old man. Also, Rebekah is not a half-sister as was Sarah; this makes Isaac a liar. Finally, Isaac and Rebekah are supposed to have two full-grown sons (chap. 25) but nothing is said about them. This episode and the rest of the chapter are meant to construct a life of Isaac parallel to that of Abraham and to make the connection between Abraham and Jacob. Apparently there were no independent traditions about Isaac for J to use.

5. The Rest of the Patriarchal Stories

We cannot deal with the rest of the patriarchal stories in the same detail. Still, the same literary process was at work, as a few general observations can demonstrate.

a. The Jacob Stories (Genesis 25, 27–35)

i. *The pre-J traditions* in this section derive from an older body of local stories about Jacob.

> *The birth of Jacob and Esau (Gen. 25:11, 21–34)* is linked genealogically through Isaac back to Abraham. The story is transparent in representing the rivalry between the two nations of Israel and Edom as that of the two brothers, Jacob and Esau. Jacob (= Israel) bargains with Esau (= Edom) for the birthright and therefore the best land. (Edom in the southern Transjordan is a much less fertile region than Israel.)
>
> *The vision at Bethel (Gen. 28:10–22*)*. In the oldest version of this story Jacob gives the site of Bethel its name ("house of God") after he has a nocturnal vision there of a great staircase with heavenly beings going up and down on it.
>
> *The story of Jacob and Laban (Genesis 29–31*)* was originally about Jacob's sojourn with his uncle Laban in the region of southeastern Syria where he

met and married his wives Leah and Rachel. It explained the historical border between the Israelites and the Arameans near the town of Ramoth-
Gilead (near the present border between Jordan and Syria).

The birth of the twelve sons (and one daughter) of Jacob (Gen. 29:31–30:24)
is an old tribal genealogy with etiologies for all the names of the tribes.

The story of the rape of Dinah (Genesis 34) is about the slaughter of the inhabitants of Shechem by the sons of Jacob as revenge for the rape of their
sister Dinah.

ii. *J's additions* to the older traditions are found throughout Genesis 27—33
and represent J's link between the Jacob and Esau story and the Jacob and Laban
story. The Yahwist developed the theme of rivalry between the brothers in Genesis 25 further by constructing a parallel story in chapter 27. (The story of Isaac in
Gerar in chapter 26 belongs to the Abraham stories and has little to do with Jacob.)
In chapter 27 Jacob steals the blessing from Esau by deceiving his blind father
Isaac. As a result Esau threatens Jacob so that Jacob is sent by his mother to her
brother's family (Laban) in Haran. On the way Jacob spends the night at Bethel
(28:10–22). J expanded the older story of the vision to include God's promises of
land, great progeny, and a safe return (28:13–15). Jacob's experiences in Haran—
his marriages, the birth of the children, the seven additional years that he worked
for Laban and by trickery became rich at his uncle's expense, and his sudden flight
—are all part of the older story. After departing from Laban, Jacob proceeds south
in Transjordan and has an encounter with a divine being at Penuel (another old
tale) in which his name is changed to Israel (chap. 32). To all of this J adds his own
story of Jacob's encounter with his brother Esau and their reconciliation (chap. 33)
before Jacob crosses the Jordan and arrives back in Canaan.

J skillfully shaped several elements into one continuous *adventure story*, a
genre common to other peoples as well. Among its typical features are the rivalry
of brothers (often over who will be heir of a kingdom), forcing one brother to flee
while the other takes control. The brother who flees goes to a foreign land, marries the daughter of the ruler, makes his fortune, and returns to claim his inheritance. The story often ends in a reconciliation of the brothers' rival claims. Especially noteworthy in this composition is J's use of the old story about the
discovery of the sacred place at Bethel as a revelation to Jacob of Yahweh, the
God of his fathers Abraham and Isaac, and the transfer of the promises of land and
becoming a great nation (28:10–20). J also adds this theme to the story of Jacob's
return from Laban's region to Canaan (35:1–8, 16–22). The story of the rape of
Dinah (chap. 34) provides the motivation for moving from Shechem to Bethel
where the promise is renewed (35:1–8). This move also gives the Jacob stories a
southern connection in anticipation of the Joseph story.

b. The Story of Joseph (Genesis 37, 39—50)

Joseph, the next-to-youngest son and the favorite of his father Jacob, is sold
into slavery by his brothers and ends up in Egypt. Through various circumstances

and adventures he rises from slave to vizier of the realm. When a famine forces the sons of Jacob to go to Egypt to buy grain, they encounter Joseph who, after a series of tests, reveals himself to them, and the whole family of Jacob migrates to Egypt to be cared for by Joseph.

This story existed in a fairly unified form at the pre-J level. (The independent story about Judah in chapter 38 was also pre-J; it is an etiology for the origins of the clans of Judah and is clearly intrusive in its present location where it interrupts the Joseph story.) The Joseph story has been modified at a few points by additions and alterations. For instance, Judah tends to replace Reuben as the older brother in charge of the rest. The Yahwist worked it into his larger account, as is evident in the theme of the divine promises in 46:1–4. The Joseph story also serves now as a bridge between the patriarchal stories and the exodus tradition to account for how the Israelites came to be in Egypt, where they became a nation (50:24–26).

c. Summary

We may recapitulate the general principles that apply to the development of the patriarchal traditions in Genesis as follows. Originally there were four separate blocks of pre-J tradition: the Abraham stories, Jacob stories, Judah story, and Joseph story. The Isaac material was never independent. J combined these with several additional episodes using genealogy, itinerary, and the promise theme as a framework to create a literary unity. Below we will discuss the final stage of this process by means of P's additions.

6. Exodus and Sinai

The exodus from Egypt is perhaps the most signficant event in the Hebrew Bible. By Yahweh's rescue of Israel from slavery and his guidance through the wilderness into a new land, Yahweh chose Israel as his own people. But the election of God is only one side of the relationship. The other side is the obligation of the people spelled out in the covenant and law of Sinai. Both God's saving action and Israel's loyalty and obedience to the law are combined in this tradition. The tradition of the exodus and Sinai is parallel to God's choosing Israel through the call of Abraham. Both are expressions of group identity through election. The covenant of *obligation* at Sinai is also parallel to the covenant of *promise* to Abraham.

In the early form of the exodus tradition as reflected in D the Israelites were simply a wandering band of nomads who went to Egypt and eventually became enslaved there. The exodus tradition originally had no connection with the patriarchs and their wanderings in the land of Canaan. It was J who developed the patriarchal stories into a major tradition and used the Joseph story as a bridge between it and the exodus. The sojourn in Egypt became a hiatus between the *promises* to the fathers and their *fulfillment* in the exodus of the people and the conquest of the land.

a. The Mission of Moses (Exodus 1-15)

Throughout the Hebrew Bible the time in Egypt is remembered as a period of oppression through slavery by Pharaoh. In fact, the notion of God as "redeemer" is related to the Hebrew idea of a kinsman (*go'el*), who rescues one from slavery by payment of a redemption. The hard labor is associated with Pharaoh's building activity. To this idea Exodus 1 adds the theme of genocide, especially in the story about the midwives who refused to do Pharaoh's cruel bidding, and the subsequent order for the Hebrew male children to be drowned in the Nile as a form of controlling their population. This provides background to the rescue of baby Moses. Beyond this there is no further mention of genocide in the rest of the story.

The story of *the birth of Moses* in Exod. 2:1–10 contains the theme of the rescue of an exposed child who later becomes famous. This theme is well known in Near Eastern and classical literature; especially similar is the story of Sargon the Great, who was rescued as a child from a basket on the Euphrates river and raised by a gardener to become a great king. It is typical of these stories that the hero who escapes the power of the wicked ruler grows up under his very protection to become his eventual undoing. In this case Moses is raised by Pharaoh's daughter in the royal palace.

Moses' first attempt to rescue his people by slaying an Egyptian who was beating a Hebrew is a failure (2:11–22), as it merely puts his life in danger from Pharaoh and forces his *flight to the land of Midian* (Arabia). There he becomes part of the family of the priest of Midian and marries one of his daughters (a non-Israelite!).

The call of Moses in Exodus 3–4 represents the long-awaited divine response to the people's oppression. In the encounter at the burning bush God identifies himself as the "God of Abraham, Isaac, and Jacob" (3:6), just as in the partiarchal stories. The story combines elements from two types of call narratives—the call of a military leader to rescue his people (e.g., Gideon in Judges 6) and the call of a prophet (like Isaiah and Jeremiah). Moses' subsequent actions are more like those of a prophet than a military leader. He confronts Pharaoh, not on the battlefield, but as a prophet would confront an irreligious king with the divine word of threat and judgment. He is also given three signs (4:1–9) to prove to the people that God has appeared to him.

One question that is much discussed is the revelation of the divine name in Exod. 3:13–15. For some scholars this episode indicates that the worship of Yahweh originated in the region of Midian with Jethro the priest (3:1).[12] However, the text will not support such an interpretation. The author understands the name *Yahweh* to be derived from the verb "to be" and therefore to mean something like "He who exists," implying that Yahweh is the only true God and other gods do not exist. The text identifies Yahweh, who appears to Moses, as the God of the fathers, Abraham, Isaac, and Jacob—which means the God of the promises. This is J's way of linking the traditions of the patriarchs and Moses.

Upon his return to Egypt Moses is joined by Aaron, and together they persuade the people by means of the signs that God has come to rescue them (Exod. 4:18–31). Their initial encounter with Pharaoh (5:1–6:1) only makes matters worse, as Pharaoh refuses to release the people and instead increases their workload. This sets the stage for the *plague stories* in 7:14–11:8 + 12:29–39. J's account originally contained a series of seven plagues (water to blood, frogs, flies, epidemic disease, hail, locust, death of the first born), to which P added three (gnats, boils, and darkness) and the contest of Aaron and the magicians (7:8–13). Since there is no plague tradition reflected in Deuteronomy, and statements in D exclude that possibility, there probably was no ancient plague tradition. The plague series in J is really a sevenfold curse (similar to Leviticus 26) that is used as a repeated warning to persuade Pharaoh to repent or be destroyed. It is similar in content to curse series that are well known in the ancient Near East. The final plague is the death of the firstborn, which leads directly to the exodus from Egypt.

b. The Exodus from Egypt (Exod. 12:29–39; 13:17–15:21)

In the account of the exodus J builds on the older tradition that the Israelites left in flight by night. He does this in two ways. First, he has Pharaoh force the Israelites to leave quickly in the middle of the night as a result of the death of the firstborn. He then has Pharaoh change his mind and pursue the Israelites in order to recapture the fleeing labor force. Within this flight/departure account we have the injunction by Moses (J) to keep the feast of unleavened bread in the land of Canaan as a remembrance of their hurried departure from Egypt (because they had no time on their journey to allow the bread to rise) and to keep the sacrifice of the firstborn of cattle as a remembrance of the sparing of the firstborn of Israel when God killed all the Egyptian firstborn (13:3–16). J does not have a passover account in Egypt, only a seven-day festival of unleavened bread in Canaan. The whole passover narrative in 12:1–28 belongs to P. The exodus event becomes the etiology for these religious practices.

For J the climax of the exodus is the event at the sea (Exodus 14). This is actually a late development in the tradition, since it is not in D or any biblical texts before the sixth century. The exodus account has been expanded to make the sea the main event of Israel's deliverance. Several issues that have been debated by scholars may be briefly summarized.

i. *Route.* There are two routes out of Egypt. A northern one, "the way of the Philistines," runs along the Mediterranean coast. But J says that Yahweh did not permit them to take this "lest they see war!" Yet all routes into Canaan will involve war. A southern route goes through the Wadi Tumeilat in which the Israelites will encounter the "sea."

ii. *Crossing site.* The sea is called the *yam suph*, literally "Reed Sea." Elsewhere in the Hebrew Bible the name refers to the Red Sea, specifically the Gulf of Aqaba and the Gulf of Suez, including the Bitter Lakes and Lake Timsah, which were joined to the Red Sea by ancient canal building. There are no reeds there.

iii. *Variants.* There are two prose accounts of the sea event (J and P) and one poetic one (chap. 15). The J version has God protecting the Israelites from the pursuing Egyptians with the pillar of cloud and causing the waters to recede by means of a strong east wind. The Israelites cross on dry ground. The Egyptians try to follow, are thrown into a panic by God, and are caught in the returning waters. P heightens the drama by having Moses split the sea with the rod of God, creating two walls of water between which the Israelites pass. When the Egyptians follow, the waters close in on them. The poem is a later composition, combining both motifs.

c. Giving of the Law at Sinai/Horeb (Exodus 19—24; 32—34)

While both Deuteronomy and Exodus stress that there was a fearful theophany at the mountain where the law was given, they differ about the specifics of the event and the laws. One difference is in the names for the sacred mountain. D uses only Horeb, but in Exodus both Sinai and Horeb designate the same place. In the present text of the Tetrateuch the account of this event goes from Exodus 19—Numbers 10, most of which is P. Here we will concentrate only on J's version in Exodus 19—24, 32—34. In J, Moses receives a promise from God of a special covenant and consecrates the people for the divine appearance (19:2–11). When the people come with Moses to the mountain there is a great storm, volcanic eruption, and the sound of a ram's horn trumpet or *shofar* (19:13b–19). The people are afraid and beg Moses to serve as their intermediary to receive all of God's instructions, which they vow to obey (20:18–21). What follows then is a series of laws (20:22–23:33) called the "book of the covenant" (24:7) and known to scholars as the "Covenant Code."

After Moses receives these laws and writes them in a book there is a special ceremony of covenant making in Exod. 24:3–8 by which the people are solemnly committed to keeping them. In contrast to D, which has two covenants—the corporate law that is part of the national covenant in Deuteronomy 12—26 and the code for individual conduct given at Horeb, which consists of only the Ten Commandments—in J there is only the one covenant at Sinai. J does not have a separate Ten Commandments (those of Exod. 20:1–17 belong to P). Instead the "book of the covenant" in 20:22–23:33 represents the whole law to which the people are committed. J also introduces a special covenant ritual that resembles the ceremony used to dedicate priests (24:3–8). But in 19:6 God declares the whole nation to be holy, a "kingdom of priests," so that they are given a special role in the mission in the world. They are to be the religious representatives of God among the nations. This seems to extend the "blessing to the nations" theme in the Abraham promises and to give to the covenant a universal perspective comparable to the mission to the nations in the message of the exilic prophet, Second Isaiah.

The account of covenant violation and renewal follows in Exodus 32—34, which is the direct sequel in J to the making of the covenant in chapter 24. (The divine instructions to Moses in chaps. 25—31 belong to P and are an expansion.) In 24:12–15a, 18b Moses is commanded to come up on the mountain, leaving Aaron in charge. Then trouble starts (chap. 32). The people complain to Aaron because Moses is delayed forty days on the mountain. They want to get on with the journey. To do this they need a god to go before them, and they ask Aaron to make them one. He collects the materials and fashions a bull image declaring, "These are your gods, O Israel, who brought you up out of the land of Egypt." They build an altar, establish a feast day for it, and bring sacrifices. This story has a close parallel in 1 Kings 12:25–33, where Jeroboam makes the *golden calves*, the feast, the sacrifices, and even uses the same words: "Here are your gods, O Israel, who brought you up out of the land of Egypt." J has taken this example of a great act of apostasy of the northern kingdom and has made the whole people responsible for the same thing at the beginning of their existence. No sooner had they sworn a solemn covenant not to make other gods of gold (cf. 20:23) than they broke the covenant.

God becomes very angry and threatens to destroy the whole people and start over again, with Moses as the forefather of a new nation. But Moses intercedes on behalf of the people and persuades God not to ruin his reputation among the nations as savior of his people and not to violate his promises to the fathers, Abraham, Isaac, and Jacob. The theme of Moses' intercession continues in chapter 33, where he pleads for God's presence with his people in spite of their weaknesses and waywardness. This divine presence is symbolized in the simple "tent of meeting" (33:7–11) where Moses receives divine guidance from time to time. Unlike the temple, the tent of meeting had no formal worship activities.

In chapter 34 J shows that because God is gracious the people can renew their covenant relationship with him despite their apostasy. The new covenant consists of a new set of laws that is a shorter version of the Covenant Code in 20:22–23:33, highlighting its religious laws. (Some scholars have mistakenly seen this as a doublet: J's version, with the Covenant Code as the E version.)

7. The Wilderness Journey

The biblical account of the wilderness journey actually extends from Exod. 15:22 to the end of Deuteronomy and includes the giving of the law at Sinai/Horeb. In the past scholars typically saw in the wilderness traditions a memory of a nomadic way of life before Israel's settlement in the land. But the wilderness stories do not reflect nomadic behavior. The people are entirely out of place and at the mercy of the elements. They lack food and water and need guides (the Midianite nomads or the divine cloud and fire). Rather, the wilderness is a great trial from which they seek to escape. All three sources—D, J, and P—treat the wilderness as a constitutional age when the essential elements of law and society were established. D's reform program is viewed as the basis of Israelite society from the beginning of the people. J presents a basic set of civil and religious laws and a simple system of governance that would work within the exilic community. We will see that in P the emphasis is on a theocratic state of priestly rule and of the temple. For J especially the wilderness illustrates God's provision and care for his people in order to encourage their trust in God. At the same time, the stories contain a warning about the consequences of faithlessness or disobedience to God. This is actually a mixture of two conflicting views of this period found in the prophetic books: Some (Hosea and Jeremiah) describe it as a time of ideal dependence upon God, uncorrupted by civilization, when they received food and drink from God; others (Ezekiel) see it as a time of testing in which Israel failed and prolonged its time there because of stubbornness and rebellion.

a. Murmurings

Several motifs surface in the wilderness traditions. The most prominent is a series of trials in which the people "murmur" against Moses and Aaron because of the need for water and food, disputes over Moses' leadership, or just discontent. Sometimes the need is genuine and God answers it by supplying food and drink. At other times the people are simply rebellious, and this brings about divine judgment. In all of these situations Moses acts as intercessor, praying in order to relieve the people's suffering or to turn back the divine punishment. In *Exodus 16*, for example, the people complain that they have nothing to eat so God provides them with manna. The present account is a mixture of J and P. But the basic story in J not only accounts for God's wondrous provision but also explains the origin of the sabbath. The people were not to gather manna on the seventh day. (For P the sabbath is linked to creation.) In *Num. 11:4–34* the people complain that they are tired of the manna and want meat. God supplies meat in the form of migrating quails. But the people are punished for their grumbling when many of them die of food poisoning. *Numbers 13—14* is a case of general rebellion. It is also a mixture of J and P. Moses prepares for an invasion of Canaan from the south by sending spies to reconnoiter the land. While they bring back evidence of the land's richness and abundant produce, they also discourage the people by recounting the strength of the enemy there (all except Caleb). The result is that the people are condemned to wander another forty years in the wilderness until the older generation has died off.

b. Institutions

The wilderness traditions also include the establishment of various civil and religious institutions under Moses. In J the law courts are created (Exodus 18) at the advice of Moses' father-in-law so that Moses does not have to judge every case himself. In Numbers 11, within the quail episode, Moses establishes a council of seventy as a governing body, inspired by God, to rule the people. These episodes build on the parallel in Deut. 1:9–18. J mentions nothing about the monarchy or the institution of the priesthood.

c. Eastern Conquest (Transjordan)

Throughout the wilderness tradition there is an itinerary that connects all the parts together. This journey finally brings them into the Transjordan (Num. 21:21–35; 32; f. Deuteronomy 2—3). They avoid any conflict with Edom and Moab but encounter two major "Amorite" kingdoms ruled by Sihon and Og, whom they defeat under Moses' leadership. The eastern tribes receive their right to this land. Moses then charges Joshua with the task of conquering the west and ascends Mount Nebo to die (Deuteronomy 34).

C. The Priestly Writer

The Priestly Writer (P) is also an antiquarian historian like his predecessor J. Many scholars do not consider P as history-writing, because it offers a minimal amount of historical narrative and shows a major preoccupation with law. But such a viewpoint does not begin from the perspective of ancient forms of history-writing that incorporated a good deal of law into their works. In fact, an account and explanation of the nation's constitution is often a major part of antiquarian historiography. Also, the priestly class seems to have had a strong preoccupation with such histories. So it is not surprising that the final major edition of the national history of Israel in Genesis–Kings should be attributed to a "Priestly Writer."

In the literary analysis of the Pentateuch adopted here, we have argued that P represents a later edition and expansion of J's history in Genesis–Numbers and not an independent source as the older documentary hypothesis had suggested. Thus, all the pieces belonging to P, when put together, do not constitute a coherent literary work. They are dependent upon their context in J. Nevertheless, there is a uniformity of style, language, and perspective that enables scholars to identify this writer, and there has been a fairly broad scholarly consensus about which texts of the Pentateuch belong to P.

1. Genesis

a. Creation (Gen. 1:1–2:4a)

A comparison of the two accounts of creation that begin the book of Genesis best illustrates the division between the two basis sources, J and P. We have already looked at the second of these (2:4b–24) in our treatment of J, so we now turn to the one in 1:1–2:4a, which is actually the later of the two and belongs to P. In contrast to J's account of creation, P describes a series of creative acts by God (Elohim), each one taking place on a single day for six days. The order is different and the pre-creation state of watery chaos and formlessness also contrasts with the desert of J. Scholars have long noted that there is a certain similarity in this account to Babylonian cosmogony (= birth of the cosmos). One version of their creation myths begins with a struggle between the monster Tiamat (= watery chaos) and the chief Babylonian god Marduk, who kills Tiamat and splits her body in two in order to create heaven and earth. While the Hebrew Bible also knows the myth about a struggle between Yahweh and a watery monster (Isa. 51:9–10; Ps. 74:12–17; 89:10), in Genesis 1 there is no opposing deity, only inanimate matter. The conception of God's power over chaos has been "demythologized." This is very much like early Greek science which, instead of speaking about the oldest pair of deities, heaven and earth, from which subsequent pairs of deities were born to make up the cosmic order, refers instead to earth, air, fire, and water and describes creation by separation. Apart from retaining the one creator deity, the rest of the account in Genesis has been demythologized.

First Day. The first act of creation is actually the creation of time by the separation of light from darkness to make a single day. It furnishes the unit of measurement for each of the next acts of creation.

Second Day. This is really the first act of cosmic creation in which the waters below (sea) are separated from the waters above (rain), which are held in place by a "firmament," a kind of dome with portals through which the rainwater can be released. This splitting of the waters corresponds to Marduk splitting the carcass of Tiamat.

Third Day. There are two stages to the creative act on this day. First is the separation of the water (= seas) from the land with emphasis on the setting of boundaries against the return to chaos. Then mother earth brings forth her yield by divine command. In Near Eastern mythology mother earth was *the* great creative power of fertility, not only of vegetation but even of the gods and humans who owed their existence to her. She and the masculine god "heaven" are the most primal pair before all the other gods are born. In contrast, in Genesis all fertility is under the single deity's control.

Fourth Day. Sun, moon, and stars are created on the fourth day rather than on the first day with light. This position is the result of dependence on the mythological tradition (such as that of Babylonia) in which these heavenly bodies are deities and receive their positions in the heavens after the destruction of Tiamat and the creation of the celestial vault. While the sun and moon are spoken of as "ruling" the day and night, this is now only a metaphor. Here the deities are demythologized as the "greater light" and the "lesser light," whose purpose is to mark times and seasons. Like the creation of day one, they become part of the history of time.

Fifth Day. Fish and birds are created from the sea, and like the earth in day three they receive the divine blessing of fertility.

Sixth Day. Again there are two separate acts of creation in one day. First animals are called forth from the earth. Then humanity is created. The term "adam" is used in a new sense to include both male and female. This new creature is made in the image and likeness of God. The plural ("Let us make humankind") contains a hint of a divine council or heavenly court. This resembles a Babylonian myth about how the king was a special creation of the gods, all of whom were called upon to contribute attributes and qualities that would equip him to rule. In Genesis 1 the myth of the first king has been democratized. All humans "have dominion over [all creation]" (see Psalm 8). The "image of God" does not refer to some special quality or aspect of humankind that is like the deity but reflects the fact that deities are represented everywhere in human form. This image is not something that was lost or destroyed because of sin, as in Christian theology. The P writer says in 5:1–3 that just as Adam was made in the image of God, so Seth, his son, was in the image of Adam. In contrast to J, where the humans become like God only after they eat the forbidden fruit, in P they are made like the deity in creation itself. Also in P when the humans are created they are given the blessing of fertility (not a curse as in J) and the guardianship of creation. And they are originally vegetarian!

Seventh Day. This is the sabbath rest for the deity. The eight stages of creation are compressed into six days (hence the double creative acts on days three and six) so that the seventh can be special. It is the etiology of a sacred institution (cf. Exod. 20:8–9). The sabbath was a special holy day for the Jews, regulated on a weekly basis only in the late monarchy. For P it becomes an act of reverence toward the creator and a sacred institution. It is not just a national institution, as in Deut. 5:12–15, but the recognition of a universal deity and an affirmation of work, productivity, and recreation in periodic cessation. The establishment of the sabbath also completes the creation of all of the units of time—day, week, month, season, year. The author finally celebrates the goodness of life. Everything is "very good."

P's account of creation is presented as the "genealogy of the heavens and the earth when they were created" (2:4a), the first part of his larger genealogy or history. Some ancient historians begin their histories with a mythical theogony or genealogy of gods—an account of how the universe came into being through the birth of successive generations of gods—that is, a genealogy of heaven and earth. Here again P has demythologized that form into a "scientific" statement, which is also a theological statement. From a modern perspective, Genesis 1 is neither science nor history. But for P there is no distinction between science, theology, and history.

We may now summarize a number of features that characterize the work of P in comparison with and in distinction from J:

—P uses God (Elohim) throughout his account; J uses Yahweh God.
—P's whole account is structured as an etiology of the sabbath with six days of divine work and rest on the seventh.
—The humans, made at one time, are in the image of God from the start, whereas in J man and woman are made separately and become like God only after eating the forbidden fruit.
—P's divine blessing "be fruitful and multiply" occurs repeatedly here and elsewhere in Genesis.
—P periodizes his history by use of the formula, "This is the genealogy of," which is found throughout Genesis.
—P's style is very formal, structured, repetitious, climactic.
—Everything is "good," "very good," optimistic. There is no story of the fall or curse on humankind and nature in P.

b. The Genealogy of Seth (Genesis 5)

The next block of P material comes in chapter 5 under the title, "the book of the genealogy of Adam." This gives the line of Seth as parallel to that of Cain in chapter 4 (J). P's genealogy also contains a *precise chronology* from a birth in one generation to a birth in the next in a linear succession of the firstborn males. This is similar to the Babylonian king list tradition in which the kings before the flood reigned in linear succession for hundreds, even thousands of years each. P also has ten generations in place of J's seven. We will see that P has a special interest in chronology in Genesis.

c. The Flood Story

As indicated earlier, P embellishes and modifies J's account of the flood. Among the differences are the fact that P has only one pair of *all* animals brought on board the ark, because there is no animal slaughter for food and no sacrifice before the flood as in J. Thus there is no need for any distinction between clean and unclean animals. Also, P's chronology is different. In P the flood lasts one full year and the date is linked with the chronological scheme of chapter 5. Noah is 600 years old when the flood begins. The most significant addition by P comes at the end of the story in 9:1–17, which contains a set of laws and a covenant. In P, major periods of history are marked by laws and covenants. Here, universal laws are set down: animal slaughter is now permitted but not the eating of blood (= raw meat), and the shedding of human blood (murder) is not permitted because humanity was made in the image of God. The covenant with Noah is a promise to all humanity that God will not bring another flood. It is an "eternal covenant" with a sign, the rainbow (cf. Genesis 17). Humankind is blessed again as at creation: "Be fruitful and multiply."

d. The Genealogy of Shem (Gen. 11:10–26)

A new genealogy of Shem is presented in this section parallel to the one in the Table of Nations (= J). This is a *linear genealogy* intended to lead directly from Shem (son of Noah) to Abraham. It provides a chronology from father to eldest son in the same way as the Seth genealogy of Genesis 5. This yields a complete chronology from Adam to the beginning of the Israelite people. It is an ingenious substitute for the scheme of the Mesopotamian king list, which is a chronology of the successive reigns of kings from before the flood. The genealogy ends with a few family notes (11:27–32) taken over from J.

e. The Patriarchs

P added more geneaologies and a precise chronology to the patriarchal stories by giving the ages of Abraham and Sarah, Isaac and Rebekah, Jacob, and so forth. In doing so, however, he created some problems for the stories to which they were attached. Thus, while the J story in Gen. 12:10–20 suggests that Sarah is young and beautiful, P says that Abraham is seventy-five and Sarah only ten years younger. Another example is the discrepancy that we noted earlier between Ishmael's age of thirteen in Gen. 17:25 and his being regarded as a young child in the story in Gen. 21:8–21. The following additions by P are noteworthy.

i. Covenant of Abraham (Genesis 17). This account by P of a covenant with Abraham is a doublet to the J version in chapter 15. Both contain the themes of numerous offspring and land. Here God appears to Abraham as El Shaddai ("God Almighty"). There are also name changes from Abram to Abraham and from Sarai to Sarah (these are merely dialectical variants). What P stresses in chapter 17 is the *sign* of the covenant, which is the circumcision of the males in the family. Failure to maintain this practice would mean exclusion from the people. For P the people of Israel is no longer just an ethnic concept. It is a religious community into which one is initiated and in which one remains by fulfilling certain rites and requirements. The covenant is "eternal," a divine institution. (The expression "eternal covenant" was also used in P's story of Noah in Genesis 9.) Participation within the covenant people is conditional upon maintaining the practice of the religion.

ii. Purchase of Sarah's Burial Place (Genesis 23). The cave of Machpelah at Hebron, purchased by Abraham in this story as a burial place for Sarah, ultimately becomes the tomb for all the patriarchs. P treats this as an entirely secular affair with no hint of any veneration for the dead, although the traditional site of this cave now has become a sacred place to both Moslems and Jews and the center of much controversy.

iii. Isaac's Blessing (Gen. 28:1–5). Here Isaac blesses Jacob in the name of El Shaddai ("God Almighty") before Jacob departs for Haran. This is parallel to J's version of the blessing in chapter 27, but it overlooks the fact that in J's version Jacob stole the blessing from Isaac. It also supplies a different motive for his migration to Haran. In addition to the reference to El Shaddai there is other language associated with P.

iv. God's appearance to Jacob at Bethel (Gen. 35:9–15). God's appearance as El Shaddai to Jacob at Bethel is a doublet to the theophany in 28:10–22 (J). There is also a change in Jacob's name to Israel and a similar set of promises to those in Genesis 17. But J has already told the story of the name change in Gen. 32:24–30.

v. Additions of P to the Joseph Story. These are minimal and consist primarily of repeating the theme of the blessing of creation ("be fruitful and multiply") to the patriarchal offspring in the land of Egypt (47:27; 48:3–6), supplying the chronology by means of Jacob's age (47:28) and specifying Jacob's burial in the patriarchal burial site in Mamre/Hebron (50:12–13). A longer addition is the genealogy of all the children and grandchildren of Jacob (seventy total) who accompanied him to Egypt (46:6–27).

In sum, for P the era of the patriarchs is marked by the revelation of God as *El Shaddai* ("God Almighty") and by the covenant of the rite of circumcision with Abraham. P continues his chronology through the ages of the partiarchs even when it does not fit the narrative contexts. P also extends the divine blessing of creation ("be fruitful and multiply") to each successive generation of patriarchs.

f. The Moses Story and the Exodus in P

All of the P units in Exodus 1—14 are again built into the older J narrative as additions. P begins by inserting a short summary of those in Jacob's family who came with him to Egypt (Exod. 1:1–5, 7*), which refers back to his longer genealogy in Gen. 46:8–27. This interrupts J's transition that extended from the death of Joseph in Gen. 50:24–26 to all his generation in Exod. 1:6 and the "new king who did not know Joseph" (v. 8). Then in 2:23–25 P adds a remark about the people's suffering and God's "hearing their groaning" and remembering his covenant with the patriarchs, which anticipates P's version of Moses' call in 6:2–7:7. This version of the call interrupts J's account of Moses' dealings with Pharaoh (chap. 5) + the first plague in 7:14–24 and includes a *second* commissioning of Moses and Aaron, this time in the land of Egypt, parallel to the call in Midian (J). The themes of announcing deliverance from the people's bondage and the connection with the patriarchs and God's promises to them are much the same as in J. Yet there are some important differences. For instance, in P the patriarchal age and the time of the exodus are presented as two distinct eras of divine revelation. Thus, according to 6:2–3 God appeared to Abraham, Isaac, and Jacob by the name El Shaddai but first became known as Yahweh to Moses. Nonetheless, P emphasizes that the motive for rescuing the people is God's remembrance of God's covenant with the forefathers, and that meant giving them the land of Canaan. Hence, the two eras are even more closely bound together than in J.

The message of deliverance that God gives Moses for the people is delivered to them in P only by Moses *without Aaron*. Yet this time the people do not receive it kindly, because of their hard service. This is different from the response in J (4:29–31), because in chapter 5 (J) Pharaoh has made matters much worse. This failure of Moses is followed in 6:10–13 by God's sending Moses, this time *with Aaron*, to Pharaoh. The action is interrupted by a genealogy of Moses and Aaron (6:14–25), after which we have P's general introduction to the plague stories in 7:1–7. In this introduction (still part of the call) God tells Moses that he is to speak to Pharaoh through Aaron to demand the people's release, but that Pharaoh will not listen because God has hardened Pharaoh's heart in order to bring divine judgment upon Egypt. This is the clearest evidence that P is a supplement to J and not, as many scholars since Wellhausen have argued, an independent source. For nowhere in the P material that follows do Moses and Aaron ever speak to Pharaoh. P's introduction to the plague story in 7:1–7, therefore, presupposes J's account where all the dialogue takes place.

We have already noted that P added three plagues (gnats, boils, darkness) to J's seven to bring the total number to ten. P also added the theme of a contest between Aaron and Pharaoh's magicians to three of the plagues (Nile water to blood, frogs, gnats) and set up the contest in 7:8–13. Next, P interrupted J's story of the departure from Egypt with an etiology of the passover as a commemoration of how God spared the Israelites' firstborn, while killing all the firstborn of Egypt (12:1–28, 40–51).[13] It is clear that the requirements of passover as detailed here could not have been observed in Egypt, because the Israelites would not have had time to prepare adequately for the festival, and they were forced to leave in the middle of the night, which would have violated the requirement of staying indoors until the morning. For P, however, it was more important that the event of the deliverance and its festal commemoration be fused into the same account. Finally, we have already shown how P's additions to J's account of the sea event (14:15–18, 21a, 22b, 26–27a) emphasized the splitting of the waters by means of the divine rod. For P the sea event is the real climax of the divine judgment of the plagues. So he makes a closer connection with them in the language he uses.

g. *Wilderness Wanderings in P*

P makes a number of additions within the wilderness tradition, mostly in the form of expansions to J's earlier stories. These may be found in the manna story of Exodus 16; the Sinai theophany of Exodus 19—20, to which P added his version of the Ten Commandments (20:1–17); the spy story in Numbers 13—14; the rebellion of Korah and its aftermath in Numbers 16—17; and the treachery of Shittim and the war on Midian in Numbers 25 and 31. In one instance P constructs a parallel account to J's story of striking the rock to produce water for the people (Exod. 17:1–7) by again having both Moses and Aaron strike the rock in disobedience to God's instructions (Num. 20:2–13) so as to explain why the two leaders died in the wilderness and not in the promised land.

h. Sinai and the Giving of the Law in P

The largest part of the P source of the Pentateuch is made up of legal material, most of it having to do with priestly or cultic matters. This will be discussed below in the section on the laws. Here I will merely point out that P has fitted his law code into the J story of the theophany at Sinai. By adding 19:12–13a, 20–25 P turns the mountain into sacred ground (like the temple precinct), on which the lay people are not permitted to trespass, in direct contradiction to J, who has Moses sanctify the people so they can come up on the mountain. Then P adds the Ten Commandments from Deuteronomy in 20:1–17 but in his own version (more on this below). Moses ascends Mount Sinai to receive the stone tablets of the laws (in J these are not the Ten Commandments but the official copy of the book of the covenant), and since Moses is on the mountain forty days, P also has God instruct him in the building of the tabernacle and issues other regulations concerning formal cultic practices. After J has Moses return to the camp for the golden calf episode and the covenant renewal (Exodus 32—34), P then has Moses build the Tabernacle "according to the pattern revealed to him on the mountain." Once this tabernacle or "tent of meeting" has been set up, Moses receives further revelations at this place. Most of the laws in the rest of the P Code are given to Israel through Moses while at Sinai before J has them break camp again in Num. 10:29–36. I will deal with the content of these laws below.

i. Acquisition of the Land (Numbers 26—27, 34—35; Joshua 13—21)

P also deals with the theme of the aquisition and distribution of the promised land. In the older presentation of the conquest in Joshua, the author was content simply to have Joshua give Israel the whole of the conquered land as an inheritance. P, however, goes into elaborate detail as to how the land was distributed among all the tribes and their clans and families according to a detailed census taken by Moses. It is then left to the individual tribes to make good their allotted claim to the land, which they attempt to do in Judges 1. The reason for this new presentation that P has in mind is the *return* of the exiles. It is no longer the conquest of the distant past that is in view but the responsibility of each Israelite family to lay claim to the territory as a religious duty (Josh. 18:1–3). The geographical boundaries and the elaborate lists of clans and families of the various tribes represent the interest and use of antiquarian lore that is a common feature of ancient historiography. Here it is put to special ideological use as part of P's program of restoration.

D. Law in the Pentateuch

As we indicated at the outset, about half of the Torah, the first division of the Hebrew Bible, consists of law in one form or other. All of the laws are attributed to Moses by tradition and most of them to the time that Israel spent at Horeb/Sinai. However, they belong to all three authors of the Pentateuch (D, J, and P) and consist of many different types, reflecting a long tradition of laws and customs from different periods of Israelite history. These laws have undergone many changes and modifications that can be seen from a comparison of those dealing with the same subject in the different sources and codes.

1. Types of Laws

The German scholar Albrecht Alt sought to establish a broad classification of the various types of laws, their origins, and their social settings.[14] His typology is still useful if modified by a consideration of the subsequent discussion.

a. Apodictic law states an absolute demand. It may be expressed as a direct command ("You shall not kill"), a curse ("Cursed is the one who does . . ."), or an indirect general principle ("whoever does . . . shall be put to death"). These three forms of apodictic law are often found in short series, such as the Ten Commandments.

b. Casuistic/case law sets forth a case or instance of an infraction and then prescribes the penalty. Thus it has the form: "If a man does thus and thus, and this causes the following damages, then he must pay . . ." This form of law is common to other Near Eastern law codes, many of them much older than Israelite law and often dealing with the same subjects. The content of these laws in the Bible reflects urban and rural life in the land of Canaan. It is, therefore, *civil law*, appropriate for life during the monarchy and later periods. Such laws could be adjudicated by law courts administered by local judges to settle property and personal injury disputes.

c. Humanitarian laws are more in the nature of moral guidelines, since they urge a mode of behavior that cannot be regulated by the courts. They often take the form of a command supported by a motivation clause: "You shall not wrong or oppress a resident alien, for you were aliens in the land of Egypt" (Exod. 22:21). Such laws reflect the influence of the ethical preaching of the eighth-century prophets.

d. Cultic laws have to do with the regulation of religious matters associated with formal worship. In the older codes they take the form of commands or statutes to the people as a whole to fulfill certain obligations, such as the keeping of religious festivals and holy days. The Priestly Code also includes a large body of elaborate instructions (directed primarily to the priests) concerning their duties, forms of sacrifice, food laws, details on the keeping of festivals, and so forth. This constitutes the largest body of laws in the Pentateuch.

2. The Law Codes

The practice of compiling laws into codes is very ancient in the Near East, and a number of codes—the most famous being Hammurabi's—have come to light through archaeology. Some of these codes have laws that are very similar to the casuistic/civil laws of the type discussed above. Within the Pentateuch there are a number of codes, some of which contain civil law but which are otherwise quite different from Near Eastern law codes. The biblical codes also contain a number of laws that are parallel but that modify each other slightly. These codes are discussed below according to the order of the sources in which they are found.

a. The D Code (Deuteronomy 12—26). As we have seen, this code is especially concerned with religious reform, beginning with the law of the altar and the centralization of worship in chapter 12 and with making the worship of another god a capital offense in chapter 13 (also see 17:2–7; 18:9–14). There are laws having to do with the administration of justice (16:18–20; 17:8–13), the monarchy (17:14–20), the priesthood (18:1–8), and the prophet (18:15–22). The ideology of holy war is set out in a detailed "law" in chapter 20. The rest of the D Code is a mixture of all the other types of laws.

b. The Covenant Code (Exod. 20:22–23:33). This is J's version of the law. In it the casuistic/civil type of law predominates, which deals with matters of everyday life, property, personal injury, and so on. But it also contains the other types as well. There are a number of laws in this code that are directly parallel to some in the D code, such as the law having to do with the Hebrew slave in Exod. 21:2–11 (// Deut. 15:12–18). Comparison of the two indicates that J's law is a later revision and modification of the law in D, intended to cover a wider range of cases of the enslavement of Hebrews by foreigners in the exilic period. The Covenant Code, in my view, is formulated to regulate life in the Jewish community of the Babylonian exile.

In the account on the covenant renewal in Exod. 34:10–27 there is a summary version of the Covenant Code. It contains a short prologue of exhortation to loyalty to Yahweh (vv. 11–16), a command against molten images (v. 17), and a list of ritual laws (vv. 18–26) parallel to those in 23:12–19. These have often been ascribed to different sources, but I consider them both to be the work of J.

c. The Holiness Code (Leviticus 17—26). This is another code similar to both the D Code and Covenant Code, and it shares some of the same laws and mixture of types in a different version. It also has a concluding exhortation (chap. 26) that is similar to the preaching style and the curses one finds in Deuteronomy. However, its major concern is for holiness (thus its designation by scholars), and it is priestly in outlook. The Holiness Code belongs to the exilic period and has close affinities with the language and perspective of the prophet Ezekiel, who was a priest and leader of the Jewish community in exile in Babylon. Originally it was an independent code, but it now finds its place within the late P Code.

Of these three codes (DC, CC, and HC), scholars have long been inclined to date the Covenant Code early, the D Code somewhat later, and the Holiness Code last. In my view this is incorrect, and I date the Covenant Code as the latest of the three and the D Code as the earliest.

d. The Priestly Code (Exod. 25—31, 35—40; Leviticus; Numbers 1—10*, 15, 18—19, 28—30). This code is of quite a different character from the other three codes. It has to do with the priestly regulations of worship: the form and furnishings of the Tabernacle, the investiture of the priests and Levites and their offices and duties, sacrifices and festivals, purity laws, and so on. Everything that pertains to the order of the cult is placed back in the time of the wilderness. Most of these laws are associated with Sinai, though some with the rest of the journey. This represents a compromise between J and D.

The Priestly Code was probably formulated by the priests of the Babylonian diaspora (under Ezra?) as a program in support of a theocracy with the high priest as head of state and supreme authority. There is no place in it for a king. The religious center, the temple, was meant to represent the entire religious community of Israel everywhere, with the priests administering the cult on behalf of the rest of the people. It did, however, permit some forms of religious life, such as the Passover, to be observed in the diaspora, a practice that was only partly carried through into later Judaism.

e. *The Ten Commandments (Exod. 20:1–17 [P] = Deut. 5:6–21 [D])* is a collection of laws that stands apart from the codes. The Ten Commandments (literally "ten words") are regarded in D as the direct utterance by God at Horeb (Sinai) to all Israel. These laws were then copied by God on two tablets of stone that Moses received from God when he later ascended the mountain. The rest of the laws were all mediated through Moses to the people because they were afraid to hear the voice of God directly. The two versions of the Ten Commandments are almost identical, with only slight differences in wording, except for the law of the sabbath. The D version is the older. It combines within it the various types of laws: strong religious sanctions against the worship of other gods, idolatry, and misuse of the divine name for evil purposes (nos. 1–3); regulations about observance of the sabbath (no. 4); moral injunction on the honoring of one's parents (no. 5); and a series of apodictic commands regarding basic social behavior (nos. 6–10). These are intended as a summation of the most basic principles of Israelite religion and ethics.

There is no separate version of the Ten Commandments in J. Instead, J included its primary elements within the Covenant Code. P, however, has restored the Ten Commandments as a separate group of laws given at Sinai, at the same time making some slight revisions, particularly in the law of the sabbath. In D the sabbath is a national law linked with the exodus; in P it is a universal law linked with creation.

The Ten Commandments continue to have a special status in both Judaism and Christianity, but they should be viewed within the context of the ancient world and not be too quickly modernized. The first command, for example, does not strictly advocate monotheism, but only that Yahweh should be the only deity worshiped by Israel. The precise wording "alongside of me" perhaps arises out of a rejection of any consort for Yahweh. However, the law does not make clear whether Yahweh could be identified with other deities, such as the creator god El. Again, the third command against taking the name of God in vain does not mean profanity in the modern sense, but the use of the divine name to curse or injure someone— swearing to another's injury or making a false or meaningless oath. The Ten Commandments were not intended to cover the whole of religious and moral teaching, nor should one make a distinction between them as universal and timeless and the "other" laws as more temporally and socially conditioned. In fact, most of the laws in the Ten Commandments are found in the other codes as well. Finally, while scholars have long recognized that the law codes do not reflect life in the wilderness, dating them long after the "time of Moses," there is still a tendency by some to consider the Ten Commandments or some earlier version of them as coming from Moses. But as with the other codes, the laws reflect settled life in the land of Canaan (see nos. 4, 5, and 10). Like all the laws, the Ten Commandments were ascribed to Moses, because he had become the symbol of the divine mediation of law and the social and religious orders of life, and his lifetime was considered the "constitutional" age of ancient Israel.

FOR FURTHER READING

Blenkinsopp, Joseph. *The Pentateuch: An Introduction to the First Five Books of the Bible.* ABRL. New York: Doubleday, 1992.

Carr, David. *Reading the Fractures of Genesis: Historical and Literary Approaches.* Louisville, Ky.: Westminster John Knox, 1996.

Noth, Martin. *A History of Pentateuchal Traditions.* Englewood Cliffs, N.J.: Prentice-Hall, 1972.

Van Seters, John. *Abraham in History and Tradition.* New Haven and London: Yale University Press, 1975.

———. *Prologue to History: The Yahwist as Historian in Genesis.* Louisville, Ky.: Westminster/John Knox, 1992.

———. *The Life of Moses: The Yahwist as Historian in Exodus—Numbers.* Louisville, Ky.: Westminster John Knox, 1994.

von Rad, Gerhard. *Genesis: A Commentary.* OTL. Philadelphia: Westminster, 1972.

Whybray, R. N. *The Making of the Pentateuch.* JSOTSup 53. Sheffield: JSOT, 1987.

———. *Introduction to the Pentateuch.* Grand Rapids: Eerdmans, 1995.

Part II

Prophets (*Nevi'im*)

2

THE FORMER PROPHETS

Joshua, Judges, 1–2 Samuel, 1–2 Kings

A. GRAEME AULD

I. OVERVIEW

The books of Joshua, Judges, 1–2 Samuel, and 1–2 Kings together tell an extended story. It begins with Joshua leading Israel across the river Jordan into the land of promise after the death of Moses on the other side. It ends with the fall of Jerusalem to the Babylonian army and the consequent removal to Babylon of the king and his court along with the valuables from the destroyed temple. The death of Moses is where the Torah ends. The Babylonian conquest is the great watershed in much of Hebrew Bible tradition—between a people in its land and a people uprooted.

Both Jewish and Christian tradition have preserved these books together and have seen them as parts of a larger whole within the Bible, though in different ways. In the Hebrew Bible, Joshua, Judges, Samuel, and Kings are four books of Former Prophets balancing a further four books of Latter Prophets: Isaiah, Jeremiah, Ezekiel, and the Twelve. Christian tradition, probably rooted in an alternative Jewish tradition, has referred to them as "historical books." Christian Bibles also include Ruth in this category (between Judges and Samuel), as well as the books of Chronicles, Ezra, Nehemiah, and Esther (after Kings). "Prophecy" and "history"—both terms derived from tradition—prepare one for important elements found in these books. Moreover, reading these books helps one to understand better what the shapers of different "canons" of biblical books meant by "prophecy" and "history."

II. THE STORY

The contents of the books in the Former Prophets may be laid out as a linear narrative. The first half of the book of Joshua reports Israel's occupation of its land west of the Jordan under Joshua's leadership. Joshua is encouraged as successor to Moses and also exhorted to base his leadership on meditation on the Mosaic Torah (chap. 1). To say that the next chapters (2—6) start with Joshua sending out spies and finish with Jericho burned and its inhabitants slaughtered is true. But its military ordinariness gives no impression of the otherworldliness of these chapters or of the surprises their stories spring on the reader. A campaign against Ai in the central hill country first fails because of ritual impropriety and then succeeds (chaps.

7—8). Then nearby Gibeon makes peace with Israel by trickery (chap. 9). Resistance to Israel led by five southern cities fails (chap. 10), and Hazor, the great city of northern Galilee, falls (chap. 11). The successful results are then summarized (chap. 12). Most of the rest of the book is concerned with the division of that land among Israel's constituent groups (chaps. 13—22). Judah in the south is treated first and in greatest detail in a lengthy chapter (15). Then Ephraim and Manasseh, jointly representing Joseph in the center, are dealt with much more schematically (chaps. 16—17). The holdings of the remaining seven tribes west of the Jordan are listed in Josh. 18:11–19:48. Around this main (west of the Jordan) delineation there is a description of a due place for Israel's people east of the Jordan River (chaps. 13, 22) and holdings for its priests and Levites (chap. 21). The book ends with farewell instruction from Joshua in two speeches prior to the report of his death (chaps. 23—24).

The book of Judges has an extended series of introductions (1:1–3:11). The lengthy first chapter is primarily a recapitulation of materials in Joshua. It stresses the greater completeness of Judah's occupation of southern Palestine over against the partial success of the central and northern Israelite tribes. The second chapter introduces the theme of Israel's repeated apostasy after Joshua's death and Yahweh's repeated response of delivering Israel. The first leader to "judge" Israel, Othniel (3:7–11), is a composite figure built from all those who follow. The central part of the book (3:12–16:31) mixes tales of major deliverers such as Ehud (3:12–30), Deborah and Barak (chaps. 4—5), Gideon/Jerubbaal (chaps. 6—8), Jephthah (10:6–12:7), and Samson (chaps. 13—16) with minor figures to whom only a couple of sentences are devoted (10:1–5 and 12:8–15). At its heart is a long story (9:1–57) critical of Jerubbaal's son Abimelech and his brief kingship in Shechem. Then, in the final five chapters, the book moves beyond the tales of judge/deliverer to two cycles of stories (chaps. 17—18 and 19—21) from a time when "there was no king in Israel," and matters were lurching from bad to worse.

The first book of Samuel opens with hope and despair (chaps. 1—6). The stories of his birth and of his vision as a lad identify Samuel as a figure of promise. This portrait of expectation is heightened against a background of foul behavior by Eli's priestly family and the loss of the divine ark to the Philistines. The next six chapters report the discussions between Samuel, Israel, and the deity about whether to establish a king in Israel and the events that lead to the choice of Saul. While Saul remains a key character throughout the book, there is also a sense in which the dispatching of his reign in only two chapters (13—14) seems quite appropriate. By the end of chapter 15, Samuel has left him in grief, never to see him again, and Yahweh has repented ever having made him king. The second half of this long book is a much more leisurely account of the rise of David—also anointed by Samuel, victorious over a Philistine giant, and sometime vassal of the Philistines. The book ends (chap. 31) with Saul dead after battle with the old enemy (the Philistines) and with David at a conveniently safe distance to the south (chaps. 29—30), neither implicated in Saul's death nor able to save him from it.

The second book of Samuel is the story of David as king. The first four chapters show him dealing with the inheritance of Saul—first publicly lamenting Saul and Jonathan—then, from his base in Hebron in the heartland of Judah, struggling with the late king's family and supporters. It is in Hebron that Israel's leaders anoint him as king. But he moves quickly north to take Jerusalem, defeat the Philistines, and bring the ark to his new capital (chaps. 5—6). Nathan prophesies two houses (chap. 7): Yahweh will give David a royal house (a dynasty) as a reward for his faithfulness, and David's son will be permitted to build a house (a temple) for the deity's name. Victories in Syria and Transjordan follow (chaps. 8—11). The last of these (in Ammon) provides the background for David's elimination of Bathsheba's husband, Nathan's parable of condemnation (chaps. 11—12), and the eventual birth of Solomon. The next eight chapters report strife within the royal house: the rape of David's daughter Tamar by her half-brother Amnon, the rebellion by Tamar's brother Absalom, another rebellion by the disaffected north, and the painful return of David to Jerusalem. It is typically ironic that these disruptive chapters should have as a leading character Absalom, whose name may be understood as "my father is peace." A final well-structured unit (chaps. 21—24) begins with a return to the topic of the relationships between David and Saul and the Philistines, has at its heart two poems embodying the royal ideology, and concludes with David failing Yahweh's test over taking a census of the people.

The first book of Kings opens with two chapters on the death of David, the succession of Solomon, and the consolidation of his power. The report of Solomon's reign (chaps. 3—11) stresses his wisdom and wealth. At its heart is the account of his building work on the temple and palace in Jerusalem and his great prayer at the dedication of the temple. But the report finishes with dissolution because of Solomon's faithlessness, and a rereading of the story reveals the seeds of dissolution even at its beginning. Division of the kingdom follows Solomon's death (chaps. 12—14): his son Rehoboam is unable to command the loyalty of the north; his one-time agent Jeroboam becomes the northern king and establishes rival temples in Bethel and Dan; and two prophets are critical of Jeroboam's sanctuaries and family while a third warns Judah against fighting with their kinfolk in Israel. Short reports of the early successors of Rehoboam and Jeroboam in Judah and Israel follow (chaps. 15—16).

The middle third of the two books of Kings (1 Kings 17—2 Kings 10) consists of very different material. The focus of these chapters is almost exclusively on the northern kingdom, and they are dominated by extended narratives featuring the prophets Elijah and Elisha. Their stories are set in the time when the house of Omri—principally Omri, his son Ahab, and Ahab's wife Jezebel—ruled Israel in Samaria. The greater struggle played out in these chapters is in fact between their divine protagonists, Yahweh and Baal. Many wonders are worked, and much blood of the devotees of Baal is shed.

The malignant influence of Omri's family does not leave Jerusalem untouched. Athaliah, the daughter of Ahab and Jezebel, usurps power in Judah upon the death of her son Ahaziah, until she is removed by a coup (2 Kings 11—12). Brief reports of the kings of Judah and Israel resume in 2 Kings 13—16. The opening of the long chap. 17 tells briefly of the fall of Samaria to Assyria, while the remainder explains at length the religious causes and results. The last chapters of 2 Kings report the final generations of the kingdom of Judah. The good kings Hezekiah (2 Kings

18—20) and Josiah (2 Kings 22—23) are dealt with at greater length, with the account of the decisively wicked Manasseh and his unrepentant son Amon in between (2 Kings 21). The final four kings are overwhelmed by either the Egyptians or the Babylonians, or are their puppets (23:31–24:20). Rebellion by Zedekiah leads to the final collapse (chap. 25).

III. THE ISSUES

One answer to the question, "What are the books Joshua to Kings about?" has just been sketched: together they tell a story from Israel's first steps in the land promised to their ancestors down to the collapse of Jerusalem to Babylon. Yet it is vital to go on and offer a second answer, for very often—and perhaps always—the story being told is an opportunity to explore significant contemporary issues.

The book of Joshua has a reputation for violence that is not entirely undeserved. However, in addition to repeatedly commending loyalty to Yahweh's Torah and covenant (1:7–9; 8:30–35; 23—24), it also devotes a great deal of space to relations between insiders and outsiders. In the first half, both Rahab (chap. 2) and the Gibeonites (chap. 9) are foreigners within Israel's land (i.e., west of the Jordan) who achieve status in the community. Then in the second half, the residents of Transjordan (chaps. 1, 13, 22) and the Levites (chap. 21), while full members of Israel, possess land outside "the land" or do not have land at all.

The introductory material in Judges begins with the relative success of Judah among Israel's constituent units and ends with Othniel, a model judge related to the southern figure Caleb. The rest of the book is set among the northern tribes, which the writer seems to regard as less successful. The story in the central chapters (3—16) is not so much linear as a downward spiral. Then by the time that we come to Samson, the final judge (chaps. 13—16), the Philistines seem so much in control of Israel, and he seems so much of a loner, however mighty in person, that it is no longer clear in what sense he is being said to have "judged Israel" (15:20; 16:31). The final chapters picture a bleak time in which "there was no king in Israel; all the people did what was right in their own eyes." They mock in advance the derivative cult in the north (chaps. 17—18) and Saul's birthplace and early leadership of Israel (chaps. 19—21). But they no longer feature judges or deliverers.

In the book of Samuel we are dealing with a single life span—or at least with the overlapping life spans of Samuel/Saul and David—as we were in Joshua, though now at more than twice the length. The onward national movement is consequently much slower, and the spotlight is directed more intensely on individuals and their characterization. There is a special interest in how the characters relate with one another, mostly in pairs: Samuel and Saul; David and Jonathan; Saul and David; David and Michal; Abigail and David; David and Absalom; Nathan and David; Amnon and Tamar; and David and his two main generals, Abner and Joab.

In the book of Kings, both Israel and Judah go into ruin at the hands of successive Mesopotamian powers, Assyria and Babylon. In each case it is the twentieth successor to David who is found treacherous and provides cause for the invasion

(2 Kings 17:4; 24:20). It is equally true that both royal regimes fall because of apostasy against their divine master Yahweh. Yet while Judah's kings are a mixture of good and bad in the eyes of Yahweh, Israel's are all bad: All "walked in the sins of Jeroboam the son of Nebat, which he made Israel to sin" and "did not depart from them." The book of Kings ends with a tantalizing glimpse (25:27–30) of a change of fortune for Jerusalem's penultimate king, Jehoiachin, who had been taken captive to Babylon after the first of two Babylonian invasions of Judah.

IV. ORIGINS

Determining why the story from Joshua to Kings was told, and was told as it was, is closely bound up with deciding whether in fact we are dealing in these "Former Prophets" of the Hebrew Bible with just one overarching story. Did they constitute one work or several? If they were conceived as a single though multipart work, one should be able to identify a controlling perspective and purpose. But if the separate books as they have come down to us were also separately written, then we would expect diverse answers to questions of aim and point of view.

The Babylonian Talmud (*b. B. Bat.* 14b–15a) teaches that Joshua wrote the book that bears his name and the final verses of the Torah, that Samuel wrote the book that bears his name and also the books of Judges and Ruth, and that Jeremiah wrote the book that bears his name as well as the books of Kings and Lamentations. The Talmud concedes that others had a part in writing some of these books: the last chapter of Joshua reports his own death, and Samuel dies well before the end of 1 Samuel (28:3). Hence, the Talmud apparently adapts the references to the books of Samuel in 1 Chron. 29:29 and informs us that Samuel's work was completed by Gad and Nathan. With Judges–Kings attributed to the prophets Samuel (and Nathan and Gad) and Jeremiah, we may suppose that Joshua was also understood to have been a prophet. But did these books come to be called "The Former Prophets" because each was already separately held to have been written by a prophet? Or were appropriate "prophetic" authors attached by tradition to each section of a collection already identified with the "former prophets" mentioned by Zech. 1:4?

Questions as to why and how the books Joshua to Kings were written have long been posed and answered in connection with similar questions about the five books of the Torah or Pentateuch. It is not just that, when read consecutively, Torah and Former Prophets tell a continuous story from the creation of the world to the fall of Jerusalem. It is also the case that they are easily joined or rejoined: Joshua picks up exactly where Deuteronomy leaves off. From early times in Christian tradition, scholars and teachers have modified the inherited term "Pentateuch"—the Greek word refers to a work that requires five scroll-jars. They have spoken instead of Genesis–Joshua as the Hexateuch, of Genesis–Ruth as an Octateuch, or even of Genesis–Kings (without Ruth) as an Enneateuch. It is hardly surprising, therefore, that several contemporary critics speak of Torah and Former Prophets together as the Bible's Primary History,[1] distinct from the first part of the Secondary History, which is supplied by the books of Chronicles. Chronicles also covers, though much more briefly, the whole story from the first human to the promise of restoration after the fall of Jerusalem to Babylon.

Before we turn to the scholarship of the last two centuries, four early modern approaches should be noted.[2] Thomas Hobbes (1651) drew on Judg. 18:30 to argue that Judges and Ruth must be dated after "the captivity of the land" and observed that an exilic date for the book of Kings was evident. Benedict de Spinoza (1670) drew attention to the many discrepancies between the books of Chronicles and Kings, and concluded "that the Bible's historical stories are not ruled by an exact chronology and that . . . these stories have been borrowed from different sources and inserted without criticism or order."[3] Richard Simon (1678), though he proposed a chain of traditions from Moses to Ezra, conservatively attributed Judges and Ruth to Samuel and Samuel and Kings to Jeremiah. Thomas Morgan (1737–1740) was critical of the Bible's theological judgments. He suggested that Samuel's attitude to Saul was motivated by jealousy, that Ahab and Jezebel were authentic humanists and heroes of tolerance in face of fanatical prophets, and that the exile was nothing but the consequence of unfortunate external politics.

The origins of the five books of Moses have been more intensively studied and debated than the writing of any other part of the Hebrew Scriptures. That process was discussed extensively in the previous chapter. It was regularly supposed by early critical scholars that the hard-won results of Pentateuchal criticism could be extended and applied to those narrative books that so obviously continued the primal story. Apparent repetition of content together with repeating clusters of language led to the detection of largely parallel "sources." The early-to-mid-monarchic "Yahwist" (J) and mid-to-late-monarchic "Elohist" (E) found in Genesis, Exodus, and Numbers were detected also in Joshua, Judges, and Samuel. Furthermore, the respective dates for these sources were determined by how far through Kings they could also be found. For a long time in more recent scholarship (the last two centuries), it was at the very least considered obvious that the books of Moses—the Pentateuch—had been shortened from an original Hexateuch. It was supposed that in the time of Ezra, who is often credited with promulgating the Torah as official law within the Persian province of Yehud, it would have been impolitic to have as a charter the complete Hexateuch, showing Israel as successful in taking and dividing all the land of promise. Therefore, scholars contended that a more primal story, extending from God's promise of land to Abraham in Genesis down to the fulfillment of that promise in the time of Joshua, must have had its conclusion removed.

V. DEUTERONOMISTIC HISTORIOGRAPHY

It had been observed for a long time that there is greater affinity between Deuteronomy and the books from Joshua to Kings than between Deuteronomy and other books of the Hebrew Bible (except perhaps for the book of Jeremiah).

This led quite early in modern scholarship to the assertion of Deuteronomic influence on the books of the Former Prophets, or to the detection of Deuteronomic portions within them. At a still earlier stage, the fact that the account in 2 Kings 22 —23 of the religious reform during the reign of King Josiah shares several leading ideas with Deuteronomy led W. M. L. de Wette (1806–1807) to date the fifth book (traditionally attributed to Moses) as late as the seventh century B.C.E.[4] This was, in fact, the crucial move that opened the way to a fresh understanding of Israel's early history and the history of its literature.

A. The Deuteronomistic History

However, it was not until 1943 that Noth published his now classic argument that, just behind the books of Deuteronomy to Kings as they now stand, one may detect a single historical work composed not many years after the exile of the Jerusalem elite to Babylon.[5] He called this history "Deuteronomistic"—in a tradition that stretched as far back as de Wette—because its key principles and language had been learned from the core of the book of Deuteronomy. The adjective "Deuteronomic" Noth reserved for material in the book of Deuteronomy itself, following Wellhausen's magisterial distinction.[6] Noth's Deuteronomist ("Dtr" for short) had been remarkably unintrusive with respect to the extended written sources available for all the periods he treated. He had coordinated these by supplying a series of linking passages. Some of these were in his own narrator's voice: Joshua 1, introducing the settlement; most of Judg. 2:6–3:6, marking the transition from Joshua's death to the period of the judges; and the extended peroration on the fall of northern Israel in 2 Kings 17. Other linking passages, while composed quite as obviously in his language, thought, and style, were put in the mouths of leading characters: Joshua's (first) farewell in Joshua 23, Samuel's retrospective in 1 Samuel 12, and Solomon's prayer at the dedication of the temple in 1 Kings 8.

Two points need to be stressed about Noth's case. The first is that, after reviewing the interconnectedness of the books Joshua to Kings, he decided that Deuteronomy rather than Joshua was the original beginning of the history. The second is his view that some substantial supplements had been added to the Deuteronomistic History before or after it was divided into the separate books we know. These included the account of the land division in Joshua 13—22; the portions of Judges at the beginning and end (1:1–2:5 and chaps. 17—21), which are not about "judging" at all; and the end of 2 Samuel (chaps. 21—24), which interrupts the story of David's court and of the succession of Solomon in 2 Samuel 9—1 Kings 2. Noth agreed with the prevailing view that the latter passage (2 Samuel 9—20 + 1 Kings 1—2) was a single original story, and he considered this to be one of the major preexisting sources available to the Deuteronomist for his history.

Two questions have dominated discussion of these issues since Noth's seminal study, and they are interrelated: (1) Was the Deuteronomistic work a unity, and (2) was the Deuteronomist (simply) an editor or (really) an author? Noth observed at the outset of his study that there was "much talk of two stages of 'Deuterono-mistic' composition in the books from Joshua to Kings." This was partly because "Dtr.'s work was subsequently added to in the same style; but this does not dis-prove the unity of the original Dtr."; and partly the result of "a too early dating of the original 'composition' of Dtr. which compels one to ascribe certain passages, which were obviously composed later, to a second Deuteronomistic author."[7] Noth accordingly proposed a sufficiently late date (mid-sixth century B.C.E.) for Dtr's work so that more of the materials from diverse periods could be reckoned among the sources that Dtr had utilized and fewer among the later additions. The fact that Dtr's work showed up so clearly as unified, against the wide diversity of the source materials used, led Noth to insist that Dtr was not merely an editor but an author who had selected and planned.[8]

A vital element in this unified plan was the chronological framework that Dtr created:[9]

> If we take even a superficial look at Dtr.'s work in Kings, we find that he is not exclusively interested in evaluating the individual kings and thus, indirectly, the monarchy *per se* . . . ; rather he is just as interested in constructing a de-finitive chronology, and for this purpose went to the trouble of taking over and reporting so many individual numbers from his sources.

There were two main foci of this work with dates. Dtr had to interweave the separate data from the monarchies of Judah and Israel into a single unbroken sys-tem. He had to relate the information available to him for the premonarchic period to the obviously round number of 480 years, which he set in 1 Kings 6:1 as the pe-riod from the exodus from Egypt to the building of Solomon's temple.

Noth's radical thesis has become widely accepted over half a century as the ba-sis for an explanation of the writing of the books of the Former Prophets and of their particularly close links with Deuteronomy. However, many critics have noted how little "Deuteronomistic" the books of Samuel are. Apart from the minor edit-ing required in the combination of his sources, Noth himself believed that the Deuteronomist had composed in these two books only 1 Sam. 7:2–8:22; 10:17–27a; and 12:1–25. Recent scholars especially have suggested that this absence of Dtr's distinctive editorial style from a large portion of the Former Prophets is fa-tal for Noth's thesis of a single historical work.[10]

B. Two or More Deuteronomists

We turn now to some modifications of Noth's arguments. Discussion has proceeded differently in English-language (especially North American) and in German-language studies, having been influenced respectively by seminal re-sponses from Frank Moore Cross and Rudolf Smend. Each began at a different end of the Deuteronomist's work.

Cross started with Kings, where he expected the historian to "express his intent most clearly" closer to his own times.[11] Cross argued that a Josianic first edition of the history represented a combination of "two grand themes or bundles of themes running through the Book of Kings":[12] the sin of Jeroboam and the faithfulness of David. The reforming king Josiah, hero of this first version, "extirpat[ed] the counter-cultus of Jeroboam at Bethel" and "attempted to restore the kingdom or empire of David in all detail."[13] These two themes, "appear to reflect two theological stances, one stemming from the old Deuteronomic covenant theology . . . and a second, drawn from the royal ideology in Judah."[14] Cross identified two main criteria for his second edition. Some passages toward the end of Kings, notably the critique of the syncretism practiced by Manasseh in 2 Kings 21:2–15, are not fully keyed into the main themes of the book. Then, while not all references to defeat and captivity need stem from an exilic edition, "a limited number of passages . . . appear to be addressed to exiles and to call for their repentance" and these "are mostly naturally regarded as coming from the hand of an Exilic editor."[15] Cross's work was elaborated by Richard Nelson, who concluded that the exilic editor had transformed a work of royal propaganda into a doxology of judgment.[16] It has also been very influential on the commentaries on Joshua and Judges by Robert Boling[17] and on many articles and monographs by Cross's Harvard students.

Smend offered his celebrated new lead in an article entitled, "The Law and the Peoples," in which he discussed certain passages in Joshua and the first two chapters of Judges.[18] He proposed that Josh. 1:7–9 represented a secondary expansion of 1:1–6 and 13:1bβ–6 of 13:1abα, 7; that Joshua 23 was a second conclusion, in the spirit of 1:7–9 and 13:1bβ–6, to the Dtr account of conquest and settlement, whose original conclusion had been provided by 21:43–45; that Judg. 2:17, 20–21, 23 were similarly secondary to their immediate context; and finally that the whole introduction to the present book of Judges (1:1–2:9) was an insertion in the same spirit into the original Deuteronomistic History. These few "nomistic" additions were only the tip of a large iceberg whose contours could be traced from Deut. 1:5 to the end of 2 Kings. In the reprint of this article, Smend noted that his former student Walter Dietrich had provided some of the analysis necessary for the books of Kings.[19]

Dietrich was unaware of the work of Cross, but he too sought answers to Dtr problems in his 1972 study of Kings entitled, *Prophecy and History*.[20] He attributed a series of reports of prophetic judgment, each followed a little later by the documentation of its fulfillment, to a further Deuteronomist: DtrP alongside—or in fact between—Smend's DtrH and DtrN. These have been conveniently summarized as follows:[21]

Prophetic Judgment	**Fulfillment**
1 Kings 14:7, 8a, 9b–11, 13b	1 Kings 15:29
1 Kings 16:1–4	1 Kings 16:11–12
1 Kings 21:19b, 20bβ–24; 22:38	2 Kings 10:17a
2 Kings 9:7–10a	2 Kings 9:36
2 Kings 21:10–14	2 Kings 24:2
2 Kings 22:15–18	

In addition to being the author of these passages and of the kernel of the story of Nathan before David (2 Samuel 12), DtrP also edited into the history preexisting materials such as the stories of Elijah and Elisha and the prophetic narratives in 1 Kings 13, 20, and 22. In a lengthy footnote Dietrich muses over 1 Sam. 2:27–36 and even Judg. 6:7–10 as candidates for the earliest insertion by this Deuteronomist.[22]

The Finnish scholar, Timo Veijola, also wrote his dissertation under Smend in Göttingen. In two volumes he concentrated more on the texts relating to the beginnings of monarchy—namely, the end of Judges and the books of Samuel.[23] He paid close attention to different ideological attitudes toward monarchy within the text. He concluded that DtrH had been favorable toward the monarchy; DtrP had been critical; and finally, DtrN had reverted to a more favorable stance provided that the kings were obedient to Mosaic Torah. Veijola was not simply hearing rival voices within the materials attributed to the Deuteronomist by Noth. Whereas Noth saw very little Dtr contribution in Samuel (in Noth's view Dtr had composed the David story largely by combining preexisting accounts of his rise and of his court and the succession of Solomon), Veijola detected more substantial contributions by each of Dietrich's three Deuteronomistic hands. Essentially he was returning to a position against which Noth had warned. Most of what Veijola attributed to DtrH was source material for Noth's Deuteronomist, and much of what Veijola attributed to DtrP and DtrN Noth had ascribed to his one and only Dtr.

One of the more influential recent writers on Deuteronomy and the Deuteronomists has been Norbert Lohfink. He has developed his ideas in an extensive series of articles,[24] and his lead has been further advanced by his former student, Georg Braulik.[25] Lohfink operates in constructive critique of both the so-called Harvard and Göttingen "schools." He agrees on the one side with Smend's followers that there have been at least two exilic reworkings of the Deuteronomistic History. But he insists, not unlike Cross, that a preexilic, proto-Deuteronomistic version of Kings and a preexilic version of Deuteronomy–Joshua was available to these exilic writers. A similar attempt at "mediation" has been made by Andrew Mayes.[26]

Cross and Smend and their former students have provided the lead, or at least the technical language, for much of the discussion of the Deuteronomist(s) that has followed in commentaries and monographs. The discussion has been reported many times, but perhaps the most useful recent presentations in English are the brief account by McKenzie in the *Anchor Bible Dictionary*[27] and the several papers presented at a jubilee celebration of Noth's work in 1993 in Washington, D.C.[28] Some of the latter review the more general impact of Noth's work; five of them deal in turn with his and subsequent work on Deuteronomy, Joshua, Judges, Samuel, and Kings. French readers now have available the comprehensive review article by Römer and de Pury.[29]

C. Quest for Deuteronomistic Unity

Although most scholars who have grappled with the inheritance of Noth have agreed that there are distinct layers or blocks of Deuteronomistic material, an attempt has been made from time to time to reappraise more positively his original vision that Dtr's work was a unity. Hoffmann offered a sustained attempt both to recognize as the Deuteronomist's own much more material within Deuteronomy–Kings than Noth had done and to argue that this represented one consistent presentation of "reform and reforms."[30] Then McKenzie, though his attention—like that of Cross, his original mentor—was concentrated on "the trouble with Kings," proposed an immediately preexilic date for the work of a single Deuteronomist.[31] But this was a much shorter work than Noth had recognized, one to whose history most of the prophetic material, including the "man of God" from Judah and Elijah and Elisha, had not yet been added. Again, like Cross, McKenzie remained convinced that the promise to the house of David for all time required that the composition of the history, or at least of Samuel–Kings, belonged before the final deportation: "I cannot believe that an exilic writer who knows that there is no Davidide on the throne in Jerusalem would include and stress such a promise."[32] It is remarkable how little Noth had to say about the divine promise to David; even if he reckoned all the relevant passages as belonging to Dtr's source material, they should have rated more discussion. (Perhaps a dissident professor in wartime East Prussia was hearing altogether too much about empires that would last a thousand years.) Yet if Dtr was faithful to his sources, as Noth contended, the old promise had to be reported even if its terms seemed called into question at the point where the story ended.

Yet it is Robert Polzin who has been providing the most substantial unified reading of these books, and this in two senses. First, his is a large-scale enterprise. Three volumes have been published dealing with Deuteronomy–Judges and 1–2 Samuel in turn.[33] A fourth volume on Kings is promised. In addition, Polzin is offering an integrated account of the complete inherited text: unity is not being achieved, as in so many other readings, by defining as secondary or additional what does not fit. He has a fine sensitivity to nuance and may have achieved a larger vision than most other readers of what these complex texts "are about." It is less clear, however, whether he uses the term "Deuteronomist" in at all a strong or in merely a conventional sense. In his earliest volume he proposes a difficult but attractive thesis about alternative and competing voices in the text, most of all in Deuteronomy, where he finds the authority of God, of Moses, and of the narrator both merged and contrasted. In his second and third volumes "Deuteronomist" seems to be little more than the accustomed name for the author of the books of Samuel.

VI. OTHER READINGS

There continue to be many useful studies of the books of the Former Prophets that completely ignore Noth's thesis and the many successor volumes. These stem largely, but not entirely, from the English-speaking world. It is the books of Samuel, and after them the book of Judges, that have generated by far the largest part of this more "literary" response. It is in keeping with this greater interest that

Polzin has dealt with Deuteronomy, Joshua, and Judges in one volume, but has devoted one volume each of his quartet to 1 Samuel and 2 Samuel.

By far the most detailed—and some would suggest relentless—literary interrogation of the books of Samuel is constituted by the four substantial volumes by the Dutch scholar, Jan Fokkelman, under the overarching title *Narrative Art and Poetry in the Books of Samuel.* The series contains this striking claim in the subtitle: *a full interpretation based on stylistic and structural analyses.* The titles of his individual volumes tell their own story: *King David (II Samuel 9—20 & I Kings 1— 2); The Crossing Fates (I Sam. 13—31 & II Sam. 1); Throne and City (II Sam. 2— 8 & 21—24);* and *Vow and Desire (I Sam. 1—12).*[34] David Clines' response must be echoed by many readers:

> One's frank disbelief at the weight [and the four volumes together contain more than 2,400 pages] so often laid upon small details of the text that are claimed to have a structural function, and one's suspicion that the text is being divinized into an object immeasurably more significant at every point than any human author could possibly have intended should not obscure for the reader the subtlety and penetration of Fokkelman's vigorous exposition.[35]

Fokkelman's work begins with the end of the section of text he has chosen to study and ends at its beginning. That section of text is essentially the book of Samuel, except that in his first volume Fokkelman discusses 1 Kings 1—2 and omits 2 Samuel 21—24. The introduction to the volume explains that

> The book concerns II Sam. 9—20 and I Kings 1—2 because this last quarter, universally recognized as the pearl of biblical prose, is a consummate whole well-suited to synchronic reading, and because it is the best text for exploiting the qualities and techniques of Old Testament narrative in order to develop interpretations as well as criteria which we shall need. . . . [36]

Yet one may argue that to bracket out 2 Samuel 21—24 and include 1 Kings 1—2 subverts or deconstructs the avowed aim of offering a synchronic reading of the final quarter of the books of Samuel.

On the other hand, it would be hard to mount a challenge against Fokkelman's claim of widespread high regard for the quality of the so-called "Succession Narrative." It has been treated as a topic on its own since the influential 1926 monograph by Leonhard Rost.[37] Rost argued that the story of David, by far the largest part of the books of Samuel, consists of two once independent units—the History of David's Rise (1 Samuel 16—2 Samuel 5) and the Succession Narrative (parts of 2 Samuel 6—7 and 2 Samuel 9—1 Kings 2). Rost's seminal study resonates through subsequent treatments of the "Succession Narrative" (also called the "Court History") by von Rad, Whybray, and Gunn[38]—to name only the most commonly cited. Despite differing views on exactly where it begins and ends and what it is about (and therefore what it should be called), there has been broad agreement over the high quality of its writing and that it was conceived separate from (and earlier than) its present context in Samuel–Kings. However, Van Seters and Auld have both urged that it was not one of the sources available to the Deuteronomist but was added to an earlier draft of David's reign.[39] Moreover, Gordon and Ho—like Carlson earlier—have argued against Rost's division of the David story between two main sources.[40]

Judges has also proved to be fertile ground for more literary approaches. Webb has offered an "integrated reading" of the whole book.[41] Mieke Bal, after two monographs on aspects of the book, has contributed the powerful *Death and Dissymmetry*.[42] This rich exploration of violence, and especially of the lethal power of men over women, is no less "integrated" for not stating such a claim. Even Joshua, which long resisted similar attempts, has yielded to readings such as *Every Promise Fulfilled: Contesting Plots in Joshua; Together in the Land: A Reading of the Book of Joshua; Narrative History and Ethnic Boundaries;* and *Joshua and the Rhetoric of Violence*.[43] There is less work of this nature on Kings as a whole, despite the lead given by Long and followed up by Savran and Wilson (1995).[44] Several interesting studies have been offered of more extended sections of Kings, and the portions on Solomon and on Elijah and Elisha have proved more congenial. Still, even as sympathetic a practitioner of literary method as Provan seems hard-pressed to produce typical rather than marginal examples for his "readerly questions" as he works at an interpretation encompassing all of Kings.[45]

VII. ONE STORY OR SEVERAL?

While the opening chapters of Samuel provide a good beginning for what follows, Samuel's retrospective in 1 Samuel 12 causes some problems for any theory, including Noth's, that views all of Joshua–Kings as a connected account, even if only part of a still longer one. In a review that begins with Jacob's departure for Egypt (12:8) and concludes with his own role (12:11), and that names many other names in between, Samuel passes over Joshua in silence. His speech even gives the impression that it was through the agency of Moses and Aaron that Israel was settled in its "place" (12:8). Somewhat reminiscent of the poem in Exodus 15 (see 15:17), Samuel also suggests more direct movement from Egypt to the "place" of settlement than we find in the canonical story familiar from Numbers, Deuteronomy, and Joshua. Then Jerubbaal, Bedan, Jephthah, and Samuel are cited (12:11) as deliverers (but not "judges"). Even if we follow several ancient versions and re-read the received Hebrew text (also called the Masoretic text or MT) as "Barak" instead of "Bedan," we have to admit that this restored Barak does not appear in the order we know: in our book of Judges, Deborah and Barak precede Gideon/Jerubbaal instead of following him. The first book of Samuel—to judge from this important chapter—may have been familiar with rather different traditions of the settlement and the period afterwards and may have been written without knowledge of our books of Joshua and Judges.

A middle position between the idea of a single connected history and the present separate books is attentive to this situation and may prove more attractive for other reasons as well. This would read only Joshua and Judges as individual works but Samuel–Kings as a single account of the monarchic period. Joshua has a particularly close connection with Deuteronomy. Its opening chapter starts, without any resumptive repetition, just where the narrative in Deut. 31:34 left off. It finishes unproblematically, noting how far the death of its hero was also the end of an era. Then the opening of 1 Samuel offers a good introduction, in promise and in threat, to everything that follows. By contrast, Judges adapts the first words of Joshua to form its own beginning at Joshua's death. Then, immediately after drawing its own implications from a review of the conquest narratives, it repeats in Judg. 2:6–9 the story from Josh. 24:28–31—the death and burial of the already departed Joshua (1:1). Looking forward, several parts of the book make allusion to or offer a mocking anticipation of episodes from the monarchy. Judges may, therefore, be read as a secondary link between Joshua and what the Greek Bible or Septuagint (LXX) describes as the four books of Reigns or Kingdoms—what the Hebrew Bible (followed by most modern English translations) calls two books each of Samuel and Kings.

Several scholars look to the Greek Bible for much more substantial clues to the origins of the books of Joshua to Kings.[46] Some early Greek manuscripts preserve versions of these books that differ in important respects from the traditional Hebrew text (MT). This has been known and evaluated differently from ancient times. The discovery, beginning in 1947, of the Dead Sea Scrolls has altered at least some of the terms in which this discussion is carried out. Among the scrolls (they are mostly in Hebrew) there are many smaller and a few larger fragments of texts that can be recognized as biblical. They vary in their wording from being almost identical to the MT to being no more different from it than the versions in Greek and other languages of the early churches that have been long available to us.

This proves at least one point that had long been contentious. We now know for certain that some discrepancies between the Hebrew (MT) and Greek (LXX) texts were not due to the mistakes or free translations that had often been supposed and blamed. Rather, the translators were providing an accurate rendering of a Hebrew text different from MT. The old polemical questions, however, are still debated, even if in new form: Was what became the standard Hebrew text (MT) always a better, more original text? How far back can we trace a distinction between an official text (possibly preserved in the Jerusalem temple as long as that stood) and unofficial, more freely altered, local copies?

VIII. FROM FORMER PROPHETS TO TORAH

Noth himself had drawn some implications for Pentateuchal study in his original 1943 book.[47] Yet these were largely negative: the older Pentateuchal sources, however far they might have originally continued, had been broken off once they had brought Moses and his people to the hills east of the Dead Sea. They are no longer available for our scrutiny. They were not represented among the sources of Joshua and the succeeding books but had been suppressed in favor of the Deuteronomistic History.

It is only more recently that several scholars, in separate but overlapping ways, have made the next radical move by taking the Deuteronomistic History as the foundation for their study of the Torah. The most comprehensive proposals have been made by Blum and Van Seters.[48] Both agree that the non-Priestly portions of Genesis–Numbers were based on themes and stories in Deuteronomy and the following narratives. While Blum writes of a D-work conceived as a fresh preface to the Deuteronomistic History, Van Seters insists on several differences of outlook and prefers to maintain "Yahwist" as the name of the primary author of Genesis–Numbers, although he explains that his Yahwist is post-Deuteronomistic (consult the previous chapter in this volume).

IX. PATTERNS

My own fresh examination of the so-called synoptic portions of Samuel–Kings and of Chronicles has led me to the conclusion that the narratives shared by the two works, which amount to some half of all the material in each, were also the major source of each and the basis upon which each was constructed.[49] This original narrative had told the story of the house (dynasty) of David in Jerusalem and of the house (temple) that Solomon built there for Yahweh from the beginnings at the death of Saul until the uprooting and removal of both by the Babylonians. This "Book of Two Houses" was then extended, supplemented, and reinterpreted independently and in very different ways in Samuel–Kings and in Chronicles.

Putting these conclusions together with the work of Blum and Van Seters makes it attractive to think of the royal story underlying Samuel–Kings as the rootwork that supports the whole tree of Genesis–Kings. The royal Davidic story was first anticipated in the Deuteronomistic account from Moses to the Judges, and then a fresh and still "earlier" preface was supplied in the groundwork of Genesis–Numbers. It has been traditional in biblical criticism to begin at the beginning with the alternative accounts of creation in Genesis 1—3, each with different language and world-views and alternative divine names, and to then work forward, developing a theory of parallel sources. What I am arguing here is that we should begin much nearer to the end and move successively earlier. At first this may appear counterintuitive. However, it is clear that early postbiblical tradition greatly elaborated the previously unexplored "lives" of early figures such as Adam, Enoch, and Noah. Hence, the idea that the history of Israel was gradually written backward from Kings via Deuteronomy to Genesis may not be so strange after all. Introductions are generally written last, and the Creator's command to "be fruitful and multiply, and fill the earth" (Gen. 1:28) was learned from exilic prophetic texts (Jer. 3:16; 23:3; Ezek. 36:11).

Two surveys of the contents of the Former Prophets have already been offered in this chapter. One reported the linear story or stories they tell. The other suggested that the text should also be read for the opportunity the story provides for exploring relationships of different sorts. A third perspective, unless it be but a variant of the second, is to note larger panels or recurring patterns in Deuteronomy–Kings. The first royal figures, David and Solomon, are handled at greater length than any who follow. The same is true of Moses and Joshua at the very beginnings. The succession of Solomon to David and that of Joshua to Moses are very similarly portrayed. The deaths of Solomon and Joshua are each followed by a breakdown in central authority. Furthermore, both Kings and Judges concentrate on the increasing disorder that ensues in northern Israel, and both contrast the north with Judah.

These repeated similarities may reinforce our impression that a deliberate pattern is being created. The new extended preface in Deuteronomy, Joshua, and Judges permits a fresh reading of the older story of David's line. We readily recall that we have encountered analogous situations before, and we are prepared for the import here and there in the royal story of values and language from the newer Mosaic narratives. The new primary stress on Torah, and no longer on king and temple, helps prepare the reader for the exilic future. The patterning already glimpsed invites us to consider whether and how Samuel and Saul fit between the end of the Moses–Judges panel and the beginning of the matching royal one. The possible parallelism of the loss of the ark to the Philistines (1 Samuel 4—6) and of the temple treasures to the Babylonians (2 Kings 25:13–17) makes the beginning of a response.

FOR FURTHER READING

Auld, A. Graeme. *Joshua Retold.* Edinburgh: T. & T. Clark, forthcoming.
———. *Kings without Privilege.* Edinburgh: T. & T. Clark, 1994.
Mayes, A. D. H. *The Story of Israel between Settlement and Exile: A Redactional Study of the Deuteronomistic History.* London: SCM, 1983.
McKenzie, Steven L. "Deuteronomistic History." *ABD* 2:160–68.
———, and M. P. Graham, eds. *The History of Israel's Traditions: The Heritage of Martin Noth.* JSOTSup 182. Sheffield: Sheffield Academic Press, 1994.
Noth, Martin. *The Deuteronomistic History.* JSOTSup 15. 2d. ed. Sheffield: Sheffield Academic Press, 1991.

3

THE LATTER PROPHETS

Isaiah, Jeremiah, Ezekiel

MARVIN A. SWEENEY

I. THE ROLE OF THE PROPHETIC BOOKS
IN THE HEBREW BIBLE

The prophetic books of Isaiah, Jeremiah, and Ezekiel constitute some of the most theologically innovative and daring books of the Hebrew Bible, and they are also some of the Bible's most enigmatic literature due to their literary complexity and their shifting historical contexts. They play a particularly key role in the literary structure and theological outlook of all forms of the Hebrew Bible, including both the Jewish Tanakh and the various versions of the Christian Old Testament. Many assume that the Tanakh and the Old Testament constitute the same Hebrew Bible, but this is true only to a certain extent. Both the Tanakh and the Protestant versions of the Old Testament contain the same books, but the Roman Catholic version of the Old Testament also contains Deuterocanonical or Apocryphal books that are grouped separately in Protestant Bibles and do not even appear in Jewish Bibles. Other versions, such as those of the Eastern Orthodox, Syrian, and Ethiopian Churches likewise contain Pseudepigraphical works that do not appear in those of the Western churches. Each Bible has its own distinctive structure and theological agenda. Because the books of the Prophets stand at the center within the literary structure of each version, they define to a large degree the respective theological outlooks and agendas of all versions of the Hebrew Bible in Judaism and Christianity.[1]

Within the Jewish Tanakh, Isaiah, Jeremiah, and Ezekiel are grouped together with the Book of the Twelve Prophets to form the *Nevi'im Aḥronim* or "Latter Prophets." Together with the *Nevi'im Rishonim* or "Former Prophets" (Joshua, Judges, 1–2 Samuel, 1–2 Kings) they form the second of the three major sections of the Tanakh. The first, *Torah* or "Instruction" (Genesis, Exodus, Leviticus, Numbers, Deuteronomy), presents the early history of the people of Israel together with the guidelines for establishing their social and religious life in the land of Israel. The second, *Nevi'im* or "Prophets," presents the period of Israel's and Judah's life in the land—from the time of Joshua, through the times of the Judges and the monarchy, and until the exile to Babylonia. The third, *Ketuvim* or "Writings" (Psalms, Job, Proverbs, Megillot/Five Scrolls, Daniel, Ezra-Nehemiah, 1–2 Chronicles), includes various works that pertain to the reconstitution of the Jewish community during the early Second Temple period in the land of Israel along the guidelines laid down by Mosaic Torah. Thus, the Hebrew acronym TaNaKh is derived from the first letter of the name of each of the three major divisions: *Torah, Nevi'im,* and *Ketuvim.* Altogether, the Tanakh presents the ideal Jewish community in the Torah, the disruption of that ideal in the Prophets, and its restoration in the Writings. As a part of the Tanakh, the Latter Prophets complement the critical history of the Former Prophets by presenting critiques of Israel's and Judah's life in the land of Israel together with projections of the reestablishment of the ideal Jewish community.

Within most versions of the Christian Old Testament, the books of Isaiah, Jeremiah, and Ezekiel are grouped together with the books of Lamentations, the Epistle of Jeremiah, Daniel, and the Twelve Minor Prophets to form the Prophets, the last of the Old Testament's four major sections. The Pentateuch (Genesis, Exodus, Leviticus, Numbers, Deuteronomy) presents the earliest history of the people of Israel in the context of the creation of the universe and the origins of humankind. The Historical Books (Joshua, Judges, Ruth, 1–2 Samuel, 1–2 Kings, 1–2 Chronicles, Ezra-Nehemiah, Esther, 1–2 Maccabees, Tobit, Judith) present the history of Israel from the time of the conquest of the land of Canaan under Joshua through much of the second temple period prior to the emergence of Christianity. The Wisdom and Poetic Books (Job, Psalms, Proverbs, Ecclesiastes, Song of Solomon, Ecclesiasticus, Wisdom of Solomon) include works that address the perennial concerns of human beings, such as the character of G-d, the nature of the world, and the meaning of human existence.* The Prophets then conclude the Old Testament and point to a future beyond the old period of Mosaic revelation (the Old Testament or Old Covenant) to a new period of divine revelation (the New Testament or New Covenant) embodied in the life and teachings of Jesus Christ. Interestingly, the structure and theological outlook of the New Testament mirrors that of the Old. The Gospels present the origins of Christianity in the life of Jesus; the Acts of the Apostles presents the history of the early Christian community following the lifetime and crucifixion of Jesus; the Epistles address the perennial concerns of the life and theology of the church; and the Revelation of John points to the future when the second coming of Christ is to be realized.

The prophetic books are constitutive for understanding the theological outlook of both the Jewish Tanakh and the Christian Old Testament in that they stand at the intersection of past and future within the structure of each. With their perspectives on the past, the prophetic books confront the reality of the exile of the Israelite and Judean nations from the land of Israel by presenting a theological explanation for the exile of the people and the loss of land, namely that Israel and Judah violated their covenant with YHWH in some way and thereby brought punishment upon themselves. Likewise, the prophetic books confront the challenges of the future by positing a means by which the covenant with YHWH, and indeed Israel and Judah as a people, could continue despite the exile, viz., YHWH will act to restore the people to the land and reconstitute the covenant with them. The major prophetic books thereby constitute a form of theodicy in that they take up the question of

---

Editor's note: In accordance with Jewish tradition, Prof. Sweeney shows respect for the Deity by not spelling out divine names but rendering them as G-d and L-rd.

G-d's righteousness: Why did G-d allow or cause destruction and exile to come upon the people of Israel and Judah? By arguing that the people of Israel and Judah violated their covenant with YHWH, they conclude that G-d is just in punishing the people for wrongdoing. By arguing that G-d will ultimately restore the people to the land of Israel, they assert that G-d is just in maintaining the covenant. The prophetic books thereby create theological constructions of Israel's and Judah's past and future. They choose not to assign responsibility for evil to G-d but to the people instead. Each prophetic book presents its own unique theological perspective on the relationship between the people and G-d, including the character of the covenant, the nature of its disruption, and the means by which it will be reconstituted or reestablished.

II. THE DEVELOPMENT OF SCHOLARLY STUDY OF THE PROPHETIC BOOKS

Before turning to individual discussion of Isaiah, Jeremiah, and Ezekiel, it is important to understand how the scholarly study of the prophetic books has developed through the course of modern times.[2] Modern historical critical scholarship on the Bible can trace its origins back into the Middle Ages, following the rise of Islam and the ensuing discussion among Muslim, Jewish, and Christian thinkers concerning the validity of their respective religious traditions and their understandings of scripture.[3] First Jewish and later Christian scholars began to take up philological-grammatical study of the Bible in order to establish the integrity and historicity of the biblical text as the basis for the truth claims of their respective traditions. In both traditions, prophecy and the prophetic books played a major role. The medieval philosopher Moses Maimonides argued that prophetic experience represented the highest degree of spiritual and intellectual consciousness by which human beings could come to understand G-d. In keeping with his concern to repristinize Christianity, Martin Luther saw in the prophets the means to move from the Old Testament to the New, to convert Jews to Christianity, and thereby to fulfill the church's role to redeem the world.

Because of its preoccupation with empirical reasoning and the task of humankind to employ reason in an effort to bring about a moral world order, the Age of Enlightenment prompted further historical study of the prophets and prophetic literature as the prophets were considered the moral and spiritual exemplars of the enlightened human being. By the latter part of the nineteenth century, the development of the field of comparative religions and the discovery and deciphering of texts from the ancient Mediterranean and Near Eastern world prompted even greater efforts to study the prophets in their ancient historical contexts. Such interests were not entirely historical, however, as the thinking of scholars during this period was dominated by Protestant beliefs that the prophets were key to understanding biblical religiosity and that the prophets pointed ultimately to the development of early Christianity. This is evident in the work of Julius Wellhausen, who argued that the Mosaic Torah, the foundation of Judaism's system of thought, was in fact composed largely in relatively late times by priestly figures who projected a ritualistic and spiritually stagnant form of religion.[4] Wellhausen posited that the earliest and truly "authentic" forms of spiritual religion in the Hebrew Bible were not to be found in the Torah but in the prophets, who in turn provided models for Christ. Later scholars have noted that Wellhausen's reconstruction of Israelite religion supported a Protestant polemic against the Roman Catholic Church and Rabbinic Judaism. In Wellhausen's view, Christ was the religious and ethical heir to the prophets. Just as Christ had been betrayed by the Roman Catholic Church, so had the prophets been betrayed by Rabbinic Judaism. Although neither of these charges was true, the prevailing intellectual climate of Western Europe during the nineteenth century focused on a progressive movement away from the traditional beliefs and institutions of the past toward an "enlightened" ethical and spiritual monotheism of the future that was styled along largely Protestant lines. Consequently, Wellhausen's work provided an appealing model for a modern progressive theology, and it thereby was foundational in motivating modern historical study of the prophets.

Whereas Wellhausen provided much of the rationale for the modern scholarly focus on prophecy, Hermann Gunkel was a pioneer in the development of form criticism or *Gattungskritik,* the study of literary forms, genres, or types as the exegetical basis for the study of prophecy and prophetic literature.[5] Gunkel was heavily influenced by the continued development of the comparative study of religions in relation to the ancient Near East on the one hand and by the focus on the study of folklore in German culture on the other. Just as German folklorists and linguists were collecting and studying the various types and functions of Germanic folk literature in conjunction with the unification and emergence of modern Germany, Gunkel sought to identify and study the literary forms in the Hebrew Bible that conveyed early Israel's self-consciousness as a distinctive people or nation with its own concept of deity. Gunkel believed that such cultural self-consciousness emerged at the earliest preliterary stages of a nation's development, and he therefore posited that the earliest literary genres were originally oral speech forms that only later had been recorded in writing after a long period of evolution in an oral tradition. Because of the prevailing belief that preliterate peoples were relatively primitive and incapable of expressing complex ideas or well-reasoned, lengthy discourses, Gunkel theorized that early speech forms must have been short, self-contained speech units that could be easily memorized by such simple folk and transmitted orally to others in well defined social or institutional settings in the life of the people. Much of his work focused on the tribal or clan folk tales of Genesis and other narrative books and the liturgical hymns of the book of Psalms. But he was especially instrumental in pointing to the fundamental genres of prophetic speech or oracles. Chief among them was the prophetic indictment form and the prophet's oracular announcement of judgment by G-d, in which a prophet publically identified the wrongdoings of the people and announced the punishment they could expect from G-d. Such a perspective presupposed the prophet's inexplicable psychological experience of the divine and pointed to the role of prophets as critics of Israelite society.

Gunkel's work prompted a multitude of studies through the mid-twentieth century that focused on the identification, classification, and evolution of prophetic oracular forms. Such work presupposed that the original oral speech forms had been modified to a certain degree over time and that they had been encased in much later literary settings by writers or scribes who did not always fully understand their original forms, functions, or settings in life. This meant that the original oral forms had to be reconstructed from their later literary contexts and that a great deal of literary material that had gathered around them at later times had to be dismissed as secondary or "inauthentic" deposits that frequently distorted or reinterpreted the original oracular forms. The identification of such later "editorial" additions constituted the basis of redaction criticism, which built upon earlier source-critical study of the Pentateuchal and Gospel literature in an effort to remove later material and thereby to expose the original "authentic" words of the prophets. Such later material was frequently judged to be theologically irrelevant because it represented the "dull and uninspired ritualism and dogmatism" of later scribes, who added their comments to the "pristine" prophetic oracles, and thereby associated them with the liturgies of the temple, the nationalistic aspirations of the Jewish people, and the legal concerns of the later priests. These concerns were deemed to be contrary to the spiritual and ethical teachings of the prophets, so that this approach reinforced the view that the prophets constituted a distinctive social movement that critiqued established societal institutions such as the monarchy, the temple, and legal institutions. Likewise, early redaction criticism reinforced Gunkel's view that prophets were exclusively speakers and not writers by positing a fundamental distinction between the oral speech forms of the prophets and written literary additions of the redactors.

As the form- and redaction-critical study of the prophets continued through the course of the twentieth century, scholars began to note the difficulties involved in reconstructing "original" oral prophetic speech forms from their present literary contexts and the supposedly later social settings that those literary contexts represented. Sigmund Mowinckel, for example, noted the relationships between prophetic oracular forms and the Psalms on the one hand (e.g., Psalms 60, 65, 82, 110) and the presence of hymnic materials in the books of the prophets on the other (e.g., Isaiah 12, 33; Nahum; Habakkuk 3).[6] This led him to posit that prophetic speech was intimately related to the liturgy of the temple in that it was performed on cultic occasions, such as the New Year festival, as a means to express the experience of YHWH and YHWH's relationship to the temple and the monarchy. He also argued that schools of the prophets' disciples transmitted and reworked this literature and employed it liturgically in the context of the temple cult. Gerhard von Rad noted the use of tradition among the prophets—particularly the Davidic covenant tradition, which posits YHWH's eternal relationship to the Davidic monarchy and the temple in Jerusalem, and the Mosaic covenant tradition, which identifies YHWH as the authority who stands behind Mosaic law—as the basis for the relationship between YHWH and the people of Israel in the various prophetic traditions.[7] Claus Westermann noted the relationship between the prophetic judgment speech form and the speech forms and functions of the Israelite law courts.[8] Hans Walter Wolff examined the interrelationship between prophetic speech forms and the wisdom literature.[9] All of these studies and those of others raised questions about the identification of prophecy as a distinctive institution within Israel that stood apart from and critiqued other elements of Israelite and Judean society. Instead, prophets frequently stood within the contexts of other Israelite institutional settings and frequently spoke out in their support.

These studies pointed out the interrelationship between posited prophetic speech forms and the literary contexts in which they appear. By the late twentieth century, scholars were increasingly viewing prophecy not simply as an oral phenomenon in ancient Israel and Judah, but as a literary phenomenon as well, in which the later editors or writers of the prophetic oracles acted as creative theologians and authors who both preserved the original prophetic speeches and reinterpreted them or rewrote them by the addition of later material that highlighted their relevance for later times as well as for those of the original prophet. This is evident, for example, in the book of Isaiah, which combines material pertinent to the eighth century prophet Isaiah ben Amoz in Isaiah 1—39 with that of an anonymous exilic prophet in Isaiah 40—55 (who spoke or wrote at the time of Cyrus's accession to the kingship of Babylon) and of various writers in Isaiah 56 66, who articulated their messages in the early Persian period. There is also considerable evidence that material from Isaiah ben Amoz in Isaiah 1—39 has been supplemented and reworked by writers from the seventh, sixth, and fifth centuries B.C.E., and that the material in Isaiah 56—66 cites texts and themes from Isaiah 1—39 and expounds on them in a much later historical and literary context.[10] Altogether, the present book of Isaiah applies the original message and words of the eighth-century Isaiah ben Amoz to approximately four centuries of Israelite/Judean history.

This points to the increasing emphasis on the study of the prophetic books as literature rather than on prophecy as an oral phenomenon or event. Obviously, such an emphasis requires a literary methodology that enables the exegete to assess the literary character and form of much larger literary units than those that Gunkel first envisioned, including entire chapters or groups of chapters and even entire prophetic books. Various methodological perspectives that focus on larger text forms are currently employed in the study of prophetic literature. Rhetorical criticism was originally developed in biblical studies by Muilenburg,[11] who attempted to analyze the poetic and thematic interrelationship of smaller formal units in an effort to determine the coherence of a prophetic text. It has been developed further by Trible and others to include assessment of the impact on an audience that a large text unit might have when delivered orally or read in written form.[12] Form and redaction criticism have expanded their horizons substantially in the work of Ackroyd, Clements, the present writer,[13] and others to include assessment of the literary form of entire prophetic books and the role of redactors as creative authors and theologians who shaped the present form of the prophetic books. Reader-response criticism has been developed by Conrad and others to evaluate the impact of a coherent prophetic composition upon a reading audience far removed in time and culture from that of the original writers.[14] Canonical critics such as Childs posit the final form of the prophetic book as the only authoritative basis for scriptural interpretation,[15] although this is disputed by others who insist that the prior history of the text must also be established and assessed.

Many scholars now argue that it is impossible to reconstruct the redactional history of the prophetic books with any certainty.[16] This is due to the difficulties that scholars face in defining reliable objective criteria for establishing the compositional stages of the text in view of the fact that a skillful redactor can successfully conceal the literary tensions that redaction critics commonly use to identify the presence of redactional layers. Despite the difficulties, such attempts at literary reconstruction must nevertheless be pursued when possible. To abandon such attempts would result in the historical decontextualization of the prophets and prophetic literature, which runs the risk of distorting a prophet's message in relation to the subjective interests of the interpreter. Redaction critics must be aware of their limits and their own subjectivity, but the recognition of these limits does not entail abandoning the attempt. It simply points to the need for the fullest assessment possible of the literary form and character of the largest possible unit of prophetic literature, the prophetic book, as the basis for redaction-critical analysis. Once such analysis is complete, attempts at reconstructing compositional stages may commence, employing evidence provided by tensions in literary form—such as grammar, syntax, and word usage; generic characteristics that point to the presence of a multilayered composition; and thematic and historical content and their relations to known historical data from outside the prophetic book. In the end, the interpreter must recognize that without independent confirmation supplied by an alternative edition of the book—and such evidence appears in the two versions of the book of Jeremiah—all such results must be considered hypothetical. Nevertheless, they are absolutely necessary to assessing the function and message of the major prophets within ancient Israelite and Judean society, both within the lifetimes of the prophets and in the centuries that followed their careers.

III. THE BOOK OF ISAIAH

The book of Isaiah generally stands at the head of the major prophets in both the Jewish and Christian versions of the Bible, although one Talmudic tradition places it as the third book of the prophets, following Jeremiah and Ezekiel (*b. B. Bat.* 14b). The superscription in Isa. 1:1 identifies it as "The vision of Isaiah son of Amoz which he saw concerning Judah and Jerusalem in the days of Uzziah, Jotham, Ahaz, and Hezekiah, kings of Judah." This is reinforced by superscriptions in 2:1, "The word that Isaiah son of Amoz saw concerning Judah and Jerusalem"; in 13:1, "The oracle concerning Babylon which Isaiah ben Amoz saw"; and references to the prophet's words and activities "in the year that king Uzziah died" (6:1), "in the days of Ahaz son of Jotham" (7:1), "in the year that King Ahaz died" (14:28), and "in the fourteenth year of King Hezekiah" (36:1). All of these references indicate that the book is identified as a presentation of the words and activities of the eighth-century prophet Isaiah ben Amoz, who lived during the reigns of Uzziah (783–742 B.C.E.), Jotham (742–735 B.C.E.), Ahaz (735–715 B.C.E.), and Hezekiah (717–687 B.C.E.). This would place the prophet historically during the years that the Assyrian empire invaded the Syro-Israelite region, destroying Aram (Syria) in 734–732 and the northern kingdom of Israel in 722/1, and subjugating Judah in 701 B.C.E.

Despite the presentation of the book of Isaiah as a portrayal of the prophet Isaiah ben Amoz, there is a great deal of evidence that much of Isaiah was in fact composed by authors working during the period of the Babylonian exile and beyond.[17] The most telling piece of evidence for this conclusion is the explicit reference to King Cyrus of Persia in Isa. 44:28 and 45:1, who is identified as YHWH's messiah as well as the one who will rebuild Jerusalem and the temple. King Cyrus ruled Persia from 559 B.C.E. until his death in 530 B.C.E. and was especially known for his defeat of the Babylonian empire and peaceful entry into Babylon in 539 B.C.E., as well as for his subsequent decree that allowed exiled Jews to return to Jerusalem in order to rebuild the temple. Other indications include the portrayal of Babylon as the chief oppressor of Israel and Judah beginning in Isaiah 40, whereas Isaiah 1—39 focuses on Assyria; the portrayal of Babylon as an enemy that is about to fall in Isaiah 40—55, whereas Assyria is an ominous threat in Isaiah 1—39; the portrayal of Israel's and Judah's imminent return to Jerusalem and the restoration of the city in Isaiah 40—55, whereas Israel and Judah either experience exile or are threatened with it in Isaiah 1—39; and the very different literary and poetic styles of writing in Isaiah 1—39 and 40—66. A further complicating factor is that Isaiah 56—66 appears to presuppose the presence of the people in the city of Jerusalem. These chapters lack the consistent literary style, seeming literary unity, and overall optimism of Isaiah 40—55, and instead anticipate YHWH's judgment against the wicked within the people and among the nations.

Beginning with the medieval Jewish exegete Abraham ibn Ezra (1089–1164 C.E.), scholars have long suspected that the book of Isaiah was not the work of a single author. Although any number of early modern scholars address this issue, the most influential major study to demonstrate that the book of Isaiah contained the work of several authors was the commentary on Isaiah published in German by Duhm in 1892.[18] Duhm argued that Isaiah was in fact the product of three major authors who wrote in different settings at different historical times. He argued that the work of the eighth-century prophet Isaiah ben Amoz is to be found exclusively in Isaiah 1—39, so that these chapters are identified as First Isaiah. The work of a second anonymous prophet from the period of the Babylonian exile who wrote in Phoenicia is found in Isaiah 40—55 and identified as Deutero-Isaiah (or Second Isaiah). The work of a third anonymous prophet who wrote in Jerusalem shortly before the time of Nehemiah in the mid-fifth century appears in Isaiah 56—66 and is identified as Trito-Isaiah (or Third Isaiah). In keeping with his methodological focus on the short, self-contained literary unit, Duhm argued that the book originally circulated as independent collections of the sayings of the three individual prophets whose words now appear in the book. In addition to several collections of oracles by Isaiah ben Amoz, Deutero-Isaiah, and Trito-Isaiah, Duhm identified several anonymous collections in Isaiah 24—27; 34; 35; 36—39; and elsewhere. There was never any intrinsic relationship between these sections; they were simply brought together over time by a relatively mechanical process, so that they eventually formed the entire book of Isaiah by the late Maccabean (Hasmonean) period, about 70 B.C.E.

Like many scholars of his time, Duhm was much more interested in recovering the words of the "authentic" prophets of the book of Isaiah and much less interested in the literary character and redactors of the book other than as a means to study the individual prophets themselves. Many scholars followed Duhm's lead through the course of the early twentieth century in attempts to reconstruct a view of the prophets Isaiah ben Amoz, Second Isaiah, and Third Isaiah. But as research continued, several problems emerged. First of all, it became clear that Isaiah 56—66 was not the work of a single prophet, but of a variety of hands. In some cases, the writings of Isaiah 56—66, especially chapters 60—62, bear a great deal of resemblance to those of Deutero-Isaiah. But others, such as the portrayal of YHWH's destruction of Edom in 63:1–6 and the scenario surrounding the destruction of the wicked in Isaiah 65—66, differ markedly. Second, it is clear that compositions such as Isaiah 24—27 and 34—35 derive from a period much later than that of Isaiah ben Amoz, and perhaps even later than that of Deutero-Isaiah. Many argue that these works represent a form of apocalyptic literature that was written during the latest stages of the composition of the book. Third, it became clear that much of the material in First Isaiah apart from these apparently independent compositions, such as the portrayal of the nations flowing to Zion in 2:2–4, the oracle against Babylon in Isaiah 13, the oracle against Tyre in Isaiah 23, and countless other texts within Isaiah 1—39, are not the product of Isaiah ben Amoz but of writers much later than the prophet. Mowinckel argues that both First Isaiah and Second Isaiah are separate traditions, but that they were assembled by schools of the original prophets' disciples who supplemented the works of First and Second Isaiah and arranged Isaiah 1—39 and 40—66 into their present forms.[19] Throughout the middle of the twentieth century, scholars tended to agree that both First and Second Isaiah were heavily redacted works that had to be critically analyzed in order to strip away the contributions of later redactors and so identify the original oracles of Isaiah ben Amoz and the anonymous prophet Deutero-Isaiah.

As redaction-critical work on Isaiah has continued through the latter part of the twentieth century, scholars have begun to note some deliberate arrangement of the materials in the book that points to an overarching theological message and perhaps to some relationship between the two parts of the book. Ackroyd argues that Isaiah 1—12 is shaped with the concerns of the Babylonian exile in mind, insofar as these chapters project an ideal future in which the exiled people of Israel and Judah would return to Jerusalem, and the nations would recognize YHWH following a period of punishment in which Jerusalem, Israel/Judah, and Assyria would suffer.[20] He likewise notes that Isaiah 1—39 is arranged to provide a deliberate contrast between the figure of King Ahaz in 6:1–9:7 and King Hezekiah in Isaiah 36—39, insofar as Ahaz refused Isaiah's guidance and led his country into disaster, while Hezekiah turned to Isaiah and to YHWH and thereby saved his city from Babylonian destruction.[21] To the degree that Isaiah 1—12 addresses exilic concerns, this raises the possibility that the portrayal of King Hezekiah in Isaiah 36—39 is intended to serve as a model of piety for the readers of Isaiah 40—66.

Much of Clements's work on Isaiah 1—39 focuses on its redactional formation during the period of the seventh-century Judean monarch Josiah and the positive message of deliverance for Jerusalem and Judah that is evident in the Josianic edition of Isaiah 1—39. But he likewise notes the presence of later theological interests, in that Isaiah 2—4 is arranged to address the problems of Jerusalem's destruction during the Babylonian exile by pointing to a bright future following a period of punishment.[22] Clements in turn notes that various themes and motifs of First Isaiah are carried over into Second Isaiah, including the concern with Babylon as enemy (Isa. 13:1–14:23; 39:1–8), the return of the exiles to Jerusalem (Isa. 11:12–16; 19:23; 27:12–13), and the motif of Israel's blindness and deafness in Isa. 6:9–10; 32:3; 35:5 versus the motif of Israel's open eyes and ears in Isa. 42:18–20; 43:8.[23] All of this suggests to Clements that the "former things" that Deutero-Isaiah announces as having come to pass must refer to the prophecies of Isaiah ben Amoz. The book of Isaiah must be read as a single book in that Deutero-Isaiah points to the fulfillment of the prophecies of Isaiah ben Amoz. Childs likewise demonstrates that such a reading is possible based upon his own assessment of "the former things" of Deutero-Isaiah and the concern in Isaiah 1—39 to point to the restoration of Israel and the deliverance of the nations in the aftermath of punishment.[24]

As a result of this earlier discussion, a great deal of current research focuses on the final form of the book of Isaiah. Scholars now address this issue from various perspectives. Overall, it points to new readings of the book of Isaiah that have significant bearing on the interpretation of its individual themes and texts. The book is clearly arranged to focus on the role of the city of Jerusalem in YHWH's plans for the world and to address some 400 years of historical experience as though it were the single vision of the eighth-century prophet Isaiah ben Amoz.

The focus on the city of Jerusalem in the book of Isaiah is evident from the formal and literary structure of the book. Although many claim that the structure of Isaiah comprises the three basic divisions identified by Duhm, that is, Isaiah 1—39, 40—55, and 56—66, this division is based not on the literary character of these sections but on their identification with historical figures who are postulated as their respective authors. Essentially, Duhm's argument is based on historical considerations pertaining to the composition of the book rather than on an analysis of its literary character and the means by which it presents its contents and message. Duhm's model employs redaction-critical criteria to define the shape and interpretation of the present form of the book, but redaction criticism requires that one first assess the present form of the text and then employ redaction-critical tools to establish its compositional history. The literary structure of the text and the stages of its composition are not one and the same. This is evident not only from these methodological considerations, but from the identification of a great deal of exilic and postexilic literary material in Isaiah 1—39 that demonstrates that the presentation of First Isaiah is shaped by many of the same concerns that were influential in the composition of Isaiah 40—66.[25]

When the literary structure of the book of Isaiah is assessed according to its literary and formal characteristics, a two-part structure emerges that focuses especially on the role of Jerusalem in relation to YHWH's plans for the future of the world or creation. The first part (Isaiah 1—33) projects judgment and subsequent restoration for Jerusalem, Israel/Judah, and the nations, whereas the second part

(Isaiah 34—66) presupposes that judgment has already taken place and that the time for restoration is at hand. It functions as an appeal or exhortation to its audience, identified with Jerusalem and Judah, to adhere to YHWH's covenant and thereby to play a role in YHWH's plans for the future. Based on the superscription and the overall arrangement of the book, it may be characterized generically as, "The vision of Isaiah ben Amoz: Prophetic exhortation to Jerusalem/Judah to adhere to YHWH."

Isaiah 1—33 is especially concerned with articulating YHWH's plans for worldwide sovereignty at Zion/Jerusalem. It begins with a prologue to the book in Isaiah 1 that lays out the basic themes of judgment and subsequent restoration for the repentant righteous in Jerusalem. These themes stand as the basic message throughout the book as a whole, so that Isaiah 1 serves as an introductory paraenesis to the audience of the book to identify with the righteous and thus with YHWH's plans. Isaiah 2—33 then presents prophetic instruction concerning YHWH's projected plans that centers around the theme of the "day of YHWH," that is, pointing to the day when YHWH's plans will be realized. Within this section of the book, Isaiah 2—4 announces the preparation of Zion for its role as the center of YHWH's world rule by pointing to the nations flowing to Zion for YHWH's instruction or Torah as the goal of YHWH's efforts to cleanse Jerusalem of evil by punishment. The section thereby stands as an invitation to Jacob/Israel to join in this plan. Isaiah 5—12 follows by providing instruction concerning the significance of Assyrian judgment against Israel/Jacob: righteous Davidic rule will follow after the arrogant Assyrian monarch is brought down for his blasphemy of YHWH, who sent him against Israel in the first place. Isaiah 13—27 announces the preparation of the nations for YHWH's world rule, including individual pronouncements against the nations and a portrayal of YHWH's gathering of the nations and the restoration of exiles of Israel to Zion in the aftermath of punishment. Isaiah 28—33 focuses specifically on YHWH's plans for Jerusalem and culminates in the announcement that a royal savior will emerge in the aftermath of Jerusalem's punishment and the destruction of Jerusalem's oppressor.

The second part of the book, Isaiah 34—66, focuses especially on the realization of YHWH's plans for worldwide sovereignty at Zion and presupposes that the oppressor of Jerusalem, now identified as Babylon rather than as Assyria, is about to fall. Isaiah 34—54 provides the initial instruction concerning the realization of this goal. Within this section, Isaiah 34—35 presents the scenario by which YHWH will return the redeemed exiles of Israel and Judah to Zion, emphasizing the fall of Edom as the symbol of oppression; the day of YHWH for Zion's recompense; the need to read the book of YHWH (i.e., Isaiah) to realize that this is coming about; and portrayal of the joy of all creation as the exiles return in a new exodus to Zion with open eyes and unstopped ears along the highway through the wilderness. Isaiah 36—39 presents royal narratives concerning Hezekiah and the Assyrian siege of Jerusalem that point to the faithfulness of Hezekiah to YHWH —in contrast to the earlier rejection by Ahaz of YHWH's word through Isaiah— as a model for the restored community in Zion. Isaiah 40—54 draws on traditional themes, such as Jacob's exile and return to the land, Sarah's barrenness and subsequent childbirth, the exodus through the wilderness, and the promise of covenant to Noah, to provide a lengthy instruction concerning the premises that YHWH is maintaining the covenant and restoring Zion. Altogether, this section argues that the restoration of Zion takes place against the background of the designation of the Persian king Cyrus as YHWH's messiah and temple-builder and the role of YHWH as creator of the entire universe. The second major section of Isaiah 34—66 appears in Isaiah 55—66, which constitutes a prophetic exhortation to adhere to YHWH's covenant. The exhortation proper appears in Isaiah 55, which assigns YHWH's eternal promise to David to the people of Israel/Judah at large and calls upon the people to join in a relationship that is as secure as all creation. Isaiah 56—66 then substantiates this exhortation by pointing to the need for righteousness on the part of the people as the final stages of YHWH's plans come to pass, including the pilgrimage of the nations to Zion and the realization of YHWH's kingship in Zion.

This overarching structure and the contents of Isaiah clearly presuppose the final form of the book, which is likely the product of the postexilic period, the fifth-century B.C.E. or later, when the Jewish community in Jerusalem was restored and the temple rebuilt. It addresses the hopes and aspirations of the community that looked to YHWH as creator and G-d of human events, who would eventually manifest divine sovereignty in Zion, or the Jerusalem temple. Nevertheless, a great deal of earlier material, written over the course of some 400 years or more, may be identified within the book. Although opinion is divided, scholars generally accept at least three, and perhaps four or more, major stages or periods of composition. The first is that of Isaiah ben Amoz from the eighth century B.C.E., whose works are found throughout Isaiah 1—33. They emphasize the threat of Assyrian invasion as YHWH's punishment of both Israel and Judah and the need for righteous rule on the part of Judah's monarchs. The second, which is not accepted by all scholars, is a late-seventh-century edition of the book that is identified with the reign of King Josiah of Judah (639–609 B.C.E.) and was designed to employ the prophecy of Isaiah in support of Josiah's program of national restoration and religious reform. This material appears throughout Isaiah 1—39, especially in Isaiah 5—12, 32, and 36—37. The third is the sixth-century edition of Isaiah that is based upon the writings of the anonymous prophet of the exile. This edition encompasses Isaiah 1—55, with special emphasis on chapters 2, 13, 24—27, 35, 40—55, and 60—62, and asserts that YHWH has placed Cyrus on the throne to redeem Israel from Babylon and return the people to Jerusalem. Finally, the fifth-century edition, identified especially with Isaiah 56—66 and materials in chapters 1, 33, and 34, calls upon people to adhere to YHWH's covenant until the wicked are destroyed and YHWH's reign is realized.

The understanding of the covenant between the people of Israel/Judah and YHWH is based upon the Davidic promise tradition, including YHWH's choice of the house of David to rule eternally and YHWH's choice of Jerusalem or Zion as the center for that rule. The book thereby portrays YHWH in royal terms as the righteous monarch of all creation and the nations at large. But the character of the book of Isaiah as a theodicy that justifies YHWH's actions in a time of disaster is evident in the means by which it employs the royal Davidic tradition to come to terms with the reality of the Babylonian exile, the destruction of Jerusalem and the temple, and the end of the Davidic dynasty. It argues that the Davidic covenant has been transformed and that this transformation was a part of YHWH's intention from the beginning. Isaiah's vision of YHWH in the temple in Isaiah 6 makes this clear when YHWH, portrayed as a monarch surrounded by the royal court of seraphim, announces plans to bring punishment upon the people until only a tenth remain to serve as the "holy seed" for restoration. This theme permeates the entire book, insofar as the book as a whole portrays the punishment and eventual restoration of the "remnant" of the people in Zion. It is especially revealing when it is applied to the royal oracles of Isaiah ben Amoz in that the various literary and historical contexts through which the book has passed provide a changing interpretative framework by which the oracles of Isaiah ben Amoz are to be read. Isaiah's oracle concerning the anticipated righteous Davidic monarch in Isa. 8:16–9:6, for example, probably looks to Hezekiah as that figure who will enable the people to move from a period of distress, darkness, and gloom into a period of light when the oppression of the Assyrians will come to an end.

When read in relation to a seventh-century Josianic edition of Isaiah, however, the parameters by which Isa. 8:16–9:6 is interpreted change. The oracle still looks forward to a period of light when Assyrian oppression will come to an end, but the righteous Davidic monarch, who will establish the throne of David and the kingdom in justice and righteousness, is now to be identified with Josiah rather than with Hezekiah. When Isa. 8:16–9:6 is read in relation to the sixth-century edition of Isaiah, the interpretative parameters change once again. The emergence from darkness into light takes place after the downfall of the Babylonian rather than the Assyrian oppressor, and the righteous monarch is Cyrus of Persia, not Josiah or Hezekiah, insofar as the Davidic covenant is applied to the people at large and not to the Davidic king. Finally, when Isa. 8:16–9:6 is read in relation to the fifth-century edition of the book, the emergence from darkness into light takes place when the wicked—both without and within the people—are destroyed, the nations stream to Zion to behold the light of Zion and the glory of YHWH, and YHWH's kingship is established in heaven and on earth.

This example may be multiplied with any number of texts that derive from Isaiah ben Amoz—and even from later writers of Isaiah—as the oracles of the book are reread, reinterpreted, and reapplied to later situations by later writers who believed that the prophet Isaiah ben Amoz was speaking, not exclusively about the eighth century B.C.E., but about their own times as well. In this regard, the expression in 40:8 points to the basic hermeneutical principle that guides later readers and writers of the book of Isaiah, "the word of our G-d will stand forever."

IV. THE BOOK OF JEREMIAH

The book of Jeremiah follows Isaiah as the second of the Latter Prophets in the Tanakh, although some Rabbinic authorities place it as the first of the Latter

Prophets (*b. B. Bat.* 14b). Jeremiah stands as the second book of the Prophets following Isaiah in the Christian Old Testament. The book of Lamentations—traditionally ascribed to Jeremiah—follows, and many traditions include the apocryphal books of Baruch and the Epistle of Jeremiah as well. The superscription of the book in 1:1–3 identifies it as "the words of Jeremiah son of Hilkiah, of the priests who were in Anathoth in the land of Benjamin" and further specifies that the word of YHWH first came to Jeremiah in the thirteenth year of the reign of King Josiah of Judah (ca. 627–626 B.C.E.), and that it also came during the reign of Jehoiakim (609–598/7 B.C.E.) and up until the captivity of Jerusalem in the eleventh year of Zedekiah (587/6 B.C.E.). Jeremiah is thus placed historically from the reform of King Josiah (627 B.C.E.), through the Babylonian subjugation of Judah in 605, the Babylonian deportation of King Jehoiachin in 597, the destruction of Jerusalem and the temple in 587/6, and the aftermath of the assassination of Gedaliah, the Babylonian appointed governor of Judah, in 582 B.C.E.

Study of the book of Jeremiah is both complicated and enhanced by the fact that the book appears in two distinct but related versions—the Greek version of the Septuagint (LXX) and the Hebrew version of the Masoretic text (MT).[26] Although the two versions contain much of the same material, the LXX version of Jeremiah is approximately one-eighth shorter than the MT, and after 25:13a they differ markedly in their order and arrangement of the materials. The most noteworthy difference between them is the placement of the oracles against the nations. They appear as chapters 46—51 in the MT and thereby stand nearly at the conclusion of the book immediately prior to the narrative concerning the destruction of Jerusalem and the exile of the people to Babylon in Jeremiah 52. In contrast to the MT, they appear as 25:14–31:14 in the LXX and thereby constitute the center of the book, so that MT Jeremiah 25—45 appears as LXX Jeremiah 32—51. The narrative in Jeremiah 52 likewise concludes the LXX version.

Scholars generally maintain that the two versions have independent transmission histories. MT Jeremiah appears to be an expanded and reworked version of the Hebrew text that stands behind LXX Jeremiah, but there are sufficient exceptions to this rule to indicate that both have gone through an extensive editorial history from the time that each was initially composed. Most scholars believe that LXX Jeremiah is the earlier version that was composed in Egypt at some time during the period 250–150 B.C.E. The earliest Greek manuscripts of the text are the Codex Vaticanus and the Codex Sinaiticus, both of which are Christian manuscripts written in the fourth century C.E. MT Jeremiah was likely composed in Babylonia during the late second temple period, but the earliest Masoretic Hebrew manuscripts of the book date to the ninth and tenth centuries C.E. Both versions appear to be attested in Qumran manuscripts of the book. The oldest of the Qumran manuscripts is 4QJer[a], which dates to ca. 225–175 B.C.E. It contains Jer. 7:1–2, 15–19; 7:28–9:2 (minus 7:30–8:8); 9:7–15; 10:9–23; 11:3–20; 12:3–16; 12:17–13:7; 13:27–14:8; 15:1–2; 17:8–26; 18:15–19:1; 20:15–18; 22:3–16; and 26:10, and appears to correspond well to MT Jeremiah, although it includes many corrections. 4QJer[b] dates to the mid-second century B.C.E., and includes Jer. 9:22–10:18; 43:3–9; and 50:4–6. The first fragment reflects the wording and verse order of LXX

Jeremiah. 4QJer^c dates to the Herodian period (30–1 B.C.E.) and contains a proto-MT version of Jer. 4:5, 13–16; 8:1–3; 8:20–9:5; 10:12–13; 19:8–9; 20:2–5, 7–8, 14–15; 21:6–10; 22:4–6, 10–28; 25:7–8, 15–17, 24–26; 26:10–13; 27:1–3, 14–15; 30:6–31:14; 31:16–26; and 33:16–20. Finally, 2QJer dates to the first century C.E. and contains a proto-MT version (with some variations) of Jer. 42:7–11, 14; 43:8–11; 44:1–3, 12–14; 46:27–47:7; 48:7, 25–39, 43-45; and 49:10. The Qumran manuscripts indicate that Hebrew texts of both versions of Jeremiah were in existence by the second century B.C.E., and they continued to develop after that time.

Study of the literary structure and theological outlook of the two versions is still relatively undeveloped. Many scholars accept the premise that LXX Jeremiah is arranged according to a relatively standard structure of prophetic books, such as Isaiah 1—39, Ezekiel, and Zephaniah, a structure that portrays an eschatological scenario of judgment against Israel/Judah (LXX Jeremiah 1—25), judgment against the nations (LXX Jeremiah 26—31; cf. MT Jeremiah 46—51), and salvation for both (LXX Jeremiah 32—52; cf. MT Jeremiah 25—52). But this pattern is problematic, in relation both to LXX Jeremiah and to other prophetic books. In LXX Jeremiah it does not account for the presentation of the Babylonian threat against Jerusalem and Judah in the third part of the book; oracles of restoration or salvation represent only a very limited part of this material. Likewise, although the pattern seems to hold for Ezekiel, it is not so clearly evident in other prophetic books. Isaiah 1—39 contains oracles of both punishment and restoration of Israel, Judah, and Jerusalem in Isaiah 1—12; oracles of punishment against the nations as well as restoration in Isaiah 13 –27; and a great quantity of judgment material directed to Jerusalem in Isaiah 28—31, followed by restoration in Isaiah 32—39. Likewise, Zephaniah contains oracles of punishment against the entire world as well as against Judah in Zeph. 1:1–2:3. The oracles against the nations in Zeph. 2:4–15 are directed only to the enemies of Judah, and Zeph. 3:1–20 combines themes of punishment and restoration for Jerusalem. Other principles underlie the structure of Isaiah 1—39 and Zephaniah that point to noneschatological concerns. This is especially clear when one realizes that the nations are not those of the entire world but are limited to specific spheres, such as the Persian empire in Isaiah 1– 39 and the enemies of King Josiah in Zephaniah. In the case of Isaiah, the structure of the book points to the realization of YHWH's kingship in the world as a consequence of the emergence of Persian power; in the case of Zephaniah, it calls for adherence to Josiah's reform. The judgment against the nations points to Persian domination in the world in Isaiah, and Judean resurgence over its neighbors and enemies in Zephaniah.

Similar principles may well inform the structure and presentation of both versions of Jeremiah. In the case of LXX Jeremiah, chapters 1—25 relate the prophet's early career, in which he argues that judgment is coming upon Jerusalem and Judah for abandoning or misconstruing their relationship with YHWH. The oracles against the nations in LXX Jeremiah 26—31 (Elam, Egypt, Babylon, Philistia, Edom, Ammon, Kedar, and Damascus) concern nations that would have comprised the general sphere of Judah during the period of the Babylonian empire and indicate the greatest potential extent of the Babylonian empire, although

Egypt was never taken. LXX Jeremiah 32—52 then portrays the realization of Jeremiah's earlier oracles, as the Babylonian empire ultimately destroyed Judah and Jerusalem, leaving Jeremiah in Egypt at the end of his life and the people of Jerusalem and Judah in Babylonian exile. This arrangement shows an interest in validating the message of Jeremiah and in portraying the reversal of Israel/Judah to their original state at the time of the exodus, that is, a people living in exile in a foreign land.

The present arrangement of MT Jeremiah includes the various visions, oracles, and laments of Jeremiah from his early career—perhaps from the time of Josiah and through the time of Zedekiah—in chapters 1—24. This material presents a highly critical view of Jerusalem, Judah, and the monarchy that anticipates YHWH's judgment against the people, although this section also looks forward to the time when YHWH will raise "the righteous branch" (that is, the Davidic monarch), who will preside over a period of peace and security in the land (23:5–6). Jeremiah 25—45 then presents a narrative account of the prophet's speeches and activities from the time of Jehoiakim, through the Babylonian destruction of Jerusalem, to the aftermath of Gedaliah's assassination, when Jeremiah was taken to Egypt against his will in order to live out his days criticizing those who abandoned Judah. Again, this material presents a largely critical view of Judah. But Jeremiah 30—33 points to the ultimate return of the people to the land and the establishment of a "new covenant" between YHWH and the people in which the Torah will be written upon their hearts and the "righteous branch" of David will rule in peace and security. The oracles against the nations in chapters 46—51 indicate that YHWH's judgment is to be equated with the rise of the Persian empire (cf. Isaiah), in that the nations listed were all subject to Persia in the early second temple period. Likewise, the nations mentioned in 25:13b–38, which are missing in LXX Jeremiah, point to Persian hegemony in a section that introduces the Jeremiah narratives as well as the oracles against the nations. Altogether, these references indicate that judgment is coming against Judah and the nations in the form of the Babylonian empire but that the Persians will see to the establishment of YHWH's punishment over Babylon as well. MT Jeremiah concludes with the notice of the destruction of Jerusalem and the Babylonian exile drawn from 2 Kings 24:18–25:30.

This arrangement is based largely on thematic and generic grounds, and many have argued that it reflects the compositional history of the book. The structure of MT Jeremiah appears to presuppose a chronological principle, but there are numerous repetitions, such as the presentation of Jeremiah's temple speech in Jeremiah 7 and the narrative concerning his trial for sedition that took place as a result of this speech in Jeremiah 26. The book begins with a narrative concerning his appointment by YHWH to serve as a prophet to the nations, which many associate with his birth or his youth, and it continues through the latter stages of his lifetime in Egypt in chapter 45. The oracles against the nations in Jeremiah 46—51 are to be realized only in the future or beyond the lifetime of the prophet. The narrative in chapter 52 summarizes the state of affairs for Jerusalem and Judah at the end of Jeremiah's lifetime. As in LXX Jeremiah, MT Jeremiah traces a process by which

Jeremiah and the people of Israel/Judah return to their origins in exile outside of the land of Israel.

There has been an extensive discussion throughout the twentieth century concerning the composition of Jeremiah. In keeping with the interests of the late nineteenth and early twentieth centuries, much of the debate initially focused on attempts to reconstruct a picture of the historical prophet Jeremiah ben Hilkiah. The issue is complicated, however, in that the book presents the scribe Baruch ben Neriah as the close associate of Jeremiah who wrote the prophet's words for him on various occasions, as in Jeremiah 36 (cf. chap. 45), when Jeremiah was prohibited from speaking publically by the king. Consequently, there is a great deal of speculation that Baruch ben Neriah could be the redactor who composed an early version of the book.

The most influential study of the early twentieth century is that of Sigmund Mowinckel, who identifies four major sources within the book of Jeremiah.[27] Source A is the poetic material of Jeremiah 1—25, which Mowinckel identifies as the words of the prophet himself, or at least presentations of the prophet's oracles. Source B is the biographical prose material in Jer. 19:1–20:6; 26; 28—29; and 36 —44, which was written by an admirer of the prophet, whom Mowinckel and others identify as Baruch ben Neriah. Source C is the sermonic prose material in Jer. 7:1–8:3; 11:1–14; 18:1–12; 21:1–10; 25:1–11a; 32:1–2, 6–16, 24–44; 34:1–35:19; and 44:1–14, which is similar to sermonic material in the book of Deuteronomy and the Deuteronomistic History. Source C also includes the various superscriptions that appear throughout the book and the prose material in 3:6–13; 29:1a, 3–9, 21–23; and 45. Source D comprises the oracles of consolation in Jeremiah 30—31, which must derive from the postexilic period. Including the oracles against the nations in Jeremiah 46—51 and the narrative drawn from Kings in Jeremiah 52, the entire book was edited and assembled into its final form at some point during the postexilic period.

Subsequent scholarship has struggled with the question of reconstructing the historical prophet from the later material of the book. For the most part, studies after Mowinckel note that the distinctions between his sources tend to blur under closer examination, as they seem to have a great deal in common with each other. John Bright questions the distinction between Mowinckel's sources B and C in that their vocabulary, modes of expression, and concepts appear to have a great deal in common, prompting him to argue that they represent a single literary stream by which the words of Jeremiah are passed down.[28] Nicholson argues that both B and C are Deuteronomic sources that were composed by Levitical circles in Babylonia who employed the figure of the prophet as a literary mouthpiece to articulate Deuteronomic teachings in the postexilic Jewish community.[29] The sermonic forms employed by these circles point to the origins of the Jewish synagogue as an outgrowth of Levitical teaching. A highly influential study published in German by Weippert argues that the prose material of Jeremiah is Deuteronomic and that it is rooted in the poetic oracles of source A that Mowinckel identifies with the words of Jeremiah.[30] This of course points to Jeremiah and his followers as the authors of the prose material and recapitulates in modern form the traditional view that Jeremiah wrote both his book and the books of Kings.

Holladay also notes the affinities between the poetic and prose materials of Jeremiah, and argues that the prose sermons constitute Jeremiah's public statements that challenge the views put forward in the public reading of the book of Deuteronomy every seven years.[31] Carroll notes the difficulties in penetrating the heavily redacted book and argues that these difficulties make it impossible to reconstruct an accurate picture of the historical prophet distinct from the redactional presentation in the current form of the book.[32] Carroll maintains that Baruch is a creation of the Deuteronomic writers of the book to assist in their presentation of a largely fictional account about the prophet. McKane contends that Jeremiah 1—20 contain the "authentic" words of the prophet but that the book must be considered as a "rolling corpus" developed in a sustained but piecemeal fashion as later writers continued to add their exegetical and editorial comments to the original "kernels" of Jeremiah.[33]

Scholarly discussion of Jeremiah clearly points to a great deal of difficulty in establishing the literary history of both versions of the book. Overall, both LXX Jeremiah and MT Jeremiah are heavily edited compositions that reflect the theological and historiographical perspectives of the later writers who composed them. Both versions attempt to portray Jeremiah as a sort of "second Moses,"[34] who served as a prophet for a forty-year period; promulgated Mosaic Torah as the basis for the relationship between YHWH and the people; suffered continuous abuse, isolation, and rebellion in carrying out his prophetic role; and ultimately died outside the land of Israel. As noted earlier, there is a sense of reversal in the presentation of Jeremiah as well, in that unlike Moses, who led the people out of Egypt to the promised land, Jeremiah presided over a period in which the people were removed from the land of Israel to exile in Egypt and Babylonia. In this regard, the book of Jeremiah constitutes a type of theodicy analogous to that of Isaiah, in that Jeremiah attempts to portray the disasters that overtake the people of Judah—the destruction of Jerusalem and the temple and the exile of the people—as righteous acts of YHWH. By defining adherence to YHWH's covenant expressed through Mosaic Torah as the criterion for the people's welfare, the book of Jeremiah overcomes the common perception that YHWH would protect the people, Jerusalem, and the temple by arguing that the people had violated the terms of their relationship with YHWH and earned exile from the land as a consequence of their actions. It thereby attempts to protect YHWH by portraying the deity as righteous and the people as guilty.

This portrayal of Jeremiah, YHWH, and the events of the time constitutes a theological construct developed by the composers of the book. The extent to which it represents a historically accurate portrayal of the views of the prophet is the subject of much discussion. Various features of the prophet and his thinking, especially his priestly or Levitical identity and his pro-Babylonian political stance, emerge from the book and point to the basis for reconstructing a portrait of the prophet. Jeremiah is a Levitical priest of the Elide line, which once served in the sanctuary at Shiloh during the premonarchic period (1 Samuel 1—3) but was banished to the village of Anathoth when King Solomon expelled the Elide priest Abiathar in favor of Zadok, apparently the founder of the Zadokite high priestly line

(1 Kings 2:26–27). Jeremiah refers to the destruction of the temple at Shiloh, an event that is not portrayed elsewhere in the Bible, as part of his diatribe against those who felt that YHWH would protect the temple in Jerusalem (Jer. 7:1–8:3). He likewise refers to Samuel (who was connected with Eli) and Moses as intercessory figures who, despite their standing, would not be able to deliver Jerusalem from its fate. His vision of the almond rod (Jer. 1:11–12), the boiling pot that represented the enemy from the north (1:16), and the baskets of good and bad figs (24:10) all indicate his priestly role. The almond rod represents the Levitical staff of the priests (Num. 17:1–11); the Levitical priests supervised the boiling of meat in pots as part of the sacrificial ritual (1 Sam. 2:11–17; Ezek. 24:1–14); and the reception and evaluation of fruit offerings at the temple was part of the priestly duties (Num. 18:1–31; Deut. 14:22–29; 18:1–5). Jeremiah's use of stereotypical lamentation language in his so-called "confessions" or "laments" (Jer. 11:18–12:6; 15:10–21; 17:14–18; 18:18–23; 20:7–18) is hardly an indication of later authorship as many claim, but may be expected from a priest who was called upon to perform such ritual duties as part of the temple liturgy in times of distress. Finally, the public teaching of Mosaic Torah is also a part of the Levitical duties (Deut. 31:9–13). It would serve as a basis for Jeremiah's critique of the people and the monarchs insofar as the Levitical priests were to supervise the writing and reading of the Torah by the king (Deut. 17:18–20).

Jeremiah is portrayed as a prophet with many enemies, but this may also be a component of his Elide priestly identity and his relationship to King Josiah's reform. His enemies include King Jehoiakim as well as men from his hometown of Anathoth (Jer. 11:1–23, esp. vv. 21–23). According to 2 Kings 23:28–30 (cf. 2 Chron. 35:20–27), Josiah closed all sanctuaries outside of Jerusalem and called for the Levites to serve in Jerusalem. The Levites refused, and Jeremiah's appearance in Jerusalem about this time may well explain the hostility with which he was viewed by his colleagues in Anathoth. Furthermore, Jeremiah's consistently pro-Babylonian political message, insofar as he called for Judah's submission to Babylon (Jeremiah 27—28) reflects the policy of King Josiah, who died at Megiddo in 609 B.C.E., attempting to stop the Egyptians from advancing north to oppose the Babylonians in their fight against Assyria at Haran.[35] King Jehoiakim, after all, was a pro-Egyptian puppet placed on the throne by Pharaoh Necho in 609 B.C.E., following Josiah's death. This political perspective is also evident in Jeremiah's close ties with the family of Shaphan: Ahikam ben Shaphan saved Jeremiah from execution for sedition as a result of his temple sermon in Jeremiah 26; Elasah ben Shaphan in Jeremiah 29 conveyed Jeremiah's letter to the exiles in Babylon advising them to build lives in Babylonian exile; Gemariah ben Shaphan provided the house in which Baruch read Jeremiah's scroll to all the people in Jeremiah 36; and Gedaliah ben Ahikam ben Shaphan was asked by the Babylonians to protect Jeremiah in the aftermath of the Babylonian victory (Jer. 39:14; 40:1–5). The father of the family, Shaphan, was a close advisor of Josiah who brought the Torah scroll found in the temple to the king; Josiah in turn subsequently employed it as the basis for his reform program (2 Kings 22:3–20). His advice to adhere to the teachings of the Ten Commandments in Jer. 7:9 (cf. 11:1–17) may well reflect his adherence to Mosaic Torah as the basis for Josiah's program.

Jeremiah's call for the return of northern Israel to YHWH and to Davidic rule in both Jeremiah 2—6 and 30—31 appears to support Josiah's program to reunify the lands of Israel and Judah under Davidic rule, with the Jerusalem temple as their religious center. Josiah's early death at Megiddo, however, apparently convinced the prophet that YHWH had determined to punish Judah as well as Israel. As understood by Jeremiah, YHWH's will was to establish Babylon as the dominant power in the world, or "enemy from the north." In addition, it called for adherence to the norms of Mosaic Torah as expressed in Deuteronomy. Jeremiah therefore calls for the just treatment of the poor and underprivileged in Judah (cf. Deut. 15; 24:17–22) and criticizes Jehoiakim for self-aggrandizement in building a sumptuous palace for himself (Jeremiah 22), contrary to the practices of his father Josiah. Jeremiah likewise condemns Hananiah as a false prophet, even though his message of deliverance for Jerusalem in two years corresponds to that of Isaiah (Jeremiah 27—28). He condemns Zedekiah for reneging on his promise to release slaves (cf. Deut. 15:1–6) when the Babylonians temporarily abandoned the siege of Jerusalem (Jeremiah 34). His redemption of family property during the lapse in the siege (Jeremiah 32; cf. Deut. 25:5–10) reflects his confidence in the future and his belief that the people must act according to Mosaic Torah to remain in the land. His warnings against flight to Egypt (Jeremiah 43—44) reflect this perspective as well as Deuteronomy's command to the king not to return the people to Egypt (Deut. 17:14–20).

Despite the emphasis on the criticism of Judah in the message of Jeremiah, the oracles in Jeremiah 30—33 point ultimately to the restoration of the people to the land under the rule of a righteous Davidic monarch when YHWH makes a new covenant with the people. The initial program of Jeremiah's commission to speak as a prophet, "to pluck up and to pull down, to destroy and to overthrow, to build and to plant" (Jer. 1:10), is thereby reiterated in YHWH's promises for the restoration of Israel and Judah in 31:28, "And just as I have watched over them to pluck up and break down, to overthrow, destroy, and bring evil, so I will watch over them to build and to plant, says the LORD."

V. THE BOOK OF EZEKIEL

The book of Ezekiel appears as the third book of the Latter Prophets in the Jewish Tanakh, although some authorities place it as the second book immediately following Jeremiah (*b. B. Bat.* 14b). Ezekiel is the third of the major prophetic books in the Christian Old Testament canon, following Isaiah and Jeremiah/Lamentations and preceding Daniel. There was apparently some question in Rabbinic tradition concerning the canonical status of the book, since it frequently stands at odds with material in the Torah. According to *b. Shabb.* 13b, Rabbi Hanina ben Hezekiah burned three hundred jars of oil working at night by the light of a lamp in order to reconcile the discrepancies between Ezekiel and the Torah. Likewise, *m. Hag.* 2:1 maintains that the inaugural vision in Ezekiel 1 is not to be expounded except by one who is a sage in his own right. Ezekiel's vision provides much of the basis for the development of the Hekhalot ("palaces") mystical tradition (e.g., 3

Enoch; Hekhalot Rabbati), which portrayed attempts to ascend through the seven levels of heaven in order to experience the divine presence and thereby to comprehend G-d's actions and intentions.[36]

The superscription in Ezek. 1:1–3 informs the reader that Ezekiel's visions of G-d came to him while he was among the exiles by the River Chebar in the land of Babylonia. The date is placed in the fifth year of the exile of King Jehoiachin of Judah, which would be approximately 593/2 B.C.E., about five years prior to the Babylonian destruction of Jerusalem and the temple. The initial reference to the thirtieth year is somewhat enigmatic in that it could refer to the prophet's age, the thirtieth year since the beginning of Josiah's reform, the thirtieth year after the prophet's initial call, or other possibilities. Since Ezekiel ben Buzi was a Zadokite priest from the Jerusalem temple who was exiled with King Jehoiachin by the Babylonians in 597 B.C.E., it seems likely that the thirtieth year refers to his age. Numbers 4:3 defines the thirtieth year as the age for beginning priestly service (contra Num. 8:23–25, which states that the initial age is twenty-five years) and the fiftieth year as the age of retirement from priestly service. It is noteworthy that, with the exception of the reference to the twenty-seventh year in Ezek. 29:17, the dated oracles of the book of Ezekiel extend through the twenty-fifth year of the exile (Ezek. 40:1), which would have been approximately 573/2 B.C.E. This would suggest that the book was designed to correlate Ezekiel's prophetic activity with his years of active service in the temple had he remained in Jerusalem. Although Ezekiel comments on events that take place in Jerusalem, he apparently remained in Babylonian exile throughout the Babylonian invasion of Judah in 588/7 and the destruction of Jerusalem and the temple in 587/6. According to Ezek. 3:15, he lived in Tel Aviv (Hebrew, "hill of spring"), an unknown site by the River or Canal Chebar near Nippur identified with the Akkadian expression *til-abubi,* "hill of flood" (perhaps a reference to flooding from the Chebar). According to the records of the Babylonian trading and banking house run by Murashu and his sons during the fifth century B.C.E., Jewish exiles settled in this region.

The Babylonian destruction of Jerusalem and the temple in 587/6 B.C.E. plays a key role in determining the structure of the book and the portrayal of Ezekiel's message. This concern is reinforced by the appearance of a series of dating formulas throughout the book that establish a chronological sequence from Ezekiel's initial vision in the fifth year, fourth (?) month, and fifth day of the exile of Jehoiachin (Ezek. 1:1–3; 3:16) through the twenty-fifth year, first month, tenth day, when Ezekiel reveals his vision of the new temple in Zion. With the exception of the above noted twenty-seventh year in Ezek. 29:17, other dates follow in roughly chronological sequence, including the sixth year, sixth month, fifth day (Ezek. 8:1); the seventh year, fifth month, tenth day (Ezek. 20:1); the ninth year, tenth month, tenth day (Ezek. 24:1); the eleventh year, unknown month, first day (Ezek. 26:1); the tenth year, tenth month, twelfth day (Ezek. 29:1); the twenty-seventh year, first month, first day (Ezek. 29:17); the eleventh year, first month, seventh day (Ezek. 30:20); the eleventh year, third month, first day (Ezek. 31:1); the twelfth year, twelfth month, first day (Ezek. 32:1); and the twelfth year, tenth month, fifth day (Ezek. 33:21). The ninth (588 B.C.E.) through the twelfth (585

B.C.E.) years are especially important in this sequence in that they highlight the death of Ezekiel's wife as a sign of the destruction of Jerusalem and the temple (Ezek. 24:1).

The chronological sequence correlates with the contents of the book. Ezekiel 1—24 focuses especially on oracles concerning the destruction of Jerusalem and Judah, beginning with Ezekiel's inaugural vision of YHWH's departure from Jerusalem and the temple and culminating with the death of his wife. Ezekiel 25—32 contains a series of oracles against the nations that Ezekiel expected would be swept up in the Babylonian advance, including Ammon, Moab, Edom, Philistia, Tyre, Sidon, and Egypt, although neither Tyre nor Egypt were ever taken by the Babylonians. Ezekiel 33—39 focuses especially on the restoration of the land of Israel and the return of the people to the land, beginning with Ezekiel's appointment as the "watchman" over the restored people and culminating in the vision of YHWH's victory over the Gog and Magog figures who oppressed Israel. Ezekiel 40—48 then portrays the establishment of the new temple in Zion as YHWH returns to the temple, which then serves as the center for a new creation with the tribes of Israel arrayed around it. Altogether, the book portrays YHWH's departure from Zion and the punishment or cleansing of Jerusalem and the world prior to YHWH's return to Zion and the establishment of Zion as the holy center of Israel and all creation.

Critical scholarship on the book of Ezekiel lagged behind that on Isaiah and Jeremiah through the early twentieth century. The highly structured and well organized presentation evident in the book, combined with the relative disinterest in priestly matters during this period, apparently convinced scholars that little would be gained from critical work in Ezekiel. This began to change with the work of Gustav Hölscher,[37] who argued that later redactors transformed the original prophet and poet Ezekiel into a priestly legalist and ritualist who served as a model for the later Jewish community. Hölscher viewed Ezekiel as a true ecstatic, comparable to the shamanistic oracle-givers that were found in primitive cultures throughout the world, and he argued that Ezekiel's authentic oracles were first delivered orally by the prophet. He therefore removed most of the book as inauthentic to the prophet, including much of chapters 6–7; 10; 12—14; 18; 20; 25—26; and all of 33—48, and retained only about one-seventh of the book, drawn from chapters 1—32. Theological dichotomies between prophet and priest and between oral prophecy and written text are clearly evident in Hölscher's work.

Subsequent work argued that Ezekiel was largely the product of writers other than the prophet. C. C. Torrey maintained that the book was a pseudepigraph written during the Hellenistic period in the third century B.C.E. in order to establish an analogy between the Seleucid period and that of King Manasseh of Judah.[38] Smith proposed that the book originally was the work of a northern Israelite prophet who addressed the situation of the exiled northern kingdom of Israel during the late eighth and early seventh centuries B.C.E.[39] It was only later transformed into a Judean work. The years following World War II saw efforts to return Ezekiel to the period of the exile and, despite the presence of some later material, to view the book largely as the product of the prophet. Thus, both Howie[40] and Fohrer[41] contended that the bulk of the book must be attributed to Ezekiel, who spoke in Babylonia during the exile.

The most influential work of modern scholarship on the book of Ezekiel is the two-volume commentary by Walther Zimmerli, first published in German in 1969 and then in English translation in 1979 and 1983.[42] Employing a thorough text-critical, traditio-historical, and form-critical analysis, Zimmerli traces the process by which the prophet's original oral statements were transformed into a written text both by the prophet himself and subsequently by his school of followers. He isolates the various oracles and speeches that lie behind the present written form of the text and demonstrates Ezekiel's interaction with a great deal of mythological, legendary, and literary material (e.g., the "Holiness Code" in Leviticus 17—26), as he developed theological insights concerning YHWH's purposes through the period of destruction and exile. The original Ezekielian "kernels" or oral texts were frequently reworked by Ezekiel and his followers through a process of *Nachinterpretation* ("later interpretation") in which the earlier *Grundtext* ("foundational text") was rewritten to address later times and concerns (e.g., Ezek. 29:17–21, which announces that Nebuchadrezzar will receive the wealth of Egypt as compensation for his labors on behalf of G-d).

Zimmerli's work in this area provides a major impetus to studies of inner-biblical exegesis in relation to the prophetic works in general and points the way to the recognition that prophecy was a literary as well as an oral phenomenon. More recent studies take the literary character of the book very seriously. Greenberg's commentary stresses the literary integrity of the book, or its "holistic" character, and argues that much of the work of revision and reapplication was carried out by Ezekiel himself.[43] Davis emphasizes the prophet's role as a writer who reflects theologically upon his own writings and employs the metaphor of "swallowing the scroll" as a means to convey the literary character of his prophetic work.[44] Darr argues that the metaphor of "swallowing the scroll" signals Ezekiel's dependence upon prior textual tradition and that the final form of the book engages in a polemical dialogue with the Isaiah tradition.[45]

A reading of the book of Ezekiel must take account of Ezekiel's identity as a Zadokite priest as well as that of a prophet. Contrary to the assertions of many scholars in the late nineteenth and early twentieth centuries, it is no longer possible to posit a fundamental distinction between the two roles without qualification. Ancient Near Eastern prophets were frequently oracle-diviners who worked in the context of the temples dedicated to the deities of the particular culture. Israelite prophets could be connected with temples as well. An example is Samuel, who was raised as a Nazirite —that is, one dedicated for service to YHWH (Numbers 6), perhaps because he was firstborn (cf. Num. 3:11–13)—and who is portrayed as a priest. Likewise, Moses is portrayed as both Levitical priest and prophet (Exod. 2:1–10; Num. 26:58–59; Deut. 18:15; 34:10). As noted earlier, Jeremiah was a priest of the Elide line, and the prophet Zechariah is identified as a priest as well (Zech. 1:1; Ezra 5:1; 6:14; Neh. 12:16).

Ezekiel's role as priest is evident throughout the book and in his articulation of his prophetic message. He is fundamentally concerned with "the glory of YHWH" (*kĕbôd yhwh*), a technical term that describes the presence of YHWH among the people (Exod. 16:7, 10–12), in the tabernacle (Exod. 40:34–38), and in the temple (1 Kings 8:10–11; 2 Chron. 7:1–3; cf. 1 Sam. 4:21–22). The expression appears in the book of Ezekiel, where it describes the prophet's vision of YHWH mounted upon the throne chariot that transports the deity through the heavens when YHWH departs from the temple in Ezekiel 1—11 and returns to the new temple in Ezekiel 40—48 (Ezek. 1:28; 3:23; 8:4; 10:3–4, 19; 11:22–23; 43:1–5). The vision of YHWH's glory in 1:4–28 is based largely on the image of the ark in the Holy of Holies at the Jerusalem temple, which a young priest would presumably study prior to commencing his duties in the temple. The description of a cloud from the north takes up the usual imagery of cloud, perhaps portrayed with the use of incense in the temple, which generally accompanies portrayals of the glory of YHWH and the designation of the north as the home of the divine in Ugaritic mythology and in biblical literature (e.g., Isa. 14:13; Job 37:22). The imagery of gleaming bronze calls to mind the gold plating of the ark (Exod. 25:1–22; 37:1–9), which perhaps in turn conveys an ideal image of the ark prior to the times when the temple was stripped of gold and replaced with bronze (1 Kings 14:25–28; cf. 2 Kings 18:14–16). The four living creatures that bear the ark in Ezekiel's vision correspond to the two cherubim who are mounted above the mercy seat of the ark (Exod. 25:18–22) and the two built by Solomon within the Holy of Holies (1 Kings 6:23–28; 2 Chron. 3:10–14).[46] The burning coals of fire in the midst of the living creatures perhaps represents the sacrificial altar or the incense altars of the temple, and the wheel within the wheel may represent the rings by which the Levites carried the ark with poles (Exod. 25:12–15) or the wheels of the cart that conveyed the ark (2 Sam. 6:3; 1 Chron. 13:7). The firmament shining like crystal above the heads of the living creatures may represent the mercy seat (Exod. 25:17) or the clear pavement beneath the throne of G-d in the narrative concerning the banquet with YHWH shared by Moses, Aaron, Nadab, Abihu, and the seventy elders (Exod. 24:9–11). Finally, the image of the bow in the cloud in Ezek. 1:28 derives from the bow that symbolizes YHWH's covenant with Noah in Gen. 9:8–17.

Other imagery from Ezekiel's initial vision likewise pertains to his priestly role. The portrayal of his eating the scroll given to him by YHWH (Ezek. 2:8–3:3) takes up the commands to the priests and Levites to read the Torah scroll in the temple at Sukkot every seven years (Deut. 31:9–13). Ezekiel's role as watchman over the people Israel may reflect the understanding of Levitical priests as gatekeepers (1 Chron. 9:17–27; 26:1–19) or perhaps as temple guards as portrayed in the Chronicler's account of Jehoiada's posting of guards in the temple supervised by the Levitical priests during the coup against Athaliah (2 Chronicles 23, esp. vv. 6, 18–19). In any case, the role of the priestly gatekeeper is to ensure the holiness or purity of those who enter the temple precincts. Ezekiel's role as watchman is to warn the people of YHWH's words so that they might avoid sins and their resulting punishment (Ezek. 3:16–21; 33:1–20), a role not unlike that of the temple gatekeepers.

The vision of YHWH's departure from the temple in Ezekiel 8—11 is particularly indicative of Ezekiel's priestly role in that it portrays the destruction of the temple and the city of Jerusalem as a sacrifice made upon the altar for purification, much as an individual would bring a sacrifice to the priests at the temple altar to atone for wrongdoing. It thereby provides the basis by which Ezekiel may be considered a theodicy in that it portrays YHWH as righteous and the people as sinful. The portrayal in Ezekiel 8 of the abominations in the temple establishes the necessity for purifying the temple, now that it has become corrupt and unclean as a result of the idolatry and weeping for the Babylonian vegetation deity Tammuz within. The process of sacrificial purification begins in Ezekiel 9 with the entry of the six men appointed for execution, each with his weapon in hand. They are supervised by a man dressed in white linen—the characteristic dress of the priests on the sacrificial altar—who is equipped with a writing case to record their actions. As the throne chariot or glory of YHWH prepares to depart from the city and temple in Ezekiel 10, the man in white linen is commanded to take coals from between the cherubim and ignite the city as a priest would ignite the sacrificial offerings on the temple altar. Following the departure of YHWH from the temple, the city is identified as the cauldron in Ezekiel 11, further establishing the analogy between the destruction of the city and temple sacrifice. Nevertheless, the prophet announces that a group of men led by Jaazniah ben Azzur and Pelatiah ben Benaiah will form the basis of the exiled community. They are promised a return to the land of Israel, the removal of iniquity, and the replacement of their hearts of stone with hearts of flesh so that they will observe YHWH's commands. Until that time, YHWH will serve as a sanctuary or temple for them during the period of exile, thereby reinforcing the priestly imagery and laying the basis for the appearance of YHWH's glory, symbolizing YHWH's presence in the temple, in the Babylonian exile.

Various other elements point to Ezekiel's understanding of the destruction of Jerusalem and the temple and the Babylonian exile as a sacrificial purification—of Jerusalem, the temple, the people, and the land of Israel. The discourse on individual moral responsibility in Ezekiel 18 presupposes the teachings of the priestly Holiness Code in Leviticus 17—26, including proper avoidance of idolatry, treatment of blood, sexual purity, restoration of a pledge to a debtor, giving food to the hungry, and so forth, as the basis for its understanding of moral action. Ezekiel's concern with the profanation of YHWH's name (Ezekiel 20, 33, etc.) likewise reflects the priestly concern for YHWH's holiness. The portrayal in Ezek. 24:1–14 of besieged Jerusalem as a burning sacrificial cauldron employs the imagery of the priests' duties at the altar, and the analogy drawn between the death of Ezekiel's wife and the destruction of Jerusalem in Ezek. 24:15–27 employs the traditional motif of Israel as bride to YHWH to convey the loss of Jerusalem. The imagery of the dry bones coming to life in Ezekiel 37 employs an image of impurity—priests are not allowed to come into contact with the dead (Lev. 21:1–3)—to convey the restoration of a purified Israel. Finally, the vision of the temple in Ezekiel 40—48 looks forward to the restoration of the purified temple as the holy center of both the world of creation at large and the tribes of Israel as the basis by which the glory of YHWH returns from exile among the nations. With the return of YHWH's glory to the temple, YHWH's name will no longer be defiled (Ezek. 43:1–9).

In sum, the book of Ezekiel presents the realization of YHWH's promises in Ezek. 36:22–32 (cf. Ezek. 11:14–21) to sanctify YHWH's name by sprinkling water on the people to remove their impurity, much as a priest must immerse himself in water to become pure for temple service. It argues that the covenant with YHWH will be maintained when the people receive a new heart, one that will enable them to observe YHWH's commandments, to live in the holy land promised to their ancestors, and to restore their relationship with YHWH as their G-d.

FOR FURTHER READING

Prophecy in General

Blenkinsopp, Joseph. *A History of Prophecy in Israel.* Rev. ed. Louisville, Ky.: Westminster John Knox, 1996.
Wilson, Robert R. *Prophecy and Society in Ancient Israel.* Philadelphia: Fortress, 1980.

Isaiah

Sweeney, Marvin A. *Isaiah 1—39, with an Introduction to Prophetic Literature.* FOTL 16. Grand Rapids: Eerdmans, 1996.
Westermann, Claus. *Isaiah 40—66: A Commentary.* OTL. Trans. D. M. G. Stalker. Philadelphia: Westminster, 1969.

Jeremiah

Carroll, Robert P. *Jeremiah: A Commentary.* OTL. Philadelphia: Westminster, 1986.
Holladay, William L. *Jeremiah.* Hermeneia. 2 vols. Philadelphia and Minneapolis: Fortress, 1986–89.

Ezekiel

Greenberg, Moshe. *Ezekiel 1—20.* AB 20. Garden City, N.Y.: Doubleday, 1983.
Zimmerli, Walther. *Ezekiel.* Hermeneia. 2 vols. Trans. R. E. Clements and J. D. Martin. Philadelphia: Fortress, 1979–83.

4

THE BOOK OF THE TWELVE/
THE MINOR PROPHETS

Hosea, Joel, Amos, Obadiah, Jonah, Micah, Nahum, Habakkuk,
Zephaniah, Haggai, Zechariah, Malachi

DAVID L. PETERSEN

I. THE BOOK OF THE TWELVE

A. Introduction

Names and labels are powerful symbols, as the title of this chapter shows. The literature subsumed under it—the final portion of the "Latter Prophets"—has routinely been known by a previous generation of biblical interpreters as the Minor, or Twelve, Prophets, a phrase that bore a slightly derogatory tone (viz., minor when compared to major prophets). By contrast, the label "Book of the Twelve" places these chapters in a position comparable to their prophetic kin: Isaiah, Jeremiah, and Ezekiel. Jeremiah is the longest prophetic book, occupying 116 pages in one edition of the Hebrew Bible, whereas Ezekiel is the shortest, occupying ninety-five pages. The Book of the Twelve stands in between, with ninety-six pages. (And, for the sake of completeness, Isaiah runs 105 pages.) Simply in terms of mass, the Book of the Twelve belongs in the same league as the other exemplars of prophetic literature.

The phrase "twelve prophets" dates to the pre-Christian era. For example, Sirach 49:10 reads, "May the bones of the Twelve Prophets send forth new life from where they lie. . . ." Hence, as early as ca. 200 B.C.E., we know that these twelve figures were viewed as a group. Moreover, there is overwhelming evidence that these twelve biblical books were viewed as a scribal unit. Perhaps the rabbis thought they belonged inextricably together. Or perhaps, as one rabbi put it, they should all be copied on one scroll so that the small books, such as Malachi, would not be lost (*b. B. Bat.* 13b). Jewish scribal practice, as stated in the Babylonian Talmud, required that four empty lines be left between biblical books, except between the minor prophets where three lines were permitted. Finally, the Dead Sea scrolls included a fragmentary leather scroll upon which the minor prophets were apparently written. So one may say conclusively that the minor prophets were viewed, as early as the Greco-Roman period, as books that were to be written together.

Even though ancient scribes clearly placed them on the same scroll, no Hebrew scroll with the title, "The Book of the Twelve," has been discovered. Neither of the two Hebrew words that might readily be translated as book or scroll (*mĕgillāh* and sēper) is associated with the Twelve (henceforth XII) in the era we have been discussing. Hence, to use the phrase "The Book of the Twelve" may involve more than the simple judgment that these books were copied as one piece. Instead, the implications of this phrase may be manifold, though perhaps the most important is the presumption that these twelve separately titled entities make up something akin to the other major prophetic books, that is, a book that coheres or has some thematic unity. Here the issue involves much more than mere scribal practice.

At the outset there is an obvious point of contrast between the XII and the other prophetic books: the presence of a sole author to whom each of the other "Latter Prophets" may be attributed. There is neither an Ezekiel nor an Isaiah to hold the XII together. So the case for "The Book of the Twelve" will have to rest elsewhere, either in the search for a theme or plot that unifies this literature or in a claim that these books were edited with an eye to each other. (We will address this issue below.)

One motif that occurs with striking prominence in the XII is the phrase, "the day of Yahweh." It is explicitly present in all but two of the XII (Jonah and Nahum, and it is implicit in the latter [Nahum 1:7]). Moreover, it is relatively infrequent in the other three prophetic books (in Isaiah it appears primarily in oracles against foreign nations [13:6; 22:5] and in later texts [e.g., 34:8]). Some of the important representative exemplars in the XII are Hos. 9:5; Joel 2:31; Amos 5:18–20; Obad. 15; Micah 2:4; Hab. 3:16; Zeph. 1:7–16; Hag. 2:23; Zech. 14:1; Mal. 4:1. As we will have occasion to note below, the day of the Lord is more than just a phrase. Those words allude to an Israelite tradition about a moment when Yahweh will act as regent, often in a military manner. If Isaiah focuses on Zion, Jeremiah on the rhetoric of lament, and Ezekiel on the glory of Yahweh, the XII highlight the day of Yahweh. The vocabulary of temporality is a key to this prophetic collection.

B. Historical Perspectives

The Book of the Twelve contains some of the earliest as well some of the latest exemplars of Israelite prophetic literature. On the one hand, Amos reflects conditions of the mid-eighth century. On the other hand, Zechariah 9—14 stems from well into the Persian period (ca. 550–330 B.C.E.). So with the XII we are dealing with a period of roughly 400 years. During these years, Israel experienced decidedly different historical contexts: (1) the period of two kingdoms; (2) the time of Judean statehood (721–587 B.C.E.); (3) exile; and (4) restoration. These centuries were times of international upheaval. With the first prophets, Israel and Judah lay on the western perimeter of the Neo-Assyrian empire. Late in the seventh century, that Mesopotamian power fell to another, the Neo-Babylonians. And then, midway through the sixth century, the Persians, an empire with its roots to the east of Mesopotamia, decimated the Babylonians.

Each of these empires at one time or another placed troops in Syria-Palestine. Hence, life in both Israel and Judah was in considerable measure a function of foreign imperial activity. The Neo-Assyrian empire destroyed Israel in 721 B.C.E.; the

Neo-Babylonian empire destroyed Judah in 587 B.C.E.; and the Persian empire allowed for and partially funded the rebuilding of Judah as one of its provinces. Each of these three nodal moments receives attention in the XII. In some sense, each could be called Yahweh's day; and yet, that day also always remained a future event.

The other three major prophetic books provide interesting points of comparison concerning the issue of historical breadth. Isaiah's inaugural vision dates to 743 B.C.E. If one may conclude that Isaiah 56—66 dates to the period immediately after the completion of the second temple, then that book represents a period of roughly 240 years. The chronological issue for Jeremiah is complicated by the various ways in which Jer. 1:2 may be understood. But the date itself is secure, namely 627 B.C.E. Apart from the so-called historical appendix (chap. 32), the book appears to conclude soon after the defeat of Judah in 587. Here the chronological sweep is decidedly shorter than for Isaiah—more like forty years. Ezekiel presents the most compressed time frame, beginning in 593 and concluding in about 570 B.C.E. (see 29:17), just a little less than a quarter century. In sum, none of the "major" prophets can compare with the historical sweep offered by the Twelve.

C. Order of the Literature

During most of the twentieth century, it has been a commonplace to assume that the minor prophets were written and edited as individual books and then collected and ordered. One of the principles for their ordering appears to have been chronological. Hosea and Amos are early books and appear early on in the collection, whereas Haggai and Zechariah are late and appear near its end. But there are troubling exceptions. Joel, which lacks any explicit historical allusions, is routinely dated to the Persian period. Yet this book appears second in the collection. Moreover, immediately before Micah, whose superscription anchors it firmly to the eighth century, come Obadiah, which dates to ca. 587, and Jonah, which, though mentioning Ninevch, is almost certainly postexilic.

The following two charts display the problematics. Chart 1 orders the books according to the dates they claim for themselves, while Chart 2 indicates the probable relative dates of origin for the books, though these judgments do not reflect a firm scholarly consensus. (A book like Zechariah involves at least two different moments: ca. 520 for chaps. 1—8; later in the Persian period for chaps. 9—14.)

Chart 1	Chart 2
Hosea	Amos
Joel	Hosea
Amos	Micah
Obadiah	Zephaniah
Jonah	Nahum
Micah	Habakkuk
Nahum	Obadiah

Chart 1	Chart 2
Habakkuk	Haggai
Zephaniah	Zechariah
Haggai	Malachi
Zechariah	Joel
Malachi	Jonah

Obviously, the XII are not in strict chronological order. There is, moreover, evidence of alternative canonical orderings. The major manuscripts of the Septuagint (the Greek translation of the Hebrew Bible, abbreviated LXX) present an order different from the Hebrew text for the first six books: Hosea, Amos, Micah, Joel, Obadiah, and Jonah. This order reflects more nearly the dates of historical origin as in Chart 2 for the first three books. But that principle breaks down with the next three. Both the Hebrew and Greek textual evidence, therefore, allows one to infer that the principle of chronological arrangement does not offer a comprehensive explanation for the ordering of the books. Other dynamics were at work. One of these was the similar phraseology at the end of one book and the beginning of another, which may have made it seem appropriate for the two books to be placed together. For example, the following lines occur near the end of Joel (3:16) and near the beginning of Amos (1:2):

> The LORD roars from Zion,
>   and utters his voice from Jerusalem.

The shared couplet may have influenced a scribe to place these two books together as they now stand in the Hebrew manuscript tradition.

The very notion of "the Twelve" requires brief comment. Why not eleven prophets? The answer that there were twelve books waiting to be included is not self-evident. The final book, known as Malachi in English, probably does not reflect a named prophet: the word *mal'āki* in Hebrew means "my messenger." It is not a typical Hebrew name. Moreover, the title of the book "an oracle, the word of the LORD . . ." is similar to the introductions that occur at Zech. 9:1 and 12:1. As a result, one may theorize that the four chapters of Malachi were split off from Zechariah 9—14 to create a separate book, thus making a total of twelve such books. The number twelve was symbolically significant for ancient Israel, as the notion of the twelve tribes readily suggests. Thus it is likely that the final portion of the XII was configured in such a way as to yield twelve prophets, not eleven or thirteen.

There is a final and related issue concerning the order of these books: the placement of the XII in the various canonical traditions. The Christian Bible concludes with the XII, whereas the Jewish scriptures place the XII at the end of the second section, "the Prophets" (*Nevi'im*), and just before the beginning of the Writings with its lead book, Psalms. As a result, the two canons conclude in different forms and with diverse tones: the Jewish canon ends with a challenge to live in Judah and worship at the temple in Jerusalem (2 Chron. 36:23) and the Christian Bible with the affirmation that Elijah will return to effect familial harmony. The one focuses on place, the other on person and relationships. Hence the very placement of the XII at one or another point in the canon affects our perceptions of this literature.

D. Formation of the Individual Books and of the XII

One may raise two different questions about literary formation when discussing the XII. On the one hand, it is appropriate to ask about the process according to which an individual book was created. For example, how did Hosea come to exist? There are some biographical and autobiographical sections at the beginning of the book that are then followed by various poetic speeches. Did someone organize the speeches, and if so, according to what principles? Were the prose pieces in chapters 1 and 3 put in their current order for some particular purpose? Answers to such questions usually result from what scholars call redaction criticism, which attempts to trace the stages in the organization and editing of literature (see section E below, on Ways of Reading the Twelve Prophets). In our sketches about each prophetic book, we will comment when appropriate about redaction-critical issues important for the interpretation of that book.

On the other hand, one may raise questions about the formation of the XII itself. In effect, we have already done this by talking about the order of these twelve books. However, that discussion presupposes a model according to which there were twelve books ready to be ordered. Other models exist. For example, some scholars have maintained that there was an early collection of minor prophets, one made up of three or four books, and that it grew to eight or nine, and then to twelve.[1] Another model involves the notion of several discrete collections. Jörg Jeremias has recently argued that Amos and Hosea exerted mutual formative influence and must have comprised an early collection.[2] In a comparable vein, Nogalski posits two such entities, a Deuteronomic collection (Hosea, Amos, Micah, Zephaniah) and the Haggai-Zechariah corpus.[3] These collections were combined and supplemented at a later time. One element that appears with increasing frequency in these discussions is the claim that there was a Deuteronomistic collection of minor prophets, a claim based in part on the conviction that a number of these books, especially Amos, Micah, and Hosea, include Deuteronomistic redactional material. (At a minimum, the superscriptions to these books reflect issues of importance to the Deuteronomist, as in the indictments in Zephaniah.) Other scholars have suggested that as the collection grew, the beginnings and endings of books were refined and revised so as to provide linkages with contiguous prophetic books (so Nogalski). Such claims, if sustained, would weigh heavily toward conceiving the XII as a book, since the material in the books, not just their order, was designed with the larger whole in view. At the moment, however, there is no scholarly consensus about these matters.

Two other items deserve some mention within the context of the formation of this prophetic literature. First, some of the books in the XII appear to have been updated, particularly with reference to the defeat of Judah in 587 B.C.E. and the experience of exile, the demise of nationhood, and the end of the Davidic kingship.

It is difficult to read Amos 9:11–15 and not imagine that these verses were written to express hope for Israel after it had suffered these catastrophes. Second, such updatings of prophetic literature are most clearly attested in the book of Isaiah, with its monumental neo-Isaianic corpuses (viz., Isaiah 24—27, 34—35, 40—55, 56—66). It may be that comparable forces were at work with the XII. O. H. Steck has argued that latter portions of the XII reflect comparable literary processes and theological concerns as late sections in Isaiah.[4] So questions about the formation of the XII are probably not easily isolated from questions about the formation of other biblical prophetic literature.

All such concerns about how the XII came to exist involve a topic inherent to the study of all prophetic literature, namely, written deposition of prophetic materials. All of the "major" prophets—Isaiah (8:1–4; 30:8), Jeremiah (32:9–15; 36), and Ezekiel (2:9–3:3) —mention in one way or another the creation or use of texts as part of the prophetic enterprise. (During the monarchic period, both leather and papyrus were probably used for inscription of longer texts.) Such practice is attested in several of the XII (Hab. 2:2–3; Mal. 3:16). Writing in the performance of the prophetic role would have been one important generator for prophetic literature. But there must have been at least one other impulse, namely, the desire to see whether that which the prophets anticipated would work itself out. The classic formulation of Deut. 18:22 virtually requires the archival preservation of prophetic utterance: "If a prophet speaks in the name of the LORD but the thing does not take place or prove true, it is a word that the LORD has not spoken." One can imagine that the words of Amos 2:13–16, when preserved and remembered after the destruction of Israel in 721 B.C.E., would have gained even greater authority than they might originally have borne. The preservation of utterances by prophets attested in the XII would ultimately have led to the formation of that larger book.

E. Ways of Reading the Twelve Prophets

Scholars have devoted considerable attention to refining the various ways in which they read and interpret biblical literature. There are certain perspectives common to all biblical literature and others of special concern for the interpretation of prophetic literature. As for the former, attention to the various manuscript traditions as well as philological matters profoundly affect the interpretation of all biblical texts. Although text-critical issues loom large for study of Jeremiah, there are no comparable text-critical problems preserved in ancient manuscripts of the XII. Still, translating the XII from Hebrew into English is no easy matter.

The problem is particularly severe for Hosea. The translators of the NRSV remark with dismaying frequency: "Meaning of Hebrew uncertain," as in Hos. 7:6, 16. Sometimes the text appears corrupt; other times the language is impenetrable. For the reader who does not know Hebrew, it is always a good idea to consult several of the recent and good translations (NRSV, Tanakh, NIV, NJB, REB, NAB are all good candidates) to gain access to the philological work of numerous scholars. If there are major differences, it may be necessary to consult a commentary or other appropriate resource. For example, the NRSV of Hos. 4:3 reads, "the land mourns," whereas Tanakh translates, "the earth is withered." The meanings are quite different: lamentation versus dessication. The translators have understood the Hebrew word in very different ways, and the reasons for such differences are made clear in major commentaries.[5]

Beyond issues involving text and translation lie questions regarding the formation of the literature. Three critical perspectives—form criticism, redaction criticism, and tradition history—have proven influential during much of the twentieth century. Form criticism is really a specialized form of literary criticism that focuses particularly on the formal and formulaic features of a text. For example, in Amos 1:3–15 there are five speeches, each directed at a foreign nation. They share a number of striking similarities including several formulas: "Thus says the LORD, for three transgressions and for four . . . , and so I will send . . . , says the LORD." Moreover, each speech is made up of essentially two parts, an indictment—what the nation did wrong—and a sentence —what God will do to them. Those sensitive to such formulas and forms will often talk about the typical form, in this case a judgment oracle. And they will theorize about reasons for the regularity of such a form. They usually argue that some social institution—the school, legal system, temple—regularly used various forms of discourse and preserved them, just as the business letter or the deed of trust is preserved in social institutions today. Those interested in form criticism will argue that the prophet used one or another form of discourse to make his point; in the case of Amos 1, the prophet chose the judgment oracle to indict and sentence certain Syro-Palestinian states.

A logical sequel to form criticism is redaction criticism. If prophets wrote or spoke in fairly brief speeches, what compositional principles were at work when they were written down? The question presumes some sort of editorial intentionality. In the case of Amos 1, one would ask why the nations were mentioned in this particular order. (There are a number of theories about this matter.) Concerning Amos 1—2, one editorial intent is patently clear, namely, that the speeches culminate with the long one addressed to Israel in Amos 2:6–16.

Tradition history is a third important tool available to students of prophetic literature. What theological ideas or ethical norms are present in the XII? Are they original with the authors or are they part of Israel's traditions? Tradition history operates with the presumption that much in Israelite culture and religion is traditional. For example, the notion of the day of the Lord almost certainly predates the book of Amos. The phrase probably alluded to a wonderful day on which Yahweh's kingship was celebrated, perhaps during the ancient New Year's celebration. For Amos, however, this day of the Lord was not something to be hoped for. Rather it was to be a day of gloom and violence (see Amos 5:18–20). One may say that Amos has creatively recast an important religious tradition in ancient Israel. Other important traditions that appear in the XII involve the covenant made between Yahweh and Israel at Sinai (see Hos. 4:1–3), holy war (Habakkuk 3), and theophany (Nahum 1:5).

More recently, scholars have explored social world and literary issues in assessing texts that make up the XII. These books offer the reader scintillating poetry (in comparison with the "major" prophets, there is minimal prose in the XII).

Any attempt to comprehend Hosea must wrestle with the way in which its figures of speech work. One may read Hosea and focus on the similes or the imagery of fertility. It is one thing to state that Israel has violated the Sinai covenant. It is another to say:

> Your love is like a morning cloud,
> like the dew that goes away early. (Hos. 6:4)

It is one thing to state that God will punish Israel. It is another to say:

> I will fall upon them like a bear robbed of her cubs
> and will tear open the covering of their heart. (Hos. 13:8)

The power of figurative speech demands a literary reading of the XII.

However, literary analysis of the XII should not be limited to an assessment of the individual books. It is possible to read the XII from beginning to end and then to contemplate the way it works. Paul House has attempted such a reading and theorized that the XII works like a comedy, according to the classical definition of this term: it begins with a crisis and concludes with a resolution.[6]

Finally, social world analysis offers many possible vantage points from which to read the XII. One may attempt to reconstruct the social and economic conditions that the prophets addressed.[7] Or, the reader may focus on the prophetic role itself, based on cross-cultural understandings of the prophets' behavior.[8] The insights from sociology and anthropology are of critical importance for such work.

II. TWELVE PROPHETIC BOOKS

Even though there are significant ways in which these twelve books may be read together, the simple fact that they occur as individual books also enables them to be treated separately. Moreover, each of these books elicits its own interpretive strategies. For example, the rich poetry of Hosea has regularly generated literary studies. By contrast, Amos's hard-hitting rhetoric has led to analysis of the social world that he addresses. As one moves through these twelve books, one or another method or combination of methods will be appropriate.

A. Hosea

Hosea is unique in the Hebrew Bible. It is the only clear case of a book that reflects the activity of a native of the northern kingdom, Israel, who assesses the life of that nation. This national rootage helps us understand why the book of Hosea is so different from Amos, which dates to roughly the same period. Amos saw Israel with Judahite eyes, whereas Hosea perceived life there from the perspective of a native.

Study of Hosea has been driven by the peculiarities of the book. This is especially true for the first three chapters, which focus on a marriage that God commands Hosea to enter. Early on debate swirled around questions of historicity: Did Hosea actually engage in such a marriage? And what is the relationship of chapter 1 to chapter 3? Do they provide two versions of the same command? Did Hosea marry the same woman twice?

After years of reflecting on these questions, many scholars have now decided that the texts in Hosea simply do not allow for ready answers. Moreover, the immediate drive to answer historical questions has preempted some more obvious, and answerable, questions. For example, a standard feature of biblical interpretation is the posing of a question about literary type: what kind of literature does the text present?

Hosea 1:2–8 and 3:1–4 are both prose reports of a prophetic symbolic action—the first biographical and the second autobiographical. Some symbolic actions are easy to perform, e.g., the buying and breaking of a ceramic pot (Jeremiah 19). Others required the prophet to involve his whole being. Isaiah fathered a child with a prophetess (Isa. 8:1–4). Jeremiah was called to a life of celibacy (Jer. 16:1–4). And Ezekiel was forbidden from mourning the death of his wife (Ezek. 24:15–24). Hosea 1 and 3 belong in this world of lived prophetic symbolic actions.

By placing Hosea's "marriage" in this context, we are able to discern that the marriage is not the message. Hosea 1:1–8 makes it clear that the children born to Hosea and Gomer, and even more the names given to them—"Jezreel," "Not Pitied," and "Not my people"—are the message that the deity intended Hosea to convey to the people. (The same is true in Isa. 8:1–4—the child's name provides the key.) Similarly, the ownership and sexual isolation of the unnamed woman in Hosea 3 symbolizes a message about Israel's isolation from necessary political and social structures. In sum, the key to understanding Hosea 1 and 3 is asking the right questions, initially literary ones.

Apart from the special problems presented by these initial chapters, the rest of Hosea has been and continues to be approached from the full arsenal of biblical studies methods. Form-critical perspectives help us discern the smaller speeches that make up the book. Divine oracles clearly outnumber prophetic speeches. However, form criticism of Hosea is far more difficult than form criticism of Amos, since there are so few introductory and concluding formulas in this first book of the XII. Still, even without such formulas, as one reads Hosea 4 it is difficult not to discern a boundary between speeches as one moves from verse 3 to verse 4. (The boundaries are less apparent when one moves through the poetry in chap. 2.)

Redaction criticism helps us understand various features of the book. First, the book is now configured in three primary parts: chapters 1—3, 4—11, and 12—14. Each of the last two sections moves from language of judgment to discourse about salvation. Such a thematization probably reflects a reading and arranging of Hosea materials after the demise of the northern kingdom (721 B.C.E.) and quite possibly after the defeat of the southern kingdom (587). David as king (3:5) and the people of Judah (1:11; 8:14; 12:1) do not reflect concerns of Hosea in eighth-century Israel. Hosea 1:7; 2:1–2; and 3:5, among other passages, reflect an interest in restoration after destruction. Moreover, Hos. 14:9 appears to be a late attempt to integrate Hosea with the wisdom tradition, comparable to the way in which Psalm 1 relates the Psalter to wisdom literature. Quite simply, Hosea is a book that emerged over time.

Tradition-history is more important than either form criticism or redaction criticism for the study of Hosea, in part because Hosea represents an area in which the traditions were different than they were for all other prophets. Zion as the seat of Yahweh's reign and David as the king played no role in the northern kingdom. Rather, the tradition about God's covenant with Israel that was made at Sinai had pride of place in the north. Hence we should not be surprised to discover in Hos. 4:1–3 an indictment that reflects the classic summary of the Sinai covenant, namely, the Ten Commandments. The Ten Commandments, or Decalogue, offers a comprehensive, though distilled, version of covenant obligations. Both religious and ethical issues are in view. One might say that if Amos focuses on ethical issues (though religious issues are mentioned), then Hosea focuses on religious issues (though ethical issues are mentioned, e.g., Hos. 4:8; 7:1). Proper and sole veneration of Yahweh is the primary issue in this book. Also significant for tradition-history is Hosea's interest in earlier Israelite history. On numerous occasions, Hosea reviews how Yahweh acted on behalf of Israel, and then how Israel, once it was in the land, rebelled (Hos. 9:10). Or, using different vocabulary, what Israel once "knew" they have since "forgotten" (so 4:6).

Finally, both literary and social world analysis may assist study of Hosea. Hosea's poetry is rich and complex. We mentioned earlier the importance of attending to the diverse figures of speech. Attention to gender issues (e.g., reading the book from a feminist perspective) casts new light on the abuse of the woman in chapters 2 and 3. The gendered social world conveyed in the text may be the subject of fruitful research.

The book of Hosea is part of Israel's literature that engages the veneration of Ba'al. While the stories of Elijah and the Deuteronomistic History are also part of that story, Hosea is the book where the challenge of Baalism is taken most seriously. As early as 2:8, 13, we learn that worship of Ba'al stands as one of Hosea's signal indictments. Scholars debate vigorously the nature of religion in Israel, and one important issue in the debate is whether Yahwism at the court or in less official contexts was inextricably bound up with the veneration of Ba'al. It is clear that many of the indictments of the book of Hosea—worship at high places (4:13) and veneration of figurines (4:12, 17) —are part of this larger critique of Ba'al worship. Hosea responds to these indictments by offering images—sometimes ambiguous (9:7–9), other times vicious (13:7–8)—of punishment. The day of the Lord will appear (9:5–6). But precisely what will happen on that day is unclear, though Assyria with all its might looms on the horizon (10:6).

Still, Hosea repeatedly expresses the conviction that because God loves Israel like a parent (or a spouse), and yet unlike a human, punishment will be more instructive than destructive.

> When Israel was a child, I loved him,
>   and out of Egypt I called my son. (11:1)

> How can I give you up, Ephraim
>   How can I hand you over, O Israel? (11:8)

for I am God and no mortal
the Holy One in your midst. (11:9)

Comparable is the marital metaphor:

Therefore I will now allure her . . .
and speak tenderly to her . . .
There she shall respond as in the days of her youth. (2:14–15)

It remains difficult to reconcile the language of punishment with this poetry expressing hopes for restoration. Some scholars have argued that the latter should not be attributed to Hosea but to a later hand. However, one of the primary motifs in the book—"love," with all its ambiguity in both Yahwism and Baalism—could, even in Hosea's time, cut against the notion of an absolute end to a relationship between Yahweh and Israel.

B. Joel

The book of Joel presents the reader with several problems. The most serious one involves the nature of the catastrophe that the book describes. Is it a locust plague described as if it were a military attack (1:4)? Or is it a military attack described as if it were a locust plague (1:6)? The difficulty of answering these questions is related to that of identifying the historical setting in which the book was composed. Unlike the prophetic books on either side, Hosea and Amos, there are no kings listed in Joel's superscription. Without allusions to a Jeroboam or an Ahaz, we are left with little data about the book's temporal setting.

However, there is language about physical setting that provides an important key to the book's interpretation. The place is Zion and the temple is situated on it. At a minimum, therefore, the book of Joel dates to a time when the temple existed in Jerusalem.

We are not accustomed to thinking about prophets and the temple. Some popular definitions of prophets contrast them with priests. However, such a judgment would fall wide of the mark in ancient Israel. Jeremiah, Ezekiel, and Zechariah were members of priestly lineages, individuals who could be both priest and prophet. Though we are told nothing about Joel's lineage, much in the book suggests that he functioned in a priestly capacity as well.

It is instructive to compare the imperative verbs in Joel 1—2 with comparable grammar in Amos. Amos tells the people:

But let justice roll down like waters,
and righteousness like an ever-flowing stream. (Amos 5:24)

But Joel admonishes the people and especially the priests:

Sanctify a fast,
call a solemn assembly. (1:14)

Sanctify the congregation;
assemble the aged. (2:16)

One searches through Joel in vain for language of ethical admonition. Instead, throughout the early portion of the book Joel challenges the people to undertake appropriate forms of lamentation at the temple by way of a response to the momentous crisis that they face.

Such consistent appeal to ritual language should elicit a way of reading the book sensitive to general religious issues, e.g., one concerned with how lamentation functioned in ancient Israel. Scholars who have addressed religious practices in ancient Israel have discovered that lamentation could be a communal as well as an individual practice. Laments are the most frequent form of psalm. (For an example of an individual lament see Psalm 28; for a communal lament, see Psalm 44 or the book of Lamentations.) Communal lamentation—the chanting of a lament, fasting, wearing sackcloth, and weeping—was almost certainly the practice for which Joel was calling. Such practices of lamentation were often undertaken at the temple. And within the context of such lamentation, a priest could offer a word on behalf of the deity, indicating that God had responded to their plight. Joel reflects temple-based worship in ancient Israel (note the reference to a specific place in the temple precinct in Joel 2:17).

Joel 1:1–2:17 focuses on the need for lamentation due to the incredible destruction the land had been suffering. Joel 2:18 reports that "the LORD became jealous for his land and had pity on his people." Joel writes as if the lamentation had actually occurred and God is now responding to the people. From this perspective, Joel was a successful prophet!

Much of the remainder of the book is written in the form of divine speech. Prior to 2:18, the only "I" from whom we hear is the prophet (1:19). Beginning with 2:19, Yahweh speaks repeatedly about what will happen as a result of his taking pity on "his people" (1:19), "the children of Zion" (1:23). Most immediately, the army/locusts will be removed. However the scale of the deity's activity enlarges: "I will show portents in the heavens and on earth, blood and fire and columns of smoke. The sun shall be turned to darkness and the moon to blood" (2:30).

To be sure, the deity responds to Israel's agricultural crisis. Whereas earlier there was drought and dessication (e.g., 1:10, 12, 17), after God acts there will be such marvelous fertility that

> the mountains shall drip sweet wine,
>   the hills shall flow with milk. (3:18)

But just as Israel receives weal, Israel's enemies suffer the deity's wrath. Whereas earlier Israel was becoming a wasteland, now Israel's enemies, Egypt and Edom, incur such a fate (3:19). Such rhetoric of international violence is of a piece with oracles against the nations found in all three of the "major" prophets. But Joel seems to highlight this element, particularly in its variation on a theme struck in both Isa. 2:2–4 and Micah 4:1–4. Whereas those prophets anticipated a time of peace and pilgrimage—a time when swords would be beaten into plowshares— Joel challenges the nations to sanctify themselves for war with God's warriors such that the nations will need to:

> Beat your plowshares into swords
>   and your pruning hooks into spears. (3:10)

Such cosmic and violent images resonate with later prophetic texts (e.g., Isaiah 24 —27; Ezekiel 38—39; Zechariah 9—14). As a result, some scholars have maintained that much of Joel 2:28–3:21 may date to a later time when something akin to apocalyptic imagery was becoming prominent in Syria-Palestine. That some of these verses are apparently written in prose (Joel 2:30–3:8) is viewed by some as a warrant for this position.

After reading Joel the inquisitive reader may well pose the following question: In what way is the author of this book acting as a prophet? The answer depends in considerable measure on one's definition of a prophet. If a prophet is an intermediary who conveys the words and plans of the deity to humans, then Joel indeed fits the bill. Moreover, as we stated earlier, the first portion of the book portrays Joel as a speaker who was able to convoke both priests and the larger populace in the lamentation, which provided their only hope. This role of prophet as mediator is also well attested, as we will see with Amos.

C. Amos

Amos and the scholarship devoted to it offer a microcosm of work on prophetic literature. Virtually every method or perspective available has been exercised on these nine chapters. As a result, no prophetic book has a bibliography comparable in size to that on Amos.

As we saw earlier, form-critical analysis of prophetic literature works particularly well on the poetry in Amos. Because of the prominence of both introductory and concluding formulas in this book, it is relatively easy to determine where short oracles or prophetic speeches begin and end. Moreover, rhetorical changes assist the reader when such formulas are absent. For example, even though a formula occurs neither at the end of Amos 3:2 nor at the beginning of 3:3, the shift from language of judgment to a series of questions makes it clear that we are dealing with two separate speeches.

Form-critical inventories of Amos reveal essentially three different kinds of speech. First, there are five autobiographic vision reports (7:1–8; 8:1–2; 9:1–4). Second, the book includes a number of prophetic speeches, instances in which the prophet speaks in his own voice and refers to the deity in the third person (e.g., 5:18–20). Third, and most prominent, Amos utters divine oracles, in which he quotes the deity directly, conveying Yahweh in first-person language (e.g., 5:21–24). The first form is essentially prose, whereas the last two appear typically as poetry.

A form-critical examination of Amos virtually demands that redaction-critical work ensue, that is, what is the significance, if any, of the ordering of the discrete speeches? Put another way, how do the rhetorical questions in 3:3–8 work well after 3:1–2? One might argue that the principle at work in the questions, namely, that things happen for a reason (a snare does not spring unless something trips it, v. 5), helps the reader understand what has been said in a far more cryptic way in verses 1–2. There is a connection between God's having chosen, "known," Israel and what will happen to them. The connection is embedded in the natural order of things; it is not due to a whimsical act of a deity. Such is the logic of redaction criticism.

There are, however, other redaction-critical issues present in the book. First, some sort of collecting of materials based on similarity of genre is present. All the oracles against the nations appear in the first two chapters. The vision reports have been put into a meaningful sequence. All the "woe" oracles appear in chapters 5 —6. Intentional collection and ordering are well attested in this book.

In addition, it appears that new literature was created to accompany Amos's original sayings. Scholars have identified diverse elements that entered the Amos tradition over time. For example, it is unlikely that Amos would have been concerned with Beersheba, a city in the far south of Judah, when he was talking to the citizens of the northern kingdom. Hence, those texts that mention Beersheba (5:5; 8:14) may derive from a time when Amos's words were being re-presented in a Judahite setting. Second, some texts may date to the late seventh- early sixth-century traditions associated with the Deuteronomic reform of Josiah, as well as to the continuing Deuteronomistic tradition. As for the former, the condemnation of the altar at Bethel (Amos 5:5) seems to be of a piece with the polemic against that ritual site in Josiah's time (2 Kings 23:15). As for the latter, the oracle against Judah (Amos 2:4–5) offers the sorts of indictments about violation of *torah* that are a hallmark of the Deuteronomistic History. Finally, Amos 9:11–15 probably reflects the defeat of Judah and Jerusalem in 587. The concern is clearly with the southern kingdom, as the specific allusion to "the booth of David" demonstrates (9:11). There are strong similarities between this oracle and other Persian period prophetic texts (compare Amos 9:13 with Joel 3:18, which has a Jerusalemite focus). Also, 9:15 alludes to exile from which Judahites would return (unlike the exile that the northern kingdom suffered, from which none would return). In sum, the words of Amos elicited other words that enabled the Amos collection to speak to ensuing generations of Israelites in different places and conditions.

In recent decades, there has been something of a counter-reaction—a dissatisfaction with attempts to discern so many refinements—that has led to a concern to read the book in its final form, often with the assumption that the book was created as one large work or composed in several major sections. The work of Shalom Paul represents this approach.[9] However, some of the most recent and impressive redaction-critical research on Amos is pointing to the formation of that literature as it may have been influenced by Hosea.[10] These claims are pushing redaction-critical study of Amos in an entirely new direction, linking it with analysis of other books of the XII.

Tradition history has also informed analysis of Amos. The very fact that there are rhetorical questions (3:3–8) has led some scholars to look throughout the Hebrew Bible for other exemplars of rhetorical questions, which they have found in wisdom literature (e.g., Job 6:22–28). Consequently, Hans Walter Wolff has argued that Amos was influenced by wisdom traditions, particularly so-called clan wisdom.[11]

Finally, scholars have been interested to know what social and economic circumstances lay behind various biblical books. Such social world concerns are especially germane for a book that overtly addresses economic issues (e.g., taxes, 5:11) and social issues (e.g., the needy, 5:12). The book of Amos allows for no easy summary. However, if one attends to the vision reports and the judgment oracles, at least three of the book's major thematic elements become clearer. The initial vision reports cluster in chapter 7. Twice, Amos sees destructive acts—the first apparently a locust plague, the second a cosmic fire that devours the salt water deep (truly a mythic image). On both occasions, Amos speaks out:

> O Lord GOD, forgive, I beg you!
>   How can Jacob stand?
>   He is so small!

Such intercession apparently worked. Amos evidently had a prophetic role of more than divine herald. He could "talk back" to the deity on behalf of the people. And, one could imagine that he could talk to the people from the same perspective, namely, as one interested in their welfare. Several sayings in chapter 5 reflect this concern:

> Seek good and not evil,
>   that you may live.

Amos's prophetic message was not always one of negative pronouncement, due in part to the diverse prophetic roles that he could exercise.

Still, the last three visions reports (7:7–9; 8:1–3; 9:1–4) do not represent Amos in an intercessory mode. In the penultimate one, he is precluded from such action due to the pun trick that the deity plays. He sees a basket of summer fruit (Hebrew *qayits*), which the deity interprets to mean the end (Hebrew *qets*). Amos does not have the opportunity to intercede before Yahweh offers the word of decisive judgment, which is intensified in the final vision report. By the end of the visionary sequence, Amos has learned that Israel will not escape God's destruction.

This conclusion to the visions cries out for an explanation. Why will the deity act in such a punitive fashion? The judgment oracles answer this question. With their classic two-part form made up of an indictment and a sentence, these oracles both explain and offer a judicial decision. When one surveys 2:6–7; 4:1; 5:10–12, it becomes clear that one major reason for the coming destruction is violation of social and economic norms, particularly the oppression of the least powerful and the poor in society. It appears that economic developments in the northern kingdom were dispossessing Israelites from their traditional position as independent land owners and creating a wealthy group who had been securing land through illicit use of the court system. Amos seems to say that there is a level of consumption that violates Israel's covenant norms of justice and righteousness (6:4–6). So those in the land should know that Yahweh's day will be coming as a direct response to the social and economic conditions that they have created.

The second element of the judgment oracle—the sentence—typically spells out what will happen. One might expect to hear Amos speak about the destruction that the Neo-Assyrian armies would wreak on the northern kingdom. And there are some allusions to destruction within the context of warfare (e.g., 5:36; 6:14). However, most of the judgments in Amos occur in divine oracles. The deity will act against Israel. The first person independent personal pronoun predominates in this rhetoric:

> I will make the sun go down at noon,
>   and darken the earth in broad daylight.
> I will turn your feasts into mourning,
>   and all your songs into lamentation;
> I will bring sackcloth on all loins,
>   and baldness on every head;
> I will make it like the mourning for an only son,
>   and the end of it like a bitter day. (8:9–10)

The one who had chosen Israel for a special relationship (3:2) will now act definitely against that nation.

Texts like Amos 8:9–10 are both frightening and baffling. They frighten because the language is so strongly negative. And it is baffling because one could not be sure exactly what it was that Yahweh would do. In these two verses, it initially sounds as if there might be an eclipse of the sun. But then the imagery shifts to that of funeral lamentation in the middle of the poem. Then, in the final two lines, the prophet uses two similes, the last of which is remarkably vague. What will Yahweh do? We are not sure, but it clearly involves death. It is not too much to claim that we learn far more about specific indictments than we do about specific forms of destruction.

The book of Amos includes three so-called hymnic fragments (4:13; 5:8–9; 9:5–6). Scholars have debated the reasons for these locations as well as whether, together, they form one coherent psalm. There is no consensus on either issue. For the final form of the book, however, these small poems, each of which share a refrain, "the LORD is his name," demonstrate that traditional language of praise, as attested in the book of Psalms, was held to be consistent with what Amos proclaimed. The God who destroys (5:8; 9:5) is also the God who creates (4:13) and who provides for continuity in the natural order (5:8; 9:6).

D. Obadiah

Because of its brevity and its subject matter, Obadiah has received little concerted scholarly attention. No other book in the Hebrew Bible is so brief.

Form-critical and general historical issues have provided the most prominent topics for the book's analysis. As for the first, Obadiah is, quite simply, one oracle against the nation of Edom. Whereas other prophetic books may include a series of such oracles devoted to the great empires and/or the smaller Syro-Palestinian states, Obadiah is directed only to a foreign nation (compare Nahum, which is directed against Nineveh). Though focusing essentially on Edom, the book may in fact be divided into two different pronouncements. Verses 1–14 castigate Edom, whereas verses 15–21, though including negative judgments about Edom, offer positive language about Israel. It is almost as if woe for Edom means weal for Israel. Finally, the literary seam between these two blocks stipulates: "for the day of the LORD is near against all the nations" (v. 15). Thus, even little Obadiah at this point adheres to the central motif of the XII, the day of the Lord.

Why does Edom come in for such enmity? It is easy to explain why the Neo-Assyrians would be subject to such fulminations as in Nahum. But what is the rationale for such rhetoric directed against this state to the southeast of Judah? Most scholars have answered this question by scouring the pages of Syro-Palestinian history to provide a context for the accusations in verses 1–14. Generic judgments, such as the one against Edom's pride (v. 3) were made about a number of other nations. But the prophet becomes far more specific, condemning Edom for standing aside when Judah was under attack (v. 11), for gloating over Judah's misfortune (vv. 12–13), and for handing over Judahites to the enemy (v. 14). Obadiah seems to have one moment in mind: the period 597–587 B.C.E. when Judah was under attack by the Neo-Babylonians and some Judahites were taken into exile. Other texts in the Hebrew Bible also attest a tradition about Edom acting improperly when Judah was defeated, most notably Ezekiel 15 and Ps. 137:7.

While the attempt to discern its particular historical context is a hallmark of much study of prophetic literature, not all particularities are historical; some are structural in the society. A social world approach to Obadiah would do more than look simply at the events surrounding 587 B.C.E. It would highlight other language, most particularly that of kinship. Edom and Judah are brothers (vv. 10, 12), designated by the names of their eponymous ancestors, Esau (vv. 6, 9) and Jacob (v. 10). Ancient enmities are at work in this oracle. This is strife that Judah places in its antiquity. Moreover, it is embedded in the family, a place where conflict can be especially intense. Neither Moab nor Ammon, other small Syro-Palestinian states, bears such a close kinship to Judah/Israel. This kinship helps explain why Edom, more than any other state, is the object of such hatred from Judah.

Just as Zephaniah anticipates that a remnant shall survive the great destruction on Yahweh's day, so too does Obadiah (v. 17). But unlike Zephaniah, there is no hope that the nations, or in this case nation, will share in the blessings of Yahweh's imperium. Mount Esau is to be dominated by Mount Zion (v. 21).

E. Jonah

Jonah is truly the odd prophet out in the XII. It is a short story, not a collection of sayings, vision reports, or written pronouncements, as we find in all eleven other books. And yet, the very first verse of the book, "Now the word of the LORD came to Jonah, son of Amittai, saying . . ." identifies Jonah implicitly as a prophet, namely, someone who receives God's words directly. Moreover, 2 Kings 14:25 identifies Jonah son of Amittai explicitly as a prophet. So, both by dint of its canonical placement and its main character, the book of Jonah is to be read as part of Hebrew Bible prophetic literature.

Though popular readings focus on the "large fish" scene in 1:17–2:10, many scholars have focused on the question of historical setting. To what period is this story to be dated? Though the question is interesting, the text provides no data that allow for a precise answer. Most scholars agree that the story postdates the destruction of Jerusalem in 587 B.C.E., primarily because the issues in the story are similar to those in texts that postdate that event. One such issue is whether or not those outside the kinship structure of Israel can be true Yahwists (cf. Isa. 56:3–8). Another is the prominence of prayer as a religious rite in the Persian period (cf. Ezra 9:5–15; Neh. 9:6–37). Still, little can be said in response to the question of the book's historical origins.

One other critical question has been prominent in the scholarly literature about Jonah: Is the psalm of thanksgiving in chapter 2 an original part of the story? Though serious questions have been raised, many interpreters now understand this poem to be an important part of the book. On one level, the hymn is appropriate since it celebrates Jonah's rescue from death by drowning. Jonah thanks Yahweh for saving his life.

Most recently, scholars have probed the book from primarily a literary perspective. Two questions have driven research: what kind of short story is it, and what is its theme or meaning? As for the former, the list of possible subtypes is daunting: parable, lampoon, and satire are only among the most prominent. In the final analysis, the choice depends upon the answer to the latter question. What is the theme or essential topic of this story? Since scholars have not reached a consensus on this question, readers are encouraged to undertake responsible literary readings of their own.

At a minimum, Jonah is a story about a successful prophet. God tells Jonah to "cry against" the city of Nineveh. In the briefest of prophetic oracles, Jonah complies: "Forty days more and Nineveh shall be overthrown" (3:4). Nineveh's king responds in remarkable fashion by commanding all living beings, including animals, to put on sackcloth and pray to God. When God perceives this action, the deity decides not to punish Nineveh as had earlier been the plan. Jonah's rhetoric works marvels.

The remainder of the book focuses on Jonah's reaction to his "success." Only here do we find out why the prophet had initially fled from undertaking his mission. He feared that God would be "gracious, merciful, slow to anger and abounding in steadfast love" (4:3). As it turns out, Jonah's premonitions were correct. And he is angry (4:1). God offers Jonah a symbolic action involving a bush, but Jonah remains upset: "It is better for me to die than to live" (4:8), the second time in the story he has been willing to give up his life (4:3). Thereafter God poses a question to Jonah: "Should I not be concerned about Nineveh?" (4:11). The reader is left to ponder how Jonah might respond.

It is probably no accident that the book of Nahum also concludes with a question; both books concern Nineveh. Nahum calls for judgment, as did the prophet

Jonah. But the book of Jonah describes a God who is merciful not only to Nineveh but to pagan mariners, and even to Jonah when he is about to drown. The notion of a God who is merciful to Israelite and non-Israelite alike provides a key to understanding this short story.

The book has more to do with theology than prophecy. One might say that the author has created a satiric version of prophetic performance—Jonah is in some ways the most "orthodox" of Israelite theologians—to make a theological point. The book is full of satire; even Jonah's name works in this way. Jonah, who is by our reckoning a hawk, has a name that means dove, even in the ancient world a symbol of purity and peace. By using such satire, the author challenges some fairly common theological notions in ancient Israel, such as the belief that those who do not comply with the deity's will shall be punished and that foreign and sinful cities (Sodom, Nineveh) will be destroyed.

Still, Jonah is part of the XII and hence is to be read in some sense as prophetic literature. And there is a kind of prophet and a kind of prophetic literature with which Jonah resonates. Like Jeremiah, Jonah is designated "a prophet to the nations." His words are directed to another nation. But they end up effecting weal rather than woe for Nineveh. To that extent, Jonah stands at odds with other prophetic rhetoric about foreign nations, which normally conveys language of destruction.

F. Micah

The oracles in Micah often sound like those in other prophetic books, especially Amos and Isaiah. This similarity should not surprise readers; Micah, like both Amos and Isaiah, was a Judahite, and, like Isaiah, was active during the latter half of the eighth century. Moreover, some of the critical problems posed by the book, especially the ways in which it grew over time, are similar to those of Isaiah. Both Micah and Isaiah achieved their final form in the Persian period.

Form-critical and redaction-critical work have been a hallmark of Micah scholarship during much of the twentieth century. Form-critical analysis has focused on lawsuit (1:2–7; 6:1–8) and wisdom-style (7:5–6) rhetoric prevalent in the book, as well as on the absence of typical introductory and concluding formulas. And redaction critics have proposed an almost dizzying number of hypotheses about the way in which the prophet's words evolved over time. However, earlier consensuses (e.g., that much of chaps. 1—3 could be attributed to Micah whereas much of 4—7 stemmed from later hands) are no longer uniformly held.

The results of tradition history and social world analysis seem more secure. As for the former, the results are both positive and negative. Though a Judahite, Micah does not seem to hold Jerusalem or Zion in the same high theological regard as did his contemporary Isaiah. So, unlike Isaiah, he anticipates the decimation of the capital and the temple:

> Zion shall be plowed like a field;
> Jerusalem shall become a heap of ruins,
>   and the mountain of the house a wooded height. (3:12)

(This judgment must have been well remembered, since it is quoted in Jer. 26:18.) Such antipathy can be explained partly by the fact that the prophet came not from Jerusalem but from a small town, Moresheth. He holds the country's leadership in the capital—"heads of Jacob," "rulers of the house of Israel," "chiefs of the house of Israel" (3:1, 9) —culpable for what is wrong. Some have maintained that he was a person who held local authority, i.e., an elder in the village who would have held out for traditional values in the face of the imperial power of the Davidic house. The norms that undergird the indictments are clear:

> He has told you, O mortal, what is good;
>   and what does the LORD require of you
> but to do justice, and to love kindness,
>   and to walk humbly with your God? (6:8)

Such a statement and question affirm traditional covenant norms as do other explicit statements about justice and equity (3:9).

Amos and Micah come from comparable social worlds—small towns in Judah. Amos, however, was a herald to Israel. By contrast, Micah speaks to his own nation. Micah 1:2–9 redirects the rhetoric of an Amos, who originally addressed Samaria and Israel, to Jerusalem and Judah, the new object of Yahweh's indictment and sentence (see also 6:9–16, which is clearly directed to "the city," Jerusalem, v. 9). Even the hopeful sections of the book look to a small town, Bethlehem Ephrathah, "one of the little clans of Judah," as the source for a new ruler (5:2). The implicit critique of Jerusalem continues, since the capital will not produce the anticipated ruler.

As one in a small, farm town, Micah was particularly concerned about land ownership, especially the ways in which people improperly lost ownership of their land:

> They covet fields, and seize them;
>   houses, and take them away;
> they oppress householder and house,
>   people and their inheritance. (2:2)

His other primary polemic was aimed at improper official disposition of duties by the nation's leaders (3:1–3; 11).

Like many prophets, Micah envisioned a time of judgment. The language of physical destruction is present in Micah (e.g., 1:7), as is that of exile (1:16; 4:10) and loss of land (2:4). But there is surprisingly little talk of physical violence against the people who are to be punished: they will lament (2:4) and be dismayed and ashamed (3:6), but they apparently remain alive. Hence, over time the book could speak about a return from exile; the people continued to live—either impoverished in the land or in exile. But they could be gathered together again; they could return.

There were certainly additions to Micah's original sayings. Virtually all of chapter 7 provides an elaborate interplay of traditional psalmic and wisdom discourse concerning the fate of Jerusalem and the people. Scholars as early as Gunkel have viewed it as a liturgy. This addition to the book clearly envisions a time of restoration for Israel. But there is also evidence of revision, not simply addition. For example, the first five verses of one oracle (5:10–15) offer words of judgment upon Judah, apparently for inappropriate religious practice. However, the final verse (v. 15) extends such destruction to "the nations"—Israel's enemies and destroyers—a view consistent with later prophetic rhetoric. The sense of an earlier oracle has been revised to meet a new situation.

Such dynamics in the additions and revisions seem to accord with portions of the book of Isaiah (Micah 4:13 or 4:6–7 or 4:8) and could as easily be found in the later chapters of Isaiah. And Micah 4:1–3 is found in Isa. 2:2–4. Still, there is a difference between the later material in these books. The prominence of good news for Zion as promulgated in Isaiah is not present in Micah. Rather, it is the people —"the remnant of Jacob" in Micah 5:7–8 or the "us" in the concluding poem of the book—who are the primary concern of this prophetic tradition. Even at the end of the book, Micah's origins outside Jerusalem inform his hopes and the hopes of those who preserved his words for the future.

G. Nahum

Nahum resembles Obadiah to the extent that it too focuses on a nation other than Israel. Whereas Obadiah was concerned with Edom, Nahum deals (as does Jonah) with a city, Nineveh. These three books attest to the international side of the prophet's task, which is confirmed by "oracles against the nations" in each of the three major prophets.

Study of Nahum has tended to dwell on the historical particulars of the Neo-Assyrian empire's demise, on the graphic depictions of warfare in a city, and on the spectacular poetry that conveys it in this book:

> The chariots race madly through the streets,
>   they rush to and fro through the squares;
> their appearance is like torches,
>   they dart like lightning. (2:4)

> Horsemen charging,
>   flashing sword and glittering spear,
> piles of dead,
>   heaps of corpses,
>   dead bodies without end—
>   they stumble over the bodies! (3:3)

Nowhere else in the Hebrew Bible is human warfare so graphically depicted. And within the ambit of ancient Near Eastern art, the best artistic analogies are the wall reliefs from Assyrian cities, like Nineveh.

One perspective that has not been utilized as fully as possible in Nahum is tradition history. What was it about Nineveh that captured this prophet's imagination and literary gifts? Part of the answer to that question hinges on an assessment about other prophetic literature concerning Nineveh. Probably the earliest texts are those in Isaiah. Early on, the king of Assyria was understood to be an instrument of God against Judah (so Isa. 7:17–18). However, a number of other texts (Isa. 10:5–19; 14:24–27; 30:27–33; 31:8–9) attest that because it overstepped its role as God's agent, Assyria itself would become the subject of God's punitive wrath. The Assyrian emperor had said:

> As my hand has reached to the kingdoms of the idols
> > whose images were greater than those of Jerusalem and Samaria,
> shall I not do to Jerusalem and her idols
> > what I have done to Samaria and her images? (Isa. 10:10–11)

From Yahweh's perspective the answer is "No," though Isaiah puts it in the form of a question:

> Shall the ax vaunt itself over the one who wields it,
> > or the saw magnify itself against the one who handles it? (v. 15)

Again, the answer is "No."

The book of Zephaniah also attests this tradition about Assyria. Zephaniah 2:13–15 also refers to Assyrian pride by quoting the personified city: "I am, and there is no one else."

These texts from Isaiah and Zephaniah help provide some of the warrant for the ferocious language in Nahum. In addition, this prophetic backdrop offers the reasons for Yahweh's anger at Assyria, reasons that are, for the most part, implicit in the book of Nahum. In that book there is more language of judgment than there is language of indictment.

If Habakkuk concludes with a hymn, and Amos has hymnic passages scattered throughout the book, Nahum begins with a hymn. Nahum 1:2–8 comprises the first portion of an alphabetic acrostic poem (Hebrew *aleph* through *kaph*). Using the imagery of theophany, a prominent feature of day of the Lord sections throughout the XII, the psalm emphasizes two features of that day. It will signal the end for Yahweh's adversaries and protection for those who seek refuge with the deity.

The hymn serves as a theological prolegomenon to the book. In fact, the entire first chapter functions this way. If one were to read Nahum 1:2–15 without the book's superscription, there is no way that Assyria would come to mind. Rather, the prophet focuses initially on the great God Yahweh and then on the interaction between Yahweh and those who plot against him (v. 9). Even here, however, the psalmic resonances are strong (cf. Ps. 2:1). One may infer that Jerusalem is being addressed in 1:12–13, but the identity of the adversary in verses 11 or 14 remains unclear until the defining moments of chapters 2 and 3.

Nahum 1:15 resonates with other prophetic literature, both earlier and later: Amos 4:13 attests the conviction that Yahweh walks on the heights of the earth; Zech. 14:4 reports that the deity steps on the heights of Jerusalem with cosmic effect; and the remarkably similar Isa. 52:7 affirms that the deity's messenger can do the same. Whether Nahum 1:15 refers to the deity or the deity's herald is uncertain. But the concluding portions of that verse demonstrate that Judah may resume its religious life since Yahweh is about to act on their behalf.

Apart from the sparkling descriptions of the attack against Nineveh, Nahum 2 —3 are characterized by direct discourse against either the city of Nineveh or its king (2:1, 13; 3:5–19). It is divine oracle—the deity in first person, rather than prophetic speech. Chapter 3 commences with the classic particle, "Woe," indicating that the context is dire. The language is full of sarcasm:

> Draw water for the siege
>> strengthen your forts;
> trample the clay,
>> tread the mortar. (3:14)

> Multiply yourselves like the locust,
>> multiply like the grasshopper. (3:15)

The threats are scatological and pornographic:

> I am against you . . .
>> and will lift up your skirts over your face; . . .
> I will throw filth [excrement] at you
>> and treat you with contempt,
>> and make you a spectacle. (3:5–6)

This book is a literature of humiliation and violence, written from the perspective of a humbled province of the Neo-Assyrian empire. Just as Israel has been destroyed and Judah subjugated by the Neo-Assyrian war machine, now, with the demise of Nineveh imminent, this Judahite prophet offers poetry that, in effect, is an answer to prayers of lament such as Psalm 89, which mentions Assyria explicitly (v. 8). This psalm, which seeks the shame and death in disgrace of Israel's enemies (v. 17), would be answered by a book such as Nahum. To say this is to suggest that Nahum's activity, as is the case with other prophets, is bound up with the worship life of ancient Israel (so Nahum 1:15).

No assessment of Nahum can stop without mention of the other book devoted to Nineveh, namely, Jonah. Both works are highly theological, and both end with questions. Many scholars have maintained that the two books should be read together in order to gain the fullest prophetic commentary on the fate of this city.

H. Habakkuk

Within the boundaries of three chapters, the reader encounters three distinct forms of literature: dialogue, woe oracle, and victory psalm. Scholars have focused on clarifying the integrity of these three elements and positing contexts, both historical and cultural, for them. For example, many have argued that chapter 3 is an ancient poem, far older than the rest of the book and replete with mythic depictions of the deity. Despite such diversity of literary style, the person responsible for composing the book has provided salutary transitions and in so doing offered an answer to the powerful theological question posed at its outset:

> O LORD, how long shall I cry for help, . . .
> Or cry to you, "Violence!" . . . (1:2)

> Justice never prevails.
> The wicked surround the righteous. (1:4)

One immediately senses echoes with Jeremiah and Job:

> Why does the way of the guilty prosper?
>   Why do all who are treacherous thrive? (Jer. 12:1)
> How long . . . .(Jer. 12:4)

> I must shout, "Violence and destruction!" (Jer. 20:8)

> Even when I cry out, 'Violence!' I am not answered;
>   I call aloud, but there is no justice. (Job 19:7)

> Why do the wicked live on? (Job 21:7)

The Hebrew Bible includes a substratum of complaint, language that has its origins in common human experience but that in Israel was refined and included in worship through the psalms of individual and communal lament. As we shall see, Habakkuk 3 makes clear that this prophet is willing to use those liturgical resources in carving out a response to these questions that appear in Habakkuk, Jeremiah, and Job.

Habakkuk complains twice (1:2–4; 1:12–2:1), and God responds each time (1:5–11; 2:2–5). Of these two sets, what the deity says is the more surprising. Habakkuk laments injustice in his world, presumably within the context of Judahite society. Yahweh responds "I am rousing the Chaldeans," as if to say that what is wrong inside Judah must be dealt with by an international force. Habakkuk has cried out "Violence" (1:2), which is exactly what the Babylonians will bring (1:9). Then Habakkuk counters by claiming that such international intervention will result in the decimation of all people not just the wicked:

> The enemy brings them all up with a hook (1:15)
>   destroying nations without mercy. (1:17)

The deity next responds by challenging Habakkuk to write "the vision." But what is this vision? The answer is not clear. Instead, God problematizes the notion that the wicked do in fact triumph (2:4–5). Then the deity cites five woe oracles (2:6b–19) that inveigh explicitly against the Babylonians but also implicitly against the evil ones whom Habakkuk identified at the beginning of the book.

In Hab. 2:20, the prophet speaks again, moving deeper into the rhetoric of lament. Lamentation involves more than complaints. In a lament, a worshiper would routinely affirm confidence in God, who is a reliable source of help. Habakkuk does exactly that:

> The LORD is in his holy temple;
> let all the earth keep silence before him!

With that affirmation the book moves to even more overt liturgical language delineated by 3:1 and 19. Inside those verses we hear the voice of the prophet (vv. 2 and 16–18). And within his testimony, we find preserved the (old) vision, vv. 3–15, that has sustained Israel from its earliest days. The vision conveys a God who appears in and disturbs the natural order:

> He stopped and shook the earth;
> he looked and made the nations tremble.
> The eternal mountains were shattered. (3:6)

This poetry depicting theophany moves to a description of the deity as divine warrior with weapons affecting the cosmic order:

> The sun raised high its hands;
> the moon stood still in its exalted place,
> at the light of your arrows speeding by. (3:11)

It was Yahweh's warfare that defeated Israel's enemies:

> You pierced with their own arrows the head of his warriors,
> who came like a whirlwind to scatter us. (3:14)

One might have thought that this poem could serve as evidence that God would save his people from the Babylonians. Habakkuk does not seem to have read it that way. Instead, he trembles and waits for calamity (3:16), affirming even at the end of the book, in traditional Psalmic images, that God is his strength (3:19).

Habakkuk is often viewed as an unusual exemplar of prophetic literature. The people of Israel are never directly addressed. Habakkuk seems as much a priest as a prophet. And yet, Habakkuk, as scribe—making the vision so plain that someone running by may read it (2:2) —is doing exactly what intermediaries were supposed to do, namely, enabling their people to understand what the deity is and will be doing with his people. The vision was clear, but the prophet would sit, waiting to see precisely what would happen, as Jonah had done before him.

I. ZEPHANIAH

Zephaniah's genealogy (Zeph. 1:1) has routinely caught the attention of biblical scholars. Is it possible that this prophet was a prince (son of Hezekiah) and/or someone of African descent (son of Cush)? No easy answers are possible, but this book does seem uniquely focused on the king's house (e.g., 1:8). Moreover, the time of Zephaniah's work is reasonably clear. It dates to reign of Josiah (640–609 B.C.E.). And since it inveighs against many of the improprieties addressed by that king's reform activities (ca. 621 B.C.E.), such as the veneration of deities other than Yahweh (1:4–5), it is likely that the prophet uttered these oracles earlier rather than later in Josiah's reign.

Form-critical analysis of the book has yielded mixed results. Although there are oracles against the nations (2:4–15), the structure of the prophetic speech both before and after this section is not at all clear. How is one to understand the structure of 1:2–2:3? Do verses 8–13 comprise one oracle or three? It is difficult to answer such questions. Tradition history has provided a better focal point in its attention to the hallmark tradition in the XII, the day of the Lord, which receives pride of place here (see especially 1:14–18). Redaction critics have suggested that the book has been updated with the addition of 3:9–20, which seems to address the people of Israel after the time of punishment has occurred (3:20, for instance, presupposes the exile). The motifs present in those verses seem consistent with post-exilic prophetic literature. Finally, literary critics have drawn attention to the intertextual resonances between Zephaniah and other portions of the Hebrew Bible (e.g., 1:2–3 and Genesis 1).

Zephaniah is a book full of dialectic, offering oppositions with no easy reconciliation. From the perspective of Israelite covenant traditions, one could say that Zephaniah speaks about both curses and blessings. One might also mention the providential freedom with which the deity acts.

The book commences with a remarkable inventory of destructive acts. Just as the deity acted and spoke to create in Genesis 1, here Yahweh will sweep away, cut off all life.

> I will utterly sweep away everything
> from the face of the earth. (1:2)

Are we to understand such an asseveration as hyperbole, an overexaggerated pronouncement, or does God really intend to kill all life—hence the reference to fish and birds as well as humans? Verse 4 suggests the attack will fall primarily on those who live in Jerusalem, especially those guilty of religious malpractice. But there is elsewhere in the book the notion that far more than Jerusalem will suffer ("all the earth shall be consumed," 3:8). Zephaniah seems to be living out of the theo-logic of covenant curses, i.e., the notion that the punishment will not be proportionate to the crime. This idea is consistent both with covenant traditions and with human experience in warfare.

One of the Ten Commandments states clearly the idea of disproportionate covenant punishment. If the Israelites venerate an image, God will punish children for the iniquity of the parents to the third and fourth generation (Exod. 20:5). To paraphrase a saying that appears in Ezek. 18:2, if a father eats sour grapes, his children's teeth are set on edge. And it precisely such religious violations that Zephaniah seems to have in mind. Perhaps one could say that Zephaniah thinks everything in Israel could be, but may not be, destroyed.

Zephaniah portrays the ominous fate of Israel using a staccato description of Yahweh's day. It will be

> a day of wrath,
> a day of distress and anguish,
> a day of ruin and devastation,
> a day of darkness and gloom,
> a day of clouds and thick darkness,
> a day of trumpet blast and battle cry. (1:15)

Such language reflects both theophany and holy war traditions—God present in the natural order and the deity as holy warrior. One should expect cosmic devastation: "the whole earth shall be consumed" (1:18).

Still, Zephaniah expresses the conviction that some will survive the day of the Lord. He allows for this possibility in the admonitions that appear in 2:1–3; it is just possible that "the humble" in Israel may be hidden on the day of Yahweh's wrath. They are admonished to seek the Lord (2:3), i.e., to use proper forms for divination, which some have not done (1:6). Although Zephaniah understands fully the punitive nature of Yahweh's day (2:16–18), involving destruction of both Judah and other nations, he mentions the survival of "the remnant of the house of Judah" (2:7) and "the remnant of my people" (2:9). The fate of the foreign nations is as ambiguous as Israel's. On the one hand, we are told that no inhabitant will be left (2:5). On the other hand, those of Ammon will be subject to Israel (2:9). And, as earlier in the book, Zephaniah utilizes traditional language to make his point. Zephaniah 2:14 presents a classical example of covenant curses, depicting what was once a city as a ruin inhabited only by wild animals.

The most subtle rhetorical move in the book occurs at the end of 2:15. We reach the conclusion of an oracle directed at Nineveh, one of the major Neo-Assyrian cities. Then, in 3:1, in a woe oracle against an unnamed city, the prophet offers a withering indictment. (Such language of woe had occurred earlier in 2:5.) Early on, one might assume that he was still addressing Nineveh, but by verse 5, it is very clear that he is now talking about another capital, Jerusalem. The fate of Israelite and non-Israelite cities will be shared—they will both incur devastation.

Zephaniah 3:9–20 tempers the hard language of punishment. The prophet clearly anticipates that Yahweh will act again on Israel's behalf. The perspective is international, resonating with other prophetic literature (cf. Zeph. 3:9 and Micah 4:5). Moreover, Jerusalem is still addressed, but in ways totally different from that earlier in the book. For the first time we hear about Zion, which is now personified, as is frequently done in Isaiah.

> Sing aloud, O daughter Zion. (3:14)

Perhaps most striking is the notion of an Israel inside Israel.

> For I will leave in the midst of you
> a people humble and lowly. (3:12)

This may well refer to a sect within post-exilic Israel—one that preserved the earlier words of the prophets and lived in the hopes for radical restoration of Yahweh's kingship (3:15).

In sum, Zephaniah deploys many Israelite texts and traditions in formulating his speeches. Day of the Lord, creation, Zion, and covenant traditions are only the most prominent of such rhetoric. Moreover, Zephaniah provides a comprehensive picture of Yahweh's interactions with Israel, by offering indictments of Israel, judgments on foreign nations, and a vision of the time beyond punishment—quite a package for so brief a book.

J. Haggai

A number of the books that make up the XII commence with a chronological formula. Hosea and Amos refer to rulers on the throne in both Israel and Judah. Micah, at a later time, specifies only Judahite kings. Haggai continues this precedent of referring to someone on the throne, but now the ruler is the Persian emperor, Darius! With this book (and Zechariah), we explicitly enter the Persian period (ca. 550–330 B.C.E.), a time when a non-Semitic civilization to the east of the classical Mesopotamian cultures (Assyria and Babylonia) exercised dominion throughout the ancient Near East, including Syria-Palestine. It was no longer possible to refer to a Davidic king, since that form of political leadership had effectively ended with the defeat in 587. Attention to this new political reality has continually informed most recent efforts to understand this small book, which dates to a three month period in 520 B.C.E. In addition, some scholars have addressed the ways in which Haggai's sayings have been incorporated into a chronological scheme rather like that present in Zechariah but also with similarities to Chronicles.

Darius's reign was one in which conquests by his predecessors (especially those of Cyrus, whom the book of Isaiah viewed as a messiah [Isa. 45:1]) were consolidated. Although Cyrus was remembered as having permitted those in exile to return to Judah (Ezra 1:1–11) and having authorized the reconstruction of the temple in Jerusalem (Ezra 6:3–5), such restoration efforts had apparently languished. Darius's reign, in part due to his administrative efforts, provided a more productive context for such work of reconstruction.

Just as there is a chronological focus, so too there is a geographical and theological focus—the temple. Haggai interprets meager crop yields and generally unsatisfactory economic conditions (1:6, 9) as due to Yahweh's response to "his house" (v. 19), which lies in ruins. Even though those living in Judah have built houses for themselves, they have not rebuilt the temple. Hence, Yahweh has called forth drought and dessication (1:10–11). However, once Haggai presents this interpretation, the people, with the high priest and governor at the lead, begin to rebuild the temple. Haggai, along with Joel and Jonah, is a successful prophet! Haggai promises that the so-called second temple will be as glorious as the one built by Solomon (2:1–9). It will also allow for purification of what is now ritually unclean (2:10–14).

The twenty-fourth day of the ninth month in 520 B.C.E. was to be of signal importance ("from this day on," 2:15). Scholars have interpreted references to one stone being placed upon another stone in the Lord's temple as an allusion to the ceremony, attested in other ancient Near Eastern cultures, in which the temple was ritually rededicated. That day signals the end of drought and the rebirth of fertility. In addition, Yahweh will begin "shaking the heavens and the earth." This shaking will allow wealth to flow into the temple. But it will also, apparently, shake up the current political order. This day in 520 B.C.E. symbolizes some aspects of Yahweh's day.

In the final oracle of the book, Haggai turns to a member of the Davidic line, Zerubbabel, who now held the office of governor. Using language that highlights the Davidic house's special place in Yahweh's polity, Haggai appears to tempt Zerubbabel to think about reviving the role of the Davidic line: "I will take you, O Zerubbabel, and make you like a signet ring; for I have chosen you, says the LORD of Hosts" (2:23). The signet ring was worn by a king as a symbol of his royal power. Moreover, earlier texts in the Hebrew Bible speak of God "choosing" David.

Thus, in the years when Judah was reconstructing not only buildings but its social, political, and religious life, Haggai seems to have been advocating a recreation of the older order orientated around temple, king, and prophet. Haggai is very much a conservative, affirming many of the traditions attested in earlier prophetic and historical books. Such perspectives have resulted from reading Haggai with an eye both to social world and political-religious traditions.

K. Zechariah

Zechariah, like Haggai, explicitly reflects Persian period realities. Darius's reign remains the frame of reference, but now the time period is a bit broader (520–518 B.C.E.), though still relatively early in Darius' reign and before the temple was rededicated (515 B.C.E.).

The latter chapters of Zechariah constitute a problem comparable to that posed by the book of Isaiah. Zechariah 9—14 presents a different literary style and reflects a later historical period from the earlier chapters (1—8). For this reason, scholars regularly talk about First and Second (or Deutero-) Zechariah. During the past two decades, given the interest in reading the "final form" of biblical books, readings that attempt to integrate these two sections have been attempted.

Zechariah 1—8 offers an adroit blend of visionary and oracular material. The relationship between the two has been explored, some suggesting that the oracles are a later addition, others maintaining that the oracles are essential for understanding the visions. In either case, the visions capture the reader's attention because they are so vivid—even colorful—and bizarre. The eight visions embedded in Zechariah 1—6 describe a universe that is initially at peace (1:7–17), moves through action (second and third visions), identifies pivotal roles for the high priest and governor (fourth and fifth visions), articulates the new world at work (sixth and seventh visions), and then returns to the world depicted in the first vision, which is now far more energized (eighth vision). The symbolism is rich and diverse, reflecting at one point the cosmic deep (1:8), at another point an oil lamp (1:2).

Those who work from the perspectives of form criticism and tradition history can place these visions within the larger context of vision reports in other prophetic books. Though vision reports appear in earlier prophetic books like Amos and Isaiah, they become more prominent in later works, most notably Ezekiel and Zechariah. Those who study even later biblical and related literature (e.g., Daniel) have observed that Zechariah's visions appear to pave the road from prophetic vision to apocalyptic vision. Unlike earlier prophetic visions, those of Zechariah include an angelic interlocutor and interpreter (e.g., 1:9; cf. Dan. 7:16), a feature present in much apocalyptic literature.

Still, Zechariah deserves to be understood as prophetic literature. Like Haggai, Zechariah's visions and oracles address the concrete issues of life in Judah ca. 520. What sort of life should Yahwists envision? Zechariah's perspective is less pragmatic than Haggai's. Rather than call for the rebuilding of the temple, Zechariah's visions put matters in a cosmic perspective. The deity is acting on Judah's behalf. Moreover, as with Haggai, the Davidic heir Zerubbabel will have an important role, more so than the high priest. The oracles tend to treat more mundane matters such as fundraising (Zech. 6:9–15) and the appropriateness of various religious practices (Zech. 7:1–5; 8:18–19).

All such attention to the concrete problems of restoration circa 520 are absent from Zechariah 9—14, which offers challenges unlike virtually any other prophetic literature. There is no clear historical background, and boundaries between poetic sections are unclear. At a fairly late date in the history of the text's formation, an editor configured these chapters into two primary entities—Zechariah 9—11 and 12—14, both of which are introduced as "an oracle." Military activity predominates in the first, with the deity often portrayed as divine warrior. Both those inside and outside "Israel" will suffer the effects of warfare. In contrast, and written in prose, Zechariah 12—14, particularly chapter 14, focuses on a day, the ominous "day of the LORD." On that day, Yahweh will appear in theophany to violent effect, and a new era will result from his rule as king. That Yahweh would rule as king is not a new theme in Israel (cf. the so-called kingship psalms). However, the radical impact of that kingship (e.g., with mountains crumbling, Zech. 14:4) is expressed in a new and intense way in these Persian period texts. It is possible to understand Zechariah 9—14 as a continuation of the cosmic perspective introduced in Zechariah's visions, but that cosmic perspective is no longer expressly related to Zechariah, the years of 520–518, or Darius's reign. However, Judah, and even more Jerusalem, remain as the primary focus of God's activity. All of this book implicitly argues on behalf of the restoration occurring in Judah.

L. Malachi

The final book of the XII may not be a separate book. As we suggested earlier, the formula with which the book begins, "An oracle, the word of the LORD to . . ." is very similar to the formulas at the beginning of Zechariah 12 and 14. Thus, the XII may at one point have concluded with three "oracles," not with a book attributed to Malachi. This case can be strengthened by observing that the Hebrew word, *mal'āki*, translated in the NRSV as a proper name, "Malachi," could as well be translated "my messenger." Put another way, there may be no individually named prophet with which to associate what we have traditionally known as the book of Malachi.

Unlike the two penultimate prophetic books, Haggai and Zechariah, Malachi offers no clear information about its point of origin. There is reference neither to Persian emperor nor to Judahite official or high priest. However, a number of scholars have agreed that the issues addressed in the book (e.g., the need for a purified priesthood, the importance of paying tithes, and concern for the Levites) are strikingly similar to those addressed in the fifth century by Ezra and Nehemiah. Following this logic, Malachi probably has its origins in the first half of the fifth century B.C.E., making it yet another prophetic book dating to the Persian period.

Malachi is made up of at least six rhetorical units devoted to diverse topics like proper sacrifice (1:6–2:9) and tithing (3:6–12). These discourses, though not sharing comparable structure, often convey a strident tone in which the opponents of Yahweh's prophet are quoted, or at least words are put in their mouths (it is hard to imagine someone saying "All who do evil are good in the sight of the LORD," 2:17), and their causes challenged. Those approaching this literature from a form-critical perspective do not agree on its nature. Some have characterized these units as disputations, other as akin to Greek diatribes. The texts do attest to a remarkably aggressive engagement within the Yahwistic community. Even 1:2–5, which refers to the Edomites, has as its goal affirming God's love for Israelites.

From a social world perspective, the book of Malachi addresses or refers to specific groups in Israel. It attacks the priests who conduct sacrifices at the temple. And it seems particularly sympathetic to the cause of the Levites, other priests who, in the Persian period, were becoming marginalized. In addition, and after the conclusion of the interchanges, the book refers to "those who revered the LORD" (3:16). Within the community, some are righteous and some are wicked, and the fate of the righteous now becomes the concern of this Persian period prophetic text. To use the imagery of Malachi 4, the wicked will be consumed by fire, whereas the righteous will "go out leaping like calves from the stall." Such an attempt to distinguish between what will happen to the righteous and the wicked is shared by Zechariah as well and appears in later biblical texts (i.e., Daniel). Moreover, such concerns are absent from earlier books in the XII, wherein prophets routinely speak about all Israel sharing the same fate.

Just as the first book of the XII, Hosea, has been expanded with a wisdom style final verse (14:9), so too Malachi concludes with two additions. The first (Mal. 4:4) integrates Malachi, and probably the XII, with the Torah or Pentateuch,

Moses' instructions to Israel. The other addition (Mal. 4:5–6) anticipates the return of Elijah, now an eschatological prophet, who will enable the people to prepare for the day of Yahweh—a motif present throughout the XII. These two verses build a link between the XII and the former prophets (Joshua–Kings) in which Elijah appears, and they imply that though the XII comprise a concluded prophetic "canon," the work of prophets will continue in the person of Elijah.

FOR FURTHER READING

The Book of the Twelve
Collins, Terence. "The Scroll of the Twelve." In *The Mantle of Elijah: The Redaction Criticism of the Prophetical Books,* 59– 87. The Biblical Seminar 20. Sheffield: Sheffield Academic Press, 1993.
House, Paul R. *The Unity of the Twelve.* BLS 27. JSOTSup 97. Sheffield: Sheffield Academic Press, 1990.
Jones, Barry. *The Formation of the Book of the Twelve: A Study in Text and Canon.* SBLDS 149. Atlanta: Scholars Press, 1995.
Nogalski, James. *Literary Precursors to the Book of the Twelve.* BZAW 217. Berlin: de Gruyter, 1993.
———. *Redactional Processes in the Book of the Twelve.* BZAW 218. Berlin: de Gruyter, 1993.

Individual Books
Auld, A. G. *Amos.* OTG. Sheffield: JSOT, 1986.
Coggins, R. J. *Haggai, Zechariah, Malachi.* OTG. Sheffield: JSOT, 1987.
Mason, Rex. *Micah, Nahum, Obadiah.* OTG. Sheffield: JSOT, 1991.
Mays, James L. *Amos: A Commentary.* OTL. Philadelphia: Westminster, 1969.
———. *Hosea: A Commentary.* OTL. Philadelphia: Westminster, 1969.
———. *Micah: A Commentary.* OTL. Philadelphia: Westminster, 1976.
Newsom, Carol A., and Sharon H. Ringe, eds., *The Women's Bible Commentary.* Louisville, Ky.: Westminster/John Knox, 1992.
Paul, Shalom M. *Amos.* Hermeneia. Minneapolis: Fortress, 1991.
Petersen, David L. *Haggai and Zechariah 1–8: A Commentary.* OTL. Philadelphia: Westminster, 1988.
———. *Zechariah 9–14 and Malachi: A Commentary.* OTL. Louisville, Ky.: Westminster John Knox, 1995.
Wolff, Hans Walter. *Hosea.* Trans. G. Stansell. Hermeneia. Philadelphia: Fortress, 1974.
———. *Joel and Amos.* Trans. W. Janzen et al. Hermeneia. Philadelphia: Fortress, 1977.
———. *Obadiah and Jonah: A Commentary.* Trans. M. Kohl. Minneapolis: Augsburg, 1986.
———. *Haggai: A Commentary.* Trans. M. Kohl. Minneapolis: Augsburg, 1988.

Part III

Writings (*Ketuvim*)

5

THE WISDOM BOOKS

Job, Proverbs, Ecclesiastes

KATHLEEN A. FARMER

I. THE WISDOM LITERATURE OF ISRAEL

In Christian Bibles, which are arranged according to the order of the early Greek translation known as the Septuagint (LXX), the narrative thread that runs from Genesis to Esther tells the story of Israel's "salvation history." This mostly prose narrative is concerned with the origins and destiny of the people of Israel. It describes God's numerous interventions and disruptions of human history and the natural order on behalf of a small segment of humanity, and it appeals to the revelation of God for the authority of its *tôrāh* (literally, "instruction"). In the prophetic books, with which the Christian canon ends, the God of Israel is said to speak directly to Israel through a variety of human agents.

But the five books of poetry that are found sandwiched in between the end of the salvation history and the beginning of the Prophets are strikingly different from the material that surrounds them in the Christian canon. Three of these five poetic texts are similar enough in content, form, and function to justify grouping them together under a single heading. Job, Proverbs, and Ecclesiastes are called the "wisdom literature" of the Bible, because they share an outlook on life that they themselves characterize as the "way of wisdom." Unlike the term *Torah* (or Law), "wisdom literature" is a modern designation that represents modern rather than ancient ways of classifying these books.

In the study of the Hebrew Bible or Old Testament the term "wisdom" can be used in various ways. The noun "wisdom" (*ḥokmāh*) and the adjective "wise" (*ḥākām*) are used in narrative texts to designate innate intelligence or shrewdness, artistic and administrative skill, or good judgment. But in Job, Proverbs, and Ecclesiastes, "wisdom" is used to describe both an attitude of mind that enables an observer to see patterns in human experience and an articulation of these observations in forms that can be taught and learned. Thus in the wisdom books "wisdom" refers both to a way of thinking and to a body of knowledge derived from that way of thinking. To be "wise," as the authors of Proverbs, Ecclesiastes, and Job use the term, means both to reflect on one's own observations and to pay attention to the observations of others, to sift through and weigh one's own experiences over against the testimonies of others (Eccl. 12:9). Merely acquiring a large body of knowledge (or knowing a large number of wisdom sayings) does not make one wise. Wisdom also includes the ability to choose which sayings are true in which contexts. "A proverb in the mouth of a fool" can be useless or dangerous (Prov. 26:7–9).

Wisdom is also invested with a certain degree of transcendence in the wisdom literature: each book acknowledges that wisdom is something that can be partially grasped but never completely apprehended by the human mind. Wisdom is attainable in part through human effort (Prov. 4:5–7) and as a gift from God (Prov. 2:6), but it is unattainable in its entirety—except by God (Eccl. 3:11; Job 28:23).

Each of the biblical "Wisdom" books attempts, in its own way, to use human reason to make sense out of human experiences. The wise in Israel search for patterns so that they can learn and teach others how to succeed in life. Each book addresses the question of what is good for human beings to do as they live out their brief lives under the sun. Those who contribute to the wisdom tradition draw upon a similar vocabulary and use similar literary forms. However, they are most alike in the way in which they draw their conclusions from human reflections upon human experience.

The Song of Solomon (also called Song of Songs or Canticles) is sometimes thought to be a product of the wisdom outlook on life. While it is true that this collection of love songs makes no mention of Israel's salvation history, only one short passage has moral or instructional overtones (8:6–7) and wisdom itself is never mentioned.[1] However, two apocryphal books known as the Wisdom of Sirach (or Ecclesiasticus) and the Wisdom of Solomon undoubtedly belong to the same genre of "wisdom literature" in Israel, even though Jewish and Protestant Christian communities do not ordinarily consider them part of their biblical canon. Many scholarly arguments about the assumptions and origins of biblical wisdom literature are based on inferences drawn from these two books, both of which were included in the Septuagint, which was the Bible of the early church.

The "mighty acts of God" in Israel's history (the exodus, the giving of the law at Sinai, the crossing of the Jordan, etc.) are neither celebrated nor remembered in Proverbs, Ecclesiastes, and Job. Unlike Israel's salvation history, which sees evidence of God's activity in extraordinary events, the wisdom writings are primarily concerned with the regularities of ordinary life. The covenant between God and Israel, which plays such an important part in the religion of Israel, is seldom if ever mentioned by the wisdom writers. The only statements they make about God's actions in the past concern the creation of the world, not the creation of Israel. Thus the wisdom writings are addressed to inquiring spirits everywhere without regard to nationality. The faithfully wise assume that God's creative activity works itself out in the normal, ordinary experiences of normal, ordinary people, wherever they may be found. Unlike other Old Testament texts, which usually appeal to special revelation for their authority ("thus says the LORD"), the wisdom books appeal to general revelation (that which can be discerned on the basis of reason and observation).

The authors of Proverbs, Ecclesiastes, and Job share an attitude of inquiry and an assumption that human experience falls into discernible patterns. However, there is no real unity of opinion among them. Each contributor to the wisdom tradition comes to his or her own conclusions, based on his or her observations and reflections on human experience, and these conclusions vary greatly from one book to another and from one speaker to another within a single book. The contributors to Proverbs, for instance, make a number of confident assertions about the way the world works that are flatly contradicted by the speakers in Job and Ecclesiastes. Rather than thinking of wisdom as a body of doctrine or a set of propositions, therefore, it is better to say that wisdom is "a method of inquiry, a use of particular forms of teaching, and a desire to compare and co-ordinate phenomena."[2]

A. The Variety of Opinions Represented

In English, "proverbs" are usually understood to be short, pithy sayings that make apt observations and generalizations about some aspect of human experience (e.g., "penny wise, pound foolish" or "a stitch in time saves nine"). But not all of the material found in the biblical book of Proverbs falls into this literary category. The first nine chapters of Proverbs contain relatively long, personalized, advice-giving speeches that are directly addressed to a listener who is called "my son" (NRSV "my child"). These speeches attempt to persuade the listener to act (or to avoid acting) in particular ways. The reader has to wait until the tenth chapter of the book to find the type of material the English title describes. In Prov. 10:1 the literature changes abruptly from long, connected speeches to short, compact sayings, each of which expresses a complete thought in one sentence, consisting of two parallel lines. Both kinds of literature (i.e., the longer speeches and the sentence proverbs) are grouped together under the larger heading, "the words of the wise" (Prov. 1:6). The plural noun for "wise" (*hăkāmîm*) is used here, indicating that many individuals have contributed to the whole. In English, the term "sage" can be used to designate these wise women and men whose opinions have been collected in Proverbs as well as in the other wisdom books. Sometimes "sage" is used to describe anyone who is particularly wise, but in recent scholarship the term has begun to assume the connotation of "one who has composed a book or piece belonging to the wisdom literature of the ancient Near East."[3]

The speakers in Proverbs 1—9 are convinced that the *tôrāh* (instruction) of wisdom is congruent with the *tôrāh* of God, because God is the ultimate source of the assumed and observable regularities from which wisdom draws its conclusions. Thus, respect for God's revelation is said to be both the origin and the goal of wisdom thinking (Prov. 1:7; 2:1–5). They also insist that whoever finds wisdom "finds life and obtains favor from the LORD," while those who hate wisdom "love death" (Prov. 8:35-36). They consider wisdom congruent with righteousness, equate wickedness with folly, and identify Wisdom's way of living with the LORD's way (Prov. 8:12–21).

But the speakers in the shorter sayings sections (Proverbs 10—29) make only a few explicit theological statements. Sayings such as, "The human mind may devise many plans, but it is the purpose of the LORD that will be established" (Prov. 19:21) and "No wisdom, no understanding, no counsel, can avail against the LORD. The horse is made ready for the day of battle, but the victory belongs to the LORD" (Prov. 21:30–31; see also Prov. 16:9; 19:21; 20:24) are far outnumbered by statements that have no explicit theological content. The sages whose words have been transmitted in Proverbs assert that human actions have consistent and forseeable consequences. They are confident that "whoever sows injustice will reap calamity," (Prov. 22:8a) and "those who sow righteousness get a true reward" (Prov. 11:18b). Their collective experiences incline them to believe that hard work, honesty, and kindness to others result in security, prosperity, and contentment, while laziness, lies, and meanness lead to predictably bad ends (Prov. 6:6–11). But the overwhelming majority of the statements that predict the consequences that will result from various forms of human behavior make no mention of God.

There is a certain degree of conditionality included in the collection that is not apparent when individual retributive sayings are looked at in isolation. Not every proverb assumes that the righteous prosper and the wicked fade away. The wise also admit that poverty is sometimes due to injustice rather than indolence (Prov. 13:23) and that riches can be gained in various evil ways (e.g., Prov. 16:8; 21:6; 28:6). But taken as a whole, the book of Proverbs leaves the reader with the overwhelmingly optimistic impression that human beings have the ability and the opportunity to make choices that have relatively predictable outcomes in their lives. Furthermore, the speakers in Proverbs are confident that "the teaching of the wise is a fountain of life, so that one may avoid the snares of death" (Prov. 13:14).

However, the sage whose voice we hear in the book of Ecclesiastes is not convinced that there really are predictable relationships between acts and their consequences "under the sun." His own observations lead him to believe that there are no guaranteed outcomes in human life. Qohelet (the Hebrew name for the primary speaker in Ecclesiastes) is convinced by his experiences in life that there is no positive correlation between moral behavior and prosperity or between immoral behavior and poverty. In his own lifetime Qohelet has seen that "there are righteous people who perish in their righteousness, and there are wicked people who prolong their life in their evildoing" (Eccl. 7:15) and that "under the sun the race is not to the swift, nor the battle to the strong, nor bread to the wise, nor riches to the intelligent, nor favor to the skillful; but time and chance happen to them all" (Eccl. 9:11).

Qohelet uses the Hebrew word for "vapor" (often translated "vanity") to describe everything "under the sun." He values wisdom and acknowledges that "wisdom excels folly as light excels darkness. The wise have eyes in their heads, but fools walk in darkness" (2:13–14a). However, unlike the speakers in Proverbs, Qohelet acknowledges that "the same fate befalls all of them . . . the wise die just like fools" (2:14b, 16b). His own reflections on human experience lead him to think that God has put unpredictability into the structure of the world, so that people cannot guarantee happiness or long lives for themselves through their own efforts (Eccl. 3:9–11). Ecclesiastes 8:16a, 17 says,

> When I applied my mind to know wisdom . . . , I saw all the work of God, that no one can find out what is happening under the sun. However much they may toil in seeking, they will not find it out; even though those who are wise claim to know, they cannot find it out.

Thus he concludes that anyone who fears God will simply avoid extremes, knowing that the future cannot be known (Eccl. 7:13–18). And, since life (like everything else under the sun) is as brief as a vapor, Qohelet advises people against toiling long hours trying to secure some distant goal of happiness for themselves. Rather than urging people to work in order to pile up riches for themselves and their heirs (as Proverbs does), Ecclesiastes encourages people to "eat and drink and find enjoyment in their toil," as God has intended for them to do (Eccl. 2:24; 3:12, 22; 5:18, etc.).

The book of Job also challenges the optimistic assumption that there is a consistent link between human behavior and the quality or length of human life. The narrative with which the book of Job begins describes Job as an admirable, faithful worshiper of the LORD (Job 1:1, 8; 2:3). It is clear from the introduction that Job has done nothing to deserve the tragedy and suffering that affects him and his family. But the "friends" who come to "comfort" Job in his misery represent the predominant proverbial opinion that God guarantees a world order in which wise and faithful choices lead to happiness, prosperity, and long life.

Job's friends ignore the nuances in Proverbs. They assume that Job's suffering is clear evidence of wrongdoing on somebody's part (e.g., Job 4:7–8). But Job's experience as an innocent sufferer and his observations that the wicked often "live on, reach old age, and grow mighty in power" (21:7) lead him to question the proverbial principle of retributive justice. If behavior and prosperity are as closely linked as Proverbs and Job's friends claim, then Job wants to know why the wicked and their children "spend their days in prosperity" and die peacefully in old age (Job 21:13a). The proverbial assertion that "the evil have no future; the lamp of the wicked will go out" (Prov. 24:20) is echoed by Job's friend Bildad (Job 18:5). But Job asks, "How often is the lamp of the wicked put out?" (Job 21:17). "Have you not asked those who travel the roads, and do you not accept their testimony, that the wicked are spared in the day of calamity, and are rescued in the day of wrath?" (Job 21:29–30).

In the final scene of the book, God says to the three friends "you have not spoken of me what is right, as my servant Job has" (Job 42:7). Thus the compiler of Job highlights the problems posed by the presence of tragedy and suffering in the lives of even the wisest and most faithful. The theory of retribution (the idea that righteousness brings material rewards and wickedness brings punishment) does not adequately explain what happened to Job. Thus the book of Job is often called a "theodicy" (meaning "an effort to interpret the origin, nature, meaning and resolution of suffering and evil within one's larger theological perspective."[4])

B. The Two Faces of Wisdom

It can be said that the speakers in Proverbs value the observable continuities in life. However, it might also be argued that the people who speak in Proverbs have benefitted from the continuities they value. What is said to "lead to life" in

Proverbs is defined by those whose prosperity and security are based on the status quo. Thus Proverbs is sometimes said to be a collection of "conservative" wisdom traditions (supporting things as they are, promoting the status quo). However, Job and Ecclesiastes challenge the prevailing viewpoints and question the dominant structures and beliefs of the society represented by the contributors to Proverbs. Thus Job and Ecclesiastes are sometimes said to be the products of "skeptical" or "progressive" thinkers who reexamine, rethink, and point out the flaws in "conservative" wisdom teachings. It might be more accurate to say that Job and Ecclesiastes challenge those who try to make the contextually relevant observations in Proverbs into statements of absolute truth. Neither Job nor Ecclesiastes questions the premise on which Proverbs is based: that certain conclusions can be drawn on the basis of human experience.

C. Ancient Near Eastern Parallels

Israel's wisdom literature has much in common with various literary traditions that have survived from Egypt and Mesopotamia (including Sumer, Babylon, Ugarit, and Assyria). It had long been assumed (even before any texts from Israel's neighbors in the ancient Near East had actually been found) that Israelites were familiar with the wisdom of other lands. Israel's own history reminds us of the many cultural and family ties that existed between Israel and the peoples of Mesopotamia and Egypt. The biblical texts trace Abraham's ancestry back to Mesopotamia and his closest relatives are said to have remained there. Abraham's first son (Ishmael) had an Egyptian mother and wife, and Moses was raised in a royal Egyptian household. Solomon had wives from all over the Middle East, and 1 Kings 4:30 claims that "Solomon's wisdom surpassed the wisdom of all the people of the east, and all the wisdom of Egypt."

But prior to the actual discovery of a variety of ancient wisdom texts from the Middle East in the late nineteenth and early twentieth centuries, the relationship between Israel's wisdom and that of her neighbors could only be assumed, not proven. However, by the end of World War I, the discovery of a variety of extant texts gave clear evidence that the wisdom of Israel was concerned with similar subjects, used similar literary forms, favored similar vocabulary, and sometimes even contained identical wording as its counterparts from neighboring societies.[5]

Like wisdom literature in Israel, Egyptian and Mesopotamian wisdom texts can be divided into "conservative" traditions, promoting the status quo (like Proverbs), and "skeptical" traditions, which question traditional teachings (like Job and Ecclesiastes). A number of conservative wisdom-teaching documents (known as "Instructions") have survived to the present day. Most wisdom Instructions contain very practical advice directed towards youths who aspire to hold positions of power at court. Perhaps the best known of these is the Egyptian "Instruction of Amenemope," which bears an extremely close resemblance to Prov. 22:17–24:22. The speaker in this Instruction is said to be a royal official who is trying to teach his youngest son how to succeed in the same profession. Amenemope's advice has moral and religious overtones. In addition to sayings, such as, "Better is bread when the heart is happy, than riches with sorrow," Amenemope says that love for "the all-knowing One" who is a compassionate god should motivate the wise to show compassion to their fellow creatures. Both the Instruction of Amenemope and the section of Proverbs that resembles it seem to be intended for the education of royal courtiers (Prov. 22:29).

In the category of "skeptical" texts we can list a Babylonian text known as the "Counsels of a Pessimist," which is reminiscent of Ecclesiastes, as well as an Egyptian composition called "A Dispute over Suicide," a Sumerian essay entitled "Man and His God," and a text known as the "Babylonian Theodicy," all of which have many characteristics in common with the book of Job.[6] The "Babylonian Theodicy" is written in the form of a debate between a sufferer, who complains that the wicked prosper while his piety brings him no benefits, and a traditionalist, who insists on the truth of the belief that good behavior is rewarded and bad behavior is punished.[7]

D. The Canonization of Wisdom

The degree to which the wisdom texts represent an attitude of faith has been debated since at least the time of Jesus. This debate affected their canonization and continues to play an important part in scholarly discussions of them in the present.

The oldest witnesses to the arrangement of the books in the biblical canon list Proverbs and Ecclesiastes next to each other and in that order. Modern Hebrew Bibles separate Proverbs from Ecclesiastes (following a tradition begun no earlier than the tenth century C.E.) in order to group the five festival scrolls together as a convenient unit. But there is evidence that Proverbs and Ecclesiastes were originally considered "companion volumes" or a single collection of the "Words of the Wise" with one introduction (Prov. 1:2–7) and one conclusion (Eccl. 12:11–14) for the whole collection.[8]

Some early rabbis questioned the sacredness of any books associated with Solomon on the grounds that they were products of Solomon's wisdom rather than divine wisdom and because they were also self-contradictory. However, Proverbs seems to have acquired a respected place in the canon of sacred Scripture well before the beginning of the Christian era,[9] while early rabbinic literature indicates that two great Pharisaic teachers, Shammai and Hillel, and their disciples continued to debate the appropriateness of including Ecclesiastes in the canon. Proverbs may have gained acceptance first because of its explicit connections with Solomon, whose wisdom was thought to be a gift from God (1 Kings 3:12; 4:29–34; 10:24; 2 Chron. 1:12) or a manifestation of God's wisdom (1 Kings 3:28). But Shammai and his disciples believed that the tenuous connection of Ecclesiastes with Solomon was not enough to justify the canonization of a book that was not only secular in outlook but also contained both contradictions and passages that tended to heresy. Well into the second century C.E. some rabbis still insisted that

Ecclesiastes represented Solomon's own wisdom rather than God's. Nevertheless, Hillel and his disciples prevailed with their argument that Ecclesiastes should be considered part of the canon, because the book both begins and ends with "words of Torah."[10]

The church seems to have accepted Ecclesiastes from its earliest times, perhaps because Paul's teacher Gamaliel (named in Acts 22:3) was one of the disciples of Hillel, and because Jerome's choice of the Latin *vanus/vanitas* to translate the central thematic statement in Ecclesiastes enabled patristic ascetics to use the book to promote "contempt of the world."

The book of Job was placed in a variety of positions within various orderings of the canon, but its claim to be a part of the sacred writings was never questioned either in early Jewish or Christian circles. In modern Hebrew Bibles (following the order of the MT), Job is the second book in the Writings, located after Psalms and before Proverbs. At least one Talmudic commentator saw the story of Job as a *māshāl* (a wisdom genre usually translated "proverb"), and the Eastern Church consistently treated it as a wisdom book. However, the majority of the Western "church fathers" (following Origen) placed Job among the historical narratives, based on the Septuagint's identification of Job with Jobab, the grandson of Esau (Job 42:17 in the LXX; Gen. 36:33–34) and Ezekiel's naming of Job as a figure whose righteousness was exemplary (Ezek. 14:14, 20).

II. A BRIEF HISTORY OF CRITICAL SCHOLARSHIP

A. The Age of the Wisdom Books

Early Jewish and Christian tradition accepted the antiquity of Proverbs without question. Even the rabbis who doubted the appropriateness of including Proverbs and Ecclesiastes in the canon still assumed that both books originated with Solomon (though Proverbs was thought to be a product of his youth and Ecclesiastes a product of his old age). In the late eighteenth and early nineteenth centuries, critical thinkers began to question whether the bulk of Proverbs really could be traced back to Solomon. After all, the text of Proverbs itself refers to "the words of the wise" (22:17), using the plural form for "wise" and so indicating that more than one wise person had contributed to the whole. One section of Proverbs is attributed to the editorial activities of "the officials of King Hezekiah of Judah" (25:1), and the final two chapters are said to contain the words of "Agur, son of Jakeh" (30:1) and those of King Lemuel's mother (31:1). Thus a closer look at Proverbs itself indicates that the book contains several identifiable subsections or collections, each with its own distinct style and point of view. Most scholars think that a variety of people had a hand in the compilation of Proverbs and that the book took shape in several stages over an extended period of time.

Although the synagogue and the church traditionally identified Ecclesiastes with Solomon, critical thinkers have often noted that the name Solomon does not occur anywhere in the book and that a number of the statements in the book are difficult to reconcile with what we are told about Solomon from other sources. In 1:12 Qohelet says that he *was* "king over Israel in Jerusalem," implying that he speaks from a time when his reign had ended. Ecclesiastes 1:16 and 2:7 imply that many other kings had preceded the speaker on the throne in Jerusalem, and both 8:2–9 and 10:16–19 sound more like the opinions of a subject than those of a king. Thus, most critical readers assume Qohelet is simply a wisdom teacher who takes on the *persona* of Solomon in order to argue that even someone as wise and as rich as Solomon was reputed to be would say what the teacher says if given a chance to do so.

By the end of the nineteenth century, even relatively conservative scholars doubted that Solomon was responsible for all of the books attributed to him, and critical scholarship in the twentieth century is almost unanimous in its agreement on this point. Many modern scholars have dated the compilation of all of the wisdom texts to the postexilic period, based on the reasoning that wisdom's lack of dependence on covenantal themes and its consistent avoidance of references to Israel's history as the "chosen" people fit well into the needs of a Jewish community trying to survive and prosper in the midst of a predominantly non-Jewish world.

The consensus in biblical scholarship from the end of the nineteenth century until the present has been to date the present form of the book of Proverbs to the early postexilic period, while acknowledging that various individual sayings or collections of sayings within the book may have been much older. Since Job and Ecclesiastes object to the retributive point of view presented in Proverbs, most critical readers have also assumed that Proverbs represents the older viewpoint to which Ecclesiastes and Job react.

The age of Ecclesiastes is a constant source of debate. However, most scholars today think the Hebrew in which its present form is written represents a very late stage in the development of the language. Several have argued that the text contains loanwords from Persian and Aramaic and uses certain vocabulary and grammatical forms that only became common shortly before the beginning of the Christian era. Thus most conclude that the present form of the book comes from the second temple period at the earliest (i.e., from *at least* four centuries *later* than Solomon), and some who think that ideas in the book reflect Hellenistic Greek culture date it as late as the third century B.C.E. Hebrew fragments of the book found among the Dead Sea scrolls indicate that it was in circulation well before 150 B.C.E.

No known historical event is mentioned in the book of Job, and the theological issues addressed in the book cannot be tied to any one particular situation in the life of Israel. Some of the early rabbis thought Job was a contemporary of either Abraham or Jacob; others thought Moses had written the book of Job; and still others argued that Job was one of the Judean exiles who returned from the Babylonian captivity. Modern opinions lean toward a postexilic dating for the final form of the book, based on the appropriateness of its subject matter to the concerns of post-exilic people, on similarities between Isaiah 40—55 and the poetic dialogues in Job, and on linguistic evidence.[11]

B. The Character of Wisdom

Modern scholars generally agree that the wisdom books differ in significant ways from the bulk of the material in the Hebrew Bible. But they often disagree over how to define that difference. Nineteenth-century scholars sometimes characterized wisdom as "practical philosophy" or "religious and moral philosophy." Around the turn of the nineteenth into the twentieth century, scholars began to argue over whether wisdom should be described as essentially a "secular," "pragmatic," or "humanistic" endeavor and whether wisdom was opposed to or congruent with the law, the priests, and the prophets.

Many of the great names associated with the study of the Old Testament in the late nineteenth and early twentieth centuries either ignored or disparaged the presence of the wisdom books in the Hebrew canon. General surveys of scholarly trends between 1925 and 1950 barely mention wisdom as a subject of investigation.[12]

Early-twentieth-century theologians interested in the history of Israel's religion found that the wisdom books had little to say about worship practices.[13] Biblical theologians seeking to define the "unifying center" of Israel's faith based on the Law and the Prophets considered wisdom a "secular" phenomenon (meaning that it lacked faith as they had defined it). Those who assumed that the faith of Israel was centered around God's acts in history[14] or around the making of a covenant between Israel and God[15] found it difficult to incorporate the wisdom books into their overall schemes. Others noted, however, that this difficulty could be due to an overly narrow interpretation of Old Testament thought rather than to a problem inherent in the wisdom texts.[16]

However, in his extremely influential work on the theology of the Old Testament, Gerhard von Rad argued that the wisdom literature (and Psalms) should be seen as part of Israel's response of obedience to God's actions on their behalf.[17] Claus Westermann argued that the Old Testament as a whole had two foci, "blessing" and "salvation history," and that wisdom, falling under the category of blessing, had an important place in Old Testament theology.[18] Finally, Samuel Terrien opened up a way for future theologians to engage the wisdom traditions in dialogue when he reframed the theological task by asking, "How does one experience the presence of God?" He then concluded that empirical observations can testify to a divine presence in human life just as visionary experiences can.[19]

In the first half of the twentieth century the perception of similarity between ancient Near Eastern and Israelite wisdom increased the average theologian's inclination to dismiss the biblical wisdom books as unreliable witnesses to Israel's "authentic" theology and faith. Similarities between Israelite and Egyptian wisdom texts led to widespread speculation about how close the assumptions of Israel's wisdom thinking might be to Egyptian concepts associated with *Ma'at*, the goddess of truth, justice, and cosmic order. *Ma'at* represented the concept of a divine order inherent in the fabric of the universe. *Ma'at* established the foundations, boundaries, and patterns of life (including those of kingship, royal government, and social structure). For an Egyptian, to live wisely meant to live in harmony with *ma'at*, the cosmic order. The wise were thought to live longer, advance in their careers, etc., because their knowledge of *ma'at* allowed them to avoid some of life's hazards.

Since numerous sayings in Proverbs speak of acts and their consequences without any reference to God, some scholars concluded that the wise men and women of Israel believed in a similar principle of cosmic order.[20] H. D. Preuss rejects any role for wisdom in Christian theology because of the presumed existence in it of a "mechanistic" belief in cosmic order.[21] The parallels between the words of Amenemope and the "thirty sayings" in Proverbs 22—24 seem to substantiate the theory that the wise in Egypt and in Israel had similar beliefs. However, other texts in Proverbs explicitly place Yahweh (as the agent of retribution) between an act and its consequences. While many of the sayings in Proverbs make no reference to God or God's involvement in human experience, other sayings are expressed in Israel's traditional religious language (22:22–23; 3:5–7; etc.). Much critical thought has been devoted to scholarly attempts to account for the inclusion of materials with such fundamental differences in outlook in a single biblical book.

C. Accounting for Contradictions in Wisdom

The self-contradictory nature of the wisdom books has been noted by critical readers from the time of the rabbincal disputes over the content of the canon to the present. The rabbis (cf. *b. Shabb.* 30b) were disturbed by conflicts that seemed impossible to harmonize. For instance, it is clear that Prov. 26:4 and 26:5 give completely opposite pieces of advice to anyone who wants to know how to respond to fools. Proverbs 15:27 clearly condemns bribery, while Prov. 17:8; 18:16; and 21:14 acknowledge its efficacy. Most critical scholars in the first three quarters of the twentieth century have attempted to explain these discontinuities as the result of multiple authorship and editorial additions.

A comparison of Prov. 13:14 and 14:27 indicates that these two sayings have a line and a half in common. But 14:27 says *"The fear of the LORD is a fountain of life, so that one may avoid the snares of death,"* while 13:14 says *"The teaching of the wise is a fountain of life, so that one may avoid the snares of death."* Scholars in the late nineteenth and early twentieth centuries found it easiest to assume that the more secular of these two statements (13:14) was the older version and that 14:27 was a "correction" made by a later, more pious editor. Thus many analysts began to assume that the more overtly religious elements in Proverbs were late editorial additions to an "earlier" core of utilitarian wisdom. The apparent piety of some and the blatant non-piety of other sayings was explained as the result of the reworking of older materials by pious redactors or editors. "Old wisdom" was thought to be essentially pragmatic in nature and later Yahwistic editing was believed to account for sayings such as Prov. 12:2, in which the LORD was said to act as the agent of retribution who stood between an act and its consequences.[22]

Similar conclusions were drawn about the contradictions in Ecclesiastes. While many of the conflicts in Proverbs could be attributed to its composite nature as a collection of loosely related or unrelated sayings, Ecclesiastes does not have any obvious indications that it should be understood as an anthology. Several passages in Ecclesiastes contain comments *about* Qohelet rather than statements by him. At the beginning (1:1–2) and at the end of Ecclesiastes (12:8–10), as well as once in the middle (7:27), someone other than Qohelet speaks in the third person *about* Qohelet and about what he was known to have said and done. However, in many places, beginning with 1:12, Qohelet refers to himself in the first person (using "I"). But a careful, thoughtful reading of the book raises the question of whether all of the statements made in the first person sections of the book could have been equally advocated by Qohelet.

In Eccl. 3:17, the speaker, who refers to himself as "I," says to himself, "God will judge the righteous and the wicked." But only two verses later he says that the fate of human beings is the same as that of beasts: "as one dies, so dies the other." The speaker in Eccl. 5:4 recommends that one pay one's vows to avoid God's displeasure, but Eccl. 9:2 asserts that "one fate comes to all, to the good and the evil . . . to those who sacrifice and those who do not sacrifice. As are the good, so are the sinners; those who swear are like those who shun an oath." On the one hand, the speaker apparently confesses "I know that it will be well with those who fear God . . . but it will not be well with the wicked" (Eccl. 8:12), but on the other hand, he asserts, "There are righteous people who are treated according to the conduct of the wicked, and there are wicked people who are treated according to the conduct of the righteous" (Eccl. 8:14).

If one assumes that Ecclesiastes is the result of (or is shaped in the form of) either a dialogue between a pupil and a teacher or a forum in which various individuals' opinions are aired, then variations in viewpoint are easily explained. Thus, Gregory the Great thought Solomon was in dialogue with a fool. There are, however, no indications in the text itself that this is the case.

In the late nineteenth and early twentieth centuries, the typical critical scholar found it

> inconceivable that a writer should say in the same chapter, that the wise man and the fool have the same fate (2:15, 16) and that there is no good but eating and drinking and enjoying one's self (2:24), and also say that God punishes the sinner and rewards the good (2:26).[23]

Thus, many readers of the text in the first half of the twentieth century felt "compelled" to conclude that those statements that *both* contain orthodox Jewish doctrine *and* contradict other statements in the book must be from the hand of one or more editors or glossators, who added phrases and/or passages to the original statements of Qohelet in order to make the original conform to their own notions of faith and piety.

More recent analysts have suggested that Qohelet's style is deliberately dialectical. Sometimes he quotes the opinions of those with whom he disagrees in order to refute them, and sometimes he uses a "Yes, but . . ." style of discussion in order to show the nonabsolute nature of many propositions his contemporaries accept as absolute truths.[24] In effect, the author of Ecclesiastes says to himself (or to his audience), "Yes, it may be true as the tradition tells us that 'it will be well with those who fear God' and 'it will not be well with the wicked' (8:12–13), *but* experience tells us that '*on earth,* there are righteous people who are treated according to the conduct of the wicked, and there are wicked people who are treated according to the conduct of the righteous'" (8:14).[25]

The discontinuities and contradictions in Job are more difficult to analyze. Since the poetic section in chapters 3—27 presents itself as a forum or a debate between Job and his three "friends," the reader is not surprised to find conflicts between Job's assertions and those made by Eliphaz, Bildad, and Zophar. However, there are also obvious discontinuities between the way Job himself is portrayed in the prose narrative (1:1–2:13; 42:7–16) and in the poetic speeches (in chapters 3—37). The image many readers have of Job as a model of piety and faithful endurance in the face of calamity is drawn from the prose narrative, which acts as a framework or as a prologue and an epilogue to the book in its present form. In the prose story, Job's inital response to the loss of his children and his livelihood is "Naked I came from my mother's womb, and naked shall I return there; the LORD gave, and the LORD has taken away; blessed be the name of the LORD" (1:21). However, Job's attitude seems to undergo a radical change with the beginning of the poetic passages that comprise the center section of the book. Almost everything Job says in the poetic sections of the book conflicts with traditional notions of faithfulness in the face of adversity. In chapters 3—31 Job complains bitterly about the injustice of God. Job says that God "mocks at the calamity of the innocent. The earth is given into the hand of the wicked; he covers the eyes of its judges" (Job 9:23b–24). Job complains that the wicked commit all sorts of crimes, causing their victims all sorts of pain and deprivation without being punished (Job 24:1–12). Either "God charges no one with wrongdoing" (according to the NIV of 24:12c) or "God pays no attention to their [the victims'] prayer" (NRSV).

While Job's poetic assertions may seem blasphemous to traditional readers (as they did to some of the early rabbis), the prose conclusion says that the LORD affirms the accuracy of Job's statements. The LORD says to Eliphaz, "My wrath is kindled against you and against your two friends; for you have not spoken of me what is right, as my servant Job has" (42:7; see 42:8). And in the end, even though Job had presented forceful poetic arguments against his friends' belief that God would always reward the faithful, the prose epilogue says Job's "faithfulness" was lavishly rewarded (42:10–17).

Thus, many scholars have concluded that the prose narrative framework could not have been composed by the author of the poetic dialogues. However, it has also been popularly assumed that the poet took an existing narrative (thought by many to have been an ancient folktale) and used it in the composition of the whole.[26] Furthermore, an overwhelming majority of scholars have considered the Elihu speeches in chapters 32—37 to be a secondary insertion into the final form of the book. Elihu (who is not mentioned either in the prologue or in the epilogue) suddenly appears in 32:1 and speaks at length without interruption. His speeches intrude, disrupting the logical continuity between the end of Job's last statement in 31:40 and the beginning of the LORD's response to Job in 38:1. No one responds to Elihu, who disappears without being mentioned again in the remainder of the book. Finally, careful readers have frequently noted that the LORD is said to "answer" Job in three different places (38:1; 40:1; and 40:6) with two different types of answers (38:1–39:30 and 40:6–41:34). Job is also said to respond to the Lord in similar ways on two different occasions (40:3–5 and 42:1–6), prompting scholars to suggest that the original composition has been augmented by later additions.

D. "Earlier" Wisdom and "Later" Wisdom?

Dividing the various wisdom books into hypothetically "earlier" and "later" segments enabled critics to disparage or ignore those portions of the material they considered "secular" or contrary to the mainstream of Israel's religious thinking. Walther Eichrodt represents a common opinion among biblical theologians in the first half of the twentieth century when he concludes that "early" wisdom in Israel was borrowed from foreign wisdom and that its strongly secular flavor represents Israel's failure to see the moral inferiority of pagan wisdom assumptions.[27]

William McKane also equated the "earliest" with the most secular aspects of the wisdom tradition and suggested that these elements could be traced back to the elder statesmen and bureaucrats who were responsible for the administration of the government in early Israel. McKane argued that the pragmatic, utilitarian advice these "wise men" gave to the Davidic kings clashed with the teachings of the prophets (e.g., Isa. 5:19–24; 10:13–19; 19:11–13; 29:14–16; 30:1–5; 31:1–3; Jer. 49:7; Ezek. 28:2). Thus, he concluded that those wisdom sayings that promoted the power of God over human plans (such as Prov. 16:9; 19:21; 20:24; 21:30) were additions made as a form of rebuttal to the claims of "old wisdom."

Others, however, challenged the thesis that the earliest forms of Israel's wisdom tradition could be characterized as secular pragmatism. In the 1970s Gerhard von Rad argued that rational and religious perceptions were one and the same in Israel and that wisdom represented a faithful form of human response to God's creative and redemptive activities.[28] Von Rad agreed that wisdom sayings probably originated in the royal bureaucracies, but he thought Yahwistic piety was inherent in wisdom from its beginnings.

Roland Murphy also questioned the legitimacy of assuming that the wise in Israel shared their Egyptian neighbors' ma'at mentality. After all, it is clear that Job blames the Lord for his situation, not some perceived basic order in the cosmos.[29]

E. The Origin of Wisdom

1. From Ancient Near Eastern Sources?

The discovery that Israel's wisdom literature had much in common with the wisdom traditions of Egypt and Mesopotamia (including Sumer, Babylon, and Assyria) led many to assume that wisdom in Israel originated and was perpetuated in the same way ancient Near Eastern wisdom was—in the royal courts and in the schools that were needed to train scribes to work in royal bureaucracies. The Old Testament associates the "wise men" of Egypt with the courtiers who advise the Pharaoh (Gen. 41:8; Exod. 7:11; Isa. 19:11), and Egyptian texts portray them in similar ways. Both Egyptian and Mesopotamian texts equate the wise with palace scribes, who used their reading and writing skills both to record and to advise the actions of kings.

Among the documents found with the remains of a Jewish community that lived in the sixth century B.C.E. on the island of Elephantine (in the middle of the Nile) is a text known as the "Words of Ahiqar." This document calls Ahiqar a "wise scribe" in the royal courts of Assyria and contains around 100 wisdom sayings, including proverbs, fables, and riddles.[30] Egyptian texts such as "In Praise of the Learned Scribes" and "The Satire on the Trade"[31] indicate that scribes in Egypt were also connected both with wisdom and with royal bureaucracies. It is also clear from ancient Near Eastern texts that there were schools in which scribes were trained to work in the governmental bureaucracies in Mesopotamia and Egypt. However, it is not clear whether Israel's wisdom literature developed in similar settings or for analogous reasons.

2. Origins within Israel?

Scholarly discussions over the past century have debated and continue to debate whether wisdom in Israel originated with a professional class of scribes and advisers to the kings or evolved from the traditions of common people, handed down in families and clans. Were the "wise" first of all heads of families and tribes,[32] or were they counselors to the kings of Israel and Judah?[33] Were the wisdom writers professionals (such as teachers in scribal schools)[34] or "intellectuals" who had the time, energy, and financial resources to devote to the production, collection, and revision of wisdom literature?[35]

Those who argue that Israel's wisdom literature originated with a professional class of wise men and women who worked for a living in the royal courts usually assume that Solomon (with his many international contacts) brought foreign forms of bureaucracy into Israel. The reference to Hezekiah's men in Prov. 25:1 seems to indicate that Solomon's descendants continued their ancestor's practice. Jeremiah 18:18 seems to list the "wise" as an identifiable group alongside priests and prophets. Second Samuel 14 and 20 refer to two women who seem to have a recognized role as "wise women"; both seem to play a role in national politics and both use proverbs as a part of their bargaining procedures (2 Sam. 14:14; 20:18).

A strong minority of scholars have argued that the connection of Proverbs and Ecclesiastes with Solomon and his administration was legendary and a product of postexilic editorial activity rather than a historically reliable tradition.[36] The presence of relatively few references to kings and their concerns in the canonical wisdom texts indicates that very few wisdom writers were royal courtiers. In Proverbs the only explicit link between the royal court and the sayings of the wise is found in the reference to Hezekiah's "men" (25:1), who either "copied" or updated the sayings now found in 25:1–29:27. The Hezekian collection begins with three sayings (each consisting of two verses) that refer to the king or his courtiers. The first (25:2–3) and third (vv. 6–7) sayings give advice on how to act in the presence of a king. The middle saying (vv. 4–5) is concerned with the characteristics of a good king. Other sayings in the Hezekian collection tie the stability of the land to the wisdom and the righteousness of its king (28:2, 16; 29:4, 12, 14). The words of Lemuel's mother (in Proverbs 31) seem to be advice from a non-Israelite queen mother to a young king or soon-to-be king.

A few sayings in Proverbs hold up high standards for a king to follow (16:12–13; 20:8, 26, 28; 21:1). Other sayings remind their listeners of the wisdom of keeping someone as powerful as a king happy (16:14–15; 19:12; 20:2; 23:1–3; 24:21; 28:15). But taken as whole, statements dealing with the administration of royal bureaucracies make up a very small part of the concerns addressed in the wisdom literature. "Of the 538 sayings in Prov 10—29, only about 30 have the courtier as the primary addressee."[37] Many more sayings are concerned with individual morals and interpersonal relationships (diligence and sloth, humility and pride, anger and arguments, hypocrisy, gossip, slander, etc.). The majority of proverbs reflect the concerns of common people who are engaged in common occupations, such as farming (e.g., 6:8; 10:5; 27:23–27; 28:19), commerce (e.g., 11:1; 16:11; 20:10, 14, 23), and the raising of children (e.g., 13:24; 19:18; 22:6; 29:15, 17).

Thus, some scholars have suggested that the "wise" were never understood to be a professional class in Israel. A close look at the way the terms "wise" and "wisdom" are used in biblical Hebrew indicates that wisdom cuts across occupational and class lines. The "wise" are those whose natural intelligence or acquired skills can be demonstrated in any profession. The "wise" might have been "intellectuals" who served the community in a variety of ways, not just as employees of the royal bureaucracy. Thus, for instance, Job's friends are not pictured as "sages" or scibes belonging to a professional class, but as "educated farmers."[38]

Since the existence of schools for the training of scribes and administrators in neighboring cultures is clearly demonstrable, some scholars argue that there must have been similar schools serving similar purposes in Israel.[39] However, there are no explicit references to schools in the Hebrew Bible. The reference to a "house of instruction" in the Apocryphal Wisdom of Sirach (51:23) stands as evidence for practices in the second century B.C.E. but says nothing about earlier periods in the history of Israel. Elisha's disciples may have been referring to a school of some sort when they complained that the place where they "sat" (also translated "lived") under the prophet's leadership was too small for them (2 Kings 6:1), and 1 Chron. 25:8 uses the terms "teachers" and "pupils" in a context that assumes there was a school for musicians connected with the temple. Proverbs 5:13 certainly seems to imply a situation of formal education, and the phrase translated "get wisdom" in Prov. 4:5, 7 could also mean "buy wisdom," implying school fees.[40] However, not all references to teachers and students necessarily imply a formal school setting. The editor who speaks about Qohelet in Eccl. 12:9 says that he "taught the people knowledge," but nothing is said about the setting in which such instruction took place. Clearly education can take place in settings other than schools. Since the listener in Proverbs is frequently called "my son" and is repeatedly urged to heed parental teachings," some readers conclude that it would be more accurate to say that the bulk of education offered by and to the "wise" took place in a family setting rather than in schools as we know them.[41]

F. Did the "Wise" Influence Other Traditions?

It is universally agreed that some stylistic features, literary forms, vocabulary, and thematic concerns can be said to be "characteristic" of the wisdom literature. But there has been great debate over the degree to which the presence of one or more of these features in historical, narrative, prophetic, poetic, or apocalyptic texts can be said to indicate "wisdom influence" on other Old Testament traditions. Gunkel's highly influential work on the categorization of psalms highlighted what he called "wisdom poetry" among the Psalms.[42] Later readers have used the term "wisdom psalms" to designate psalms that manifest themes, forms, vocabulary, or worldviews characteristically associated with the wise in Israel. Psalms 1 and 37 resemble Proverbs 1—9 in the way they distinguish between the respective fates of the righteous and the wicked. Psalm 49 begins like a wisdom Instruction, specifically mentions speaking wisdom (v. 3), and contains themes that are similar to Ecclesiastes (vv. 10–12, 17, 20). Psalm 73 struggles with the problem of retribution in a way that is reminiscent of Job. However, there is little scholarly agreement about the criteria that might be used to decide which psalms can be called wisdom psalms.[43]

Gerhard von Rad suggested that the Joseph narrative in Genesis belonged to the category of early wisdom writing. He argued that Joseph was pictured as a model wisdom student whose virtue, piety, and learning enabled him to become an administrator in Pharaoh's court and that Joseph's statement to his brothers in Gen. 50:20 ("You meant evil against me, but God meant it for good") reflected the wisdom way of thinking about the events of human history.[44] Others, following in von Rad's footsteps, argued that the "succession narrative" in 2 Samuel 9—1 Kings 2 was a dramatization of the wisdom ideals presented in Proverbs,[45] that Genesis 1—2 contained a number of "sapiential motifs,"[46] and that Deuteronomy was formulated in scribal circles associated with the Judean monarchy.[47]

Like Proverbs, Deuteronomy asserts that good behavior will be rewarded and bad behavior punished. Proverbs 1—9 and Deuteronomy both insist that a clear distinction can be made between actions that will enhance and lengthen life and those that will not. Both are concerned with *tôrāh* (teaching or instruction), which must be handed down from parent to child in order to guarantee the survival of future generations (compare Deut. 6:6–8 with Prov. 1:8–9; 3:1–4; 6:20–22). However, in some ways, Deuteronomy and Proverbs seem diametrically opposed. In Deuteronomy, the *tôrāh* (instruction) that promises long life, security, and prosperity to those who heed it comes directly from God through the mediation of Moses (Deut. 5:33; 6:3, 20–25, etc.). But in Proverbs such life-giving instruction (*tôrāh*) comes from wisdom (i.e., from human reflection on the observable regularities of life) through the mediation of the wise. Only the forms of speech are similar. The underlying assumptions upon which the speakers base their exhortations are quite different. And only those who assume the Instructions in Proverbs 1—9 are older than Deuteronomy can ignore the possibility that it was the sages who used Deuteronomy as a model for their writings rather than the other way around.

The question of whether wisdom traditions might have influenced the prophets also generated a flood of scholarly theories. Up until the middle of the twentieth century, most scholars would have argued that Israel's prophets were diametrically opposed to wisdom ways of thinking. While the prophets may have known and made use of vocabulary and forms of expression that more commonly occur in wisdom literature, it was generally assumed that the prophetic and the wisdom traditions were inherently antithetical. Prophets in Israel and Judah often stood over against the policies and practices of the kings. If the "wise" consisted mostly of professional courtiers and scribes, involved with royal administration, then it would not be surprising to find evidence of some degree of enmity between the prophets and the royal bureaucrats.[48] However, one prominent scholar who studied Isaiah's use of vocabulary and forms of speech that might be said to be characteristic of wisdom traditions (e.g., "wise," "understanding," and "counsel" in Isa. 9:5; 11:2) concluded that Isaiah had begun his career as a sage, but that he eventually turned against his origins in order to take a strong stand against the self-reliance preached by the wisdom teachers.[49]

Critical arguments have been mustered both for and against the supposition that the prophets' use of wisdom genres and wisdom rhetoric indicated "wisdom influence" in the prophetic tradition.[50] For instance, Amos uses the "consecutive numerals" form found in Prov. 30:15–31,[51] and there are similarities between the doxologies of Amos and Job. Does this mean that Amos was "influenced" by wisdom traditions? Could it be said that Amos modeled his "admonition speeches" on early clan wisdom admonitions?[52] Or would it be more accurate to say that both the sages and the prophets drew from a common pool of social, cultural, linguistic, and rhetorical resources?[53] Since Israelite prophets used forms of speech drawn from the culture in which they lived (taunt songs, dirges, hymns, legal indictments, etc.), the mere use of a parable or a wisdom admonition does not make a prophet into a sage. "It is not a question of the direct influence of the sages or of the wisdom literature, but rather of an approach to reality that was shared by all Israelites in varying degrees."[54]

G. Current Issues and Trends

As the twentieth century draws to a close, it is no longer widely assumed that scholars can either define or find the origins of a discrete wisdom tradition in Israel. It is now generally acknowledged that neither wisdom nor prophecy were static traditions. Both developed over the course of time. Instead of trying to find wisdom "influence" on the hypothetical "original" prophet, scholars today are more likely to explain the presence of a wisdom-like utterance in the final form of a prophetic book as an addition made by later editors or scribal compilers.[55]

1. The Place of Wisdom in Israel

Recent decades have brought about remarkable changes in how wisdom is valued and how it is seen to fit into the overall picture of Israel's history and theology. While there is still some debate over the "social location" of wisdom (whether wisdom thinking and texts developed in family, in clan and tribe, or among the elite, in royal courts and scribal schools), the dominant current opinion seems to be that "No single sociological group was responsible for the sapiential corpus, whether family or royal court."[56] Instead it is commonly agreed that the "social groups responsible for the writing of the wisdom traditions span epochs and class settings. . . . It is this diversity of origins . . . that contributes to the ecumenicity of wisdom's worldview."[57]

Instead of looking for specific instances of wisdom vocabulary, rhetoric or themes in nonwisdom texts, biblical scholars today typically emphasize ways in which "wisdom insights have affected both the shaping of the Hebrew canon and the reading strategy recommended in certain parts of it."[58] Instead of looking for discrete units of wisdom "influence," interpreters today are more likely to see wisdom supporting all of the religious thinking of Judaism in the postexilic period. Thus, recent scholars have argued that when the destruction of the temple discredited the cultic world view that prevailed up until the end of the monarchy, wisdom ways of thinking helped people to "theologize" and spiritualize their religion, so that intentions and attitudes could be counted as important as the actual performance of ritual actions.[59] "That Yahweh could speak through the world of experience as well as through the mouths of his prophets was wisdom's distinctive contribution to Hebrew theology."[60]

2. The Valuing of One's Own Experience

The wisdom texts emphasize the validity of human experience as a basis for thinking theologically. Scholars have long recognized that both Job and Ecclesiastes use their own and other peoples' experiences to argue that neither the righteous nor the wicked regularly receive their "just deserts" (e.g., Job 21:7–34; Eccl. 2:11; 3:16; 4:1–8, etc.). Only recently have critical readers begun to recognize the essentially experiential nature of proverbial sayings. Unlike laws or commandments that *advocate* certain types of behavior, most proverbs simply *describe* a type of human behavior that occurs often enough to be familiar to both the speaker and the listener. And unlike theological or philosophical statements, most proverbs are understood by their users to express contextually limited truths. Thus, for instance, the users of a common English proverbs such as "penny wise, pound foolish" know that this saying does not claim universality for the truth it contains. No speaker of proverbs asks us to believe that every person who handles small amounts of money wisely is invariably shortsighted or deals unwisely with larger amounts. Nor does the user of this proverb imply that such behavior is desirable or condoned by the speaker. Understanding the nature of proverbs allows the reader to see that the sentence proverbs comment and generalize on the basis of their observations, but they do not always approve of what they see. Sayings such as, "The poor are disliked even by their neighbors, but the rich have many friends" (Prov. 14:20), are observations about human experience. Such observations may prove true in many human settings, but not in all. Furthermore, the speaker who makes this observation based on his or her experiences does not necessarily approve of the reality it describes.[61]

While some proverbs do seem to advocate or prohibit a certain course of action, even these "prescriptive" sayings are clearly meant to be carefully matched to fit appropriate settings. Thus, the wise can deliberately list two completely opposite pieces of advice, one right after the other (as in Prov. 26:4–5), because they know that circumstances differ. Sometimes it is wise to "answer fools according to their folly" (26:5), and sometimes it is wiser not to do so (26:4). The wisdom sayings are not "rules" but generalizations based on observations. The wise in Israel articulate perceived patterns in experience, but they also recognize that experiences differ. No one set of human experiences can be taken as universally true. Sometimes, however, observations get absolutized. But when people (such as the friends of Job) mistake the contextually based observations of the wise for statements of absolute truth, then the wisdom tradition corrects itself. Job and Ecclesiastes protest the *misuse* of the "words of the wise" collected in Proverbs.

3. Feminist Appropriations of Wisdom

One of the most distinct developments in wisdom studies in the last quarter of the twentieth century is the degree to which wisdom ways of thinking have begun to appeal in particular to women and others whose experiences are not congruent with traditional "norms." In spite of the fact that Proverbs 1—9 is addressed to "my son," and in spite of the well-known and often quoted misogynistic portions of the sentence literature (e.g., 21:9, 19; 25:24), the book of Proverbs offers women ways to see positive reflections of their roles in the production of wisdom. Women as well as men are counted among the wise in Israel. Mothers are pictured as playing an important part in their children's education (Prov. 1:8; 4:3; 6:20; 10:1; 15:20; 17:25; 19:26; 23:22, 25; 30:17), and women are accepted as a source of instruction in the framework sections of Proverbs. A "woman of strength" is highly praised in the final chapter (Prov. 31:10–31), and Wisdom is personified as a skilled, articulate and powerful woman in Prov. 1:20–33 and 8:4–36.

Personification is a literary technique in which an inanimate quality is said to speak and act like a human being. In Hebrew the word translated "wisdom" is grammatically feminine, so when wisdom takes on a life of its own, seeming to achieve a degree of independence from the wisdom teacher, Wisdom speaks as a woman (1:20–33; 8:1–31). In the Hebrew version of Proverbs it is fairly clear that Wisdom was not understood to be an entity in its own right. Wisdom was the personification of a quality that Yahweh demonstrated in the creation of the universe (Prov. 3:19–20). However, ambiguities in the meaning of several words used in Wisdom's self description in Prov. 8:22–31 allowed the Greek translation of this passage to be used as a proof text by opposing parties in the early church's debates on Christology and trinitarian theology.

In the Gospel of John and in some of Paul's christological statements, Jesus Christ is described in terms that closely resemble the description of Wisdom personified in Proverbs. Paul said that Christ crucified was "the wisdom of God" (1 Cor. 1:24), and Wisdom imagery seems to have helped shape John's concept of Christ as the *Logos* (Word). By the middle of the second century c.e. (the time of

Justin Martyr), most Christians associated Wisdom (*Sophia* in Greek) and the Word (*Logos* in Greek) with the pre-existent character of Christ.

In the early fourth century C.E. opponents on both sides of the debate that ended in the Council of Nicaea assumed that what was said about Wisdom in Prov. 8:22–31 could be applied to Jesus Christ. Their difference of opinion centered around their different ways of reading the passage. The Arians argued that Wisdom (equated with Jesus Christ) was "created" by God and thus was a creature, not fully divine. Those who won the debate and established the orthodox trinitarian doctrine argued that the term the Arians translated "created" in this passage meant "begotten" not "made." Thus a number of early Christian theologians argued that the Son was the Wisdom and the Word of the Father, fully divine and of the same substance with the Father.[62] Wisdom could be used in prayer as a name for the triune God[63] and could function as simply another name for the second person of the Trinity.[64]

In the Eastern Church, through the medieval period and into the modern era, both Orthodox and Catholic Christians continued to use Wisdom (under the Greek name *Sophia*) as an image of God. The numerous eastern churches named Hagia Sophia or Saint Sophia refer not to a human saint but to Jesus Christ as the Holy Wisdom of God. In Western Christianity (both Catholic and Protestant) interest in the Wisdom/Sophia of God waned until feminists in the last quarter of the twentieth century began to see the imagery of Wisdom/Sophia as an alternate and less exclusively masculine way of speaking about the triune God.

Women are not sympathetically portrayed in Ecclesiastes, and they are mentioned only in the prose narrative framework of Job. However, taken as a whole, all these texts encourage the valuing of one's own experience. Wisdom texts can nourish and support the argument that neither the experiences of males nor those of the ethnically dominant portions of a given society are normative for all human beings. The wisdom literature encourages its readers to test traditional formulations of "truth" over against their own experiences. Wisdom ways of thinking encourage women (and others whose experiences vary from the "norm" in their society) to use their own observations of reality to measure the truths of traditional dogmas. Feminists and other minority-group readers have begun to use the wisdom writings in a fashion worthy of the wise by adopting wisdom ways of thinking rather than accepting the conclusions reached by wisdom writers as expressions of absolute truth.[65]

4. Earlier and Later Wisdom?

In the late nineteenth and early twentieth centuries, it was generally thought that Israel's earliest (or "original") forms of Wisdom were secular or utilitarian in nature and that the statements with explicit theological content found in the final forms of Proverbs and Ecclesiastes were later additions that attempted to repudiate or to reinterpret the profane material. In the last quarter of the twentieth century, scholars have been more inclined to believe that "wisdom contained a religious element from the beginning,"[66] that the explicitly theological statments in proverbial wisdom are "an elucidation of mundane wisdom's fundamental religious grounding,"[67] and that "the God-sayings [in Proverbs] should be regarded as an intrinsic part of the wisdom tradition."[68] It is now generally acknowledged that there is no way to prove that either the explicitly religious or nonreligious sayings can be assigned to different groups from different time periods. Even evidence from non-Israelite sources, such as the Egyptian Instructions of Amenemope and the Aramaic sayings of Ahiqar, is now seen to indicate that "wisdom literature conventionally incorporated religious elements long before it reached Israel, if, indeed, it ever lacked them."[69]

5. Wisdom and Faith

There has not as yet developed any widely recognized consensus about the place of wisdom thinking in Israel's faith. However, people today are no longer so much inclined to think that wisdom ways of thinking are less than faithful. Wisdom's appeal to general revelation is now commonly understood to constitute an act of faith rather than "secular humanism." A few radical writers have continued to maintain that biblical wisdom is inherently pagan.[70] But most recent interpreters have moved away from earlier tendencies to disparage wisdom or to relegate it to the outer edges of Israel's theological circles. Wisdom is now most frequently seen as one of the several distinct and essential witnesses or theological forces that contributed to the shaping of the biblical canon.[71] Scholars today are more likely to say that "appeals to reason, tradition, and common sense do not need to be understood as standing in opposition to theological thinking"[72] or that "the worldview of wisdom in Proverbs does not represent a sharp break with the rest of ancient Israel's society, but only reflects a difference in emphases and interests."[73]

6. Creation Theology

While creation thelogy has long been identified with wisdom,[74] it has only been in the last decades of the twentieth century that influential theologians have attempted to build theologies that take God as Creator (rather than God as Savior or Redeemer) as the organizing principle of Israel's faith. If creation is seen as the lens through which the various strands of tradition are examined, then the wisdom literature moves from the periphery into the center of Israelite theology.[75]

If God is viewed first of all as Creator, then it becomes clear that God is not only concerned with Israel, but with humanity as a whole. Furthermore, it becomes apparent that God the Creator is not only concerned with the well-being of humanity but with the well-being of the cosmos as a whole. The LORD's speeches in Job 38—41 emphasize the care and concern God lavishes on the natural world. The animals with whom the LORD is intimately involved are not the domesticated kind that can be of any use to humankind. These speeches imply that God's interest and God's actions are not focused exclusively on humankind.[76] Thus, in the last decades of the twentieth century, wisdom literature and wisdom ways of thinking have both stimulated and supported a growing ecological theology that insists on valuing the needs of the rest of creation as well as the needs of humankind.

FOR FURTHER READING

Camp, Claudia V. *Wisdom and the Feminine in the Book of Proverbs.* Sheffield: Almond, 1985.

Crenshaw, James L. *Old Testament Wisdom: An Introduction.* Atlanta: John Knox, 1981.

Farmer, Kathleen A. *Who Knows What Is Good? A Commentary on the Books of Proverbs and Ecclesiastes.* Grand Rapids: Eerdmans,1991.

Good, Edwin M. *In Turns of Tempest: A Reading of Job with a Translation.* Stanford, Calif.: Stanford University Press, 1990.

Murphy, Roland E. *The Tree of Life: An Exploration of Biblical Wisdom Literature.* ABRL. New York: Doubleday, 1992.

Perdue, Leo G. *Wisdom and Creation: The Theology of Wisdom Literature.* Nashville: Abingdon, 1994.

Zuck, Roy B., ed. *Learning from the Sages: Selected Studies on the Book of Proverbs.* Grand Rapids: Baker, 1995.

6

THE SONGS OF ISRAEL

Psalms and Lamentations

JOHN H. HAYES

The books of Psalms and Lamentations are "poetical" in character. This factor can be seen in all modern translations in their attempts to print the text in arranged lines. The exact character of Hebrew poetry, however, is still a disputed matter, with some scholars denying that we should speak of poetry per se. Lines or half-lines, for example, do not rhyme and there are disputes about what role word count, the number of accented syllables, and meter play. Nonetheless, one factor is clear: the balancing of lines, repetition, and parallelism occur frequently in bib-lical "poetry." Part of a line or more than one line may repeat, modify, or expand a previous statement. For example,

> When Israel went forth from Egypt,
>   the house of Jacob from a people of strange language,
> Judah became God's sanctuary,
>   Israel his dominion. (Ps. 114:1–2)

> How lonely sits the city
>   that once was full of people!
> How like a widow she has become,
>   she that was great among nations!
> She that was a princess among the province
>   has become a vassal. (Lam. 1:1)

A simple reading of these passages allows one to see the repetition and parallel-ing of expressions and ideas and the balancing of material.

I. THE BOOK OF PSALMS

A. Content and Structure

The Hebrew Bible and English translations based on the Hebrew contain 150 psalms. The ancient Greek translation (the Septuagint, abbreviated LXX), still in use in the Greek Orthodox Church, contains a Psalm 151. This psalm also appears in one of the psalms scrolls from Qumran (the so-called Dead Sea Scrolls) but divided into two psalms. In some traditions of the Syriac Bible there are 155 psalms. (Of these additional psalms, Psalms 154 and 155, as well as 151, are found in 11QPs^a, a fragmentary scroll from cave 11 at Qumran that is dated near the beginning of the Common Era.) The content of the Hebrew Bible with its 150 psalms has been the standard content of Jewish and Western Christian canons.

Four general doxologies appear in the book of Psalms and divide it into five sub-books. These are:

> Blessed be the LORD, the God of Israel,
> from everlasting to everlasting.
> Amen and Amen. (Ps. 41:13 [Heb. 41:14])

> Blessed be the LORD, the God of Israel,
> who alone does wondrous things.
> Blessed be his glorious name forever;
> may his glory fill the whole earth.
> Amen and Amen.
> The prayers of David son of Jesse are ended. (Ps. 72:18–20)

> Blessed is the LORD forever
> Amen and Amen. (Ps. 89:52 [Heb. 89:53])
> Blessed be the LORD, the God of Israel,
> from everlasting to everlasting.
> And let all the people say, "Amen."
> Praise the LORD. (Ps. 106:48)

That these doxologies divide the overall book into five smaller divisions or books is evinced by the fact that none of the doxologies really belongs as an integral component to the psalms to which they have been attached and by the appearance of the "amens" that are found nowhere else in the Psalms. Many modern translations recognize this fivefold division of the book and add headings designating these subunits as Book 1 (Psalms 1—41), Book 2 (Psalms 42—72), Book 3 (Psalms 73—89), Book 4 (Psalms 90—106), and Book 5 (Psalms 107—150), although such headings are not found in the Hebrew text.

This division into five books is probably to be understood as an editing device employed by the final redactors to make the book of Psalms similar in pattern to the fivefold division of the Torah or Pentateuch. Rabbinic teachers commented on this fivefold division and its parallel to the Pentateuch: "As Moses gave five books of law to Israel, so David gave five books of Psalms to Israel" (the midrash on Psalm 1).

Many of the individual psalms have headings or superscriptions. In fact, 116 of the 150 psalms have such superscriptions or titles. (Even more psalms have titles in the Greek and Syriac versions.) These titles range from lengthy comments (see Psalm 18, which is identical to 2 Samuel 22) to a single word (Psalm 98). Psalm 10 has no title because it was originally a continuation of Psalm 9; the two together form an alphabetic (acrostic) poem. Psalm 43 has no title since it is a continuation of Psalm 42, as the refrains indicate. The untitled or "orphan" psalms are found in four of the five books:

Book 1:   Psalms 1, 2, and 33
Book 2:   Psalm 71
Book 3:   all have titles
Book 4:   Psalms 91, 93—97, 99, 104—106
Book 5:   Psalms 107, 111—119, 135—137, 146—150

These titles contain varied forms of information.

1. Some appear to be musical directions perhaps addressed to the "leader" (or "choirmaster," which appears in over a third of the psalm titles). These include such statements as "with stringed instruments" (Psalms 4, 6, 54, 55, 61, 67, 76), which indicates that some of the directions probably referred to the manner of musical accompaniment, and such notations as "according to lilies" (Psalms 45, 69, 80), which may have referred to commonly used tunes.

2. Some terms appear to refer to the type of composition: "a psalm," which occurs fifty-seven times, and "song," appearing thirty times. Other such terminology is often left untranslated.

3. Other information refers to the occasion for using the psalm: Psalm 30—"a song at the dedication of the temple"; Psalms 38 and 70—"for the memorial offering"; Psalm 92—"a song for the sabbath day"; Psalm 102—"a prayer of one afflicted, when faint and pleading before the LORD."

4. Other information in the titles refers to individuals. The most commonly occurring name is David, which appears in 73 titles. This led in the course of time to the assumption of David's authorship of the psalms. Later versions, like the Greek and Syriac, have his name in even more titles than the Hebrew. In a prose insert in a fragmentary psalm scroll from cave 11 at Qumran, David is described as the psalm writer par excellence:

> David, the son of Jesse, was a wise man and a light like the light of the sun and a writer and discerning and perfect in all his ways before God and men. And Yahweh gave to him a spirit of discernment and enlightenment. And he wrote 3,600 psalms (*těhillîm*); and songs (*shîr*) to sing before the altar over the burnt-offering, the daily regular burnt-offering, for all the days of the year, 364; and for the sabbath offerings, 52 songs; and for the offering of the new moons and for all the days of the assemblies and for the day of atonement, 30 songs. And all the psalms which he spoke were 446, and songs to make music over the afflicted, 4. And the total was 4,050. All of these he spoke through prophecy which was given to him from before the Most High (11QPs[a] col. 17, lines 2–11).

Other names and groups are mentioned in the titles: sons of Korah (Psalms 42—49, 84—85, 87—88), Asaph (Psalms 50, 73—83), Solomon (Psalms 72, 127), Heman (Psalm 88), Ethan (Psalm 89), Moses (Psalm 90), and Jeduthun (Psalms

39, 62, 77). This led the rabbis of the Babylonian Talmud to note, "Who wrote the Scriptures? . . . David wrote the book of Psalms, including in it the work of the ten elders, namely, Adam, Melchizedek, Abraham, Moses, Heman, Jeduthun, Asaph, and the three sons of Korah" (*b. B. Bat.* 15a).

Thirteen psalm titles have historical statements that relate the content of the psalms to various circumstances in the life of David. The number of historical settings provided for some of the Davidic psalms has been expanded in the Greek and even more so in the Syriac text and the Aramaic Targum. The following are the thirteen psalms that specify a particular historical episode in the life of David that supposedly provided the occasion for composition. The parallels to these historical references from the books of Samuel are provided in the right-hand column.

Psalm 3	2 Sam. 15:1–18:33
Psalm 7	without parallel
Psalm 18	2 Samuel 22
Psalm 34	1 Sam. 21:10–15 (but where he feigned madness before Achish not Abimelech)
Psalm 51	2 Sam. 11:1–12:14
Psalm 52	1 Sam. 22:6–10
Psalm 54	1 Sam. 23:14–24
Psalm 56	1 Sam. 21:10–15; 27:1–4 (in neither of these passages is David seized by the Philistines)
Psalm 57	1 Sam. 22:1; 24:1–7
Psalm 59	1 Sam. 19:8–17
Psalm 60	2 Sam. 8:3–8; 10:15–20; 1 Kings 11:15–16
Psalm 63	1 Sam. 24:1–7; 2 Sam. 15:1–16:14
Psalm 142	1 Sam. 22:1; 24:1–7

B. The Form-Critical Approach

Anyone reading the book of psalms straight through for the first time is apt to be impressed by both the diversity and similarity of the material. The diversity is reflected in the fact that the work contains prayers and petitions and sometimes praise directly addressed to God, praise of God that speaks of the divine in the third person, proclamation addressed to human audiences, thanksgiving addressed either to God or humans, divine speech addressed to humans, shifts back and forth between singular and plural speakers, and addresses and texts that appear to be scripts written to accompany ritual activity. The similarity and repetitiveness of the material is found in the fact that many psalms repeat or parallel themes, descriptions, and even terminology found in other psalms.

This similarity of outline and mood in the psalms has led scholars to try and arrange the psalms into groups so as to discuss them in classes. Psalms studies in the twentieth century have thus strongly emphasized genre analysis. Here the attempt is made to classify the psalms into various classes or literary types on the basis of their form, structure, and content. Already in his 1811 Psalms commentary,

Wilhelm de Wette (1780–1849) had divided the psalms into various classes primarily on the basis of content. He wrote of the following groupings: (1) hymns in praise of God, (2) national psalms concerned with the history of Israel and Judah as the people of God, (3) Zion and temple psalms, (4) royal psalms, (5) various forms of laments, and (6) general religious and moral psalms.

This approach reached its apex in the writings of Hermann Gunkel (1862–1932), whose work remains foundational for practically all contemporary psalms research. Decades of his work on the psalms were summed up in his *Einleitung in die Psalmen: Die Gattungen der religösen Lyrik Israels* (1933; completed during Gunkel's final illness by his student Joachim Begrich). Although this work has never been translated into English, Gunkel's main views are presented in an English-language booklet published in 1967, which contains a translation of one of his dictionary articles on the topic.[1] The finest discussion of his approach can be found in the survey by A. R. Johnson.[2]

Gunkel divided the psalms into five primary literary types.

a. The first of these genres was the *hymn,* which contains the following elements:

1. *Introductory call to praise* (which was originally addressed to the choir, nation, or other praising group) or *an affirmation of praise.*
2. The *main body* of the hymn praising Yahweh's attributes and deeds. These might be given expression in the form of participial phrases, separate sentences, rhetorical questions, or other grammatical forms.
3. *Conclusion,* which might parallel the introductory formula or express a wish, petition or blessing.

Gunkel argued that the hymn was originally intended for use in worship services at the sanctuaries, especially at the great and important annual festivals and national celebrations. Psalms 8, 19, 29, 33, 46, 48, 65, 67, 68, 76, 84, 87, 96, 98, 100, 103, 104, 105, 111, 113, 114, 117, 122, 135, 136, 145, 146, 147, 148, 149, and 150 were placed in this general class.

Gunkel separated out a special subgroup within the larger category of hymns. He called these "hymns/songs of Yahweh's enthronement." Into this special group he placed Psalms 47, 93, 96:10–13; 97, and 99. These hymns celebrate the rule and kingship of Yahweh. Gunkel believed that these psalms proclaimed the final, eschatological rule of God and that this was a motif the psalm writers had picked up from the prophets. Gunkel argued that these hymns were especially dependent upon the preaching of Second Isaiah (Isaiah 40—55).

b. The second genre or *Gattung* Gunkel discussed was the *community laments.* Unlike the hymn, in which Yahweh is praised, the lament has its center in the appeal or petition for aid and assistance. Of the community lament, Gunkel wrote:

> The content of these laments may be divided into three parts. First, there is the lament proper, the purpose of which is to move Yahweh to compassion. . . . Then comes the prayer to Yahweh to remove the calamity, whatever it may be. At this point, all kinds of arguments are put before Yahweh with the intent of

moving him to think graciously upon his people and intervene in their behalf.
Here belong especially the reminders of their close relationship with Yahweh,
which he should not forget, or the memory of the past, in which he has so often helped them. Finally, there is the certainty of hearing.[3]

Gunkel placed Psalms 44, 74, 79, 80, 83, and, to a lesser degree, Psalms 58, 106,
and 125, into this group. He argued that this genre of psalms was employed on
days of community fasts that were proclaimed and observed when the whole community was threatened with some major calamity such as drought, famine, war,
pestilence, or foreign invasion. The community assembled at the sanctuary, and
along with signs of fasting, wearing sackcloth and ashes, weeping and wailing,
and sacrifice, poured out its soul to Yahweh in pleas for deliverance. In the communal laments "the woeful plight of the people is depicted; it is bewailed and
lamented with copious tears. These are the vengeful cries of a tormented people,
affronted in that which they consider most holy."[4]

c. A third class of psalms, according to Gunkel, is a group in which the earthly
king appears to have been the principal focus of concern. These he designated
royal psalms and placed the following in this category: Psalms 2, 18, 20, 21, 45,
72, 101, 110, 132, and 144:1–11. Gunkel recognized that this classification was
not strictly a form-critical assessment, since the only unifying element in these
psalms was the fact that all of them were concerned in one way or another with the
king. Of these psalms, Gunkel wrote:

> Psalm 20 was performed by the royal choir when the king went forth to bat-
> tle. The royal lament, Psalm 144:1–11, is to be assigned to the same setting.
> Psalm 18 is the thanksgiving prayer of a king upon his return from a cam-
> paign. Psalm 45 is a spirited and very ancient song sung to glorify the wed-
> ding of the sovereign. A song performed in the royal sanctuary on the occa-
> sion of the anniversary of the establishment of that sanctuary and the founding
> of the kingdom is Psalm 132. Most frequent are those poems which were
> sung at the king's enthronement or at the annual royal festival (Pss. 2, 21, 72,
> and 110); on the day of his enthronement the king himself made a solemn vow
> [Ps. 101].[5]

d. The largest category of psalms, according to Gunkel, consists of the psalms of
individual lament. These psalms all refer to conditions or situations of personal
distress and trouble. The component features of this genre are:

1. The *invocation or address to the deity* often with a personalizing appellation
   such as "Yahweh, my God" or "my God" and frequently with an initial
   statement of plea.
2. The *complaint,* in which the worshiper describes the conditions of distress.
3. The *petition* or *request for help,* which forms the heart of the lament, generally stated in an imperative form. Sometimes this section appears in the
   form of a wish with Yahweh spoken of in the third person. The petition or request prayed for the rescue and redemption of the worshiper and for the destruction of one's enemies.

4. The *motivations for divine intervention,* which contain references to such things as the grace and the righteousness of God.
5. The *affirmation of confidence,* which contains the worshiper's statements of confidence in the divine ability to help. These might be addressed with references to Yahweh in either second or third person.
6. *Assertion of innocence* or *confession of sin.*
7. *Conclusion* often expressing a statement of assurance and/or a vow plus hymnic elements.

Gunkel assigned the following psalms to this type: 3, 5, 6, 7, 13, 17, 22, 25, 26, 27:7–14; 28, 31, 38, 39, 42, 43, 51, 54, 55, 56, 57, 61, 63, 64, 69, 70, 71, 86, 88, 102, 109, 120, 130, 140, 141, 142, 143.

Gunkel also associated what he called "psalms of confidence" (4, 11, 16, 23, 27:1–6; 62, 131) with this class and saw them as independent expressions of the affirmation of confidence (see number 5 above). The individual psalms of lamentation have a

> very pronounced style; almost invariably the same thoughts and images recur. The peculiar and recurring situation in this psalm type is that of the supplicant who, in the midst of some illness which is a matter of life and death, must at the same time complain about his enemies who are persecuting and slandering him.[6]

e. A second class of individual psalms are those of *personal thanksgiving* (18, 30, 32, 34, 40:2–12; 41, 66, 92, 116, 118, 138). These psalms, according to Gunkel, had their origin in rituals of sacrificial thanksgiving as references in them to sacrifice and fulfillment vows suggest. The following elements appear in these psalms:

1. *Introductory statement of thanksgiving or praise.*
2. *Description of the distress and redemption* from which the person had been saved. This might contain references to God in the second or third person.
3. *Confession of Yahweh as redeemer.*
4. *Proclamation of thanksgiving sacrifice.*
5. *Conclusion* often containing hymnic or petitionary elements.

In describing the usage of these psalms, Gunkel wrote:

> The scene which we must try to visualize is something like this. The person who is to offer the sacrifice prostrates himself before the temple (Ps. 138:2). A number of relatives and acquaintances who expect to participate in the sacred meal stand around him (Ps. 22:26). Then, with a sacred goblet in his hand (Ps. 116:13) and prior to the actual sacrifice, he sings his song with a loud

voice. He may turn first to the bystanders and say something to this effect: "Listen, this is the way it was with me; so now thank Yahweh with me."[7]

In addition to these five major types of psalms, Gunkel distinguished a number of lesser or minor types, most represented by only a small number of examples in the Psalter. One of these was the category of *pilgrim psalms* (Psalms 84 and 122), which Gunkel thought might have been sung by pilgrims in their preparation, along their journey to, or at the time of their arrival at the sanctuary. Pilgrimages are occasionally referred to in the Hebrew Bible and the influence of the pilgrim's song may be reflected in some of the prophetical books.

A second class of the minor types are *victory songs,* which were employed in praise of military victories and heroes and/or Yahweh the granter of victory. No independent species of this form are found in the psalms, although remnants and the influence of such songs Gunkel noted in Psalms 46, 48, 66, 76, and 118.

A third minor category is the *communal thanksgiving psalms* represented by Psalms 66:8–12; 67, 124, and 129. In structure these are very similar to the individual psalms of thanksgiving, and their usage he located in special cultic services of thanksgiving.

A fourth minor category was the *legend,* in which narrative is the dominant characteristic. No true legends are represented in the Psalter although Psalms 78, 105, and 106 reflect their influence. Gunkel considered the legend or narrative style to be similar to the thanksgiving psalm with its report of past events.

Another minor category of psalms Gunkel designated as *wisdom poetry.* There is some uncertainty as to how many psalms he placed in this division, although the following seem certain: 1, 37, 49, 73, 112, 127, 128, and 133. Gunkel considered wisdom poetry to be an independent literary form ranging from simple proverbs to poems and whole books. According to Gunkel, wisdom psalms are characterized by their instructional content and by phrases and expressions of an instructional nature that have parallels in the wisdom books of the Hebrew Bible (Proverbs, Ecclesiastes, Job).

A sixth minor type of psalms Gunkel called *liturgies and dialogues.* This type of literary form he saw as a development out of situations in which there was responsive singing with refrains, in which there were questions by the laypeople and responses by priests, and in the pronouncement of divine oracles as responses to laments. When various elements from different types of psalms or worship situations were brought together to form a new unit in which dialogue or response was a characteristic feature, Gunkel labeled the literary form "a liturgy." For him, there were both priestly and prophetical antecedents utilized in the composition or construction of the liturgies now found in the Psalter. Psalms 15 and 24 reflect a type of liturgy employed when worshipers sought instruction on the requirements for entry to the sanctuary, perhaps on the occasion of an annual festival; the latter psalm should be understood in the context of a procession accompanied by the ark. In these two psalms, the priestly response consists of legal or torah pronouncements; so, Gunkel denoted these as torah liturgies. Psalm 134 is similar to Psalms 15 and 24 with the response being a priestly blessing. Some of the royal psalms (2,

20, 110, 132) contain oracular proclamations which Gunkel explained as oracles spoken by a priest or choir soloist. Similar to these is Psalm 121, which Gunkel understood as a dialogue between a priest and a supplicant but which he thought might have been an imitation of rather than a psalm actually used in the cult. Psalm 60 with its dialogue and oracular form Gunkel considered to be an authentic cultic and preexilic psalm.

Several of the psalms (12, 75, 85, 126) combine laments with an oracular response. In these cases Gunkel saw the influence of the prophets who, he argued, had borrowed the original liturgical form from the cult and imitated it only in turn to have their imitations influence the cult. These he designated prophetical liturgies. The influence of the prophets he detected in Psalms 81 and 95 with their blending of hymn and oracle and in Psalms 14, 50, 53, and 82 with their strong pronouncements of judgment modeled after the oracles proclaimed by the prophets.

A final category of psalms distinguished by Gunkel was what he called *mixed poems,* which display a blending or combination of elements from originally different psalm types. These mixtures or inner transformations he considered to be late developments in the history of psalmody and representive of a decay in the forms. Laments might be combined with thanksgiving (Psalm 22) or thanksgiving with a hymn (Psalms 66 and 103) or the lament with hymnic elements (Psalms 44 and 104). Some of these may have been, he suggested, derived from the adaptation of earlier materials (Psalms 40, 89, 90, 107, 108, 144, and perhaps 36 and 77) or through imitation and free composition (Psalms 9—10, 78, 94, 123, 129, 137, 139).

C. The Psalms and Worship

Gunkel was one of the first interpreters to see a close connection between the psalms and Israelite worship and to utilize this principle as a tool for understanding and expounding the psalms. (A similar approach was carried out by the American John P. Peters [1852–1921], but his work was not as thorough, exhaustive, or well known as Gunkel's and thus had little impact.) Gunkel's Protestant pietism, however, expressed itself in his psalms work. He wanted to see behind some of the psalms a lone individual in contact with God in prayer without benefit of priest or ritual. He wrote:

> Very many of the psalms which have come down to us do not belong to the poetry of the cult. They presuppose no particular cultic acts. They were not intended to be sung only on specific occasions but could be sung or prayed anywhere. Accordingly, out of the Cult Songs have grown Spiritual Poems. Here a kind of piety which has freed itself of all ceremonies expresses itself, a religion of the heart. Religion has cast off the shell of sacred usage, in which, until now, it has been protected and nurtured: it has come of age.[8]

> The Spiritual Laments of the Individual constitute the largest group of songs in the Psalter. Here, and in the Wisdom Literature, is the place where individuality is expressed in the Old Testament. These songs, above all, are the prototypes of Protestant hymnody. From the standpoint of poetry, they are not

always outstanding; but from the standpoint of religion, they are the imper-
ishable treasure in the Psalter.[9]

Other scholars assumed the task of trying to determine what Gunkel called the
Sitz im Leben of the psalms. By this he meant the "situation in life" that had given
rise to the material and in which it was used. Gunkel himself had pointed to the
cult or worship as the original *Sitz im Leben* for most of the psalm types.

A pioneer in the association of the psalms with worship was the Norwegian
scholar Sigmund Mowinckel (1884–1965), whose work has cast a shadow over recent and contemporary Psalms study second only to Gunkel, under whom he studied for a time. The major presentations of Mowinckel's approach are found in his
six-volume *Psalmenstudien* (1921–24, written in German and never translated into
English), and his later 1951 work *Offersang og sangoffer* ("The Offering of Song
and the Song of Offering"), which bears the English title *The Psalms in Israel's
Worship*.[10]

Mowinckel accepted as valid Gunkel's form-critical methodology in analyzing
the Psalter. For him, however, Gunkel's work had suffered from his adherence to
remnants of the literary-historical treatment of the psalms, particularly in Gunkel's
view that the psalms as we now possess them frequently reflect a spiritualized
stage one step removed from the cultic sphere and are, therefore, literary compositions modeled on older cultic prototypes. In addition, Mowinckel felt that
Gunkel's analysis of Israelite religion into its formal cultic aspects on the one hand
and its personal noncultic aspects on the other hand introduced an unnecessary and
erroneous dichotomy both in his analysis of the psalms and in his reconstruction
of Israelite religion.

Mowinckel brought to the psalms not only Gunkel's interest in their form-
critical analysis and generic description but also a greater interest in and understanding of the cult and a greater willingness to interpret Israelite religion and the
psalms in the light of Near Eastern, and especially Babylonian, parallels. Mowinckel's work on the psalms was influenced in its formative stages by two thrusts
in religion that were far more advanced at the time he began his writing on the
psalms than was the case with Gunkel. These two influential elements were the
emphasis on the comparative study of religion and its practices through the use of
materials drawn from "primitive religions" and the advancements in the study
of Near Eastern religion, especially in the case of Babylonian studies. For the first
of these, Mowinckel was indebted to his outstanding Danish professors, Vilhelm
Grønbech and Johannes Pedersen, who were interested in the social, psychological, and institutional form of primitive religion and the creative and mysterious
powers of the individual and communal primitive mentality.

The basic and innovative contributions of Mowinckel to psalms research were
twofold: his association of practically all of the psalms in their present form with
cultic services and his theory of an annual reenthronement of Yahweh as king during the fall festival, which coincided with the autumn new year. Mowinckel called
his approach "cult-functional." In his earlier writings, he distinguished only three
originally noncultic psalms, although this number was later extended to twelve

(Psalms 1, 19B, 34, 49, 105, 106, 111, 112, 127) and over forty different psalms were associated with the ritual of Yahweh's enthronement (Psalms 8, 15, 24, 29, 33, 46—48, 50, 65, 66:1–12; 67, 75—76, 81, 84—85, 87, 93, 95—100, 118, 120 —134, 149).

Beginning from Psalms 47, 93, 95—100, Mowinckel argued that many psalms suggest that Yahweh was annually enthroned as king in Jerusalem in a great religious drama. According to him, the basic elements in this drama were: (1) a sacred procession around the temple by worshipers and priests carrying the ark-throne of Yahweh; (2) the dramatization of the triumph of Yahweh over the mythological and historical enemies of creation and Israel, presented as a repetition and renewal of the original, primeval creation and as judgment over the nations of the earth; and (3) the proclamation and celebration of Yahweh's assumption and reign as king over creation, the world, and Israel. Mowinckel argued that these psalms did not reflect any historical events, nor were they composed in anticipation of the coming kingdom and reign of God. They referred instead to the actual realization of Yahweh's kingship dramatized and actualized in the celebrations of the autumn festival. He proposed that the Hebrew expression *Yahweh mālak,* found as the opening words of some of the enthronement hymns (see Pss. 93:1; 97:1), should be translated "Yahweh has become king" and not "Yahweh reigns." Thus, for Mowinckel, year by year, Yahweh reassumed kingship and was reenthroned as king in the Jerusalem ritual drama.

D. Contemporary Issues

The work of Gunkel and Mowinckel raised numerous issues still being discussed in present day scholarship. The following are of special significance.

1. If the cult was the location for the use of the majority of the psalms, what was the nature of that cult? Some have argued that the "I" who speaks in a great number of the psalms was the king, so that in the basic worship occasions in ancient Israel, the king was a central actor.[11] Even the psalms of lament and suffering are assumed to reflect a royal drama in which the reigning monarch underwent ritual humiliation as in the Babylonian *akitu* festival.[12]

Mowinckel spoke of this position as

> a theory . . . to the effect that in the royal psalms of lamentation we do not have real dangers and sufferings, which have befallen the king; and that the king is not really suffering, but only "suffering in the cult," that is to say he is taking part in a cultic "play" or drama, where he suffers, only to be later exalted."[13]

In spite of his emphasis on the mythical aspects of the Jerusalem cult, Mowinckel refused to accept such a theory and argued that what the royal psalms reflect "are real human historical conditions, and real historical distress and affliction and suffering, and no ritual sham suffering."[14]

One's acceptance or rejection of the view that sees the king as the "I" speaking in many of the psalms will depend upon how one understands the culture and cult of ancient Israel and the role of the monarchy in these and the relevance of the Babylonian cultic material to the interpretation of the Hebrew Bible.

Others have suggested that when speaking of the cult, one should not think so much about the preexilic cult dominated by the monarchy and the royal court but rather some other manifestation of worship. Tournay and others have related the development of the Psalter to the worship of the second temple.[15] Gerstenberger and others have stressed family and small group rituals as the *Sitz im Leben* for the psalms.[16] This approach emphasizes popular folk culture as the determinative context.

Some interpreters have examined the psalms without much regard to the cult.[17] Westermann wrote:

> The "categories" of the Psalms are not first of all literary or cultic in nature. They are this of course, but it is not the essential element. They designate the basic modes of that which occurs when man turns to God with words: plea and praise.[18]

> This whole tendency to explain as many as possible or even all of the Psalms . . . by a cultic schema . . . seems to me . . . to have produced meagre results for the understanding of the individual Psalms.[19]

Brueggemann has chosen to speak of the psalms in terms of poems of orientation (the hymns and psalms that affirm the wholeness and positive side of life), disorientation (mainly the laments in which the negativity of life is expressed), and re-orientation (as in the thanksgiving psalms where troubles have been overcome and life acquired an equilibrium).[20]

This type of reading takes the book of psalms as a collection for use in meditation and instruction (see further below), a perspective present throughout the history of the synagogue and church. Brevard Childs has written:

> With all due respect to Gunkel, the truly great expositors for probing to the theological heart of the Psalter remain Augustine, Kimchi, Luther, Calvin, the long forgotten Puritans buried in Spurgeon's *Treasury,* the haunting sermons of Donne, and the learned and pious reflections of de Muis, Francke and Geier. Admittedly these commentators run the risk, which is common to all interpretation, of obscuring rather than illuminating the biblical text, but because they stand firmly within the canonical context, one can learn from them how to speak anew the language of faith.

> John Calvin, in the preface to his commentary, described the Psalter as . . . "the anatomy of all the parts of the soul, for not an affection will anyone find in himself whose image is not reflected in this mirror. All the griefs, sorrows, fears, misgivings, hopes, cares, anxieties, in short all the disquieting emotions with which the minds of men are wont to be agitated, the Holy Spirit hath here pictured exactly." The canonical shape of the Psalter assured the future generations of Israelites that this book spoke a word of God to each of them in their need. It was not only a record of the past, but a living voice speaking to

the present human suffering. By taking seriously the canonical shape the reader is given an invaluable resource for the care of souls, as the synagogue and church have always understood the Psalter to be.[21]

2. As many scholars have noted, the so-called "wisdom psalms" present problems for those who relate the origin and use of the psalms to cultic life.[22] These psalms do not seem to presuppose cultic activity but are instructional in nature. There is a wide diversity of opinion about which psalms belong in this category; a minimum list generally includes Psalms 1, 32, 34, 37, 49, 112, and 128. Gunkel suggested that these psalms became part of the collection due to the pressure of lay activity on the temple priesthood. Mowinckel spoke of "learned psalmography," which he associated with a school for scribes with connections to the temple.[23] These learned psalmographers were the authors of the wisdom psalms and the collectors and editors of the other psalms.

3. The question of the collecting and final editing of the psalms dominates much of the current work in psalms research.[24] The main concerns here are to explain how the diverse collections that we noted earlier came to be included in a single work and to determine the central thrusts and intentions behind the production of the book. These concerns have come to be referred to as the study of the "canonical shape" of the Psalter (see the above quote from Childs).

The placement of particular psalms and the overall pattern or flow of the psalms have attracted much attention. Psalms that extol the law and law-piety, for example Psalms 1, 19, and 119, have been seen as indicating that the book of Psalms was put together to be read as a book of instruction appealing for observance of the torah. Westermann has suggested that an early form of the book began with Psalm 1 and ended with Psalm 119. Brueggemann has argued that the book's theological intentionality can be seen in its structure: the first two books (Psalms 1—72) tend to focus on laments, troubles, etc., while the latter books move more to hymnic and praise material. The book was thus structured to lead the reader from obedience to praise. Wilson has noticed the placement of royal psalms at strategic points in the collection: Psalm 2 at the beginning, Psalm 72 at the close of book two, and Psalm 89 at the close of book three. These royal psalms at the "seams" of the book are taken as statements about the monarchy, its failure in the past, and yet the expectation for the future messianic age.

This focus on the "canonical shaping" of the Psalter assumes that the final collection was intended to be read as a book, as a guide to living, and as an encouragement to observance of torah-piety. Instruction, meditation, and reflection were its intentions. Childs has referred to the thirteen psalms whose headings relate the psalms to events in the life of David as typical of the purpose behind the final editing of the book. He writes:

> Psalms which once functioned within a cultic context were historicized by placing them within the history of David. Moreover, the incidents chosen as evoking the psalms were not royal occasions or representative of the kingly office. Rather, David is pictured simply as a man, indeed chosen by God for

the sake of Israel, but who displays all the strengths and weaknesses of all human beings. He emerges as a person who experiences the full range of human emotions, from fear and despair to courage and love, from complaint and plea to praise and thanksgiving. Moreover, by attaching a psalm to a historical event the emphasis is made to fall on the inner life of the psalmist. An access is now provided into his emotional life. One now knows how his faith relates to the subjective side of his life. The effect of this new context has wide hermeneutical implications. The psalms are transmitted as the sacred psalms of David, but they testify to all the common troubles and joys of ordinary human life in which all persons participate. These psalms do not need to be cultically actualized to serve later generations. They are made immediately accessible to the faithful. Through the mouth of David, the man, they become a personal word from God in each individual situation. In the case of the titles the effect has been exactly the opposite from what one might have expected. Far from tying these hymns to the ancient past, they have been contemporized and individualized for every generation of suffering and persecuted Israel.[25]

Studies on the canonical shape of the Psalter have tended to assume that individuals read the psalms consecutively for edification purposes and that the structuring of the Psalter has a theological and practical intentionality. (In this regard, Psalm 73, taken as the pivotal, central psalm in the book, has taken on special significance.[26])

There are problems with this position. Whybray has evaluated the arguments for "reading the Psalms as a book" and the impact this intended purpose might have had on the editorial process. He concludes that

it is not possible to give a confident answer to the question whether the final redaction of the Psalter was undertaken in order to make it into a single, coherent book to be read privately from beginning to end by devout persons for their instruction or as an aid to their devotion. . . . That it was so used in the worship of some kind of 'cultic' assembly is improbable, since nothing is known of such a practice, and the Psalter is too long for such use.[27]

There is no evidence that individuals in early Judaism and Christianity read the book of Psalms privately and devotionally. There is some evidence that memorized psalms were sung in times of distress (see 4 Maccabees 18:15). In addition, the book or codex form was not in use until after the book of Psalms reached its final form. It would have been difficult to sense the "center" of a work reading it in scroll form. Overlooked in the modern discussion of the problem of "canonical shaping" is the old view that the five books of David were produced to be read in a triennial lectionary along with the five books of Moses.[28]

II. THE BOOK OF LAMENTATIONS

The book of Lamentations is composed of five poems, each consisting of a chapter. The first four poems are alphabetic acrostics. That is, the poems are written so that the first word in the first verse begins with the first letter of the Hebrew alphabet and the successive verses begin with the successive letters of the alphabet. Chapter 3 is a triple alphabetic acrostic with three verses beginning with the same Hebrew letter before moving to the next subsequent letter. Since there are twenty-two letters in the Hebrew alphabet each poem has twenty-two verses except for chapter three which has sixty-six. Chapter 5 is not written in this alphabetic style but nonetheless is composed of twenty-two verses. Later, we will return to the issue of why such an alphabetic scheme may have been utilized. (Several psalms are also alphabetic acrostics: Psalms 9—10 [read together]; 25, 34, 37, 111, 112, 119, and 145.)

Early tradition, both Jewish and Christian, considered Lamentations to have been written by the prophet Jeremiah. Various early translations—the Greek Septuagint, the Syriac Peshitta, the Aramaic Targum, and the Latin Vulgate—contain notations at the opening of the book attributing the work to the prophet. The statement in the Latin Vulgate is typical:

> After Israel was led into captivity and Jerusalem laid waste, Jeremiah the prophet sat weeping, and lamented with this lamentation over Jerusalem. And with a sorrowful mind, sighing and moaning, he said . . .

In Hebrew, the book has no such introduction, in fact, no title; it is called after its opening word 'êkāh.

Three factors probably explain this association of the book with Jeremiah. (1) At the time of the fall of Jerusalem to the Babylonians and the city's destruction, Jeremiah was the best known prophet in Jerusalem and a proclaimer of the city's destruction. (2) The book of Jeremiah contains a number of laments analogous in genre to the content of the book of Lamentations. (3) 2 Chronicles 35:25 reports that Jeremiah wrote laments: "Jeremiah composed laments for [King] Josiah which all the singers, male and female, recited in their laments for Josiah, as is done to this day; they became customary in Israel and were incorporated into the laments" (author's translation). This statement probably greatly contributed to the idea of Jeremiah as the author of the book of Lamentations, especially when Lam. 4:20 was understood as speaking about King Josiah.

This association with Jeremiah influenced Christians to place the book immediately following the book of Jeremiah. This was done in the ancient Greek and Latin versions of the Hebrew Scriptures and remains the case in modern Christian translations of the Bible.

Although ancient Jewish rabbis associated the book with the prophet Jeremiah, the organizers of the Hebrew canon did not attach Lamentations as an appendix to the book of Jeremiah. (The Babylonian Talmud [b. B. Bat. 15a] notes that "Jeremiah wrote the book which bears his name, the book of Kings, and Lamentations.") In manuscripts and early printed editions of the Hebrew Bible, Lamentations always appears in the third section of the Hebrew Scriptures, the Ketuvim or Writings. As a general rule the book of Lamentations appears in the Jewish biblical tradition along with the Song of Songs, Ruth, Ecclesiastes, and Esther, although there appears to have been no set order among these books. These five writings were called the Megilloth ("scrolls") and were read at the times of major festivals: Song of Songs at the spring festival of Passover, Ruth at the early summer feast of Weeks, Lamentations on the Ninth of the month Ab in the summer recalling the destruction of Jerusalem, Ecclesiastes at the fall festival of Tabernacles (Sukkoth), and Esther at the late winter festival of Purim. This is the order of the books in the New Jewish Publication Society Version. In the modern critical edition of the Hebrew text, the *Biblia hebraica stuttgartensia,* which is based on the early-eleventh-century Codex Leningradensis, the books of the Megillot appear in an order apparently based on chronological considerations: Ruth (from the period of the Judges), Song of Songs (the young Solomon), Ecclesiastes (the old Solomon), Lamentations (from the time after the destruction of Jerusalem by the Babylonians), and Esther (from the time of the Persian empire).

Jeremiah's authorship of the book of Lamentations was first challenged by H. von der Hardt in 1712, but it has only been in the twentieth century that the book has been generally interpreted without reference to him as author. The RSV published in 1952 still contained the heading "The Lamentations of Jeremiah." The NRSV (1989) and other recent translations have now dropped this heading.

Today, scholars are in general agreement on two matters about Lamentations. (1) The book was probably not written by Jeremiah and can be interpreted apart from any connection with the prophet. (2) The events of 586 B.C.E. form the background for the work that responds to these events. In 586 B.C.E., the Babylonians captured Jerusalem for the second time after a lengthy siege during which the city's population suffered from severe famine. The events attendant upon and following the capture of the city are reported in 2 Kings 25 and Jeremiah 52: the reigning Judean king, Zedekiah, was captured and carried into exile after witnessing the slaughter of his sons before having his eyes put out; royal officials were executed; the treasures and artifacts in the Jerusalem temple were confiscated and the temple burned; the city was torched; and many Judeans were taken to Babylonia into exile.

The poems in the book do not fit into any clear-cut genre typology. Scholars have debated whether they are laments—communal or individual—or dirges or some mixture of the two. As was noted above in the discussion of psalm genres, laments are addressed to the deity describing a situation of trouble and distress and pleading for redemption, a return to normalcy. Clearly much of the material in these poems fit into this category. A special use of the lament was employed in the ancient Near East to bemoan the fall and destruction of a city.[29] Such laments focused on the divine abandonment of the city leading to its destruction but followed by a description of the return of the divine to restore the city to its former state. Some motifs of this city-lament are clearly evident in the book of Lamentations.

Parts of the book also parallel the funeral dirge in which the bereaved bewails the departed and even addresses the deceased. The clearest example in the Bible of such a dirge is found in 2 Sam. 1:17–27 where David wails over the deaths of Saul and Jonathan.

Various voices are heard in the poems of Lamentations. One is the voice of the poet. This voice describes the destruction and desolation of the city and the misery of its inhabitants (1:1–11a, 17; 2:1–19; 4:1–16) and addresses Zion/Jerusalem calling upon the city to weep and pour out its heart to Yahweh (2:18–19). Zion is described as an abandoned widow exposed to numerous dangers.

A second voice is that of the destroyed city (1:11b–16, 18–22; 2:20–22). The speeches of the city appear only in the first two chapters.

A third voice is that of the community. It occurs in those sections where the first-person plurals appear (4:17–22; 5:1–22). All of chapter 5 is a communal lament depicting the community's dire straits (vv. 1–18) and pleading to Yahweh for restoration (vv. 19–22).

A final voice is that of an individual male found in chapter 3. Here the person describes the suffering that Yahweh has inflicted (vv. 1–18) but follows this with a statement of trust defending the actions of Yahweh as both just and beneficial (vv. 19–39). Others are called upon to turn to Yahweh and join the worshiper in prayer (vv. 40–48). After a statement of continued turmoil (vv. 49–54), the chapter ends with a prayer for Yahweh's help for the worshiper and vengeance against the person's adversaries (vv. 55–66). In the book generally, the victim is presented in feminine imagery. This has made acute the issue of the identity of the male speaker in chapter 3. When the book was associated with Jeremiah, it was easy to see the prophet as the speaker. Until modern times, Christians saw in the figure a prophetic depiction of Christ and his suffering. Many have taken this chapter as the key for understanding the entire book, since it offers the most extensive rationale for God's action against Jerusalem and shows a greater confidence and hope in the future than the rest of the book.

The voice totally missing from the book is that of God. Yahweh nowhere is allowed to speak in the book in spite of the numerous speeches and appeals addressed to him.

For what occasion in ancient time the book of Lamentations was written remains uncertain. A likely theory suggests that the material was originally written to commemorate the fall of Jerusalem, a usage that became traditional in later Judaism.

Anyone reading the book is naturally confronted with the issue of the central thrust of the work. Was it written as a theodicy, to justify the disaster of Jerusalem's fall? There are places where sin and wrongdoing are acknowledged as the basis for God's actions against the city (1:8–9a, 18; 2:14, 17; 3:40–42; 5:7). Nonetheless, the depiction of the severity of Yahweh's actions seems to overwhelm the admission of guilt in the book. Rarely is there a confession of sin in the speeches/laments addressed to God, but there is a recital of Yahweh's acts when Yahweh acted "like an enemy" (2:5).

Is the book a call for patience in the present and hope in the future? Chapter 3 gives some expression to this viewpoint (see especially vv. 21–39). The book, however, does not end with chapter 3, but with chapter 5, which concludes with an emphasis on divine abandonment that accuses Yahweh in direct speech: "You have rejected us, Bitterly raged against us" (author's translation).

Recent study has pointed to the tragic dimension of the book[30]—that the degree of suffering of the people is presented as undeserved and that expectations of a future resolution and redemption are minimal, to say the least. As tragedy, the book allows the various voices to take up, heroically, their complaints against God and to verbalize the depth of their suffering. Perhaps the acrostic form, going from A to Z as we would say, gives expression to the totality of the situation's despair. That the book of Lamentations strikes a chord in contemporary, post-holocaust times should be no surprise.

FOR FURTHER READING

Psalms
Brueggemann, Walter. *The Psalms and the Life of Faith.* Minneapolis: Fortress, 1995.
Croft, S. J. L. *The Identity of the Individual in the Psalms.* JSOTSup 44. Sheffield: JSOT, 1987.
Day, John. *Psalms.* OTG. Sheffield: JSOT, 1990.
Eaton, J. H. *Kingship and the Psalms.* 2d ed. Sheffield: JSOT, 1986.
Gerstenberger, E. S. "Psalms." In J. H. Hayes, ed., *Old Testament Form Criticism,* 178–223. San Antonio, Tex.: Trinity University Press, 1974.
———. *Psalms: Part I: With an Introduction to Cultic Poetry.* FOTL 14. Grand Rapids: Eerdmans, 1988.
Gillingham, S. E. *The Poems and Psalms of the Hebrew Bible.* Oxford: Oxford University Press, 1994.
Gunkel, Hermann. *The Psalms: A Form-Critical Introduction.* Facet Books: Biblical Series 19. Philadelphia: Fortress, 1967.
Holladay, William L. *The Psalms through Three Thousand Years: Prayerbooks to a Cloud of Witnesses.* Minneapolis: Fortress, 1993.
Johnson, A. R. "The Psalms." In H. H. Rowley, ed., *The Old Testament and Modern Study,* 162–209. Oxford: Clarendon Press, 1951.
Keel, Othmar. *The Symbolism of the Biblical World: Ancient Near Eastern Iconography and the Book of Psalms.* New York: Seabury, 1978.
McCann J. C., ed. *The Shape and Shaping of the Psalter.* JSOTSup 159. Sheffield: JSOT, 1993.
Mowinckel, Sigmund. *The Psalms in Israel's Worship.* 2 vols. Sheffield: JSOT, 1992 [1962].
Seybold, Klaus. *Introducing the Psalms.* Edinburgh: T. & T. Clark, 1990.
Tournay, R. J. *Seeing and Hearing God with the Psalms: The Prophetic Liturgy of the Second Temple in Jerusalem.* JSOTSup 118. Sheffield: JSOT, 1991.
Westermann, Claus. *The Praise of God in the Psalms.* Richmond: John Knox, 1965.
———. *Praise and Lament in the Psalms.* Atlanta: John Knox, 1981.
Whybray, R. N. *Reading the Psalms as a Book.* JSOTSup 222. Sheffield: JSOT, 1996.
———. "Wisdom Psalms." In J. Day, R. P. Gordon, and H. G. M. Williamson, eds., *Wisdom in Ancient Israel: Essays in Honour of J. A. Emerton,* 152–60. Cambridge: Cambridge University Press, 1995.
Wilson, G. H. *The Editing of the Hebrew Psalter.* SBLDS 76. Chico, Calif.: Scholars Press, 1985.
Wittstruck, T. *The Book of Psalms: An Annotated Bibliography.* Garland Reference Library; Books of the Bible 5. New York: Garland, 1994.

Lamentations
Dobbs-Allsopp, F. W. *Weep, O Daughter of Zion: A Study of the City-Lament Genre in the Hebrew Bible.* BibOr 44. Rome: Pontifical Biblical Institute, 1993.
———. "Tragedy, Tradition, and Theology in the Book of Lamentations." *JSOT* 74 (1997): 29–60.

Hillers, Delbert R. *Lamentations.* AB 7a. 2d ed. Garden City, N.Y.: Doubleday, 1992.

Lanahan, W. F. "The Speaking Voice in the Book of Lamentations." *JBL* 93 (1974): 41–49.

Provan, Iain W. *Lamentations.* NCB. London: Marshall, Morgan & Scott/Grand Rapids: Eerdmans, 1991.

Salters, R. B. *Jonah and Lamentations.* OTG. Sheffield: JSOT, 1994.

Westermann, Claus. *Lamentations: Issues and Interpretation.* Minneapolis: Fortress, 1994.

7

OTHER WRITINGS

Ruth, Song of Songs, Esther, Daniel

KIRSTEN NIELSEN

I. THE BOOK OF RUTH

A. Contents

On the surface, the book of Ruth is a plain and charming narrative about two women who manage to survive under difficult conditions. It is a folk tale, but it is also much more. It explains how it happened that precisely David's family was chosen by the God of Israel. The story about Ruth the Moabitess who marries Boaz of Bethlehem was therefore used as a defense of the claims of that family to political power.

The book of Ruth consists of four chapters. The first deals with a famine that forces Elimelech, his wife Naomi, and their two sons to leave their hometown of Bethlehem. In order to survive they go to Moab; but Elimelech and both of the sons die there. After ten years in Moab, the widow Naomi decides to return to Judah where food is again available. She urges her daughters-in-law to stay in Moab where they belong, but one of them, Ruth, decides to accompany Naomi back to Bethlehem.

In the second chapter Ruth is gleaning in a field to gather food for herself and her mother-in-law. The field turns out to belong to a man named Boaz, who shows favor to her and sees to it that she can collect plenty of grain. When Ruth comes back to her mother-in-law in the evening, Naomi tells her that Boaz is a relative of Elimelech and therefore one of their kinsman-redeemers.

Chapter 3 is the crucial chapter: Naomi suggests that Ruth seek out Boaz at night at the threshing floor and lie down next to him. Then "he will tell you what to do," the older woman promises (Ruth 3:4). Night falls and Ruth lies down next to the sleeping Boaz. When Boaz awakes, Ruth makes him promise to marry her. The only difficulty, says Boaz, is that there is a kinsman-redeemer who is actually nearer to Ruth than himself, and so he must be approached first.

Chapter 4 begins with Boaz negotiating with the other kinsman-redeemer the next morning at the town gate. Boaz offers the other kinsman the opportunity to redeem a field that Naomi has for sale. But then he surprises the people present by disclosing that he himself intends to marry Ruth to provide her late husband with an heir who can perpetuate their family line and keep the property of the family. Suddenly, the field is not so attractive for the other kinsman, and so he refrains from buying it, and Boaz marries Ruth and takes over everything that belonged to

Elimelech. Ruth becomes pregnant, gives birth to a son named Obed, and the book ends with a genealogy reciting the family line of David from Judah and the son of Tamar, Perez, through Boaz and Obed up to David himself.

B. Place in the Old Testament and Hebrew Bible

The book of Ruth can be read in various ways. How one reads it depends in part on whether it is read in its position in the Hebrew Bible or in its position in modern translations. Following the Septuagint (LXX), most modern translations place Ruth between Judges and 1—2 Samuel. The Ruth narrative thus forms a kind of transition between the period of Judges, which is described as a period of lawlessness with rape and murder, and the monarchy, which begins when Samuel anoints the first king of Israel, Saul. The book of Ruth can thus be considered the legend of the birth of the monarchy.

When reading Ruth in the light of the last chapters of the book of Judges, a clear contrast emerges between the time when women were misused and abused and the narrative about Ruth, who is chosen to be the ancestress of David's family. In this order the book of Ruth also anticipates the events in the first chapters of 1 Samuel, where the woman Hannah becomes the mother of one of Israel's greatest leaders, the prophet Samuel. In this context, the reader understands that the book of Ruth is actually a story about women.

In the Hebrew Bible the book of Ruth is one of the five scrolls (Ruth, Song of Songs, Ecclesiastes, Lamentations, and Esther) that were read at the Jewish festivals. Ruth was read at the Feast of Weeks (Pentecost). According to Jewish tradition, this festival was held not only because of the wheat harvest but in memory of God giving the law to Israel at Mount Sinai. Just as the Israelites had pledged loyalty to God's commandments, so Ruth assumed all the duties belonging to Judaism by saying, "Where you lodge I will lodge. Your people shall be my people and your God my God" (Ruth 1:16). Thus, the rabbis portray Ruth as the ideal example of a proselyte for non-Jews who choose to convert to Judaism.

C. The Book of Ruth as a New Patriarchal Narrative

The book of Ruth consists of the beautiful narrative about a foreign woman who renounces everything to follow her mother-in-law (Ruth 1:1–4:17) and of the final genealogy (Ruth 4:18–22). For decades, scholars treated these two parts separately, since the genealogy was considered a later addition, a genealogical appendix to the older story.[1] However, recent studies have shown that the genealogy cannot simply be neglected. As a matter of fact, it has a very important function in the book, for the very purpose of the story is to show how it happened that the God of Israel chose *David and his family* to sit on the throne in Jerusalem. In this connection, it is therefore important that the genealogy starts with Perez, as this refers to one of the patriarchal narratives, Genesis 38, which also deals with God's surprising selection, and in the light of which the reader should understand the book of Ruth. The intertextual link to the story about how the mother of Perez, Tamar, became pregnant by Judah is thus a key to the understanding of the book of Ruth.[2]

The book of Ruth in many ways resembles the patriarchal narratives. Abram also had to travel to a foreign country because of a famine (Gen. 12:10–20), and repeatedly in these stories we see the motif about the ancestress who remains childless for several years despite God's promises. Ruth is thus included in a network of stories about ancestresses. When Ruth and Boaz get married, the witnesses express the wish for Boaz that the LORD may "make the woman who is coming into your house like Rachel and Leah, who together built up the house of Israel . . . through the children the LORD will give you by this young woman, may your house be like the house of Perez, whom Tamar bore to Judah" (Ruth 4:11–12). Here, some of the names of Israel's ancestors are repeated, and the reader is indirectly asked to consider Boaz and Ruth among the ancestors who are to build the house of Israel. But not until after the birth of Obed do we learn that the house to which these two contribute is the house of David.

Much of the story of Ruth takes place in Bethlehem. The apparent meaning of the name Bethlehem, "house of bread," implies that it is a fertile area. Ironically, this of all places is hit by a famine (Ruth 1:1), which forces Elimelech and his family to go to Moab. While Judah and Bethlehem have positive connotations, the country of Moab is negatively loaded in the Bible. In Gen. 19:37 the Moabites are described as the product of an incestuous relationship between Lot and his firstborn daughter. That something good should come from Moab thus demands an explanation. From a literary point of view, one of the purposes of the book of Ruth is to give this explanation, which is that just as the daughters of Lot save the family line by something as extraordinary as letting themselves become pregnant by their father, so Ruth had to choose the extraordinary means of lying down next to Boaz at night and asking him to marry her.

There is another reason for reading the book of Ruth in the light of motifs from the patriarchal narratives. Why was it precisely famine that forced Elimelech away from Bethlehem? Why not war or something else? Again the answer can be found in intertextual reading. For in the patriarchal narratives the problem is not just the lack of seed (grain) during famine but also the infertility of the ancestresses. The patriarchal narratives make it easier to see that also in the book of Ruth there is a connection between the lack of fertility of the land and the lack of fertility of the women.

Chapter 3 of the book of Ruth is the crucial chapter. It is the chapter where Ruth goes to see Boaz at night. Naomi instructs Ruth to wash and anoint herself before she lies down with him and then to uncover herself at Boaz's feet. These last words are usually translated as a request to uncover Boaz's feet or the place at his feet. That they refer to a place is clear from verses 8 and 14. Isaiah 57:8 furnishes a good parallel of a woman uncovering herself, but there is no example in the Hebrew Bible of a woman uncovering a man. It seems best, therefore, to translate this as Ruth uncovering herself at Boaz's feet. This interpretation also seems the most appropriate in the light of the Tamar narrative in Genesis 38. Both the story of Tamar and the book of Ruth are about women who have lost their husbands and who engage in trickery. By means of law alone they cannot get the husband they need to make them pregnant. In both cases the trick is also closely connected with the fact that they are women. Both women show their intentions by the way they dress. Tamar puts on the veil of a harlot when she presents herself to her father-in-law. Ruth does the opposite; she removes the clothing from her genitals ("feet") and asks Boaz to cover her with the corner of his garment. Each in her own way, by means of her clothes, signals the same message: intercourse. However, Tamar only wishes to become pregnant, whereas Ruth would like to have a lasting relationship when she asks Boaz to spread the corner of his garment over her. That this means marriage is clear from a comparison with Ezek. 16:8, where God finds Jerusalem as a nude woman and marries her by spreading the corner of his garment over her. Similarly, in the book of Ruth the nude woman is covered by the man's garment.

Chapter 4 also contains a series of motifs that refer to the patriarchal narratives. First, as mentioned earlier, there is a reference to Rachel and Leah, the two wives of the patriarch Jacob. Secondly, the chapter is quite clearly about a field that should remain family property and about descendants. The theme here, therefore, is identical with that of the dual promise of people and land (Gen. 17:6–8).

D. The Book of Ruth as Literature

The Ruth narrative has often been defined as a short story or an idyll. By the word idyll the German scholar Gunkel meant to stress the poetic and thus the literary qualities of the short story.[3] This aspect of the book of Ruth is especially worth noticing, for the book is extremely well composed. It consists of four chapters, each of which consists of three smaller sections; but these twelve parts create a unity that convinces the reader that the book ends precisely as intended.

Throughout the entire book there is a constant movement between the village of Bethlehem and other places: Bethlehem–Moab–Bethlehem–the field–Bethlehem–the threshing floor–Bethlehem–the town gate–Bethlehem. So the book ends where it began: in the town linked to the name of David. The author has a clear preference for such circle compositions. This is seen at its clearest in the general structuring of the book, which begins with detailed information about family background and ends with a genealogy. A comparison of the individual parts of the book shows that the first and the fourth chapters are interrelated and that the two middle chapters reflect each other. The author's preference for such chiastic structures is important for an interpretation of the text, since it enables the reader to see where the central statements are to be found. It is therefore no mere coincidence that in chapter 2, as well as in chapter 3, Boaz's wish that the LORD should bless Ruth forms the fulcrum (2:12 and 3:10).

The structure of the book is marked by efforts to create both a roundedness and a forward drive in the narrative. Even though each of the four chapters, for example, is well-rounded, the reader is given a clear signal at the end of the chapter as to the topic of the next scene. The structure of the book thus creates a feeling of conscious control, without the reader knowing beforehand *how* the unhappiness at the beginning of the book will be transformed into a happy ending. The fact that the rounded form does not create a closed circle is also evident in the book's ending in a genealogy. The list of names rounds off the story but at the same time inspires the reader to ask for more stories. What happened to this David who ends the book? The book may have come to an end, but it is clearly part of a much wider network of texts.

E. The Legal Aspects

A crucial problem for scholarship has been the tension between the legal background that appears to be assumed in the book and the laws that are actually known from the Old Testament, especially those concerning levirate marriage. The marriage between Ruth and Boaz has often been understood as a levirate marriage. because its purpose is to "maintain the dead man's name on his inheritance in order that the name of the dead may not be cut off from his kindred and from the gate of his native place" (Ruth 4:10). The marriage between a widow and her deceased husband's brother has the same purpose according to Deut. 25:5–10. But Boaz is not Ruth's brother-in-law, and indeed the entire book concerns how the two widows have to choose untraditional means to get a husband for Ruth. If Boaz had a legal duty to marry Ruth, the mother-in-law could merely have brought the matter before the courts and would not have had to send Ruth to Boaz under cover of night. There is thus no reason to try to make the laws of Deuteronomy 25 apply to the book of Ruth.

The purpose of the laws of the Old Testament is to describe how to handle a normal situation. The effects of the laws are thus predictable. However, a good story like the book of Ruth is not supposed to be predictable. The reader may expect it to end well but must be anxious to know *how* it ends well. The problems experienced by scholars trying to find agreement between legal texts and the story of Ruth are therefore due to faulty interpretation of the book of Ruth as a piece of law. More recent interpretations have begun to emphasize the literary qualities of the book rather than using it to explain the legal conditions of that time.

F. The Book of Ruth as Political Instrument

The fact that Ruth is a well composed literary work does not necessarily mean that it is pure fiction. On the contrary, the author wishes to relay information about a family that the audience knows and is interested in. We do not know when the story about Ruth and Boaz was written. Scholars have based their arguments in favor of specific dates on language and style, on the references to Israelite legal practice, and on the theology of the book. However, these criteria have resulted in very different dates: from the time of David to the last centuries before the Common Era.[4] What is more important than finding a specific date for the book, however, is to identify the kind of political situation that could give rise to it. For it is the placement of the text in such a context that can provide an understanding of the purpose(s) the book.

To examine Ruth's historical context, we must first ask when there were reasons to tell about David's family background and his Moabite ancestress. Even though the Old Testament gives the impression that David was the king of all kings, there are also traditions that indicate that there was some controversy as to whether David's family had the right to the throne. According to 1 Kings, the kingdom began to crumble during the reign of David's son, Solomon. When Solomon died, his son Rehoboam traveled to the ancient shrine at Shechem to be crowned as his father's successor. But when Rehoboam refused to accede to the demands of the northern tribes for tax relief, they rejected him, and only the tribe of Judah (to which David belonged) remained to accept Rehoboam as their king. We do not know if the supporters of the Davidic dynasty in this situation told about Ruth and Boaz to support Rehoboam's claim to kingship, but it is a possibility. At least this allows us to use 1 Kings 12 as an example of a situation in which the book of Ruth would have a clear political function, namely, to justify David's lineage. If opponents contemptuously referred to the family's somewhat doubtful relation to Moab, supporters emphasized that even though David's ancestress derived from Moab, she came to Bethlehem because God wanted her to come and chose her to be the ancestress of the Davidic dynasty. Thus, it was this very ancestress who guaranteed God's will.

G. Theological Themes

The discovery that the book of Ruth was originally written as a contribution in a political struggle does not exhaust the significance and application of the book. For a book that deals with how God chooses and looks after an individual person is significant in many other connections. There is no direct reference in Ruth to Yahweh controlling the course of events. Only twice does it mention God as intervening, namely when the famine ends (1:6) and when Ruth becomes pregnant (4:13). But these two verses are also essential for any conversation about Israel's God: he provides bread and babies. In another place, namely when Ruth "accidentally" comes to Boaz's field (2:3), the author strongly hints that God is behind the events. This may not be so accidental!

In opposition to the patriarchal narratives, God is silent in the book of Ruth. There are no direct meetings with God; there are no dreams or angels. God acts indirectly through the people, as when Boaz looks after Ruth and marries her. God guides and controls events, but from beneath the surface. On the surface itself, it is Ruth, Naomi, and Boaz who move. They plan and act and try to shape their existence as best they can. However, their plans are never fully coordinated. For example, Boaz and Naomi never meet to make plans; each of them thinks individual thoughts. But out of all their individual plans grows a unity that leads the reader to sense that in this way not human will, but the will of God is being carried out.

Naomi's plan for the meeting at the threshing floor and Ruth's execution of it are serious breaks with contemporary norms. But just as Tamar was rewarded by becoming the mother of twins, so Ruth and Naomi are rewarded for their faithfulness to the family. This emphasizes that God is on the side of the marginalized, conducting their case even where the law is inadequate, and they must resort to trickery in order to gain justice.

Many scholars have emphasized that Ruth as a foreigner becomes part of Israel. Thus, they see a link between the book of Ruth and other Old Testament texts, such as the book of Jonah, that present Yahweh as God of the whole world. Seen from this angle, it is precisely the conversion motif and God's goodness to foreign peoples that are the focus of Ruth. This perspective on the image of God is also found in the patriarchal narratives, as is clear from God's words to Abram in Gen. 12:1–3, where not only Abram himself is blessed, but the culmination of the blessing is reached in the promise, "All peoples on earth will be blessed through you." Considered in a wider perspective, these words could just as well apply to David's ancestress, Ruth.

II. SONG OF SONGS

A. Contents

Song of Songs, with its heading "Solomon's Song of Songs," is a collection of love lyrics. Two voices, one female and one male, succeed each other, sometimes interrupted by other voices. The woman initiates the collection and the theme of love by wishing that he whose love is more delightful than wine will kiss her. Throughout the poems, the voices in the dialogue alternate, and this dialogue form is characteristic of Song of Songs. They are in love with and praise each other but do not praise love as such.[5] The two lovers long to meet (1:7–8) and repeatedly express their affection by praising each other. He compares her with a lily among thorns, and she replies by comparing him with an apple tree among the trees of the forest (2:2–3). In the poems, the intimate presence where she can express, "His left arm is under my head and his right arm embraces me" (2:6, author's translation), alternates with the intense search for the missing person, when she runs through the streets of the city looking for her lover until, eventually, she finds him and holds him (3:1–5). Presence, absence, and longing; that is love!

The beloved's figure is described by a wealth of similes in some of the poems. The beauty of the woman recalls images from the shepherd's daily life, as when her hair is compared with "a flock of goats moving down the slopes of Gilead" and her teeth to "a flock of shorn ewes that have come up from the washing" (4:1–2). The images visualize the feelings that the lovers have for each other and at the same time justify their love. When the woman is like a fragrant garden, an orchard of pomegranates, then the man must obviously come into the garden and taste its fruits (4:12–5:1). Nothing is more natural or more fitting.

The garden motif in chapter 4 is just one important feature in this collection of poems. In the succeeding chapters earlier motifs are taken up again. There are repetitions and variations, as when we again hear about the woman searching for her lost lover in 5:2–8. However, whereas in chapter 3, after the woman's searching, there is a description full of images about Solomon's carriage coming up from the desert, her search in chapter 5 ends with a description of the man. With an abundance of imagery she evokes a picture of the ideal man, whose head is purest gold, whose "lips are like lilies, distilling liquid myrrh," and whose "appearance is like Lebanon, choice as the cedars" (5:10–16). Then follows another series of descriptions of her. One of the most significant appears in the verses about the dancing woman with beautiful sandaled feet and hair like royal tapestry; "a king is held captive in its tresses" (7:1–6). Then the image of the woman as the countryside is resumed. Her stature is like that of the palm, her breasts are like clusters, and thus her lover exclaims, "I will climb the palm tree and take hold of its fruit" (7:7–8, author's translation).

It appears from various descriptions throughout the poems that it is a problem for the lovers to meet. However much they would like to, they cannot always be together. Suddenly he has disappeared and must be found again, or outside factors that threaten their love obstruct their being together. In chapter 2 the threat appears in the shape of little foxes that ruin the vineyards (2:15). Opposition to their relationship makes her wish that he were her brother so that she could meet with him freely at her mother's house (8:1–2). Also, her brothers may interrupt and declare that they know how to protect their young sister if she receives an offer of marriage. For if she were a door, they would bar it with panels of cedar (8:8–10). The reader knows that neither this nor anything else can part them, "for love is strong as death, passion fierce as the grave" (8:6). Even if she were a wall (8:10), when she met him she would have to surrender; the two of them belong together. Consequently, Song of Songs ends with a dialogue between them in which he asks her to call him. He would love to hear her say, "Make haste, my beloved, and be like a gazelle or like a young stag on the mountains of spices" (8:14).

While the Song ends this way, at the same time it continues. We simply have to start from the beginning and read the poems once more. Then we will see that she calls him; we will hear her encourage him to take her hand and run away with her (1:4), and she almost literally fulfills his prayer when she begs him, "Until the day breathes and the shadows flee, turn, my beloved, be like a gazelle or like a young stag on the cleft mountains" (2:17). The structure of Song of Songs is like a circle; hardly have we finished before we start again. For love is like a circle; it never ends.

B. Place in the Hebrew Bible and Old Testament

Song of Songs in the Hebrew Bible is one of the five festival scrolls (the *měgillôth*) along with Ruth, Ecclesiastes, Lamentations, and Esther. Song of Songs was recited during the Passover festival, but of course with the interpretation that the poems are about God's love for Israel. In a discussion during the second century C.E. about the canonization of Song of Songs, Rabbi Aqiba emphasized that "the whole world is not worth the day on which the Song of Songs was given to Israel, for all the Scriptures are holy, but the Song of Songs is the Holy of Holies."[6]

He thereby categorically rejected any profane use of Song of Songs at public drinking places.

In the Greek translation, the Septuagint (LXX), and in the modern translations used in Christian churches, Song of Songs is found after the books of Proverbs and Ecclesiastes. It is thus placed with two other books that tradition has attributed to King Solomon. This position makes it possible to see Song of Songs in the light of the wisdom traditions and their reflections about how God made the world and what is good for humanity. In this light, it seems more natural to interpret the songs in the book as poems about love between man and woman and not as images of the relationship between God and God's people. Yet it is not as simple as this. Within Christian tradition, the allegorical interpretation was in fact preferred for centuries.

C. Song of Songs as Poetry

However Song of Songs is interpreted, it must be read as a poetic work.[7] We must therefore look for the poetic devices used in the text. Song of Songs is written in concise, rhythmic language, which is achieved by omitting some of the particles found in normal Hebrew prose. An unusual word order is also used sometimes to ease rhythm and the poetic style. Alliteration and assonance are common in the book, and one finds a variety of parallelisms, a well-known stylistic device in the Bible. There is also an abundance of similes and metaphors. Many of these are conventional, but the widespread use of imagery is still a continuous challenge to the reader. Even a conventional image must be interpreted from its context. Images are ambiguous, so that just as the two lovers are in continuous dialogue with each other, the reader is invited to enter into a dialogue with Song of Songs in order to interpret it.

However, the reader is invited not only to interpret Song of Songs but also to react emotionally to it. One of the numerous features of Song of Songs is its appeal to the human senses. The highly visual descriptions appeal to the sense of sight, whereas the sense of hearing is caught not just by the reciting of the text but also by the actual dialogue form. The lovers talk with each other and thereby address us, who are listening, "Listen! My beloved!" (5:2; cf. also 2:8). The woman charges the daughters of Jerusalem and thus her audience (2:7; 3:5; 5:8; 8:4), and the man longs to hear her voice (2:14; 8:13). If the senses of sight and hearing mark a certain distance between the two lovers, the senses of smell, touch, and taste suggest their intimacy. Song of Songs repeatedly appeals to these senses by describing the woman as a fragrant garden, the fruits of which the man longs to taste (4:12–16), just as she expresses her longing to kiss her lover (1:2; 8:1), refers to him as a sachet of myrrh resting between her breasts (1:13), and describes how she will hold him and bring him to her mother's house (3:4; 8:2). This appeal to the senses figures significantly in the structure of Song of Songs, which presents the constant change between distance and intimacy as a beating rhythm. She sees him from a distance, hears his voice, grabs hold of him. He looks at her admiringly, expresses his longing to touch her, to enjoy the fragrance of her breath, to taste the wine from her mouth. Sometimes the wish for intimacy is fulfilled: his arms embrace her and she feels pleased that "I am my beloved's, and his desire is for me" (7:10).

While scholars agree that Song of Songs is poetry, there is no consensus about whether it is one poem or an anthology. It is possible to read Song of Songs as though the two voices belong to one couple. But there are just as many, if not more indications that it is an anthology of poems that have been written in various situations and compiled later. In this case, there is no point in talking about the two recurrent voices being identified with one specific man and one specific woman. The woman is any woman, the man any man. The poetry of Song of Songs is meant to be used. The variety of metaphors and similes provides a text that can be recited repeatedly. Hence, Song of Songs is not bound to one specific historical situation or one specific interpretation. It is, therefore, no wonder that attempts to date this text range from 950 to 200 B.C.E. and that many different interpretations are found in the history of research on the book. In what follows we will consider some examples.

D. Song of Songs as an Allegory of God's Love

In their attempts at tracing the original use of Song of Songs, scholars have made many proposals.[8] In the twentieth century, when scholars showed great interest in the Israelite cult, the possibility was mentioned that the book's songs were originally used in fertility rituals. The searching woman in Song of Songs would then refer to the cultic motif of the goddess searching for her lover as in Egyptian, Mesopotamian, and Ugaritic practice. However, this interpretation is problematic, since Song of Songs does not have a mourning motif, which is closely connected to the death and resurrection of the god in the fertility cult. Similar difficulties arise for Pope's position that Song of Songs was used in connection with ancient funeral rites.[9]

While it is difficult to show a religious origin for these love songs, it is easy to see the religious application of them within Jewish and Christian traditions. Historically, different songs within the book have been reinterpreted separately by different groups of people, so that after their canonization—if not earlier—they came to be considered more comprehensive than a literal interpretation would indicate. These songs have been reused as striking images of the relationship between God and Israel, an interpretation that the Christian church has continued by interpreting Song of Songs as an allegory. Allegorical interpretation takes advantage of the openness of imagery and its suitability for reinterpretation. Here, the man is God (or Christ within Christian tradition), and the woman is the Jewish community or the Christian church, respectively. Within both traditions there are also interpretations that consider the relationship to be between the individual person and God, as well as other variations: God and God's Shekinah (Jewish mysticism) or Jesus and Mary (Christian mysticism).

This interpretation touches something crucial in Jewish and Christian tradition. The Jewish creed, the Shema, says, "Hear, O Israel: The LORD is our God, the

LORD alone" (Deut. 6:4). The phrase, "the LORD alone" means that he is the one and only. The crucial aspect of Judaism has thus been phrased as a declaration of love. Similarly, in one of the most significant verses in the New Testament there is a reference to God who "so loved the world that he gave his only Son, that everyone who believes in him may not perish but have eternal life" (John 3:16).

Another feature of Song of Songs that makes it natural to use as an image of the relationship of persons to God is its continuous change between presence and absence. The lovers long for each other, but their being together is repeatedly obstructed. They lose each other; they call to each other and are reunited.

Allegorical interpretation obviously regards Song of Songs as a unity. There is only one male voice, God himself, and only one woman, whom God loves. Song of Songs, therefore, is also read as a narrative or a drama describing the development of the relationship between those two. To extract as much significance as possible from the texts, there has been a tendency to interpret even the slightest detail as an image of the religious relationship.

One reason for the allegorical interpretation of Song of Songs was of course that in the Old Testament marriage was a well-known metaphor for the relationship between God and Israel. Viewed in the light of passages such as Hosea 1—3; Jeremiah 3; Ezekiel 16 and 23, to mention only the most important, the allegorical elaboration is self-evident. In the marriage imagery employed by these prophetic writings it is the man, representing God, who is always in control and takes the initiative to betrothe as well as to divorce. The situation is different, however, in Song of Songs. Here the woman shows just as much initiative as the man. This has induced especially feminist scholars to warn against transferring the traditional view of the divine/human relationship to Song of Songs and thus making the woman a passive object, which she is certainly not in Song of Songs.[10] Her love is just as fervent as the man's love, and she is just as active as he in their love relationship. Therefore, many scholars believe that Song of Songs cannot possibly be interpreted as the relationship between God and the world. Nevertheless, when read in the light of the allegorical interpretation of Song of Songs, the controlling God of the prophetic writings also appears to be loving; he is a husband who loves too much and thus keeps taking back his beloved.

Allegorical interpretation was, of course, often motivated by anxiety over the erotic character of Song of Songs, so that it was reinterpreted as a reflection of *spiritual* love. Modern research has evinced a clear tendency to reject the allegorical interpretation and to read Song of Songs as poetic expression of the secular love between man and woman. The tendency is at least as old as Herder (1807) who directly challenged his readers on the matter: "If you are ashamed of the Song of Songs, hypocrite, then you are ashamed of the woman who conceived you and the child that your wife has born you, but first of all, you are ashamed of yourself."[11]

E. Song of Songs as Poems about Love between Man and Woman

Showing the influences behind a certain interpretation is not enough to reject it. However, if we read Song of Songs in the light of other Near Eastern love songs, it becomes clear that the nonallegorical interpretation makes the most sense. A majority within recent scholarship, thus, also believes that Song of Songs is about love between man and woman and not about the relationship to God, who is actually not mentioned in Song of Songs. Thus understood, the poetry of Song of Songs has its origin in ancient wedding feasts or simply belongs to the popular songs from antiquity. Many scholars therefore believe that the poems originate from different eras and that they were compiled at a late date. In recent years, however, it has also been generally accepted that Song of Songs is a literary unity. Thus, Exum argues that the sophisticated structure of Song of Songs implies that either a group of authors working together or one individual created it.[12]

One of the basic problems of the book is the limits of each poem. Some scholars divide it into as many as thirty-one individual poems.[13] Exum, on the other hand, distinguishes only six poems, which are paired with one another: 1:2–2:6 with 8:4–14; 2:7–3:5 with 5:2–6:3, and 3:6–5:1 with 6:4–8:3.[14] This analysis is obviously subject to debate, but the achievement of Exum and others has been to show that the poems in Song of Songs have not been compiled at random. On the contrary, an attempt has been made to create cohesion and dialogue between the individual poems within the book, which itself reflects a deliberate, poetic design. Whether the demonstration of such a deliberate structure, however, is sufficient to claim that there is a single author still remains to be clarified.

F. Intertextuality

As shown, the interpretation of Song of Songs very much depends on the intertextuality within which it is read: Near Eastern cultic texts, Old Testament wisdom literature, the prophets' marriage imagery, or other Near Eastern love songs. The fluidity of the imagery makes the context in which the songs are read crucial for interpretation. One final approach to interpretation should be mentioned. It is based on the idea that biblical texts form an interrelated network. Song of Songs can therefore also be read in relation to another biblical text. For example, Phyllis Trible refers to the narrative about the Garden of Eden as "A Love Story Gone Awry."[15] The relationship between man and woman begins in Genesis 2 with life, harmony, and mutual attraction, but ends in Genesis 3 with mutual mistrust, division into separate roles, and death. What begins as a fairy tale, ends as a tragedy. However, this is not the only Old Testament narrative about man and woman in a paradisiacal garden. In Song of Songs man and woman meet again. It may not be the morning of the creation measured by the standards of history, but perhaps it is by the personal standards of the two leading characters of the Song. Its poems are full of life, harmony, and mutual attraction; they are songs that, due to their date-lessness, remove the societal division into separate domains and the ranking of social superiority and inferiority. The words said to the woman in the narrative about the Fall, "your desire shall be for your husband, and he shall rule over you" (Gen. 3:16), are here repeated, in contrast, when she can shout with joy, "I am my beloved's, and his desire is for me" (Song 7:10). Seen within this intertextuality, the contents of Song of Songs is the realization of the words in Gen. 1:27, "God created humankind in his image, in the image of God he created them; male and female he created them." That was what God intended—a love relationship between equals.

III. THE BOOK OF ESTHER

A. Contents

The book of Esther is about how Esther succeeded not only in preventing a threatened pogrom against the Jews living in the reign of the Persian king, Ahasuerus, but also in taking revenge on their enemies. In order for this event to be remembered, letters are sent to all Jews urging them to observe a joyous celebration, known as Purim, annually at a fixed time.

The book both begins and ends with a banquet. The king of Persia invites all his nobles to a feast, and during this extravagant drinking party commands his queen to appear before his guests so that they can admire her beauty. Queen Vashti, however, refuses, and her disobedience sets in motion the chain of events in the book. She is not only dismissed as queen, but the king also issues an edict to prevent such a lack of female submission from occurring again in his reign (chap. 1). A young Jewish woman named Esther is chosen in a beauty contest to become the new queen. Esther is the adopted daughter of Mordecai, and following his advice, she does not reveal her Jewish identity. Then the story about Mordecai uncovering a conspiracy against King Ahasuerus begins (chap. 2). After this, the king decides to elevate Haman the Agagite. When Haman finds out, however, that the Jew Mordecai refuses to kneel down and pay him honor, Haman asks the king's permission to destroy all Jews. Ahasuerus agrees, and another edict is issued (chap. 3). When the news reaches Mordecai, he encourages Esther to use her position as queen to save her people, for "Who knows? Perhaps you have come to royal dignity for just such a time as this?" (4:14). She reluctantly accepts the proposal (chap. 4). Esther then approaches the king and invites him and Haman for a banquet the next day. Haman is honored by this invitation, but when he sees Mordecai, who still does not pay him suitable homage, he is filled with rage. As advised by his friends, he erects a gallows, on which he intends to hang Mordecai (chap. 5).

That night Ahasuerus cannot sleep, and he has his servants read to him from the royal annals. He discovers that Mordecai was never rewarded for having rescued the king from the earlier conspiracy. Much against his will, Haman is commanded to see to it that Mordecai receives the honor and recognition he deserves (chap. 6). Esther repeats her invitation. When Ahasuerus and Haman come the second time, Esther reveals that the edict about the destruction of all Jews, which Haman advanced, will strike her and her people. The king punishes Haman by having him hanged on the gallows that he had erected for Mordecai (chap. 7). Subsequently, the king issues an edict granting all Jews the right to protect themselves when the previously decreed assaults occur. This new edict is received with joy among the Jews and with fear among their enemies (chap. 8). The Jews take advantage of the right to take up arms and kill their enemies by the thousands. Both Esther and Mordecai now send letters to all Jews asking them to celebrate the anniversary of these events as days of feasting and joy. These days are called Purim to remind them that Haman cast a lot ("*pur*") for the destruction of the Jews (chap. 9). The last chapter of the book refers to the annals of the kings of Media and Persia. These include an account of Mordecai, who was not only elevated to be second in rank to the king, but was also held in high esteem by the Jews because he worked for the good of his people (chap. 10).

B. Place in the Hebrew Bible and Old Testament

The book of Esther, like the book of Ruth, is named after the female main character. Both books are among the five festival scrolls. But unlike the book of Ruth, Esther is a festival legend telling how one of the Jewish feasts, Purim, was established. Its close connection to this popular festival is probably the most significant reason why the book, despite continuous opposition, was accepted into the Hebrew canon. Opposition to the book of Esther was especially due to the absence from it of any reference to Israel's God and the lack of any mention of Purim in the Torah. The book shows no sign of Jewish virtues such as mercy and forgiveness. Indeed, Christians have opposed it because of its description of the joy among the Jews at the bloodbath against their enemies as well as its lack of religious content. The book only sporadically mentions a single religious custom, namely the "lot." It is also a relatively late composition, so that it does not possess the authority attributed to age. Despite these features, the book of Esther became very popular, and according to Rabbinical tradition, Esther is counted as one of the seven prophetesses in Israel (Sarah, Miriam, Deborah, Hannah, Abigail, and Huldah).

What is missing in the Hebrew version of Esther in terms of religious content can be found in the Greek translation, the Septuagint (LXX), which contains whole sections that are not in the Masoretic text (the received Hebrew text).[16] Included in these sections are prayers by Mordecai and Esther. Mordecai expresses his trust that Yahweh will save his people as he delivered them from captivity in Egypt. Esther emphasizes that there is no other savior than Israel's God and that God must remember that she only lives at the court of a pagan because she is forced to do so, for she hates to share a bed with an uncircumcised man. These prayers, which may originally have been in Hebrew, mention the name of God repeatedly and thus make the Greek text much more Jewish.

C. Genre

The book of Esther has traditionally been considered as history, and at first glance many events described in the book look historical. The author refers in detail to times and places; the persons have names; there are references to edicts, letters, and annals; and the descriptions of the Persian court at the time of King

Ahasuerus also indicate a certain knowledge of the conditions at Susa. However, most modern scholars regard the book as fiction—a short story—particularly since no extrabiblical sources confirm the events described in it. Indeed, some details of the story are contradicted by information in outside sources. For example, according to the Greek historian, Herodotus, the queen of King Xerxes (=Ahasuerus) was the daughter of a Persian general named Amestris, rather than either Vashti or Esther.

If the Purim festival originated in the Persian period, it is also surprising that this festival is not mentioned in the late Priestly laws in the Bible. Neither is it plausible that Xerxes would have issued an edict to exterminate the Jews (eleven months before the actual time of the pogrom!) and later issued a second edict allowing the Jews to massacre large parts of the Persian population. Together with the fact that the book has qualities of a novel, the conclusion must be that the author intended to historicize the story in order to justify the celebration of Purim. The short story about Esther and Mordecai should therefore not be read as a description of a historical event, but as a story about how a Jewish woman succeeded in getting sufficient influence at a foreign court to help her own people.

D. Intertextuality

Scholars have long recognized that the book of Esther belongs with a body of literature, including the stories of Joseph, Moses, and Daniel, about Jews living at the court of foreign kings. Gerleman even argues that Esther is patterned after Exodus 1 —12.[17] Both contain stories of deliverance by God, and both are festival legends to be read at Passover and Purim, respectively. A closer analysis shows that the two texts are so different that Esther is unlikely to have been modeled on Exodus. Nevertheless, it is still fruitful to consider them as belonging to the same intertextuality, so that we can read the stories about Esther, Joseph, Moses, and Daniel in light of each other. This makes the special features of each individual story stand out more clearly.

Joseph and Daniel are both examples of Jewish men who through their wisdom (both are described as interpreters of dreams) gain great influence at the courts of foreign kings. Esther differs from these stories in some striking ways. For Esther may be regarded as a wise woman,[18] but it is because of her femininity rather than her wisdom that she manages to influence King Ahasuerus. This makes Esther appear more like Sarah, who, according to Gen. 12:10–20, is included in the harem of the king of Egypt (see also Genesis 20 and 26). Sarah's stay at the foreign court is a serious threat to the promise that it is Abraham's family who will become a great people and receive the promised land. This is precisely the reason why the deliverance from the foreign king is so vital. Regarded in this intertextuality, Esther's role becomes more evident. She is the wife of the foreign king and cannot therefore have been chosen as an ancestress in Israel. She does not raise a family, but she does help to preserve the "family line" by preventing the pogrom against the Jews in Persia.

According to some scholars, the narrative features in the book of Esther, which are also known from other texts, are due to the folktale character of the book. Studies in folklore have uncovered a number of motifs that are repeated in folktales, and several of these can be found in Esther. These motifs are used over and over in folktales about "underdogs" and "tricksters."[19] They include the wife's obedience test,[20] the fair maiden of lowly status who becomes the king's wife, the offer to have a wish fulfilled, the upright and wise hero as opposed to the treacherous villain, the "foolish king," court intrigues, and attempts to destroy a "threatening rival." Finally, the basic theme of the book—Esther's use of her influence on the king to save her people—can also be traced to a folklore motif.

E. Narrative Style and Message

That the book of Esther should be read as a literary work is also emphasized by the very conscious use of narrative style in the book. The author frequently uses repetitions and duplications.[21] When Queen Vashti refuses to follow the king's command, not only she but all women in the country are punished through the king's edict (1:22). And when Mordecai stands up to Haman by refusing to show him honor, all Jews in the country again feel the impact of the king's edict (3:12–15). The repetitions can also be oppositions, as when Haman is hanged on the gallows that was intended for Mordecai (5:14 and 7:10) or when Mordecai receives the honors that Haman himself expected to receive (6:7–9 and 6:10–12). Some repetitions thus express irony.

One of the recurrent themes in the book of Esther is the holding of feasts. It should be noted, however, that the feasts always come in pairs. There are two at the beginning (1:1–8, 9), two in the middle (5:5–8; 7:1–8) and two at the end (9:17–18, 20–22). The festival theme thus helps to structure the story. First, there is the detailed description of the king's extravagant drinking party with the nobles of Persia and Media and the brief note about the queen's banquet for the women in the palace. The contrast is striking, and the reader knows immediately which feast is the more significant. From other stories we know that important things can happen and vital decisions be made when a king has a party: Pharaoh decides to have his baker hanged on the gallows but to restore his cupbearer to his former position (Gen. 40:20–23), and Belshazzar learns about his coming fall through Daniel's interpretation of the writing on the wall (Daniel 5).

Another important stylistic phenomenon is the use of chiastic structures. The best example is the description of how events turned in the opposite direction after the sending out of the second letter: "on the very day when the enemies of the Jews hoped to gain power over them, but which had been changed to a day when the Jews would gain power over their foes" (9:1). This structure is very important in the book of Esther, where the contrast between Haman and Mordecai is one of the recurrent features.[22]

The many oppositions also help to characterize the persons in the story. Haman and Mordecai are described as classic rivals in conflict, and only one of them can be the victor. Vashti is described as the disobedient queen and is thus opposed to the obedient Esther. Vashti's independence in relation to the king contrasts with Esther's submissiveness when she approaches Ahasuerus. The Greek additions to

Esther suggest that even so some found the similarities of Esther to Vashti offensive. For here, in Esther's prayer, it is emphasized that only against her will did she share a bed with a non-Jew and that she had definitely abstained from dining at Haman's table, just as she had not drunk libation wine.

The author's preference for duplications also appears from the description of Vashti and Mordecai. Both display disobedience which has unexpected dramatic consequences: Vashti becomes the direct cause of an edict commanding all women to submit to their husbands, while Mordecai causes an edict to be issued about the extermination of all Jews. One person's disobedience thus results in collective punishment of the group to which the person belongs. If the reader does not realize the absurdity of this phenomenon the first time it occurs when it is "only" the women who suffer, then the repetition, where all Jews have to pay with their lives, illuminates the injustice of this procedure to such an extent that everybody must react.

One of the chief figures in Esther is the Persian king Ahasuerus. The description of him is near comical because he is so inept. Repeatedly, his counselors, Esther or Mordecai, make the proposals that continue the story (compare Haman, who lets others like his wife and friends, control his acts). Who, however, is the counterpart for this inept king? Do the other persons in the story alternately act in this role? Or is it the absent God acting in the background, who, after all, controls events according to his will?[23]

Read in the light of other stories about God saving people at the last moment, it is striking that there is no direct reference to Yahweh interfering and providing a happy ending to the story of Esther. In this respect Esther is similar to Ruth: Yahweh's control is not explicitly mentioned but is clear from the composition of the book. Both books have tight structures. The cause of events is carefully planned and at vital points the author places signals indicating to a Jewish reader that what is happening is not incidental. This is most evident in the correspondence between Mordecai and Esther in 4:14, where Mordecai is confident that relief and deliverance for the Jews will arise from another place if Esther does not realize her purpose in coming to her royal position. On the other hand, there is the external form of the book, which signals order and planning. The text brilliantly takes the reader through the many individual parts of the plot, and the many repetitions strengthen the feeling of being under conscious control. So I agree with Brenner who, after having discussed the style and language of Esther, summarizes: "It would be naive to assume, I think, that such repetition techniques do not constitute a message as well as a medium."[24]

F. The Purposes of the Book of Esther

While scholars agree that the purpose of the book of Esther in its present form is to justify the Purim festival, there is no agreement about the origin of Purim. Attempts to explain the festival on the basis of the word "pur," after which it is named, according to Esther, have not resulted in any agreement among scholars. Neither have attempts to connect it to Babylonian religion and to read the book as a story about the gods Marduk (Mordecai) and Ishtar (Esther). Others, without great success, have tried to find a connection to the Persian New Year festival or a special feast for the dead. Because of the book's central plot, a pogrom against the Jews, it has also been discussed whether the background could have been a historical event such as Judas Maccabeus's victory over the Syrian general Nicanor (1 Macc. 7:39–50). This event, however, was celebrated separately on 13 Adar "the day before Mordecai's day" (2 Macc. 15:36). The origin of the Purim festival is therefore still a mystery.

Recent studies of the book of Esther indicate that, apart from being related to the Purim festival, it has had a more general function, namely to tell Jews how to survive in a diaspora environment. Esther is described as living in a very difficult situation. Despite belonging to a minority in the Persian kingdom and being a woman, she gained an advantageous position in the court of the king. The achievement of this position, however, was not without costs. She submitted to the king's authority, unlike Queen Vashti, and participated in a beauty contest, thus exposing her own beauty, which conflicted with the norms with which she grew up as a Jewish woman. In addition, she became the wife of a non-Israelite. Thus, Esther clearly adapted herself to the customs of the foreign country, and she only reluctantly complied with Mordecai's request to appear uninvited before the king in disobedience to the rules set by the king. That her loyalty towards Ahasuerus as her husband and her loyalty towards her own Jewish background clash with each other is the basic experience for all Jews living in diaspora. This conflict is intensified by the fact that Esther, as a Jewish woman, is marginalized in a twofold sense: both because of her race and because of her sex. The message of the book to the diaspora Jews then is that concern for the whole justifies compromising one's own norms. Esther becomes assimilated, but it serves a purpose: to save her people. Behind this purpose, God is seen faintly when Mordecai indicates that she may have come to royal position precisely for that purpose (4:14). It is thus not only possible to reach a high social position in a foreign country, it is also legitimate.

In this respect, it is worth noting that the Jewish identity of Mordecai is untouched; he does not have to bow to Haman. For Esther, however, it is a different matter. As a Jewish woman she has to sacrifice part of the honor, which is her identity. This makes Esther the loser, as also appears at the end of the book, where it is Mordecai who is elevated to be second in rank to the king, and not Esther.[25] From a feminist viewpoint, therefore, Esther cannot be seen as a pure tribute to the woman who saves her family from persecution. This is where Esther differs from a figure like the Moabitess Ruth, who chooses Naomi's country, people, and God rather than her own and within Jewish tradition is represented as a model proselyte. In contrast, Esther is neither completely a Jew nor completely a wife for her husband. On the other hand, Esther can be a model for the woman in a foreign country who, at the proper time and place, has to use the system from within, by playing her part as the sexually attractive and humble woman, to reach the goal of saving her people. Esther is instrumental in solving the problem of the Jews; but the problem of the women is not solved. For whereas the book of Esther invalidates the edict on behalf of the Jews, the edict that was issued following Vashti's revolt is not invalidated. The man is still supposed to be the master of the house. Even though King Ahasuerus gave Esther the estate of Haman, even though Esther immediately appointed Mordecai over the estate (8:1–2), and even though it was Mordecai as well as Esther who sent letters about the Purim festival, it is Mordecai and not Esther who, at the end of the book, stands as the second in rank to the king.[26]

The book of Esther, therefore, describes indirectly how Jewish communities considered their possibilities of survival in the diaspora. Seen in this perspective the book intends to inspire confidence that if one just accepts a certain degree of assimilation then even Jews can obtain favorable conditions in a foreign country. This seems to be a plausible attitude in a period when the Jews have still not lived through the Greek rule and the savage struggles against foreigners during the Maccabean wars. This makes it plausible that the book, at least its principal contents, can be traced to the end of the Persian era.

IV. THE BOOK OF DANIEL

A. Contents

The book of Daniel unfolds in two parts. Part one, chapters 1—6, contains legends about Daniel and his three friends. Part two, chapters 7—12, recounts Daniel's visions. In chapter 1 we are introduced to Daniel as the main character. He and his friends belong to the group of Israelites who were exiled to Babylon around 600 B.C.E. They became servants in the court of King Nebuchadnezzar, where they have distinguished themselves by their good looks, piety, obedience to the law, and wisdom.

Chapter 2 introduces the theme of Daniel as a dream interpreter. In contrast to the wise men of Babylon, Daniel not only describes to Nebuchadnezzar the king's own dream but also explains that the statue in it represents the coming empires and their declines. When Nebuchadnezzar hears Daniel's interpretation, he praises Daniel's God and gives Daniel and his friends extensive authority in the country.

While Daniel's wisdom is a significant motif in chapter 2, it is the piety of his three friends that is emphasized in chapter 3. Daniel's friends are reported to Nebuchadnezzar, because they refuse to worship the image of gold that the king has set up. During the interrogation they maintain that even if their God will not save them from the fiery furnace, they will still not obey the king's decree. Then they are thrown into the fiery furnace. However, the flames of the fire do not harm them, for with them is one who looks like a son of the gods. Nebuchadnezzar praises their God, and the friends are restored to their positions.

The motif of Daniel as a dream interpreter is resumed in chapter 4, where Nebuchadnezzar has a dream about a large tree that is cut down. Daniel interprets the dream as an image of the king's own destiny—for a period the king will be removed from his throne. The dream is fulfilled, and the narrative ends with Nebuchadnezzar's sanity being restored and his praising of Israel's God, who humbles those who walk in pride.

In chapter 5 the son of Nebuchadnezzar, Belshazzar, has become king. During a banquet he sees some incomprehensible words being written on the wall. Again, Daniel acts in the role of the wise man. By God's help he is able to interpret the mysterious words as a message about King Belshazzar and the decline of his kingdom.

The last of the legends, chapter 6, takes place during the reign of King Darius and emphasizes Daniel's piety. Some of Daniel's competitors jealously report to the king that Daniel does not pay attention to the king's decree but continues to pray to his own God. As punishment, he is thrown into the lions' den but is rescued by God. Darius, who only reluctantly imprisoned Daniel in the lions' den, punishes his jealous enemies and declares that all people must fear Daniel's God.

The common purpose of these legends is to assure readers that during days of distress God takes care of those who continue to believe in him. Daniel and his friends are thus role models for those in a foreign country who want to live in obedience to the God of Israel. The legends were probably written in the eastern diaspora (Mesopotamia) during an era when it was still possible to live with the dual loyalty demanded from a diaspora Jew.

Whereas the legends are clearly directed to those who want to hold on to Israel's God under difficult conditions, the visions in the second half of the book have a more specific audience, namely those who are wise. The visions address Jews who live under foreign rule and oppression in Judah. The situation is much more difficult here, for whereas the kings in the legends are not necessarily considered as opponents, the foreign kings in the visions are presented as rapacious tyrants. The common theme of Daniel's visions is the predetermination of world history, and the time references in these chapters show that we are dealing with the period from approximately 600 to 160 B.C.E. The first vision, chapter 7, concerns four great beasts, which symbolize the kings of Babylon, Media, Persia, and Greece. Each in turn will establish a "world" empire until God's saints inherit the kingdom. The central features of the vision are the Ancient of Days, who sits on his throne flaming with fire (7:9), and the one like a son of man, coming with the clouds of heaven (7:13).

In chapter 8, Daniel sees a ram and a goat fighting with each other. This vision, the meaning of which is made clear to Daniel by the angel Gabriel, concerns the time of the end. The two-horned ram symbolizes the kings of Media and Persia, whereas the goat is the king of Greece. The small horn is the last tyrant who will be destroyed, but "not by human hands" (8:25). However, Daniel is told to seal up the vision.

In chapter 9, Daniel confesses his sin and the sin of his people and prays to God to show mercy to the destroyed city of Jerusalem. Gabriel then comes to tell Daniel about God's plans—following the words of the prophet Jeremiah—that Jerusalem will become a desolate wasteland for 70 years. These 70 years are expressed as 70 weeks of years (i.e., 490 years) that will pass from Jeremiah until the time of the end.

Chapters 10—11 describe how a message came to Daniel in a vision about the predetermination of history. One king will succeed another, and the troubled times that follow will be many. Under the last king (the small horn) the Temple will be desecrated, the abomination that causes desolation will be set up, and the king will say unheard-of things against the God of gods (11:31–36).

The beginning of chapter 12 promises that at that time Michael will arise and fight for Israel. Many of the dead will be raised. The righteous will be rewarded and the godless punished. When Daniel asks for more details about the time schedule, he is told that it will be for a time, times, and half a time (cf. Dan. 7:25). However, Daniel must be silent about what he has heard until the time of the end, when those who are wise will understand. Then it is made clear that from the time that the abomination that causes desolation is set up, there will be 1,290 days. When all this happens, Daniel himself will rise from the dead.

B. Place in the Hebrew Bible and Old Testament

In the Hebrew Bible, the book of Daniel is found in the last part of the canon, among the Writings. In the Greek translation of the Bible, the Septuagint, and in the modern translations used in the Christian church, however, Daniel follows the three Major Prophets, Isaiah, Jeremiah, and Ezekiel. According to some scholars, Daniel's placement among the Writings in the Hebrew Bible was because of its late date of writing. According to others, the book is placed with the other wisdom books in the Writings because the Jewish community in Palestine saw Daniel primarily as a wise man able to interpret dreams, i.e., the Daniel of the legends. The book's position in the Septuagint, on the other hand, stresses Daniel's ability to predict future events, i.e., Daniel as a prophet.

Daniel is not an unknown figure within the Old Testament tradition. In Ezek. 28:3 the ruler of Tyre is said to be "wiser than Daniel" because of his wisdom and understanding of secrets. And in Ezek. 14:14, 20, Daniel's righteousness is compared to that of Noah and Job. Both passages may build on old Canaanite traditions, since the Ugaritic texts (ca. 1400 B.C.E.) mention a king named Dn'il, who was renowned for his righteous judgments. These references about Daniel, together with his role in the legends, indicate that Daniel was a legendary figure rather than a historical person.

Daniel's fame can also be seen in the Apocrypha, which contains some additions to the Book of Daniel. "The Prayer of Azariah" and "the Hymn of the Three Young Men" are both additions to the narrative in Daniel 3 about the friends in the fiery furnace. And in "Bel and the Dragon," we are first told how Daniel by a trick exposes the priests of the god Bel, and then we are given a version of the narrative about Daniel in the lions' den (cf. Daniel 6). Finally, the story about the beautiful Susanna, whom Daniel saves by his wisdom, may be read as an addition to Daniel 12.

C. Date and Genre

The book of Daniel is about Daniel's experiences during the Babylonian exile. Chapter 1 begins with Nebuchadnezzar's siege of Jerusalem, which takes place in the third year of the reign of King Jehoiakim (606 B.C.E.), and Daniel's last vision (Dan. 10:1) takes place in the third year of the reign of Cyrus king of Persia (536 B.C.E.), i.e., seventy years later. However, there are many indications that the final form of the book did not come into existence until much later in the 160s B.C.E., when the Maccabees revolted against Antiochus IV Epiphanes.[27] In general, all the time references in Daniel point to the Maccabean period. It is evident that this is the period the author knows, since the book's historical information grows more concrete and accurate as it approaches the 160s but less specific and correct when it deals with the exilic period in the sixth century when the legends are set. As examples of historical inaccuracies, one may note the following: (1) Nebuchadnezzar cannot have besieged Jerusalem in the third year of the reign of Jehoiakim (contra Dan. 1:1), since he was campaigning at Carchemish in the far north at the time (cf. Jer. 46:2); (2) Belshazzar was neither the son of Nebuchadnezzar nor the king of Babylon, as claimed in Dan. 5:1–2; (3) Darius was not a Mede; he did not succeed the last Babylonian king; he did not rule before Cyrus; and his father was not Ahasuerus (Dan. 6:1, 28; 9:1); and (4) no Median kingdom existed between the Babylonian and the Persian kingdoms.

Evidence of a late date for the Book of Daniel also appears indirectly from the fact that Ben-Sira, whose work is from ca. 180 B.C.E., does not mention Daniel but only Isaiah, Jeremiah, Ezekiel, and the twelve "minor" prophets. In addition, Daniel 2—7 is written in Aramaic, a language that only became the everyday language of the Jews in the centuries following the exile. Indeed, scholars often date the completion of the book of Daniel precisely to 167–164 B.C.E. based on two grounds: (1) the description of the desecration of the temple and the setting up of the abomination that causes desolation and (2) matters that the author does *not* mention. In 167 B.C.E. Antiochus IV Epiphanes desecrated the temple in Jerusalem and erected a pagan altar on sacred ground, and this must be the event referred to in Dan 11:31. However, the author does not mention that Antiochus died late in 164 B.C.E. while campaigning in Persia, but rather predicts his death in Jerusalem. This indicates that the book of Daniel was given its final shape before 164. The author then looks back and interprets the things that had happened since the exile as part of God's plan. On the basis of this plan, he can prophesy that now the end is near; the evil powers will be destroyed and God's kingdom will come. This author, like the classical prophets, addresses his own age and prophesies God's plans for his people during this critical period.

Thus, the decisive argument in favor of the book's late date is its message, aimed at those facing the turbulent events during the reign of Antiochus IV Epiphanes. The author attempts to comfort them and convince them that God controls the progress of history and will provide a happy ending for those who endure the tribulation. The author effectively combines two well-known literary genres— legends and visions—in order to lead the audience to trust in God's plan. Whereas the legends emphasize Daniel's piety and wisdom and thus his credibility, the visions emphasize that Daniel does not prophesy his own words but what God has revealed to him. That the message is delivered by a legendary figure from the past further endows the prophecy with authority. Relative to the time when the events are set, the book is a literary fiction. But this form of fiction was both known and acknowledged in the centuries just before the Common Era. Other contemporary books such as 1 Enoch, 4 Ezra, 2 Baruch, 3 Baruch, 2 Enoch, and the Apocalypse of Abraham were also ascribed to ancient figures whose words were considered valuable and dependable.

D. Apocalypticism

The book of Daniel, like the other writings just mentioned represents apocalyptic literature. The apocalyptic features appear most clearly in the second part of the book but are also found in chapter 2, where Daniel interprets Nebuchadnezzar's dream of the large statue, which predicts how the four kingdoms will be crushed and replaced by the Kingdom of God. What is characteristic of apocalyptic literature is the strong conviction that God has created an organized world and planned the progress of history. Hence God can reveal (apocalypse is the Greek word for revelation) what course world history will take. In apocalyptic writings heavenly secrets are disclosed to the hero either through a heavenly journey, or, as in the book of Daniel, through a number of visions that show that history is predetermined. The times of the world rulers are limited, and then the final age will come when the powers of evil will be defeated and God's kingdom established. In Dan. 12:4, Daniel is instructed to be secretive about what has been revealed to him until the time of the end. This is also a well-known motif of apocalyptic literature used by the author to explain why Daniel's visions have not been made generally known earlier.

By focusing on the future, apocalypticism resembles the eschatological expectations found in the works of the prophets. But besides that, it is influenced by the wisdom traditions with regard to their interest in the world order. Therefore, it is not enough for the apocalyptic writer to refer to a new time in some distant future; the writer also wants to have an insight into God's schedule for world history. In apocalyptic writings there is often a reference to time periods that will succeed each other. One example is the four great beasts in Daniel 7, which represent four successive kingdoms; the considerations in Daniel 9 about the seventy weeks of years; and the reference in Daniel 12 to time, times, and half a time, i.e., years that in v. 11 are prolonged to 1,290 days.

The book of Daniel, like other apocalyptic works, is a composite phenomenon. Features from Old Testament prophecy and wisdom traditions have had an influence on Daniel. In chapter 9 there is a direct reference to Jeremiah's prophecy that Jerusalem will be destroyed for seventy years. Daniel ponders this prophecy and is told its true meaning by the angel Gabriel, who acts as a mediator between this world and the world to come. The man dressed in linen in Dan. 10:5 and 12:6 is known from Ezek. 9:3, and the one who looks like a man, who touches Daniel's lips (10:16), probably derives from the stories about the calls of Jeremiah (Jer. 1:9), Ezekiel (Ezekiel 1, esp. v. 26; 2:8–10), and maybe Isaiah (Isa. 6:6–7). The scene in Daniel 7 with the Ancient of Days on his flaming throne is based on Isaiah's and Ezekiel's visions. And the large tree in Daniel 4 reminds one of Ezekiel 31, where the destiny of the great king is described by the image of a tree that is cut down, an image that is also found in the Isa. 6:13 and 10:33–11:1.

The author's use of literary motifs and conventions also appears from the book's basic narrative: a young Israelite thrives in a foreign court and by his piety and wisdom survives the attempts on his life. The actual theology is well-known from traditional wisdom literature, emphasizing that God looks after the pious, whereas the godless are condemned. Narratives like the story of Joseph (Genesis 37—50) and the book of Esther have the same structure despite their differences.[28] The author's use of well-known literary conventions can also explain some of the numbers in the book. Daniel's experiences take place over seventy years, the same number as the seventy years in Jeremiah's prophecy. The number seventy indicates perfection and must therefore be understood as a large, round number. Similarly, the number four is used to express a well-known convention. The four quarters of the globe express unity, and the book of Amos, for instance, has several examples of the structure 3 + 1 (Amos 1:3–2:3), in which the fourth item is the most significant. This is also the case when the book of Daniel refers to the fourth beast or the fourth kingdom. And maybe even Daniel himself is to be seen as the fourth one in relation to his three friends.

E. "The Son of Man"

Whereas Jewish communities in Palestine emphasized Daniel's wisdom, within Christian tradition the book has especially been read as a prophecy about the time to come. The reference in Dan. 7:13–14 to one like a son of man coming with the clouds of heaven is significant for the interpretation in the New Testament of Jesus as the Son of Man, meaning the Messiah. Similarly, the time references in the book of Daniel have been used to determine the anticipated second coming of Christ and the final judgement.

The expression "a son of man" in Daniel 7 has been interpreted in various ways. According to some scholars, this figure is an image of the people of Israel;[29] according to others, it refers to an individual person. It appears clear from the context that we have to do with imagery. The great beasts rising from the sea (the author probably wants to arouse associations with the deep and the giant chaos beasts) are images of the kingdoms of the world. Opposite the beasts is the one who looks like a man (but is actually not a man). Just as the beasts are images of the kings and their kingdoms, this figure must be the image of God's kingdom which will succeed the human kingdoms. However, when God's kingdom is described through the image of one looking like a man, it may reflect the author's thoughts about Israel's guardian angel Michael.

In Daniel, angels—who are also called "the saints"—are actually referred to as beings who look like people. Daniel 8:15 describes the angel Gabriel as one "who looked like a man," and in Dan. 10:16 the one who touches Daniel's lips is referred to as "one who looked like a man." The author, therefore, seems to be imagining an angel. Whereas the beasts represent world powers, the angel represents the heavenly world and thus the coming kingdom of God that will be realized on earth. That the angel is Israel's guardian, Michael, can indirectly be seen from Dan. 7:27, which says that power will be handed over to "the people of the saints of the Most High," i.e., God's angels' people. This interpretation of the text is not in opposition to Dan. 7:14, where the kingdom is given to the one like a son of man, i.e., Israel's guardian angel Michael, or Dan. 7:27, where power is given to the people, of whom Michael is the guardian angel, but who are here referred to as the people of the saints of the Most High.[30]

F. Language

The book of Daniel is a book marked by dualities. As mentioned, it consists of two parts, a collection of legends and a collection of visions. It operates at two time levels, the time of the narrative and the time during which and to which the author writes. As an apocalyptic work, Daniel builds on two well known traditions: prophecy and wisdom.[31] Finally, the book is written in two different languages: Hebrew and Aramaic. It would have been simple and understandable if the two parts of the book were written each in a different language. Then there would have been good reason to believe that the book had originally consisted of two independent texts that were later compiled into a unit. However, this is not the case. Whereas 1:1–2:4a and 8:1–12:13 are written in Hebrew, 2:4b–7:28 is written in Aramaic. This means that the majority (but not the entirety) of the legends is in Aramaic, whereas the majority (but not the whole) of the visions is in Hebrew.[32] Scholars have formed various hypotheses to explain this strange phenomenon.[33] Some believe that the legends were originally all in Aramaic, whereas the visions were all in Hebrew, and that the editor translated chapter 1 into Hebrew and chapter 7 into Aramaic in order to combine the sections. According to others, chapter 1 was translated into Hebrew to facilitate the inclusion of the book in the Hebrew canon. A German scholar has argued that the Aramaic chapters (2—7) never existed in any other language, which would mean that an independent book of Daniel written in Aramaic must have existed at some time.[34] However, since the editor during the time of the Maccabees related this book to the visions written in Hebrew (chaps. 8—12), he himself wrote (or translated from Aramaic) an introduction to the entire book (i.e., chapter 1) in Hebrew.

The thesis about an independent Aramaic book on Daniel's experiences in the Babylonian court and his great vision of the end of times is supported by the structure of chapters 2—7, which form a chiasmus: chapters 2 and 7 share the theme of the kingdoms; chapters 3 and 6 are both deliverance narratives; and chapters 4 and 5 are interpretation narratives. The position of the chapters in relation to each other is thus deliberate, which suggests that they were originally a unit and that the division between legend and vision is not as sharp as it first appears.[35] That chapters 2—7 are written in Aramaic is probably due to the linguistic development throughout the period when Aramaic became more and more popular at the expense of Hebrew. The author of chapters 8—12 (and perhaps chap. 1) still chose Hebrew, probably because of the struggle during the time of the Maccabees to maintain what was specifically Jewish. Since the two languages are closely related, it was not difficult for readers to shift from one to the other.

G. Theological Themes

Daniel may be the latest book in the Hebrew Bible, and it is different from the other writings in certain aspects. It is the only example of an actual apocalypse in the Hebrew Bible. In contrast to the pseudepigraphal apocalypses, which were not included in the canon, the book of Daniel tells about this world. The kingdom to come will be an earthly kingdom in the same way that the classical prophets expected a new Davidic kingdom. Also the belief in the resurrection of the dead is new in relation to the previous understanding of death, though the author does not envision a general resurrection but only a resurrection of the martyrs.

The book of Daniel was written in a period of persecution, and it has proven suitable for rereading and reinterpretation in similar situations. The Revelation to John in the New Testament is a good example of this. Considering its size, the book of Daniel is quoted quite frequently in the New Testament, and 70 percent of the quotations are found in Revelation. That Daniel's prophecies of the end of the world had still not come true did not induce the Christian church to reject the book; instead they made the necessary reinterpretations. The many images of hostile powers were still just as relevant: the Romans could easily be compared with great and cruel beasts, and the book's encouragement to endurance made sense during the persecutions of the early era of Christianity. Different communities could therefore reread the book in the light of their own situations trusting that God was still the lord of history who would one day sit on the throne and call for justice over the enemies. The legends in the book of Daniel taught these communities the meaning of endurance, and the visions taught them to think and speak using images, when they were tormented by the nagging question, "How long, O LORD?"

FOR FURTHER READING

Ruth

Campbell, Edward F., Jr. *Ruth*. AB 7. Garden City, N.Y.: Doubleday, 1975.

Fewell, Danna Nolan, and David Miller Gunn. *Compromising Redemption: Relating Characters in the Book of Ruth*. Literary Currents in Biblical Interpretation. Louisville, Ky.: Westminster John Knox, 1990.

Gow, Murray D. *The Book of Ruth: Its Structure, Theme and Purpose*. Leicester: Apollos, 1992.

Hubbard, Robert L., Jr. *The Book of Ruth*. NIC. Grand Rapids: Eerdmans, 1988.

Nielsen, Kirsten. *Ruth: A Commentary*. OTL. Louisville. Ky.: Westminster John Knox, 1997.

Sasson, Jack M. *Ruth: A New Translation with a Philological Commentary and a Formalist-Folklorist Interpretation*. Biblical Seminar 10. 2d ed. Sheffield: JSOT, 1989.

Song of Songs

Brenner, Athalya. *The Song of Songs*. OTG; Sheffield: JSOT, 1989.

Brenner, Athalya, ed. *A Feminist Companion to the Song of Songs.* Feminist Companion to the Bible 1. Sheffield: Sheffield Academic Press, 1993.

Exum, J. Cheryl. "A Literary and Structural Analysis of the Song of Songs." *ZAW* 85 (1973): 47–79.

Falk, Marcia. *Love Lyrics from the Bible: A Translation and Literary Study of the Song of Songs.* BLS 4. Sheffield: Almond, 1982.

———. "Song of Songs." *Harper's Bible Commentary*, ed. J. L. Mays, 525–28. San Francisco: Harper & Row, 1988.

Fox, Michael V. *The Song of Songs and the Ancient Egyptian Love Songs.* Madison: University of Wisconsin Press, 1985.

Murphy, Roland. *The Song of Songs.* Hermeneia. Minneapolis: Fortress, 1990.

Pope, Marvin H. *Song of Songs.* AB 7C. Garden City, N.Y.: Doubleday, 1977.

Trible, Phyllis. *God and the Rhetoric of Sexuality.* OBT. Philadelphia: Fortress, 1978.

Esther

Berg, Sandra. *The Book of Esther: Motifs, Themes and Structure.* SBLDS 44. Missoula, Mont.: Scholars Press, 1979.

Brenner, Athalya, ed. *A Feminist Companion to Esther, Judith and Susanna.* Sheffield: Sheffield Academic Press, 1995. Note the bibliography on pp. 324–36.

Clines, David J. A. *The Esther Scroll: The Story of the Story.* JSOTSup 30. Sheffield: JSOT, 1984.

Fox, Michael V. *Character and Ideology in the Book of Esther.* Studies in Personalities of the Old Testament. Columbia: University of South Carolina Press, 1991.

Gerleman, Gillis. *Esther.* BKAT 21. Neukirchen-Vluyn: Neukirchener Verlag, 1973.

Larkin, Katrina J. A. *Ruth and Esther.* OTG. Sheffield: Sheffield Academic Press, 1996.

Levenson, Jon D. *Esther.* AB. New York: Doubleday, 1998.

Daniel

Collins, John J. *The Apocalyptic Vision of the Book of Daniel.* HSM 16. Missoula, Mont.: Scholars Press, 1977.

———. "Daniel, Book of." *ABD* 2: 29–37.

Davies, Philip R. *Daniel.* OTG. Sheffield: JSOT, 1985.

Hartman, Louis F. and Alexander A. Di Lella. *The Book of Daniel.* AB 23. Garden City, N.Y.: Doubleday, 1978.

Talmon, Shemaryahu. "Daniel." In R. Alter and F. Kermode, eds., *The Literary Guide to the Bible,* 343–56. London: Collins; Cambridge, Mass.: Belknap, 1987.

8

THE "CHRONICLER'S HISTORY"

Ezra-Nehemiah, 1–2 Chronicles

M. PATRICK GRAHAM

I. NAME AND PLACE IN THE CANON

The Hebrew Bible begins with the "Primary History" (Genesis—2 Kings) and ends with the "Secondary History" (1–2 Chronicles, Ezra-Nehemiah). The former is a tragic narrative that begins with the creation of the world by God and ends with God's destruction of Jerusalem and the exile of his people. While the "Secondary History" also begins with creation ("Adam" is the first word in 1 Chronicles), it moves beyond the destruction of Jerusalem and the monarchy to describe the return of Jewish exiles to Jerusalem, the rebuilding of the temple and city walls, and the commitment of the people to live under the guidance of God through the law. It is a story that ends with hope and the formation of a people to serve God faithfully (cf. Neh. 13:30–31).[1]

In the Hebrew Bible, 1–2 Chronicles goes under the title, "Events of the days" (*dibrê hayyamîm*) and also appears as two books. This title recurs elsewhere in the Hebrew Bible, where it is often translated "Chronicles" and used to designate annalistic sources of which biblical authors were aware (e.g., "the Book of the Chronicles of the Kings of Israel," 1 Kings 14:19). The application of the title to 1–2 Chronicles probably reflects the Jewish community's sense of the genre of the work as "history." Its division in the Hebrew Bible into two separate books can be traced back to the fifteenth century, but before that it was treated as a single book, as shown by the fact that it was counted as only one of the twenty-four books that constituted the canon of the Hebrew scriptures. Similarly, Ezra and Nehemiah were counted as a single book with the name "Ezra" in Hebrew Bibles before the fifteenth century. In the LXX, though, Chronicles appears as two books under the designation Paraleipomenon ("omitted things") alpha and beta, thus reflecting an observation about the content of the work: it included many things omitted from Samuel–Kings. This understanding of the work is also reflected in its title in the Vulgate, "Paralipomenon," and has been influential in traditional Christian evaluation of the work. The title of the work in English Bibles may be traced back through Luther's designation of the work as "Chronica" in his translation of the Old Testament into German and ultimately to Jerome's reference to the work as "the *chronikon* of the whole of sacred history" in the prologue to his translation of Samuel–Kings.[2] The more complex state of affairs in the case of Ezra-Nehemiah may be illustrated by the following table:[3]

LXX	Vulgate	Modern Bibles
Esdras alpha	III Esdras	1 Esdras
Esdras beta	I Esdras	Ezra
Esdras gamma	II Esdras	Nehemiah
	IV Esdras	2 Esdras

1 Esdras is a Greek translation of 2 Chronicles 35—36; Ezra 1—10; and Neh. 8:1–13, along with supplementary material at 1 Esdr. 3:1–5:6. The Vulgate's IV Esdras is a compilation of a Jewish apocalyptic work (chaps. 3—14) with Christian additions (chaps. 1—2 and 15—16).[4] It is clear, however, that Ezra and Nehemiah were treated as a single work in the earliest Hebrew and Greek manuscripts, and it was not until the time of Origen and Jerome that the two were treated as separate books.[5]

Apart from the Syriac tradition in the Christian church, there seems to have been no problem with the acceptance of Chronicles and Ezra-Nehemiah into the Jewish or Christian canons, and both were lodged in the Writings (*Ketuvim*), the third division of the Hebrew canon. In the Hebrew Bible, the Palestinian tradition (Aleppo Codex; Leningrad B19a) places Chronicles at the first and Ezra-Nehemiah at the end of the Writings, while the Babylonian tradition set both Ezra-Nehemiah and Chronicles at the end of the Writings. The LXX, however, set Chronicles with the other historical books of the Old Testament, between Kings and Ezra-Nehemiah, probably on the basis of their content, although some LXX manuscripts inserted 1 Esdras between Chronicles and Ezra-Nehemiah. The inclusion of the works in the LXX points to their incorporation into the canon by the mid-second century B.C.E., and it also appears that canonization occurred separately for Chronicles and Ezra-Nehemiah.[6]

II. STRUCTURE AND CONTENTS

Chronicles divides neatly into four parts: 1 Chronicles 1—9, genealogies; 1 Chronicles 10—29, the reign of David; 2 Chronicles 1—9, the reign of Solomon; and 2 Chronicles 10—36, the reigns of the kings of Judah from Rehoboam to Zedekiah. The final two verses of Chronicles (2 Chron. 36:22–23) reproduce the opening of Ezra-Nehemiah (Ezra 1:1–3a) and so link the two works together. Ezra 1—6 deals with the return of the exiles and the rebuilding of the Jerusalem temple; chaps. 7—10 detail the work of Ezra himself and are typically designated the "Ezra Memoir" because of their narration in the first person; Nehemiah 1—7 describes how Nehemiah came to Jerusalem and rebuilt the city walls under great adversity; chaps. 8—10 describe the reading the law by Ezra, celebration of the Feast of Booths, and the making of a covenant; and chaps. 11—13 treat several matters: the distribution of the Jewish population in Judea and Jerusalem (chap. 11), lists of priests and levites (12:1–26), dedication of Jerusalem's walls (12:27–13:3), and Nehemiah's second visit to Jerusalem (13:4–31).

III. CRITICAL ISSUES

A. Relation of Chronicles to Ezra-Nehemiah

Although Rabbinic Judaism and medieval Christianity typically considered Ezra as the author of Chronicles and Ezra-Nehemiah,[7] it was Leopold Zunz in 1832 who argued that "the Chronicler," rather than Ezra, composed these works,[8] and two years later, F. C. Movers interpreted the correspondence of 2 Chron. 36:22–23 and Ezra 1:1–3 to mean that those two books were written by the same author.[9] These publications signaled a shift in the scholarly treatment of Chronicles and Ezra-Nehemiah, and it was Zunz's view that became almost uniformly accepted in scholarly circles until 1968, when Sara Japhet published the findings of her M.A. thesis before a broader audience.[10] Japhet identified four principle arguments for Zunz's thesis: (1) Ezra 1:1–3a also appears at the end of Chronicles (2 Chron. 36:22–23); (2) 1 Esdras duplicates 2 Chron. 35—36 and Ezra 1—10; (3) there is a linguistic resemblance between the three books, as is shown in vocabulary, syntax, and style; and (4) the three works share a certain uniformity in theological concepts, which is expressed in the material itself and in its selection.

While Japhet's article examined only the matter of the linguistic resemblance among the three books, other scholars followed her example, treating the linguistic arguments, as well as the other three "legs" of Zunz's thesis. The argument about material shared between Ezra 1:1–3a and 2 Chron. 36:22–23 has not been decisive in the debate. While some argue that the duplication supports the thesis of common authorship for the two works, others regard it as supporting the opposite position, i.e., it was added later to signal the reader about where the story continued.

Similarly, the collocation of 2 Chronicles 35—36; Ezra 1—10; and Neh. 7:38–8:12 in 1 Esdras has not been decisive in the debate, since so many questions remain about the relation of 1 Esdras to 1–2 Chronicles and Ezra-Nehemiah. Some have explained 1 Esdras as the original LXX translation of a part of the Chronicler's history (Chronicles and Ezra-Nehemiah) before those parts came to be separated into individual books. Others have argued more convincingly that the author of 1 Esdras did not simply translate a single earlier, coherent document but created a new composition from material in separate books (Chronicles and Ezra-Nehemiah).[11] Therefore, 1 Esdras simply attests the obvious: that the events of Ezra 1—7 should be read as following those of the books of Chronicles.

As for the linguistic similarities between Chronicles and Ezra-Nehemiah, Japhet's article classified them differently and saw them as: linguistic opposition, variation in technical terms (the stage of development represented in Chronicles was later than that of Ezra-Nehemiah), and stylistic traits peculiar to Chronicles and Ezra-Nehemiah respectively. Williamson's research confirmed Japhet's findings.[12] He investigated the list of 140 items drawn up by earlier scholars to affirm the existence of a Chronicler's history (Chronicles and Ezra-Nehemiah)[13] and eliminated all but six as either irrelevant to the question or as actually showing that Chronicles differed from Ezra-Nehemiah. He did not claim that disunity had been proven but that the linguistic argument for unity had been removed and that the burden of proof still remained with those arguing that Chronicles and Ezra-Nehemiah were a unified composition.[14] Two complications in the linguistic analysis undertaken by Japhet and Williamson are these: (1) much of the textual material with which they work is taken from other sources (e.g., about seventy percent of Ezra-Nehemiah is from other sources); and (2) the chronological periods that are the subject of the narratives are also different (Chronicles dealing with the preexilic and Ezra-Nehemiah with the postexilic era).[15] Therefore, while there remains a difference of opinion about the linguistic relationship of Chronicles to Ezra-Nehemiah, the balance of opinion has certainly shifted—to the point that the linguistic argument is no longer a compelling reason in favor of a single author of Chronicles and Ezra-Nehemiah.

Finally, although Chronicles and Ezra-Nehemiah seem generally congruent in their focus on priestly and cultic matters, there are areas of disagreement. First, while Chronicles repeatedly shows God participating in the life of his people—punishing their unfaithfulness on one occasion, and delivering them from hostile neighbors on another—the God of Ezra-Nehemiah is not portrayed as so immediately involved in the life of the Restoration community. Second, Ezra-Nehemiah advances a much more restrictive view of the people of God than does Chronicles. While Chronicles uses "Israel" for all twelve tribes and is open to the participation of the Northern tribes and even foreigners in the worship of God at Jerusalem (cf. 2 Chron. 30:25), Ezra-Nehemiah uses "Israel" only for Judah, Benjamin, and the descendants of Levi and excludes all others from involvement in the Jerusalem cult (cf. Ezra 4). Third, the temple servants appear repeatedly in Ezra-Nehemiah (e.g., Ezra 2:43, 58, 70) but only once in Chronicles (1 Chron. 9:2).[16]

Therefore, three positions on the existence of a Chronicler's history have come to dominate the discussion. First, some affirm that such a history existed and believe that it included either all or part of Ezra-Nehemiah. Others believe that Chronicles and Ezra-Nehemiah were written by different authors. Finally, still others think that Chronicles and Ezra-Nehemiah were written by the same author but at different times and issued as separate works.

B. Chronological Order of Ezra and Nehemiah

Perhaps the most vigorously debated issue in the interpretation of Ezra-Nehemiah is that of the chronological order of the two primary figures in the work. In addition to the fact that the canonical sequence itself suggests that Ezra's activity occurred before Nehemiah's, there are two other factors that favor this sequence. First, Ezra 7:8 reports that Ezra arrived in Jerusalem in the fifth month of

Artaxerxes' seventh year, while Neh. 2:1–9 indicates that Nehemiah left for Judea in Artaxerxes' twentieth year. If the Artaxerxes mentioned in both texts was Artaxerxes I, then Ezra arrived in Jerusalem in 458 and Nehemiah in 445 B.C.E. In addition, Nehemiah 8—9 describes a ceremony in Jerusalem in which Ezra reads the law in the presence of Nehemiah, who served as governor.

Since 1890, however, when Van Hoonacker proposed that the sequence of the two leaders should be reversed (Nehemiah went to Jerusalem under Artaxerxes I, but Ezra's activity was spent under the reign of Artaxerxes II),[17] debate on the issue has continued, and it has typically focused on the dating of Ezra's return, since scholars usually agree that Nehemiah's activity in Jerusalem began in 445 B.C.E. Among the arguments favoring van Hoonacker's reconstruction are the following. First, while Nehemiah 7 credits Nehemiah with rebuilding the walls of Jerusalem, Ezra 9:9 notes that Ezra found the walls already rebuilt when he arrived in Jerusalem. Second, the presence of Nehemiah alongside Ezra in Neh. 8:9 and 12:26 seems superficial. In the first text it may be observed that the entire chapter was originally part of the Ezra Memoir but has been moved to its present position. In the case of Neh. 12:26, Nehemiah's name may have been added to the episode by the editor, since the verb in Neh. 8:9 is in the singular, and Nehemiah is unmentioned in the parallel passage in 1 Esdras 9:49, which some regard as a witness to a more original form of the text. Similarly, in Neh. 12:26 Ezra's involvement is superficial, and his name may have been inserted secondarily. Third, in Nehemiah's review of the census of people who returned with Zerubbabel, none of the approximately 5,000 returning with Ezra are mentioned (cf. Neh. 7:5–73 and Ezra 8:1–14). Finally, Nehemiah was a contemporary with the high priest Eliashib (Neh. 3:1), while Ezra lived in the time of Jehohanan ben Eliashib (Ezra 10:6), who was the grandson, not the son, of Eliashib. Opponents of this view have argued that: (1) the reference to Jerusalem's walls was intended to be understood figuratively rather than literally; (2) though it is usually conceded that the reference to Nehemiah in Neh. 8:9 is secondary, this is not the case with Neh. 12:26, where the author is "working with a text that has already fused the two reformers' activities";[18] and (3) since Eliashib was a common name (three are listed in Ezra 10:24, 27, 36), it is not necessarily the case that the Eliashibs of Ezra 10:6 and Neh. 3:1 are the same person. Therefore, in spite of the support that van Hoonacker's view has attracted, it has not succeeded in overthrowing the traditional sequence of Ezra followed by Nehemiah.

A third proposal to resolve this issue has been popularized by John Bright, who emends "seventh year" in Ezra 7:7–8 to "thirty-seventh year," explaining that the error arose because of a scribe's error copying the text (three consecutive words would have begun with the Hebrew letter *shin*, and this would have provided ample opportunity for such a mistake). This reconstruction has Ezra arrive in 428 B.C.E. and allows him to have been a contemporary of Nehemiah's. The latter was initially in Jerusalem from 445 to 433 B.C.E. and returned for a second visit later. It was during this second visit that Ezra arrived, and the two undertook their reforms simultaneously.[19] This view has failed to win significant support.[20]

C. Sheshbazzar and Zerubbabel

Another frequently debated issue in this material is that of the relationship between Zerubbabel and Sheshbazzar. Both are called governors of Judah and receive credit for laying the foundation of the Jerusalem temple (cf. Ezra 1:8; 3:8–10; 5:14–16; Hag. 1:1). Some have proposed that the two names refer to a single person or that Sheshbazzar was in fact Shenazzar, Zerubbabel's uncle (1 Chron. 3:19). The most likely explanation is that Sheshbazzar began work on the temple foundation first and that later Zerubbabel made his own contribution to the effort.[21]

D. Identity of Ezra's Lawbook

Artaxerxes commissioned Ezra to "make inquiries about Judah and Jerusalem according to the law" of God (Ezra 7:14) and to teach the law and see that it is obeyed (7:25–26). The remainder of the book (chaps. 8—10) describes Ezra's actions to carry out his charge, and Neh. 7:72b–8:12 (EVV 7:73b–8:12) sketches a scene in which Ezra reads the law before the people. Such an initiative on the part of the Persian government seems entirely possible in light of the tradition of Darius's efforts to codify laws for his subjects in Babylon and Egypt.[22] While it is clear that "the law of Moses" was already being followed to some extent in Judah before Ezra's arrival (e.g., Ezra 3:2), the precise nature of Ezra's "book of the law of Moses" (Neh. 8:1) remains unclear. Among the various proposed identifications that have been made, four have received the most attention.[23]

Some have suggested that the book was some form of Deuteronomy, and indeed there are several clear allusions to Deuteronomy in Ezra's reform (e.g., cf. Ezra 9:2 with Deut. 7:3; and Neh. 8:18 with Deut. 31:9–13). Others have proposed that Ezra's law was only the Priestly Writing, a work that probably derives from the Persian period and finds some role in Ezra's reform (e.g., cf. Neh. 8:14–15 with Lev. 23:42–43; and Ezra 3:4 with Num. 29:12–28). Still others have suggested that Ezra's law has not come down to the present intact, but that its laws have been scattered in the Pentateuch and can no longer be retrieved and reconstructed into a whole. The most popular suggestion, however, has been that Ezra's book was the Pentatuech (or some close approximation thereof), since it is clear that the law was associated with Moses and that it contained at least segments of Deuteronomy and the Priestly writing.[24]

IV. SOURCES: CHRONICLES

In the study of Chronicles great attention has been given to the matter of determining what sources the author used for his work. Much of this discussion has been driven by historical concerns, viz., did the Chronicler draw on ancient and reliable sources of information for his narrative, or did he simply fabricate the details of his history? Even if it is agreed, though, that the Chronicler made use of previous literary and historical works, there is still the matter of how he used them: did he follow them faithfully, or did he willfully distort them to serve his own purposes? The debate on these and related issues continues to be vigorous, and there are strong differences of opinion among scholars.

One point on which all agree, however, is that the Chronicler drew on other books in the Hebrew Bible for his narrative. His genealogies, for example, incorporate material from Genesis, Exodus, Numbers, Joshua, Judges, Samuel, and Ruth; 1 Chronicles 16 quotes Psalms 95, 105, and 106; and the body of 1 Chronicles 9—2 Chronicles 36 relies on the books of Samuel and Kings. While some have argued that Chronicles and Samuel–Kings rely on a common source,[25] most scholars have concluded that the Chronicler has largely followed the course of the Samuel–Kings narrative, often incorporating large sections with few changes (cf. 2 Chron. 10:1–19 with 1 Kings 12:1–19). There is less certainty, however, about the form of the text of Samuel and Kings that the Chronicler used. It appears that he did not use the MT of Samuel but the form of the Hebrew text that is attested in the LXX and perhaps 4QSam[a].[26] This state of affairs makes it hazardous to assume that all differences in the material held in common between Chronicles and Samuel–Kings are due to the Chronicler's deliberate editorial activity.

In addition to the foregoing canonical materials, there are indications that the Chronicler used certain noncanonical sources. Instead of rigid uniformity in the genealogies of 1 Chronicles 1—9, one finds tribal genealogies of vastly differing length and a variety of genealogical genres. Some genealogies, for example, are horizontal, others vertical, and the rich variety of features that one encounters in the various tribal genealogies points to the fact that this material has been gathered from sources that differ in kind (e.g., family genealogies, military census lists) and that the Chronicler has allowed many of these differences to remain as he composed his narrative.[27] In addition, there are the events and people in Chronicles that are not mentioned elsewhere in Scripture. The developments described in 1 Chron. 4:38–43, for example, which seem reasonable, are not reported elsewhere in Scripture and so may indeed have been taken by the Chronicler from an earlier source. Similarly, the story of the capture and repentance of Manasseh (2 Chron. 33:10–13) is unique in Scripture to Chronicles, and in this instance the Chronicler cites a source for his information ("the Chronicles of Hozai"). Since the report of Manasseh's repentance, though, completely reverses the picture of the king that one finds in 2 Kings 21 and may be explained as the Chronicler's attempt to account for Manasseh's long, peaceful reign (at fifty-five years, the longest of any Judean king), it has been called into question. Did the Chronicler simply fabricate it? Did he rely on an earlier source, which itself had no historical basis? Or is it the Deuteronomistic Historian who should be challenged for excluding this event from his narrative because of his own disgust for Manasseh's idolatry?[28]

Finally, there is the matter of the source citations in Chronicles. While this would seem to settle the matter and lead all readers to conclude that the Chronicler proceeded in a methodical way to gather reliable historical information for his narrative and that he clearly used many nonbiblical resources for his task, this has not at all been the case. Most of the Chronicler's source citations occur at the end of his account of a king's reign and often follow the pattern of 2 Chron. 25:26, "And the rest of the acts of Amaziah, the first and the last, are they not written in

the Book of the Kings of Judah and Israel?" (The source citations in Samuel–
Kings follow a similar pattern.) Aside from minor variations to this pattern, there
are references to the chronicles of the prophets Samuel, Nathan, and Gad (1
Chron. 29:29; cf. 2 Chron. 9:29), the prophecy of Ahijah the Shilonite and the vi-
sions of Iddo the seer (2 Chron. 9:29), the chronicles of Shemaiah the prophet and
Iddo the seer (2 Chron. 12:15), etc. Although it could be that the Chronicler and
the Deuteronomistic Historian are using and so citing the same "Chronicles of the
Kings" source, it seems more likely that the Chronicler is using some form of the
Deuteronomistic History and largely copying the latter's source citations.[29] Similarly, it seems that the references to the chronicles of the prophets are also citations
of Samuel–Kings but reflect the Chronicler's view that these reports arose from
the hands of the prophets. In the case of Samuel, for example, it is clear that the
prophet died before David began to reign and so could not have written a description of his reign, as 1 Chron. 29:29 would suggest.

Therefore, it appears that the Chronicler made use of certain canonical books
(especially Samuel–Kings) and that he probably had access to certain noncanonical works, whose nature may be only generally surmised but whose date, origin,
and reliability are unknown. Most scholars then proceed on a case by case basis,
attempting to determine whether reports found only in Chronicles derive from reliable, extra-biblical sources. As might be expected, opinions often differ sharply,
and there is always the temptation for the interpreter to accept the Chronicler's account when it supports a cherished theory or historical reconstruction but reject information from Chronicles when it clashes with the model at hand.

At any event, it is also important to note the use that the Chronicler made of his
sources, something that can be determined with some (though not absolute) certainty
by comparing Chronicles with Samuel–Kings. It is clear, for example, that the
Chronicler made only selective use of his source material, omitting reports that were
of no interest to him (e.g., accounts of the reigns of rulers of the northern kingdom
of Israel) or that did not advance his agenda (e.g., the omission of information about
David's sin against Uriah [2 Samuel 11—12]). The Chronicler also sometimes har-
monized contradictions in his sources or otherwise resolved difficulties in them (cf.
2 Chron. 7:9–10 with 1 Kings 8:65; Deut. 16:13–15; and Lev. 23:33–36), ignored
the context of material in a source and rearranged its order (cf. 2 Chron. 34:3–18
with 2 Kings 23:1–10), and used various literary techniques (chiasmus, repetition,
inclusio, etc.) to construct a coherent narrative.[30] It is clear from the foregoing that
the Chronicler was no mere copyist but a creative and skillful author who used earlier materials to advance his own purposes. In the subsequent discussion it will be
shown that the Chronicler was driven primarily by theological—rather than histori-
cal-critical—concerns and that his effort was to instruct and encourage his readers.

V. SOURCES: EZRA-NEHEMIAH

The discussion of sources for Ezra-Nehemiah has some parallels with that of
Chronicles (the concern with determining the historical reliability of the biblical

text, for example), but there are two important differences: Ezra-Nehemiah does not have the frequent source citations that are met in Chronicles, and there is no earlier, additional narrative that substantially parallels that of Ezra-Nehemiah. Consequently, researchers must use less direct means to identify the sources behind Ezra-Nehemiah, and it is much more difficult to determine how the author used the sources.

There is general agreement that the author made use of two extensive documents, the Nehemiah Memoir and the Ezra Memoir. Though it is common practice to designate these "memoirs" because of their first-person narratives, it is not believed that either of them is in fact an actual "memoir" of Nehemiah or Ezra. In addition, there are various opinions about what constituted each of them. One proposal is that the Nehemiah Memoir included Neh. 1:1–7:73a; 11:1–2; 12:31–43; 13:4–31, though there is debate about whether parts of this material were added by later editors.[31] At any rate, it appears as a first person narrative by Nehemiah about the events in which he was involved as Persian governor. The document shows little signs of editorial revision, and it is unclear whether the document was originally composed as an address to God, votive inscription, biographical tomb inscription, prayer of the falsely accused, or as a legal defense in the royal court. Whether the Nehemiah Memoir itself drew on other sources is debatable (e.g., Nehemiah 3 is a list of wall builders and Neh. 7:6–73a is a list of returnees; alternatively, each list may have been added to the Nehemiah Memoir at a later time).[32]

The Ezra Memoir apparently was the source behind Ezra 7—10 and Neh. 8:1–9:15—perhaps first-person sections (7:27–9:15) derive from Ezra himself, and third-person sections are by the author of Ezra-Nehemiah. Since the styles of first- and third-person narratives are similar—and similar also to other postexilic Hebrew documents—it is difficult to separate on stylistic grounds the works of various authors. Lack of clarity also exists about the purpose of the Ezra Memoir—was it written as a defense/apology by/for Ezra, or composed for the edification of the Jewish community? The Ezra Memoir itself seems to draw on the firman of Artaxerxes (Ezra 7:12–26, written in Aramaic and widely regarded as authentic), the list of those returning with Ezra (8:1–14), and the list of those making mixed marriages (Ezra 10:18–43).[33]

The Aramaic chronicle of Ezra 4:7–6:18 is another source used by the author of Ezra-Nehemiah. It is an Aramaic writing that contains several purportedly authentic documents strung together with linking narrative. This correspondence fits what is known regarding Aramaic correspondence of the fifth century B.C.E. There are also lists that may derive from the temple archives: a listing of family heads (Neh. 11:3–19), a list of country towns with Jewish populations (Neh. 11:25–36), a list of priests and Levites from Zerubbabel's day (Neh. 12:1–9), a list of high priests from Jeshua to Jaddua (Neh. 12:10–11), a list of priests and Levites from the time of Joiakim (Neh. 12:1–21, 24ff.), and the Nehemian pledge (Nehemiah 10), probably derived by the author of Ezra-Nehemiah from an archival document.

VI. AUTHOR AND DATE: CHRONICLES

Chronicles is an anonymous work that seems to derive from Jerusalem in the Persian period. That Levitical circles in Jerusalem are responsible for the composition is suggested by its strong focus on Jerusalem and its temple and the elevated importance of the Levites in the work ("Levites" occurs more often in Chronicles than in any other part of the Hebrew Bible). Extensive genealogical material is supplied for the Levites (1 Chronicles 6), great attention is given to David's organization of them for temple service (1 Chronicles 23—26), and they play an important role at several points in the narrative (e.g., as teachers sent out by Jehoshaphat in 2 Chron. 17:7–9). As for the date of the work, opinion ranges from the sixth to the second century B.C.E. The reference to "darics" (a Persian coin not in use until 515 B.C.E.) in 1 Chron. 29:7 and the apparent citation of Zech. 4:10 in 2 Chron. 16:9 point to a time after 515 B.C.E. The continuation of the genealogy of "the sons of Jeconiah the captive" (King Jehoiachin was taken prisoner by the Babylonians in 597 B.C.E.) for at least six generations (some extend this to fourteen generations) would push the date of composition at least into the fifth century, and many scholars place it in the last half of the fourth century. It may well be that Chronicles was written after Ezra-Nehemiah and that 2 Chron. 36:22–23 was drawn from Ezra 1:1–3 in order to link the two compositions.

VII. PURPOSE AND THEOLOGY: CHRONICLES

While various theories have been proposed to explain the purpose of the author of Chronicles, ranging from anti-Samaritan polemic[34] to the legitimation of the Levites[35] or of the Davidic dynasty[36] in the Second Temple period, none has won overwhelming support as establishing the central reason for the composition of Chronicles. Each has failed to do justice to the breadth of the material in the work. The movement of the narrative as a whole, as well as the interpretive commentary that one finds emerging at various points in the book, suggest a broader, more pointedly theological intent on the part of the author: to persuade the restoration community to serve God with singleness of purpose.[37]

It is, of course, clear that the Chronicler viewed David and his descendants in Judah as the succession chosen by God to lead Israel (2 Chron. 13:5); that he saw the Jerusalem cult, as led by its priests and Levites, to be the center for authentic worship of God (2 Chron. 13:10–11; 20:6–9); and that he regarded the northern kingdom as essentially apostate and corrupt (2 Chron. 13:8–9; many of its faithful had fled to the south, according to 2 Chron. 11:13–17), so that the true people of Israel was embodied in the southern kingdom of Judah. In spite of these convictions and the focus on king and temple in Jerusalem, the Chronicler develops an understanding of the people of God—"all Israel"—that is inclusive enough to encompass not only the tribes of Judah, Benjamin, and Levi, but also all those from the northern tribes and even foreigners ("sojourners") who were willing to commit themselves to the worship of God in Jerusalem (cf. 2 Chron. 30:25).[38] What the

Chronicler makes increasingly clear as his narrative progresses, though, is that the story of "all Israel" is filled with trouble, ambiguity, and unevenness. Rulers and priests cannot simply be divided into the good and the bad, because life is more complex than that. Even the revered founder of the Israelite monarchy, David, "sinned greatly" when he instituted a census of the people (1 Chron. 21, esp. v. 7). Similarly, his successors would now be devoted to God and then abandon him (e.g., Rehoboam, 2 Chron. 11:17; 12:1–2; Asa, 2 Chron. 14:1–2; 16:7–10, 12), and Manasseh—that king about whom the Deuteronomistic Historian had nothing good to say (2 Kings 21:1–18)—appears in 2 Chronicles to repent of his evil and institute a religious reform (33:12–17). Even the priests and Levites are negligent at times (cf. 2 Chron. 24:4–6; 30:1–3).

This community is related to the rest of Adam's descendants and received from God the land of Canaan as their allotment and dwelling among the nations (1 Chron. 16:15–18 [// Ps. 105:8–11]; 2 Chron. 6:25 [cf. 1 Kings 8:34]; 20:7).[39] Israel had been shaped by God's word, both the law (1 Chron. 22:12; 2 Chron. 17:9) and the proclamation of the prophets (2 Chron. 12:5–8). This word instructed king and people not only in political affairs but also in how the community was to memorialize, celebrate, and live out its covenant with God (cf. 2 Chron. 23:18–9; 24:6; 30:1–27). The books of Chronicles show that God is active in the life of his people—to deliver Israel from oppressors (2 Chron. 14:9–15) and to punish the nation for unfaithfulness (cf. 2 Chron. 12:1–12 with 1 Kings 14:21–28). Similarly, God's word is alive, as well: the law of Moses continues to set Israel's moral and religious compass (2 Chron. 23:18; cf. 25:3 4), and through prophets and other inspired speakers that law is interpreted and applied to later circumstances (2 Chron. 17:7–9; 19:8–11; 24:20).[40] It is the king's response to the proclamation of God's word, therefore, that determines the ensuing course of his reign, whether to prosperity (2 Chron. 15:1–19) or destruction (2 Chron. 24:17–26). In all this, it is the Chronicler's teaching about the justice and retribution of God that rises to great prominence—especially in the speeches that the Chronicler composes to such great effect to represent his theology. The principle of God's justice is spelled out clearly in speeches by kings (David to Solomon in 1 Chron. 28:9) or prophets (Shemaiah to Rehoboam in 2 Chron. 12:5; Azariah to Asa in 2 Chron. 15:2), and it is demonstrated repeatedly in the course of the Chronicler's narrative, even to the point of correlating God's judgment with the precise point in the king's reign when the ruler led his people into sin (2 Chron. 12:1–2; 24:1–2, 17–24). And so, just as the earlier traditions in Scripture provided a narrative to shape Israel, Chronicles emerges as a continuation of this story of God's deeds and words in order to remind the restoration community of God's power and role as the author of Israel's story.

In Chronicles worship appears as the natural expression of the people's reverence, gratitude, and joy as they live in faith and enjoy God's blessings (1 Chron. 29:9; 2 Chron. 29:25–30; 30:13–27). Such worship is a reflection of the community's identity, and such a people can do nothing else but give expression to their faith in cultic activity. The Chronicler's hope is that Israel will serve God with a "whole heart" and that consequently their lives and community will be characterized by integrity and coherence of belief, will, and behavior (1 Chron. 22:11–13; 28:9–10; 29:9). And when such coherence of disposition and action follow, the community does not become arrogant or proud of its members' achievement, but God is praised as the one who has accomplished this in their midst (1 Chron. 29:10–19). The institutions that gave shape to this worship—the system of festivals, regulations regarding purity, and the cultic infrastructure provided by temple personnel and facilities—were established by the law of Moses and the early provisions of her kings, David and Solomon (1 Chronicles 23—26; 2 Chron. 23:16–21; 30:13–27). It was Israel's faith and worship that defined the community, and the role of the monarchy was to support and enable this aspect of national life (1 Chron. 22:13; 2 Chron. 6:16; 7:17). The Chronicler's narratives about David, Solomon, and their successors make this abundantly clear by virtue of the enormous attention given to the cultic activities of these kings (1 Chronicles 23—26; cf. 2 Chron. 8:12–16 with 1 Kings 9:25; and 2 Chron. 29—31 with 2 Kings 18:4). Through the Chronicler's idealized description of the reigns of David and Solomon it is clear that these kings establish the religious and political institutions that those who follow them will inherit, and it is their fidelity to God that sets the standard against which all later kings will be judged (2 Chron. 11:17; 29:25–30; 30:26; 35:4). The remainder of the narrative (2 Chronicles 10—36) shows the relative success or failure of later kings and the corresponding judgment of God upon their reigns. It comes as no surprise then to find that when kings failed in this regard and so led their people into idolatry God punished them and their people. This usually occurred through the military action of foreign powers and illustrates the Chronicler's view of foreign nations/leaders as God's instruments (e.g., Pharaoh Neco, 2 Chron. 35:20–24; the Babylonians, 2 Chron. 36:17). When corruption became overwhelming, the land of Judah, Jerusalem, and even the temple itself were destroyed and the people taken away into exile (2 Chron. 36:17–21). Yet, even with this terrible turn of events there is hope for the exiles, since God remains sovereign and is able again to use a foreign ruler, this time Cyrus of Persia (2 Chron. 36:20–23), to bring his people back to the land and shape them through the law and rebuild their institutions.

Therefore, it seems far more consistent with the books of Chronicles themselves to see as their primary purpose that of religious instruction for the postexilic community in Jerusalem and Judea. They show through Israel's history that God blesses her faithfulness and punishes her sin. This is not presented woodenly as an enterprise that mechanically rewards a cold and calculating legalism. Rather it portrays a patient and merciful God who consistently holds his rulers and their people accountable for their dispositions and behavior. In this way, the narrative attempts to persuade the restoration community to serve God wholeheartedly and so to shape its character and guide its behavior.

VIII. AUTHOR AND DATE: EZRA-NEHEMIAH

Although Ezra-Nehemiah appears to include materials that derive from the men whose names have been assigned to the books, it is unclear who produced the work itself. As for the date of Ezra-Nehemiah, there are several indications that help the reader determine the earliest time at which it could have been written. Ezra returned to Palestine in 458 (or possibly as late as 398) and Nehemiah arrived in 445 B.C.E. Nehemiah left Jerusalem in 433 but returned for a brief period, probably before 423 when Artaxerxes I died (Neh. 5:14; 13:6). This means that a date toward the end of the fifth century is the earliest one possible, but it also allows for a fourth century date.

IX. PURPOSE AND THEOLOGY: EZRA-NEHEMIAH

The purpose of Ezra-Nehemiah seems to have been to set forth the theological significance of the events associated with the rebuilding of Jerusalem and provide the restoration community with a clear identity. The story about the rebuilding of the temple and that of the refortification of the city are interwoven so as to show the expansion of the holy precincts of the temple until they encompass the entire city, thus transforming Jerusalem into the holy city of earlier vision (cf. Isa. 48:2; 52:1; Jer. 31:38).[41]

This restoration of the city and temple of Jerusalem was accompanied by a religious and spiritual restoration: strong leaders and a willing community committed themselves to a careful observance of the law of Moses and so they became a holy people, fit to live in a holy city. Ezra appears as the great teacher of the law (Ezra 7:6, 10; Nehemiah 8), and both Ezra and Nehemiah are represented as fiercely insistent on the Jewish people observing the law. The people's resistance to the law's proscriptions of marriage with foreign peoples (Ezra 9; Neh. 13:23–29; cf. Deut. 7:3–4), work on the sabbath (Neh. 13:15 22; cf. Deut. 5:12–15), and heartless economic exploitation of one's fellow (Nehemiah 5; cf. Lev. 25:35–38) is finally overcome, and there is a renewal of the law's ordinances regarding great religious festivals (e.g., Feast of Booths in Ezra 3:1–7; Neh. 8:13–18; cf. Lev. 23:33–43; Passover and Unleavened Bread in Ezra 6:19–22; cf. Deut. 16:1–8). All this is accomplished under the vigorous leadership of Zerubbabel, Ezra, and Nehemiah and with the assistance of assemblies of the people and their other leaders (e.g., Ezra 3:1; 10:1, 7–9; Neh. 7:73b–8:1; 9:1). The grand traditions of Israel's shared experience (cf. Ezra's sermon in Neh. 9:6–38) form the backdrop for these events (see below) and infuse them with rich theological significance.

Out of these developments grew the restoration community's sense of identity as the people of God, and by these events were the boundaries of ethical behavior and religious practice established, which were to mark this people off from their neighbors. The lines of continuity with earlier generations are evident: the genealogical connection ("the heads of the fathers' houses of Judah and Benjamin," Ezra 1:5; Ezra stood in the priestly lineage of Hilkiah, Zadok, and Aaron, 7:1–5) was accompanied by geographical (they settled in the ancestral lands of Jerusalem and Judah; Ezra 2:1), legal (at the heart of Ezra's mission was the application of the law to the restoration community; Ezra 7:25–26), and cultic (worship and the organization of the cult was arranged according to the law of Moses; e.g., Ezra 3:2; 6:18; Neh. 7:1, 8) linkages. In addition, there were obvious parallels or typologies that connected the events of the restoration community's life with the great events in the life of ancient Israel.[42] Compare, for example, the statements about the Jewish exiles being "brought up" to their homeland (Ezra 1:11) with those about the exodus generation being brought up out of Egypt by Moses (Exod. 33:1); the descriptions of the collection of wealth for the building of the second temple (Ezra 1:5–11) with those about the furnishing of the sanctuary in the wilderness (Exod. 25:1–9) and the building of Solomon's temple (1 Chron. 29:1–9); and the place of Ezra's prayer in Neh. 9:6–37 within the long tradition of public historical recitals in preparation for enacting covenant (e.g., Josh. 24:1–15) and psalmic recitals of history for confessional purposes (e.g., Psalm 106).

Therefore, the restoration of Jerusalem's architectural remains was accompanied by the restoration of her religious institutions and her people's commitment to God. In this way, the community of returnees stood in continuity with the founding documents and religious practices of earlier generations of Israel, and this rebuilding of the temple and Jerusalem as a holy city made it possible for this community to express its faith in authentic worship of God and be nourished accordingly.[43] Finally, even though Persian imperial power remained in place as an ever present consideration for Zerubbabel, Ezra, Nehemiah, and the other leaders of the restoration community, the institutions, worship, and faith of Jerusalem set that authority in perspective and made it possible for the restoration community to assume its role in a holy place where God both remembered and was remembered (Neh. 1:8; 4:14; 5:19; 13:14, 22, 31).

FOR FURTHER STUDY

Although relatively little interest was shown in Chronicles and Ezra-Nehemiah by Jewish and Christian interpreters before the nineteenth century, the critical studies of de Wette and Zunz changed all this dramatically.[44] De Wette vigorously attacked the usefulness of Chronicles as a source of information about the preexilic period of Israelite history, concluding that the author's prejudices (in favor of Judah and the Levites, for example) and lack of reliable sources made his work useless.[45] This debate dominated Chronicles studies in the nineteenth century and has continued to occupy the attention of scholars to the present.[46] Zunz proposed that a single author was responsible for Chronicles and Ezra-Nehemiah, and this view held sway until the publication of Japhet's study in 1968, as mentioned earlier. While nineteenth- and early-twentieth-century study of Chronicles was largely occupied with historical issues of the work as a whole (e.g., historical reliability, sources available to the author), the study of Ezra-Nehemiah was more tightly focused on certain specific historical and literary issues (e.g., the historical sequence of the activity of Ezra and Nehemiah, the identity of Ezra's lawbook).

Scholarly interest in the study of the second temple period generally and so in the books of Chronicles and Ezra-Nehemiah, too, has increased sharply in the last thirty years. In addition to earlier studies that sought to identify the place of Chronicles in the ancient Jewish political world (see above, Purpose and Theology: Chronicles), much recent research has attempted to understand Chronicles and Ezra-Nehemiah as literary, theological, and historiographical works in their own right. Rather than approaching Chronicles, for example, as little more than a supplement to Samuel–Kings, the books are regarded as a valuable part of the Hebrew canon, representing the language and idiom of late biblical Hebrew, considerable literary artistry on the part of the author, and a theological perspective that deserves to be heard.

Several studies in particular have promoted the study of this literature. The bibliography of Isaac Kalimi[47] on the books of Chronicles, for example, provides an excellent entrée into this body of scholarly literature, and the recent works that set the parallel texts of Samuel–Kings and Chronicles alongside one another have greatly facilitated the study of these parallels.[48] Similarly, those interested in the study of the Chronicler's theology now have an excellent guide in Sara Japhet's *The Ideology of the Book of Chronicles and Its Place in Biblical Thought*, and for English readers needing a solid commentary on these books, there are those on Chronicles by Williamson, Braun, Dillard, and Japhet and those on Ezra-Nehemiah by Clines, Williamson, and Blenkinsopp.[49] Finally, it should be noted that research on the Persian period generally has continued to increase, and the discussion of its sociological aspects has generated considerable interest.[50]

NOTES

PREFACE

1. The most recent such work of which I am aware is *The Hebrew Bible and Its Modern Interpreters*, edited by Douglas Knight and Gene Tucker (Bible and Its Modern Interpreters 1; Chico, Calif.: Scholars Press, 1985.) It reflects the state of scholarship in the late 1970s and so is now about twenty years old, though it remains a very useful book. Its format is also somewhat different from the present volume.

CHAPTER 1: THE PENTATEUCH

1. Julius Wellhausen, *Prolegomena to the History of Ancient Israel* (Scholars Press Reprints and Translations Series; Atlanta: Scholars Press, 1994 [German original, 1883]).
2. The epoch-making work of W. M. L. de Wette appeared in 1806–1807 with the title, *Beiträge zur Einleitung in das Alte Testament: I, Kritischer Versuch über die Glaubwürdigkeit der Bücher der Chronik mit Hinsicht auf die Geschichte der Mosäischen Bücher und Gesetzgebung; II, Kritik der Israelitischen Geschichte, Erster Theil: Kritik der Mosäischen Geschichte* ("Contributions to an introduction into the Old Testament: I, A critical investigation into the credibility of the Books of Chronicles with respect to the history of the Books of Moses and the giving of the law; II, A critique of Israelite history, Part One: A critique of the history of Moses").
3. Hermann Gunkel, *The Legends of Genesis* (New York: Schocken, 1964 [translated from the introduction of his German commentary on Genesis, 1901]); Hugo Gressman, *Mose und seine Zeit: Ein Kommentar zu den Mose Sagen* (Göttingen: Vandenhoeck & Ruprecht, 1913); Albrecht Alt, "The Origins of Israelite Law," *Essays in Old Testament History and Religion* (Oxford: Blackwell, 1966), 81–132. German original published in 1934.
4. Gerhard von Rad, "The Form-Critical Problem of the Hexateuch," *The Problem of the Hexateuch and Other Essays* (Edinburgh and London: Oliver & Boyd, 1965), 1–75.
5. Martin Noth, *A History of Pentateuchal Traditions* (Englewood Cliffs, N.J.: Prentice-Hall, 1972 [German original, 1948]).
6. Claus Westermann, *The Promises to the Fathers* (Philadelphia: Fortress, 1980); George W. Coats, *Genesis, with an Introduction to Narrative Literature* (FOTL 1; Grand Rapids: Eerdmans, 1983).
7. Richard E. Friedman, *Who Wrote the Bible?* (Englewood Cliffs, N.J.: Prentice-Hall, 1987); Antony F. Campbell and Mark A. O'Brien, *The Sources of the Pentateuch* (Minneapolis: Fortress, 1993).

8. Rolf Rendtorff, *The Problem of the Process of Transmission in the Pentateuch* (JSOTSup 89; Sheffield: JSOT, 1990 [German original 1977]).

9. For a more detailed discussion of the land promise in the Old Testament see John Van Seters, *Prologue to History: The Yahwist as Historian in Genesis* (Louisville: Westminster/John Knox, 1992), 227–45.

10. Earlier discussions of this development of the patriarchal traditions may be found in Gunkel, *Genesis*, and Noth, *History of Pentateuchal Traditions*. For more details see my *Abraham in History and Tradition* (New Haven, Conn.: Yale University Press, 1975) and *Prologue to History*.

11. R. E. Clements, *Abraham and David: Genesis XV and Its Meaning for Israelite Tradition* (London: SCM, 1967).

12. This is the basic thesis of Gressmann in *Mose und seine Zeit*. A full review of this hypothesis may be found in Roland de Vaux, *The Early History of Israel* (Philadelphia: Fortress, 1978), 330–38.

13. Some scholars want to make 12:21–27 part of the J source. But it does not fit the J narrative any better than the rest of the passover law, and the language in it is P. Also, the provisions for the non-Israelite participation in the passover are not appropriate for Egypt and so are appended in vv. 40–51.

14. Alt, "The Origins of Israelite Law."

CHAPTER 2: THE FORMER PROPHETS

1. See especially David Noel Freedman, "Deuteronomic History," *IDBSup*, 226–28.

2. These are selected and treated by Thomas Römer and Albert de Pury, "L'historiographie deutéronomiste (HD): Histoire de la recherche et enjeux du débat," in A. de Pury, T. Römer, and J.-D. Macchi (eds.), *Israël construit son histoire: L'historiographie deutéronomiste à la lumière des recherches récentes* (La Monde de la Bible 34; Geneva: Labor et Fides, 1996), 14–17.

3. Cited in Römer and de Pury, "L'historiographie deutéronomiste," 15.

4. W. M. L. de Wette, *Dissertatio critica-exegetica qua Deuteronomium a prioribus Pentateuchi libris diversum* (Jena: Literis Etzdorfii, 1805).

5. Martin Noth, *Überlieferungsgeschichtliche Studien: Die sammelnden und bearbeitenden Geschichtswerke im Alten Testament* (Halle: Niemeyer, 1943). The portion dealing with the Deuteronomistic History is now available in English as *The Deuteronomistic History* (JSOTSup 15, 2d ed.; Sheffield: Sheffield Academic Press, 1991).

6. Julius Wellhausen, *Prolegomena to the History of Ancient Israel* (Atlanta: Scholars Press, 1994 [German original, 1883]).

7. Noth, *Deuteronomistic History*, 20.

8. Noth, *Deuteronomistic History*, 26.

9. See Noth, *Deuteronomistic History*, 34–44. The quotation is from p. 34.

10. Claus Westermann, *Die Geschichtsbücher des Alten Testaments: Gab es ein*

deuteronomistisches Geschichtswerk? (TB 87; Gütersloh: Chr. Kaiser, 1994); Ernst Axel Knauf, "L' 'Histoire Deutéronomiste' (DtrG) existe-t-elle?" 409–18 in de Pury, Römer, and Macchi (eds.), *Israël construit son histoire.* See also A. Graeme Auld, "The Deuteronomists and the Former Prophets; or, What Makes the Former Prophets Deuteronomistic?" presented in the Deuteronomistic Section of the 1996 SBL meeting in New Orleans and forthcoming in L. S. Schearing and S. L. McKenzie (eds.), *Those Elusive Deuteronomists* (Sheffield: Sheffield Academic Press).

11. Frank Moore Cross, *Canaanite Myth and Hebrew Epic: Essays in the History of the Religion of Israel* (Cambridge, Mass., and London: Harvard University Press, 1973), 217–89.

12. Cross, Canaanite Myth, 278.

13. Cross, Canaanite Myth, 283.

14. Cross, Canaanite Myth, 284.

15. Cross, Canaanite Myth, 285–87.

16. Richard D. Nelson, *The Double Redaction of the Deuteronomistic History* (JSOTSup 18; Sheffield: JSOT, 1981), 121–23.

17. Robert G. Boling, *Joshua* (AB 6; Garden City, N.Y.: Doubleday, 1982), and *Judges* (AB 6a; Garden City, N.Y.: Doubleday, 1975).

18. Rudolf Smend, "Das Gesetz und die Völker: Ein Beitrag zur deuteronomistischen Redaktionsgeschichte," in H. W. Wolff, ed., *Probleme biblischer Theologie: Gerhard von Rad zum 70. Geburtstag* (Munich: Chr. Kaiser, 1971), 494–509.

19. Rudolf Smend, "Das Gesetz und die Völker: Ein Beitrag zur deuteronomistischen Redaktionsgeschichte," *Die Mitte des Alten Testaments: Gesammelte Studien,* Band 1 (BET 99; Munich: Chr. Kaiser, 1986), 137 n. 58.

20. Walter Dietrich, *Prophetie und Geschichte: Eine redaktionsgeschichtliche Untersuchung zum deuteronomistischen Geschichtswerk* (FRLANT 108; Göttingen: Vandenhoeck & Ruprecht, 1972).

21. De Pury and Römer, "L'historiographie deutéronomiste," 52.

22. Dietrich, *Prophetie und Geschichte,* 132–33.

23. Timo Veijola, *Die ewige Dynastie: David und die Entstehung seiner Dynastie nach der deuteronomistischen Darstellung* (AASF, Ser. B 193; Helsinki: Suomalainen Tiedeakatemia, 1975) and *Das Königtum in der Beurteilung der deuteronomistischen Historiographie: Eine redaktionsgeschichtliche Untersuchung* (AASF, Ser. B 198; Helsinki: Suomalainen Tiedeakatemia, 1977).

24. A representative selection has been reprinted in three volumes: Norbert Lohfink, *Studien zur Deuteronomium und zur deuteronomistischen Literatur* (SBAB 8, 12, 20; Stuttgart: Katholisches Bibelwerk, 1990, 1991, and 1995).

25. Georg Braulik, *Studien zur Theologie des Deuteronomiums* (SBAB 2; Stuttgart: Katholisches Bibelwerk, 1988).

26. A. D. H. Mayes, *The Story of Israel between Settlement and Exile: A Redactional Study of the Deuteronomistic History* (London: SCM, 1983).

27. Steven L. McKenzie, "Deuteronomistic History," *ABD* 2: 160–68.
28. S. L. McKenzie and M. P. Graham (eds.), *The History of Israel's Traditions: The Heritage of Martin Noth* (JSOTSup 182; Sheffield: Sheffield Academic Press, 1994).
29. Römer and de Pury, "L'historiographie deutéronomiste," 9–120.
30. H.-D. Hoffmann, *Reform und Reformen: Untersuchungen zu einem Grundthema des deuteronomistischen Geschichtsschreibung* (AThANT 66; Zurich: Theologischer Verlag, 1980).
31. Steven L. McKenzie, *The Trouble with Kings: The Composition of the Book of Kings in the Deuteronomistic History* (VTSup 42; Leiden: Brill, 1991).
32. McKenzie, "The Books of Kings," in McKenzie and Graham (eds.), *The History of Israel's Traditions*, 303.
33. Robert Polzin, *Moses and the Deuteronomist: Deuteronomy, Joshua, Judges* (ISBL; Bloomington: Indiana University Press, 1980); *Samuel and the Deuteronomist* (ISBL; Bloomington: Indiana University Press, 1989); *David and the Deuteronomist* (ISBL; Bloomington: Indiana University Press, 1993).
34. J. P. Fokkelman, *Narrative Art and Poetry in the Books of Samuel: A Full Interpretation Based on Stylistic and Structural Analyses*, vol. I, *King David (II Samuel 9—20 & I Kings 1—2)* (SSN 20; Assen: Van Gorcum, 1981); vol. II, *The Crossing Fates (I Sam. 13—31 & II Sam. 1)* (SSN 23; Assen: Van Gorcum, 1986); vol. III, *Throne and City (II Sam. 2—8 & 21—24)* (SSN 27; Assen: Van Gorcum, 1990); vol. IV, *Vow and Desire (I Sam. 1—12)* (SSN 31; Assen: Van Gorcum, 1993).
35. D. J. A. Clines, Review of J. P. Fokkelman, *Narrative Art and Poetry in the Books of Samuel*, vol. II, *The Crossing Fates (I Sam. 13—31 & II Sam. 1)*, in *Society for Old Testament Study Book List*, 1987, p. 63.
36. Fokkelman, *King David*, 1.
37. Leonhard Rost, *The Succession to the Throne of David* (trans. D. M. Gunn; Sheffield: Almond, 1982 [German original 1926]).
38. Gerhard von Rad, "The Beginnings of Historical Writing in Ancient Israel," *The Problem of the Hexateuch and Other Essays* (Edinburgh: Oliver & Boyd, 1966), 166–204; R. N. Whybray, *The Succession Narrative: A Study of II Samuel 9—20, I Kings 1 and 2* (SBT 2,9; London: SCM, 1968); David M. Gunn, *The Story of King David: Genre and Interpretation* (JSOTSup 6; Sheffield: JSOT, 1978).
39. John Van Seters, *In Search of History: Historiography in the Ancient World and the Origins of Biblical History* (New Haven, Conn., and London: Yale University Press, 1983), 277–91. A. Graeme Auld, "Prophets through the Looking Glass: Between Writings and Moses," *JSOT* 27 (1983): 3–23.
40. R. P. Gordon, *1 & 2 Samuel* (OTG; Sheffield: Sheffield Academic Press, 1984); Y. S. (Craig) Ho, "Conjectures and Refutations: Is 1 Samuel xxxi 1–13 Really the Source of 1 Chronicles x 1–12?" *VT* 45 (1995): 82–106; R. A. Carlson, *David, the Chosen King: A Traditio-Historical Approach to the Second Book of Samuel* (Stockholm: Almqvist & Wiksell, 1964).

41. B. J. Webb, *The Book of Judges: An Integrated Reading* (JSOTSup 46; Sheffield: JSOT, 1987).
42. Mieke Bal, *Death and Dissymmetry* (Chicago Studies in the History of Judaism; Chicago: University of Chicago Press, 1988).
43. L. Daniel Hawk, *Every Promise Fulfilled: Contesting Plots in Joshua* (Literary Currents in Biblical Interpretation; Louisville, Ky.: Westminster/John Knox, 1991); Gordon Mitchell, *Together in the Land: A Reading of the Book of Joshua* (JSOTSup 134; Sheffield: Sheffield Academic Press, 1993); E. Theodore Mullen, *Narrative History and Ethnic Boundaries: The Deuteronomistic Historian and the Creation of Israelite National Identity* (Semeia Studies; Atlanta: Scholars Press, 1993); Lori L. Rowlett, *Joshua and the Rhetoric of Violence: A New Historicist Analysis* (JSOTSup 226; Sheffield: Sheffield Academic Press, 1996).
44. Burke Long, *1 Kings with an Introduction to Historical Literature* (FOTL; Grand Rapids: Eerdmans, 1984) and *2 Kings* (FOTL; Grand Rapids: Eerdmans, 1991); George Savran, "1 and 2 Kings," in R. Alter and F. Kermode (eds.), *The Literary Guide to the Bible* (Cambridge, Mass.: Belknap, 1987), 146–64; Robert R. Wilson, "The Former Prophets: Reading the Books of Kings," in J. L. Mays, D. L. Petersen, and K. H. Richards (eds.), *Old Testament Interpretation, Past, Present and Future: Essays in Honor of Gene M. Tucker* (Nashville: Abingdon, 1995), 83–96.
45. Iain W. Provan, *1 & 2 Kings* (OTG; Sheffield: Sheffield Academic Press, 1997).
46. See especially Julio Trebolle Barrera, *Centena in Libros Samuelis et Regum: Variantes textuales y composición literaria en los libros Samuel y Reyes* (Textos y estudios "Cardinal Cisneros" de la Biblia Poliglota Matritense 47; Madrid: CSIC, 1989). Cf. also Raymond F. Person, Jr., *The Kings-Isaiah and Kings-Jeremiah Recensions* (BZAW 252; Berlin: de Gruyter, 1997) and A. Graeme Auld, *Joshua Retold* (Edinburgh: T. & T. Clark, forthcoming).
47. Noth, *Überlieferungsgeschichtliche Studien*, 211–16.
48. Erhard Blum, *Studien zur Komposition des Pentateuch* (BZAW 189; Berlin: de Gruyter, 1990); John Van Seters, *Prologue to History: The Yahwist as Historian in Genesis* (Louisville: Westminster John Knox, 1992) and *The Life of Moses: The Yahwist as Historian in Exodus–Numbers* (Louisville: Westminster John Knox, 1994).
49. A. Graeme Auld, *Kings without Privilege* (Edinburgh: T. & T. Clark, 1994).

CHAPTER 3: THE LATTER PROPHETS

1. For discussions of the various canonical forms of the Hebrew Bible, see James A. Sanders, "Canon," *ABD* 1: 837–52; M. J. Mulder (ed.), *Mikra: Text, Translation, Reading, and Interpretation of the Hebrew Bible in Ancient Judaism and Early Christianity* (Philadelphia: Fortress, 1990); Marvin

A. Sweeney, "Tanak versus Old Testament: Concerning the Foundation for a Jewish Theology of the Bible," in H. T. C. Sun and K. L. Eades (eds.), with J. M. Robinson and G. I. Moehller, *Problems in Biblical Theology: Essays in Honor of Rolf Knierim* (Grand Rapids: Eerdmans, 1997), 353–72.

2. For an overview of the study of prophetic literature, see Joseph Blenkinsopp, *A History of Prophecy in Israel* (rev. ed.; Louisville: Westminster John Knox, 1996), 7–39 and Gene M. Tucker, "Prophecy and the Prophetic Literature," in D. A. Knight and G. M. Tucker (eds.), *The Hebrew Bible and Its Modern Interpreters* (Bible and Its Modern Interpreters 1; Chico, Calif.: Scholars Press, 1985), 325–68.

3. For a brief overview of the history of biblical interpretation, see J. W. Rogerson and Werner G. Jeanrond, "Interpretation, History of," *ABD* 3:424–43.

4. Julius Wellhausen, *Prolegomena to the History of Ancient Israel* (Scholars Press Reprints and Translations Series; Atlanta: Scholars Press, 1994 [German original, 1883]).

5. Hermann Gunkel, "The Prophets as Writers and Poets," in D. L. Petersen (ed.), *Prophecy in Israel: Search for an Identity* (Issues in Religion and Theology 10; Philadelphia: Fortress; London: SPCK, 1986), 22–73. Translated from *Die Propheten* (Göttingen: Vandenhoeck & Ruprecht, 1923), 34–73.

6. See his "Cult and Prophecy" in Petersen (ed.), *Prophecy in Israel*, 74–98. Translated from *Psalmenstudien III: Kultprophetie und prophetische Psalmen* (Kristiania: Jacob Dybwad, 1929), 4–29.

7. Gerhard von Rad, *Old Testament Theology*, vol. 2, *The Theology of Israel's Prophetic Traditions* (trans. D. M. G. Stalker; New York: Harper & Row, 1965).

8. Claus Westermann, *Basic Forms of Prophetic Speech* (trans. H. C. White; Louisville, Ky.: Westminster John Knox; Cambridge: Lutterworth, 1991).

9. See for example his *Amos, the Prophet: The Man and His Background* (trans. F. R. McCurley; Philadelphia: Fortress, 1973).

10. See Marvin A. Sweeney, *Isaiah 1—39, with an Introduction to Prophetic Literature* (FOTL 16; Grand Rapids: Eerdmans, 1996).

11. James Muilenburg, "Form Criticism and Beyond," *JBL* 88 (1969):1–18.

12. Phyllis Trible, *Rhetorical Criticism: Context, Method, and the Book of Jonah* (GBS; Minneapolis: Fortress, 1994).

13. Peter R. Ackroyd, *Studies in the Religious Tradition of the Old Testament* (London: SCM, 1987); Ronald E. Clements, *Old Testament Prophecy: From Oracles to Canon* (Louisville, Ky.: Westminster John Knox, 1996); Marvin A. Sweeney, "Formation and Form in Prophetic Literature," in J. L. Mays, D. L. Petersen, and K. H. Richards (eds.), *Old Testament Interpretation: Past, Present, and Future Essays in Honor of Gene M. Tucker* (Nashville: Abingdon, 1995), 113–26.

14. Edgar W. Conrad, *Reading Isaiah* (OBT 27; Minneapolis: Fortress, 1991).

15. Brevard S. Childs, *Introduction to the Old Testament as Scripture* (Philadelphia: Fortress, 1979).

16. See Robert Carroll, *Jeremiah: A Commentary* (OTL; Philadelphia: Westminster, 1986).

17. For overviews of the study of the book of Isaiah and its component parts, see the relevant sections of Blenkinsopp, *A History of Prophecy*; Marvin A. Sweeney, "The Book of Isaiah in Recent Research," *CRBS* 1 (1993): 141–62 and "Reevaluating Isaiah 1—39 in Recent Critical Research," *CRBS* 4 (1996): 79–113; C. R. Seitz, W. R. Millar, and R. Clifford, "Isaiah, Book of," *ABD*3: 472–507.

18. Bernhard Duhm, *Das Buch Jesaia* (HKAT 3.1; Göttingen: Vandenhoeck & Ruprecht, 1892).

19. E.g., Sigmund Mowinckel, *Prophecy and Tradition: The Prophetic Books in the Light of the Study of the Growth and History of the Tradition* (Oslo: Dybwad, 1946).

20. Ackroyd, "Isaiah 1—12: Presentation of a Prophet," *Studies in the Religious Tradition of the Old Testament,* 79–104.

21. See his essays, "Isaiah 36—39: Structure and Function," and "An Interpretation of the Babylonian Exile: A Study of II Kings 20 and Isaiah 38—39," in *Studies in the Religious Tradition of the Old Testament*, 105–20, 152–71.

22. R. E. Clements "The Prophecies of Isaiah and the Fall of Jerusalem in 587 BC," *VT* 30 (1980): 421–36.

23. See his essays, "The Unity of the Book of Isaiah" and "Beyond Tradition History: Deutero-Isaianic Development of First Isaiah's Themes," in *Old Testament Prophecy*, 93–104, 78–92.

24. Childs, *Introduction to the Old Testament as Scripture*, 328–30.

25. See H. G. M. Williamson (*The Book Called Isaiah: Deutero-Isaiah's Role in Composition and Redaction* [Oxford: Clarendon Press, 1994]), who argues that Deutero-Isaiah is the redactor of First Isaiah.

26. For an overview of Jeremiah studies, see Blenkinsopp, *History*, and J. R. Lundbom, "Jeremiah," *ABD* 3. 684–98 and "Jeremiah, Book of," *ABD* 3:706–21.

27. Sigmund Mowinckel, *Zur Komposition des Buches Jeremia* (Vidcnskapsselskapets Skrifter II; Hist.-filos. Klasse, 5; Oslo: Dybwad, 1914).

28. John Bright, "The Date of the Prose Sermons of Jeremiah," *JBL* 70 (1951): 15–29 and *Jeremiah* (AB 21; Garden City, N.Y.: Doubleday, 1965).

29. E. W. Nicholson, *Preaching to the Exiles: A Study of the Prose Tradition of the Book of Jeremiah* (New York: Schocken, 1970).

30. Helga Weippert, *Die Prosareden des Jeremiabuches* (BZAW 132; Berlin and New York: de Gruyter, 1973).

31. William L. Holladay, *Jeremiah* (Hermeneia, 2 vols.; Philadelphia and Minneapolis: Fortress, 1986–89).

32. Carroll, *Jeremiah.*

33. William McKane, *A Critical and Exegetical Commentary on Jeremiah*, vol. 1: *Introduction and Commentary on Jeremiah I-XXV* (ICC; Edinburgh: T. & T. Clark, 1986).

34. C. R. Seitz, "The Prophet Moses and the Canonical Shape of Jeremiah," *ZAW* 101 (1989): 3–27.
35. See Jay Wilcoxen, "The Political Background of Jeremiah's Temple Sermon," in A. Merrill and T. Overholt (eds.), *Scripture in History and Theology: Essays in Honor of J. Coert Rylaarsdam* (Pittsburgh: Pickwick, 1977), 151–66.
36. For overviews of the study of the book of Ezekiel, see Blenkinsopp, *History*; Katheryn Pfisterer Darr, "Ezekiel among the Critics," *CRBS* 2 (1994): 9–24; L. Boadt, "Ezekiel, Book of," *ABD* 2:711–22.
37. Gustav Hölscher, *Hesekiel, der Dichter und das Buch: Eine literarkritische Untersuchung* (BZAW 39; Giessen: Töpelmann, 1924).
38. C. C. Torrey, *Pseudo-Ezekiel and the Original Prophecy* (YOS 18; New Haven, Conn.: Yale University Press, 1930).
39. J. Smith, *The Book of the Prophet Ezekiel: A New Interpretation* (London: SPCK, 1931).
40. C. G. Howie, *The Date and Composition of Ezekiel* (JBLMS 4; Philadelphia: Society of Biblical Literature, 1950).
41. Georg Fohrer, *Die Hauptprobleme des Buches Ezechiel* (BZAW 72; Berlin: Töpelmann, 1952).
42. Walther Zimmerli, *Ezekiel* (Hermeneia; 2 vols.; trans. R. E. Clements and J. D. Martin; Philadelphia: Fortress, 1979–83).
43. Moshe Greenberg, *Ezekiel 1—20* (AB 22; Garden City, N.Y.: Doubleday, 1983).
44. Ellen F. Davis, *Swallowing the Scroll: Textuality and the Dynamics of Discourse in Ezekiel's Prophecy* (BLS 21; JSOTSup 78; Sheffield: Almond, 1989).
45. Darr, "Ezekiel among the Critics," 20.
46. Whether there were actually four cherubim in the Holy of Holies is debatable, but a close reading of the extant biblical sources points to a total of four when the Exodus and Kings/Chronicles traditions are read together, perhaps indicating the literary basis of Ezekiel's knowledge.

CHAPTER 4: THE BOOK OF THE TWELVE

1. So Barry Jones, *The Formation of the Book of the Twelve: A Study in Text and Canon* (SBLDS 149; Atlanta: Scholars Press, 1995).
2. Jörg Jeremias, *Hosea und Amos: Studien zu den Anfängen des Dodekapropheton* (FAT 13; Tübingen: Mohr, 1996).
3. James Nogalski, *Literary Precursors to the Book of the Twelve* (BZAW 217; Berlin: de Gruyter, 1993) and *Redactional Processes in the Book of the Twelve* (BZAW 218; Berlin: de Gruyter, 1993).
4. Odil Hannes Steck, *Der Abschluss der Prophetie im Alten Testament: Ein Versuch zur Frage der Vorgeschichte des Kanons* (BTS 17; Neukirchen-Vluyn: Neukirchener Verlag, 1991).

5. E.g., Hans Walter Wolff, *Amos* (Hermeneia; Philadelphia: Fortress, 1974), 68.
6. Paul R. House, *The Unity of the Twelve* (BLS 27; JSOTSup 97; Sheffield: Sheffield Academic Press, 1990).
7. J. Andrew Dearman, *Property Rights in the Eighth Century Prophets: The Conflict and Its Background* (SBLDS 106; Atlanta: Scholars Press, 1988).
8. Robert R. Wilson, *Prophecy and Society in Ancient Israel* (Philadelphia: Fortress, 1980).
9. Shalom Paul, *Amos: A Commentary on the Book of Amos* (Hermeneia; Minneapolis: Fortress, 1991).
10. So Jeremias, *Hosea und Amos.*
11. Hans Walter Wolff, *Joel and Amos* (Hermeneia; Philadelphia: Fortress, 1977).

CHAPTER 5: THE WISDOM BOOKS

1. See Nicolas J. Tromp, "Wisdom and the Canticle," in M. Gilbert (ed.), *La Sagesse de l'Ancien Testament* (BETL 51; Leuven: Leuven University Press, 1979), 88–95.
2. R. E. Clements, "Wisdom and OT Theology," in J. Day, R. P. Gordon, and H. G. M. Williamson (eds.), *Wisdom in Ancient Israel: Essays in Honor of J. A. Emerton* (Cambridge University Press, 1995), 280.
3. See the preface to John G. Gammie and Leo G. Perdue (eds.), *The Sage in Israel and the Ancient Near East* (Winona Lake, Ind.: Eisenbrauns, 1990), x–xi.
4. Tyron Inbody, *The Transforming God: An Interpretation of Suffering and Evil* (Louisville: Westminster John Knox, 1997), 30.
5. The Aramaic fragments of Ahiqar and the Egyptian Instruction of Amenemope, both treated below, became available to scholars in 1906 and 1922, respectively.
6. See John Gray, "The Book of Job in the Context of Near Eastern Literature," ZAW 82 (1970):251–69.
7. See W. G. Lambert, *Babylonian Wisdom Literature* (Oxford: Clarendon Press, 1960).
8. Gerald H. Wilson, "'The Words of the Wise': The Intent and Significance of Qohelet 12:9–14," *JBL* 103 (1984):175–92.
9. Roger Beckwith, *The Old Testament Canon of the New Testament Church and Its Background in Early Judaism* (Grand Rapids: Eerdmans, 1985), 318–19.
10. A good summary of the arguments and their sources can be found in Beckwith, *The Old Testament Canon*, 274–337.
11. David Noel Freedman, "Orthographic Peculiarities in the Book of Job," *EI* 9 (1969): 35–44; and Avi Hurvitz, "The Date of the Prose-Tale of Job Linguistically Reconsidered," *HTR* 67 (1974):17–34.

12. A. S. Peake (ed.), *The People of the Book: Essays on the Old Testament* (Oxford: Clarendon Press, 1925); and H. W. Robinson (ed.), *Record and Revelation: Essays on the Old Testament* (Oxford: Clarendon Press, 1938).

13. E.g., Ernst Sellin, *Alttestamentliche Theologie auf religionsgeschichtlicher Grundlage* (Leipzig: Quelle & Meyer, 1933–1936).

14. E.g., G. Ernest Wright, *God Who Acts: Biblical Theology as Recital* (SBT 8; London: SCM, 1952).

15. E.g., Walther Eichrodt, *Theology of the Old Testament* (2 vols.; OTL; trans. J. A. Baker; Philadelphia: Westminster, 1961, 1967).

16. Lawrence E. Toombs, "Old Testament Theology and Wisdom Literature," *JBR* 23 (1955):195.

17. Gerhard von Rad, *Old Testament Theology* (2 vols.; New York: Harper & Row, 1962, 1965).

18. Claus Westermann, *Blessing in the Bible and the Life of the Church* (OBT 1; trans. K. R. Crim; Philadelphia: Fortress, 1978).

19. Samuel Terrien, *The Elusive Presence: Toward a New Biblical Theology* (Religious Perspectives 26; San Francisco: Harper & Row, 1978).

20. See, e.g., Helmut Gese, *Lehre und Wirklichkeit in der alten Weisheit: Studien zu dem Spruchen Salomos und zu dem Buche Hiob* (Tübingen: Mohr, 1958); and H. H. Schmid, *Wesen und Geschichte der Weisheit: Eine Untersuchung zur altorientalischen und israelitischen Weisheitsliteratur* (BZAW 101; Berlin: Töpelmann, 1966).

21. H. D. Preuss, "Alttestamentliche Weisheit in christlicher Theologie," pp. 165–81 in C. Brekelmans (ed.), *Questions disputées d'Ancien Testament: Méthode et théologie* (BETL 33; Leuven: Leuven University Press, 1974).

22. See William McKane, *Prophets and Wise Men* (SBT 44; Naperville, Ill.: Allenson, 1965); and R. N. Whybray, *Wisdom in Proverbs: The Concept of Wisdom in Proverbs 1—9* (SBT 45; Naperville: Allenson, 1965). Whybray argues the same point in more detail in "Yahweh Sayings and Their Contexts in Proverbs 10:1–22:16," in Gilbert (ed.), *La Sagesse de l'Ancien Testament*, 153–65, as does R. B. Y. Scott in "Wise and Foolish, Righteous and Wicked," in G. W. Anderson et al. (eds.), *Studies in the Religion of Ancient Israel* (VTSup 23; Leiden: Brill, 1972)146–65.

23. George A. Barton, *A Critical and Exegetical Commentary on the Book of Ecclesiastes* (ICC; Edinburgh: T. & T. Clark, 1908), 44.

24. Kathleen A. Farmer, *Who Knows What Is Good? A Commentary on the Books of Proverbs and Ecclesiastes* (ITC; Grand Rapids: Eerdmans, 1991).

25. For a thorough survey of various approaches to the contradictions in Ecclesiastes, see Michael V. Fox, *Qohelet and His Contradictions* (JSOTSup 71; BLS 18; Sheffield: Almond, 1989), 19–28.

26. Georg Fohrer, *Das buch Hiob* (KAT 16; Gütersloh: Mohn, 1963).

27. Eichrodt, *Theology of the Old Testament*, 2:81–82.

28. Gerhard von Rad, *Wisdom in Israel* (Nashville: Abingdon, 1972).

29. Roland Murphy, "Wisdom—Theses and Hypotheses" in John G. Gammie et al. (eds.), *Israelite Wisdom: Theological and Literary Essays in Honor of Samuel Terrien* (Missoula, Mont.: Scholars Press, 1978), 36.

30. H. L. Ginsberg (trans.), in J. B. Pritchard (ed.), *Ancient Near Eastern Texts Relating to the Old Testament* (3d ed.; Princeton, N. J.: Princeton University Press, 1969), 428.

31. John A. Wilson (trans.), in Pritchard (ed.), *Ancient Near Eastern Texts*, 431–34.

32. E. Gerstenberger, *Wesen und Herkunft des sogennanten 'apodiktischen Rechts' im Alten Testament* (WMANT 20; Neukirchen-Vluyn: Neukirchener Verlag, 1965) and Carole R. Fontaine, *Traditional Sayings in the Old Testament: A Contextual Study* (BLS 5; Sheffield: Almond, 1982).

33. William McKane, *Proverbs: A New Approach* (OTL; Philadelphia: Westminster, 1970).

34. André Lemaire, *Les écoles et la formation de la Bible dans l'ancien Israël* (OBO 39; Fribourg: Éditions Universitaires, 1981).

35. R. N. Whybray, *The Intellectual Tradition in the Old Testament* (BZAW 135; Berlin: de Gruyter, 1974).

36. R. B. Y. Scott, "Solomon and the Beginnings of Wisdom in Israel," in M. Noth and D. W. Thomas (eds.), *Wisdom in Israel and in the Ancient Near East: Presented to H. H. Rowley* (VTSup 3; Leiden: Brill, 1955), 262–79.

37. W. Lee Humphreys, "The Motif of the Wise Courtier in the Book of Proverbs," in Gammie et al. (eds.), *Israelite Wisdom: Theological and Literary Essays in Honor of Samuel Terrien*, 187.

38. Whybray, *The Intellectual Tradition*, 65.

39. André Lemaire, "The Sage in School and Temple," in Gammie and Perdue (eds.), *The Sage in Israel*, 165–81.

40. James L. Crenshaw, "Education in Ancient Israel," *JBL* 104 (1985): 602.

41. Crenshaw, "Education in Ancient Israel," 602.

42. Hermann Gunkel, *Einleitung in die Psalmen: Die Gattungen der religiösen Lyrik Israels* (GHAT; Göttingen: Vandenhoeck & Ruprecht, 1933).

43. Roland E. Murphy, "A Consideration of the Classification 'Wisdom Psalms,'" in J. L. Crenshaw (ed.), *Studies in Ancient Israelite Wisdom* (New York: Ktav, 1976), 456–67; and R. N. Whybray, "The Wisdom Psalms" in Day, Gordon, Williamson (eds.), *Wisdom in Ancient Israel*, 152–60.

44. Gerhard von Rad, "The Joseph Narrative and Ancient Wisdom," in *The Problem of the Hexateuch and Other Essays* (Edinburgh: Oliver & Boyd, 1953), 292–300.

45. R. N. Whybray, *The Succession Narrative: A Study of II Samuel 8—20; I Kings 1 and 2* (SBT 2/9; London: SCM, 1968).

46. Luis Alonso-Schökel, "Sapiential and Covenant Themes in Genesis 2—3," in Crenshaw (ed.), *Studies in Ancient Israelite Wisdom*, 468–80.

47. Moshe Weinfeld, *Deuteronomy and the Deuteronomic School* (Oxford: Clarendon Press, 1972). See also Calum M. Carmichael, *The Laws of Deuteronomy* (Ithaca, N. Y.: Cornell University Press, 1974).

48. So McKane, *Prophets and Wise Men*.

49. Johannes Fichtner, "Jesaja unter den Weisen," *TL* 74 (1949): 75–80; translated into English as "Isaiah among the Wise," in Crenshaw (ed.), *Studies in Ancient Israelite Wisdom*, 429–38.

50. J. William Whedbee, *Isaiah and Wisdom* (Nashville: Abingdon, 1971).
51. Samuel Terrien, "Amos and Wisdom," in B. W. Anderson and W. Harrelson (eds.), *Israel's Prophetic Heritage: Essays in Honor of James Muilenburg* (New York: Harper, 1962), 108–15.
52. Hans Walter Wolff, *Amos the Prophet: The Man and His Background* (Philadelphia: Fortress, 1973).
53. James L. Crenshaw, "Method in Determining Wisdom Influence upon 'Historical' Literature," *JBL* 88 (1969): 129–42.
54. Roland Murphy, "Wisdom—Theses and Hypotheses," 39. For a history of research, see R. N. Whybray, "Prophecy and Wisdom," in R. Coggins, A. Phillips, and M. Knibb (eds.), *Israel's Prophetic Tradition: Essays in Honour of Peter R. Ackroyd* (Cambridge: Cambridge University Press, 1982), 181–99.
55. H. G. M. Williamson, "Isaiah and the Wise," in Day, Gordon, and Williamson (eds.), *Wisdom in Ancient Israel*, 136.
56. James L. Crenshaw, "The Sage in Proverbs," in Gammie and Perdue (eds.), *The Sage in Israel*, 214.
57. Carole Fontaine, "Wisdom in Proverbs," in L. G. Perdue, B. B. Scott, and W. J. Wiseman (eds.), *In Search of Wisdom: Essays in Memory of John G. Gammie* (Louisville, Ky.: Westminster/John Knox, 1993), 111.
58. The introduction to Day, Gordon, and Williamson (eds.), *Wisdom in Ancient Israel*, 1. See also G. T. Sheppard, *Wisdom as a Hermeneutical Construct: A Study in the Sapien-tializing of the Old Testament* (BZAW 151; Berlin and New York: de Gruyter, 1980).
59. R. E. Clements, "Wisdom and Old Testament Theology," 269–86.
60. Frederick M. Wilson "Sacred and Profane? The Yahwistic Redaction of Proverbs Reconsidered," in K. G. Hoglund et al. (eds.), *The Listening Heart: Essays in Wisdom and the Psalms in Honor of Roland E. Murphy* (JSOTSup 58; Sheffield: JSOT, 1987), 330.
61. Kathleen A. Farmer, *Who Knows What Is Good?* 67–68.
62. Athanasius, *Orations against the Arians*, 1.16.
63. Marius Victorinus, *Against Arius*, 1B, 56, 64.
64. Augustine, *On the Trinity* 4.5.27.
65. See Claudia V. Camp, *Wisdom and the Feminine in the Book of Proverbs* (BLS 11; Sheffield: Almond, 1985); and articles on "Proverbs," by Carol R. Fontaine, and "Job," by Carol A. Newsom, in C. A. Newsom and S. H. Ringe (eds.), *The Women's Bible Commentary* (Louisville: Westminster/John Knox, 1992).
66. James L. Crenshaw, *Old Testament Wisdom: An Introduction* (Atlanta: John Knox, 1981), 92.
67. Wilson, "Sacred and Profane?" 318.
68. Lennart Boström, *The God of the Sages: The Portrayal of God in the Book of Proverbs* (ConBOT 29; Stockholm: Almqvist & Wiksell, 1990), 136.

69. Stuart Weeks, *Early Israelite Wisdom* (Oxford Theological Monographs; Oxford: Clarendon Press, 1994), 73.

70. H. D. Preuss, "Das Gottesbild der alteren Weisheit Israel," in Anderson et al. (eds.), *Studies in the Religion of Ancient Israel*, 117–45, and idem, *Einführung in die alttestamentliche Weisheitsliteratur* (Kohlhammer Urban-Taschenbücher 383; Stuttgart: Kohlhammer, 1987).

71. Brevard S. Childs, *Biblical Theology of the Old and New Testaments: Theological Reflection on the Christian Bible* (Minneapolis: Fortress, 1993).

72. Boström, *The God of the Sages*, 36.

73. Fontaine, "Wisdom in Proverbs," 111.

74. Walther Zimmerli, "The Place and Limit of the Wisdom in the Framework of the Old Testament Theology," *SJT* 17 (1964):146–58, reprinted in J. Crenshaw (ed.), *Studies in Ancient Israelite Wisdom*, 314–25.

75. See Rolf Knierim, "Cosmos and History in Israel's Theology," *HBT* 3 (1981): 59–123, and Leo G. Perdue, *Wisdom and Creation: The Theology of Wisdom Literature* (Nashville: Abingdon, 1994).

76. See Tyron Inbody, *The Transforming God: An Interpretation of Suffering and Evil* (Louisville, Ky.: Westminster John Knox, 1997), 41, 73–74, 83.

CHAPTER 6: THE SONGS OF ISRAEL

1. Hermann Gunkel, *The Psalms: A Form Critical Introduction* (Facet Books: Biblical Series; Philadelphia: Fortress, 1967).

2. A. R. Johnson, "The Psalms," in H. H. Rowley (ed.), *The Old Testament and Modern Study* (Oxford: Clarendon Press, 1951), 162–209.

3. Gunkel, *The Psalms*, 32.

4. Gunkel, *The Psalms*, 32.

5. Gunkel, *The Psalms*, 24.

6. Gunkel, *The Psalms*, 19–20.

7. Gunkel, *The Psalms*, 17–18.

8. Gunkel, *The Psalms*, 26.

9. Gunkel, *The Psalms*, 33.

10. Sigmund Mowinckel, *The Psalms in Israel's Worship* (2 vols., 1962; repr. with an introduction by R. K. Gnuse and D. A. Knight; Sheffield: JSOT, 1992).

11. See J. H. Eaton, *Kingship and the Psalms* (2d ed.; Sheffield: JSOT, 1986) and S. J. L. Croft, *The Identity of the Individual in the Psalms* (JSOTSup 44; Sheffield: JSOT, 1987).

12. On this festival and the humiliation and exaltation of the reigning king, see J. Klein, "Akitu," *Anchor Bible Dictionary* 1 (1992): 138–40.

13. Mowinckel, *The Psalms in Israel's Worship*, 1:242–43.

14. Mowinckel, *The Psalms in Israel's Worship*, 2:255.

15. R. J. Tournay, *Seeing and Hearing God with the Psalms: The Prophetic Liturgy of the Second Temple in Jerusalem* (JSOTSup 118; Sheffield: JSOT, 1991).

16. E. S. Gerstenberger, *Psalms: Part I: With an Introduction to Cultic Poetry* (FOTL 14; Grand Rapids: Eerdmans, 1988). See also S. E. Gillingham, *The Poems and Psalms of the Hebrew Bible* (Oxford: Oxford University Press, 1994), 184–86.

17. For example, Claus Westermann, *The Praise of God in the Psalms* (Richmond: John Knox, 1965) and *Praise and Lament in the Psalms* (Atlanta: John Knox, 1981), and Walter Brueggemann, *The Psalms and the Life of Faith* (Minneapolis: Fortress, 1995). See also Gillingham, *The Poems and Psalms of the Hebrew Bible*, 186–89.

18. Westermann, *The Praise of God in the Psalms*, 153.

19. Westermann, *Praise and Lament in the Psalms*, 21.

20. Brueggemann, *The Psalms and the Life of Faith*.

21. Brevard S. Childs, *Introduction to the Old Testament as Scripture* (Philadelphia: Fortress, 1979), 523.

22. See the discussion in R. N. Whybray, "Wisdom Psalms," in J. Day, R. P. Gordon, and H. G. M. Williamson (eds.), *Wisdom in Ancient Israel: Essays in Honour of J. A. Emerton* (Cambridge: Cambridge University Press, 1995), 152–60 and *Reading the Psalms as a Book* (JSOTSup 222; Sheffield: JSOT, 1996), 15–35.

23. Mowinckel, *The Psalms in Israel's Worship*, 2:104–25.

24. For the issues, see the articles in J. C. McCann (ed.), *The Shape and Shaping of the Psalter* (JSOTSup 159, Sheffield: JSOT, 1993) and Whybray, *Reading the Psalms as a Book*.

25. Childs, *Introduction to the Old Testament as Scripture*, 521.

26. See most recently Walter Brueggemann and Patrick D. Miller, "Psalm 73 as a Canonical Marker," *JSOT* 72 (1996): 45–56.

27. Whybray, *Reading the Psalms as a Book*, 123–24.

28. This view is summarized by A. Arens, *Die Psalmen in Gottesdienst des Alten Bundes* (Trier Theologische Studien 11; Trier: Paulinus, 1968), 160–202.

29. See F. W. Dobbs-Allsopp, *Weep, O Daughter of Zion: A Study of the City-Lament Genre in the Hebrew Bible* (BibOr 44; Rome: Pontifical Biblical Institute, 1993).

30. See Dobbs-Allsopp, *Weep, O Daughter of Zion,* for a summary.

CHAPTER 7: OTHER WRITINGS

1. Edward F. Campbell, Jr., *Ruth* (AB 7; Garden City: Doubleday, 1975), 170.

2. Cf. Kirsten Nielsen, *Ruth: A Commentary* (OTL; Louisville, Ky.: Westminster John Knox, 1997).

3. Hermann Gunkel, "Ruth," in *Reden und Aufsätze* (Göttingen: Vandenhoeck & Ruprecht, 1913), 84–86.

4. According to Murray D. Gow (*The Book of Ruth: Its Structure, Theme and Purpose* [Leicester: Apollos, 1992], 206), the book of Ruth was written during David's reign, when it was used in defense of his Moabite origin. On the other hand, Erich Zenger (*Das Buch Ruth* [ZB 8; Zurich: Theologischer Verlag, 1986], 28) is of the opinion that the final version of the book belongs to the second century B.C.E.

5. Song of Songs is thus different from Egyptian love poetry, where the dialogue feature is missing and where love as such, rather than the beloved, is the main focus. See Michael V. Fox, *The Song of Songs and the Ancient Egyptian Love Songs* (Madison, Wis.: University of Wisconsin Press, 1985) and "Love, Passion, and Perception in Israelite and Egyptian Love Poetry," *JBL* 102 (1983): 219–28.

6. See further Marvin H. Pope, *Song of Songs* (AB 7C; Garden City, N. Y.: Doubleday, 1977), 19.

7. A fine introduction to poetic literature is David L. Petersen and Kent Harold Richards, *Interpreting Hebrew Poetry* (GBS; Minneapolis: Fortress, 1992).

8. See further Athalya Brenner, *The Song of Songs* (OTG; Sheffield: JSOT, 1989), 67–77.

9. Pope, *Song of Songs*, 210–29.

10. See for example Athalya Brenner, "To See Is to Assume: Whose Love Is Celebrated in the Song of Songs?" *BI* 1 (1993): 265–84, and the various feminist readings of Song of Songs in A. Brenner (ed.), *A Feminist Companion to the Song of Songs* (Feminist Companion to the Bible 1; Sheffield: Sheffield Academic Press, 1993).

11. Johann Gottfried Herder, *Sämtliche Werke zur Religion und Theologie*, VII (Tübingen: J. G. Cotta, 1807), 96.

12. J. Cheryl Exum, "A Literary and Structural Analysis of the Song of Songs," *ZAW* 85 (1973): 47–79.

13. So Marcia Falk, *Love Lyrics from the Bible: A Translation and Literary Study of the Song of Songs* (BLS 4; Sheffield: Almond, 1982), and idem, "Song of Songs," pp. 525–28 in J. L. Mays (ed.), *Harper's Bible Commentary* (San Francisco: Harper & Row, 1988).

14. See the further development of this model in Williams H. Shea, "The Chiastic Structure of the Song of Songs," *ZAW* 92 (1980): 378–96.

15. Phyllis Trible, *God and the Rhetoric of Sexuality* (OBT; Philadelphia: Fortress, 1978), 72–165.

16. On the different versions (A and B) of the Greek text of Esther, see David J. A. Clines, *The Esther Scroll: The Story of the Story* (JSOTSup 30; Sheffield: JSOT, 1984).

17. Gillis Gerleman, *Esther* (BKAT 21; Neukirchen-Vluyn: Neukirchener Verlag, 1973), 43.

18. See Shemaryahu Talmon, "Wisdom in the Book of Esther," *VT* 12 (1963): 419–55, who classifies the book of Esther as "a historicized wisdom tale" (p. 426).

19. Susan Niditch, "Esther: Folklore, Wisdom, Feminism and Authority," pp. 26–46 in A. Brenner (ed.), *A Feminist Companion to Esther, Judith and Susanna* (Feminist Companion to the Bible 7; Sheffield: Sheffield Academic Press, 1995).

20. See Maryse Waegeman, "Motifs and Structure in the Book of Esther," in M. Augustin and K.-D. Schunck (eds.), *"Wünschet Jerusalem Frieden": Collected Communications to the XIIth Congress of the International Organization for the Study of the Old Testament, Jerusalem 1986* (BEATAJ 13; Frankfurt am Main: Peter Lang, 1988), 371–84.

21. This feature of narrative style has been seen by some scholars as an indication that the book has been compiled from two different narratives, a Mordecai story and an Esther story. For a thorough discussion of this matter, see Clines, *The Esther Scroll*, 115–38.

22. See further J. A. Loader, "Esther as a Novel with Different Levels of Meaning," *ZAW* 90 (1978): 417–21.

23. So Athalya Brenner, "Looking at Esther through the Looking Glass," in Brenner (ed.), *A Feminist Companion to Esther*, 76.

24. Brenner, "Esther through the Looking Glass," 73.

25. Honor and shame are two decisive elements in the book of Esther. See further Lillian R. Klein, "Honor and Shame in Esther," in Brenner (ed.), *A Feminist Companion to Esther*, 149–75.

26. The issue of the incomplete emancipation of Esther is discussed by Bea Wyler, "Esther: The Incomplete Emancipation of a Queen," in Brenner (ed.), *A Feminist Companion to Esther*, 111–35.

27. This has been the general opinion of critical scholarship during the last 200 years on the issue of the book's date. In addition to the standard introductions to the Old Testament, see John J. Collins, "Daniel, Book of," *ABD* 2:33–34.

28. See Shemaryahu Talmon, "Daniel," in R. Alter and F. Kermode (eds.), *The Literary Guide to the Bible* (London: Collins; Cambridge, Mass.: Belknap, 1987), 350–55.

29. See for example Louis F. Hartman and Alexander A. Di Lella, *The Book of Daniel* (AB 23; Garden City, N.Y.: Doubleday, 1978), 218–19, and Philip R. Davies, *Daniel* (OTG; Sheffield: JSOT, 1985), 101–4.

30. Cf. Benedikt Otzen, "Michael and Gabriel: Angelological Problems in the Book of Daniel," in F. García Martínez, A. Hilhorst, and C. J. Labuschagne [eds.], *The Scriptures and the Scrolls: Studies in Honour of A. S. van der Woude on the Occasion of his 65th Birthday* [VTSup 49; Leiden: Brill, 1992]), 114–24. Otzen continues Collins's thesis that "the son of man" is the archangel Michael (J. J. Collins, *The Apocalyptic Vision of the Book of Daniel* [HSM 16; Missoula: Scholars Press, 1977], 144–47).

31. Davies (*Daniel*, 70–72) discusses this matter and rightly points out that prophecy and wisdom were not in opposition during the Hellenistic era.

32. Among the numerous fragments of Daniel found in the Dead Sea Scrolls at Qumran, one fragment contains the text in Dan. 2:4, where the language changes from Hebrew to Aramaic.

33. See the discussion in Davies, *Daniel*, 2:35–39, in this respect.
34. Jürgen-Christian Lebram, *Das Buch Daniel* (ZB 23; Zurich: Theologischer Verlag, 1984), 21. According to Collins ("Daniel," 30–31) only Daniel 2—6 was originally an Aramaic unit, maybe including chapter 1, which was then later translated into Hebrew. Chapters 7 + 8—12 were added in the time of the Maccabees.
35. A. Lenglet, "La Structure littéraire de Daniel 2—7," *Bib* 53 (1972): 169–90.

CHAPTER 8: THE "CHRONICLER'S HISTORY"

1. Cf. Joseph Blenkinsopp, *Ezra-Nehemiah: A Commentary* (OTL; Philadelphia: Westminster, 1988), 36–38.
2. Ralph W. Klein, "Chronicles, Book of 1–2," *ABD* 1:992; "Ezra-Nehemiah, Books of," *ABD* 2:731; H. G. M. Williamson, *1 and 2 Chronicles* (NCB; Grand Rapids: Eerdmans, 1982), 3.
3. Blenkinsopp, *Ezra-Nehemiah*, 38.
4. Klein, "Ezra-Nehemiah," 732.
5. H. G. M. Williamson, *Ezra, Nehemiah* (WBC 16; Waco: Word, 1985), xxi–xxiii.
6. Sara Japhet, *I & II Chronicles* (OTL; Louisville, Ky.: Westminster/John Knox, 1993), 2; Williamson, *1 and 2 Chronicles*, 4–5.
7. Japhet, *I & II Chronicles*, 3.
8. Leopold Zunz, *Die gottesdienstlichen Vorträge der Jüden* (Berlin: A. Asher, 1832).
9. F. C. Movers, *Kritische Untersuchungen über die biblische Chronik* (Bonn: T. Habicht, 1834), 11–14.
10. Sara Japhet, "The Supposed Common Authorship of Chronicles and Ezra-Nehemia Investigated Anew," *VT* 18 (1968): 330 71.
11. Williamson, *1 and 2 Chronicles*, 4–5.
12. H. G. M., Williamson, *Israel in the Books of Chronicles* (Cambridge: Cambridge University Press, 1977), 37–59.
13. S. R. Driver compiled a list of forty-six examples of the linguistic style of Hebrew in Chronicles and Ezra-Nehemiah (*An Introduction to the Literature of the Old Testament* [International Theological Library; 7th ed.; Edinburgh: T. & T. Clark, 1898], 535–39), not presented as evidence for common authorship for the books but in his discussion of postexilic Hebrew. The list was expanded to 136 items in Edward L. Curtis and A. A. Madsen, *A Critical and Exegetical Commentary on the Books of Chronicles* (ICC; Edinburgh: T. & T. Clark, 1910), 28–36. Others used the list as an argument for the literary unity of the books.
14. Williamson, *Israel*, 59.
15. Blenkinsopp, *Ezra-Nehemiah*, 48-49.
16. Klein, "Chronicles," 993.
17. A. van Hoonacker, "Néhémie et Esdras, une nouvelle hypothèse sur la chronologie de l'époque de la restauration," *Le Muséon* 9 (1890): 151–84,

317–51, 389–401; "La succession chronologique Néhémie-Esdras," *RB* 32 (1923): 481–94; 33 (1924): 33–64.

18. Williamson, *Ezra, Nehemiah*, 366.

19. Bright, *A History of Israel* (3d ed.; Philadelphia: Westminster, 1981), 400–401.

20. J. A. Emerton has pointed out the flaws in Bright's reconstruction in "Did Ezra go to Jerusalem in 428 B.C.?" *JTS* new series 17 (1966): 1–19.

21. For a concise treatment of the various aspects of this problem, see the excellent summary of Tamara C. Eskenazi, "Sheshbazzar," *ABD* 5:1207–1209.

22. See Blenkinsopp, *Ezra-Nehemiah*, 157.

23. For surveys of the literature on this issue, see: U. Kellermann, "Erwägungen zum Esragesetz," *ZAW* 80 (1968): 373–85; R. W. Klein, "Ezra and Nehemiah in Recent Studies," in *Magnalia Dei: The Mighty Acts of God*, ed. F. M. Cross, W. E. Lemke, and P. D. Miller (Garden City, N. Y.: Doubleday, 1976), 361–76; C. Houtman, "Ezra and the Law," *OTS* 21 (1981): 91–115.

24. Williamson, *Ezra, Nehemiah*, xxxviii–xxxix.

25. See, e.g., A. Graeme Auld, *Kings without Privilege: David and Moses in the Story of the Bible's Kings* (Edinburgh: T. &T. Clark, 1994), and Anson F. Rainey, "The Chronicler and his Sources—Historical and Geographical," in M. P. Graham, S. L. McKenzie, and K. G. Hoglund (eds.), *The Chronicler as Historian* (JSOTSup 238; Sheffield: JSOT, 1997), 37–43.

26. See Steven L. McKenzie, *The Chronicler's Use of the Deuteronomistic History* (HSM 33; Atlanta: Scholars Press, 1985).

27. Klein, "Chronicles," 997.

28. Klein ("Chronicles," 997) also mentions Hezekiah's tunnel (2 Chron. 32:30), Pharaoh Neco's goal in his battle against King Josiah (2 Chron. 25:20), and the list of Rehoboam's fortresses (2 Chron 11:5–11).

29. While the author of Kings refers to the "Book of the Chronicles of the Kings of Judah," the Chronicler regards the king of Judah as heir to the kingdom of Israel and so adjusts the last part of the citation to express this: "Kings of Israel and Judah." Cf. Klein, "Chronicles," 997.

30. See Isaac Kalimi, *Zur Geschichtsschreibung des Chronisten: Literarisch-historiographische Abweichungen der Chronik von ihren Paralleltexten in den Samuel- und Königsbüchern* (BZAW 226; Berlin: de Gruyter, 1995).

31. An alternative definition of the Nehemiah Memoir is that it consists of Neh. 1—2; 4—6; 7:1–5; elements of 12:31–43; and 13:4–31. Cf. H. G. M. Williamson, *Ezra and Nehemiah* (OTG; Sheffield: JSOT, 1987), 15–17.

32. David J. A. Clines, *Ezra, Nehemiah, Esther* (NCB; Grand Rapids: Eerdmans, 1984), 4–9.

33. Klein, "Ezra-Nehemiah" 733: Nehemiah 8 presents Ezra and Nehemiah as contemporaries, but some have proposed that the chapter originally dealt only with Ezra and was situated between Ezra 8 and 9 (or after Ezra 10).

34. Martin Noth, *The Chronicler's History* (JSOTSup 50; Sheffield: JSOT, 1987).

35. Gerhard von Rad, *Das Geschichtsbild des chronistische Werkes* (BWANT 54; Stuttgart: Kohlhammer, 1930).

36. David Noel Freedman, "The Chronicler's Purpose," *CBQ* 23 (1961): 436–42.
37. Rodney K. Duke, *The Persuasive Appeal of the Chronicler: A Rhetorical Analysis* (JSOTSup 88; Sheffield: Almond, 1990).
38. See the development traced by H. G. M. Williamson, *Israel in the Books of Chronicles* 130–31.
39. Israel's traditions about the exodus, wilderness wandering, and conquest of Canaan seem to play a much less important role in Chronicles than in Samuel-Kings, so that one can even speak of Israel's "uninterrupted settlement in the land." On this point, see Sara Japhet, *The Ideology of the Book of Chronicles and Its Place in Biblical Thought* (BEATAJ 9; Frankfurt am Main: Peter Lang, 1989), 363–86.
40. On this point, see most recently William M. Schniedewind, *The Word of God in Transition: From Prophet to Exegete in the Second Temple Period* (JSOT-Sup 197; Sheffield: Sheffield Academic Press, 1995).
41. Tamara Cohn Eskenazi, *In an Age of Prose: A Literary Approach to Ezra-Nehemiah* (SBLMS 36; Atlanta: Scholars Press, 1988).
42. See Williamson, *Ezra and Nehemiah* (OTG; Sheffield: JSOT, 1987), 84–86; *Ezra, Nehemiah*, 306–7.
43. See Clines, *Ezra, Nehemiah, Esther*, 25–30.
44. For the history of research into Chronicles and Ezra-Nehemiah, see respectively: Sara Japhet, "Chronicles, Books of" and H. G. M. Williamson, "Ezra and Nehemiah," both in John H. Hayes (ed.), *Abingdon's Dictionary of Biblical Interpretation* (Nashville: Abingdon, forthcoming).
45. W. M. L. de Wette, *Beiträge zur Einleitung in das Alte Testament,* 2 vols. (Halle: Schimmelpfennig, 1806, 1807) It was the first volume of this work that dealt with Chronicles and its reliability for historical reconstruction of the preexilic period.
46. On the discussion of Chronicles' usefulness for the reconstruction of preexilic history, see most recently: Kai Peltonen, *History Debated: The Historical Reliability of Chronicles in Pre-Critical and Critical Research,* 2 vols. (Publications of the Finnish Exegetical Society 64; Helsinki: Finnish Exegetical Society; Göttingen: Vandenhoeck & Ruprecht, 1996).
47. Isaac Kalimi, *The Books of Chronicles: A Classified Bibliography* (Simor Bible Bibliographies; Jerusalem: Simor, 1990).
48. E.g., Jürgen Kegler and Matthias Augustin, *Synopse zum Chronistischen Geschichtswerk* (2d ed.; BEATAJ 1; Frankfurt am Main: Peter Lang, 1991).
49. Those not cited in earlier notes are: Roddy Braun, *1 Chronicles* (WBC 14; Waco: Word, 1986) and Raymond B. Dillard, *2 Chronicles* (WBC 15; Waco: Word, 1987).
50. For recent assessments on Chronicles and Ezra-Nehemiah, see: John W. Kleinig, "Recent Research in Chronicles," *CRBS* 2 (1994): 43–76, and Tamara C. Eskenazi, "Current Perspectives on Ezra-Nehemiah and the Persian Period," *CRBS* 1 (1993): 59–86. See especially pp. 66–71 in Eskenazi for a concise summary of recent discussion on Judah's socioeconomic structures during this period.

INDEX OF AUTHORS